SHAREPOINT® 2013

BRANDING and USER INTERFACE DESIGN

Randy Drisgill

John Ross

Paul Stubbs

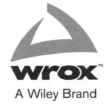

wrox™

A Wiley Brand

SharePoint® 2013 Branding and User Interface Design

Published by
John Wiley & Sons, Inc.
10475 Crosspoint Boulevard
Indianapolis, IN 46256
www.wiley.com

Copyright © 2013 by John Wiley & Sons, Inc., Indianapolis, Indiana

Published simultaneously in Canada

ISBN: 978-1-118-49567-4
ISBN: 978-1-118-49561-2 (ebk)
ISBN: 978-1-118-71073-9 (ebk)

Manufactured in the United States of America

10 9 8 7 6 5 4 3 2 1

For general information on our other products and services please contact our Customer Care Department within the United States at (877) 762-2974, outside the United States at (317) 572-3993 or fax (317) 572-4002.

Wiley also publishes its books in a variety of electronic formats and by print-on-demand. Not all content that is available in standard print versions of this book may appear or be packaged in all book formats. If you have purchased a version of this book that did not include media that is referenced by or accompanies a standard print version, you may request this media by visiting http://booksupport.wiley.com. For more information about Wiley products, visit us at www.wiley.com.

Library of Congress Control Number: 2012956398

Dedicated to waffles (thank you for staying delicious) and to Jackie (the love of my life) for always being there to eat them with me.

—Randy Drisgill

To my mom, thanks for always correcting my grammar.

—John Ross

To my daughter, Julia, the artistic one in the family.

—Paul Stubbs

About the Authors

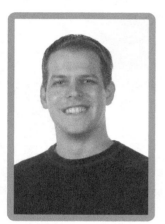

Randy Drisgill has more than a decade of experience developing, designing, and implementing web technologies for clients ranging from small businesses to Fortune 500 companies. For the past 5 years, he has been working exclusively with SharePoint branding projects at SharePoint911, which was subsequently acquired by Rackspace in 2012. During this time, Randy has worked on more than 50 internal and public-facing SharePoint branding projects.

Randy is an active member of the SharePoint community, having contributed to several articles and books on the topic, as well as being the cofounder/comanager of the Orlando SharePoint User Group (OSPUG). In 2009, Randy was recognized by Microsoft as an authority on SharePoint branding by being awarded MVP status for SharePoint Server.

Randy lives in Orlando, Florida, with his wife. You can find Randy online on Twitter as @Drisgill or at his blog at http://blog.drisgill.com.

John Ross is a Senior Consultant with Rackspace and has more than eight years of experience implementing solutions for clients ranging from small businesses to Fortune 500 companies as well as government organizations. He has worked with all project phases from analysis to implementation and has been involved with a wide range of SharePoint solutions that include public-facing Internet sites, corporate intranets, and extranets.

John is an active member of the community and has presented at conferences all around the world. He is the cofounder/comanager of the Orlando SharePoint User Group (OSPUG). In 2009, John was awarded Microsoft's MVP award for SharePoint Server for his community contributions.

John lives in Orlando, Florida with his wife and two children. Visit his blog at http://johnrossjr.wordpress.com or follow his SharePoint adventures on Twitter @JohnRoss.

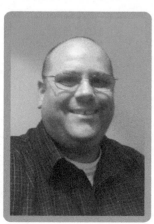

Paul Stubbs is a Microsoft Architect for Windows Azure focusing on cloud solution development and SharePoint. Previously, Paul worked with the SharePoint community developing SharePoint, Office, and Silverlight solutions and training. Paul has also worked as a Senior Program Manager on the Visual Studio team in Redmond, Washington. Paul is a Microsoft Certified Trainer (MCT) and has received Microsoft Certified Applications Developer (MCAD) and Microsoft Certified Solution Developer (MCSD) certifications. He has authored several books on solution development using Microsoft Office, SharePoint, and Silverlight, wrote several articles for MSDN Magazine, and has also spoken at many conferences such as Tech-Ed, Build, MIX, and the Professional Developers Conference (PDC) and Tech-Ready. Paul has a passion for new technologies and sharing those experiences with the community on his blog at http://blogs.msdn.com/pstubbs.

About the Contributor

Ryan Keller has been working with SharePoint technologies since 2007, and he has worked as a SharePoint consultant since 2009 when he joined SharePoint911, a consulting company from Cincinnati, Ohio. In 2012, Rackspace Hosting acquired SharePoint911, and he is now part of the SharePoint team at Rackspace. He has helped write and edit material related to SharePoint 2010 for Microsoft, wrote as a contributing author to the popular Professional SharePoint 2010 Administration, and served as a technical editor for Beginning SharePoint Designer 2010, *Professional SharePoint 2010 Branding and User Interface Design*, and for this book, *Professional SharePoint 2013 Branding and User Interface Design*. He is also a contributing author on Professional SharePoint 2013 Administration. Since 2011, Ryan has focused his consulting efforts exclusively on SharePoint branding and has worked on projects ranging from simple designs to complex custom branding solutions. Ryan lives in Firestone, Colorado, with his wife Brittany and two kids, Kylie and Nathan.

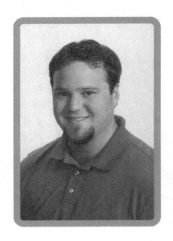

About the Technical Editors

Heather Waterman is the Director of Synteractive Studio, a subsidiary of Smartronix based in Hollywood, Maryland. She is responsible for leading the designers and developers with an emphasis on web design for SharePoint. She has over 12 years of web design and development experience, the past six with a primary focus on SharePoint branding. With these skills she has quickly become a leader in the SharePoint branding community. Her past SharePoint Branding projects include the award-winning Recovery.gov and Treasury.gov among others. Prior to joining Synteractive, she was the president and CEO of the Waterman Design Group, during which time she developed website templates for resell and provided SharePoint branding for clients including Shell and Merck. When she is not working on client projects, she actively contributes design and branding time to the community by developing blogs and sites for other community leaders. You can find her on twitter @hwaterman or via her blog www.heatherwaterman.com.

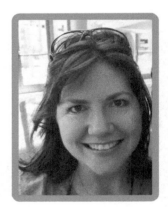

Larry Riemann has over 18 years of experience architecting and creating business applications for some of the world's largest companies. Larry is an independent consultant who owns Indigo Integrations and SharePoint Fanatics. He is an author, contributing author, and technical editor on three other SharePoint books and is an occasional speaker at conferences. For the last several years he has focused on SharePoint, creating and extending functionality where SharePoint leaves off. In addition to his expertise with SharePoint, Larry is an accomplished .Net Architect and has extensive expertise in systems integration, enterprise architecture, and high-availability solutions. You can contact Larry at larry@spfanatics.com.

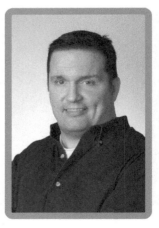

Credits

Acquisitions Editor
Mary James

Project Editor
Victoria Swider

Contributing Author
Ryan Keller

Technical Editors
Heather Waterman
Ryan Keller
Larry Riemann

Production Editor
Daniel Scribner

Copy Editor
San Dee Phillips

Editorial Manager
Mary Beth Wakefield

Freelancer Editorial Manager
Rosemarie Graham

Associate Director of Marketing
David Mayhew

Marketing Manager
Ashley Zurcher

Business Manager
Amy Knies

Production Manager
Tim Tate

Vice President and Executive Group Publisher
Richard Swadley

Vice President and Executive Publisher
Neil Edde

Associate Publisher
Jim Minatel

Project Coordinator, Cover
Katie Crocker

Interior Designer
Ed Cross

Compositor
Lissa Auciello-Brogan, Abshier House

Proofreader
Lowell Kim, Abshier House

Indexer
Kelly Dobbs-Henthorne, Abshier House

Cover Designer
Elizabeth Brooks

Photographer
Erik Wieder

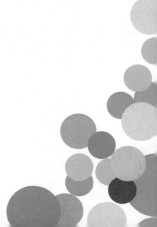

Acknowledgments

Well, here we are again, a new version of SharePoint and a new branding book to go along with it. This is the third SharePoint branding book I've worked on, and every time I forget exactly how much work goes into putting these things together. With each new book there are, of course, new concepts to learn in a short amount of time, but new challenges also arise. For this book, the new challenge began when Jim Minatel from Wrox came to me with the crazy idea that we could produce a highly designed, full-color SharePoint branding book. The idea of making something that looks entirely different from any other SharePoint book on the market got me excited to jump back in to the writing process. There is absolutely no way this full-color book could be a reality without the help of many people that I need to thank.

First, I want to thank the author team for helping me put together the best collection of SharePoint 2013 branding knowledge that exists today. This includes my coworker, copresenter, and good friend, John Ross, as well as my buddy, Paul Stubbs, Sr. Architect at Microsoft. We also had assistance from my co-worker, Ryan Keller, who worked both as a contributing author and technical editor. Another big thanks goes out to Heather Waterman, who tech edited some of the more advanced branding chapters and went above the call of duty to make sure the book turned out awesome. Thanks to Larry Riemann and Mark Watts for tech editing chapters as well.

Along with the writing team, another obvious big thanks goes out to everyone at Wrox Press who helped us get this book to you. This includes Jim Minatel, Mary James, Victoria Swider, San Dee Phillips with Apostrophe Editing Services, Debbie Abshier, Lissa Auciello-Brogan, Kelly Henthorne, and probably several other people behind the scenes. They not only helped us sound intelligent, but also put together a really great-looking book. We also owe a great deal of thanks to our designer Ed Cross for creating the amazing look of the chapters and Erik Wieder for lending his photography skills to take that look even further. Special thanks to Jon Duckett for paving the way for a full-color technical book at Wiley.

I want to personally thank several folks from Microsoft without whom this book may have never seen the light of day. These people provided some of the best help and information that I have ever seen for a product that was still being developed. Primarily, this help came from the wonderfully talented Alyssa Levitz (SharePoint Program Manager at Microsoft), who never failed to find us the answers no matter how stupid the question may have seemed at the time, even if it meant answering a question over Facebook while she was on vacation! Topics like the Design Manager, composed looks, and the minimal download strategy would not have been described nearly as well without her help. Some of the other Microsoft folks that helped us understand SharePoint 2013 better include, in no particular order: Mark Kashman, Ethan Gur-esh, Kevin Gjerstad, Josh Stickler, Lionel Robinson, Jeremy Kelley, Jonathan Kern, Manfred Berry, Cindy Liao, Arye Gittelman, Petru Moldovanu, Tom Werner, Matt Evans, Reagan Templin, Nina Ruchirat, Stephen Howard, Kevin Davis (AWESOME), and anyone else I'm forgetting. These people all helped make SharePoint 2013 the best version of SharePoint ever.

Special thanks go out to everyone I work with at Rackspace, both new coworkers and the old Share-Point911 family. I don't think anyone could ask for a better set of coworkers or a more talented team of SharePoint experts. Also, thanks to my bosses Jeff DeVerter, Shane Young, and Walt Leddy for all their support during the transition to SharePoint 2013 and their support of this writing effort.

Lastly, I need to thank all my friends and family who put up with me working long hours throughout several months to put together this book. Most of them have no idea what I do for a living and will probably never read past this paragraph, but I couldn't have done it without all your friendship and support throughout the years. This includes my beautiful wife Jackie Drisgill, my parents Pat and Tom Drisgill, my in-laws Debbie and Dave Auerbach, my grandparents George and Mary Shea and Thomas and Elsie Drisgill, my friends Adam McCard and Marcela Errazquin, Jenn and Mark Clemons, John and

Vanessa Ross, Josh and Rachel Witter, and all my friends from Orlando, New York City, San Antonio, Boston, and throughout the SharePoint community; you know who you are!

The soundtrack for the writing of this book can be found at `http://drisgill.com/go/spotify-playlist`.

—Randy Drisgill

When we first learned that the next version of SharePoint was going to place a big focus on enhancing the design experience, and when Jim Minatel from Wiley presented the idea of doing a highly designed, full-color SharePoint book, it seemed like the stars were aligning. Bringing all of the new technical concepts together in a new format wouldn't have been possible without the help and support of many people.

I'd like to thank the rest of the author team; this book has your blood, sweat, and tears all over it. Big thanks to my good friend Randy Drisgill for being the driving force behind this book and dragging it across the finish line. It has been a wild and strange journey since our days back on the 8th floor to today. To Paul Stubbs, I appreciate all of your help and insight throughout the years. Big thanks to our coworker Ryan Keller for all his hard work as both a contributing author and technical editor.

To the technical editors, Heather Waterman and Larry Rieman, thanks once again for keeping us honest. This book is better because of your efforts. Thank you both!

With this release, I was completely blown away by the help and support from so many people at Microsoft; I hope we've done you proud. To Alyssa Levitz, I don't think anything written here in these acknowledgments could convey everything you've done to help make this book what it is. You're the best! There are so many others at Microsoft who have been generous with their time, including: Mark Kashman, Ethan Gur-esh, Josh Stickler, Lionel Robinson, Manfred Berry, Tom Werner, Reagan Templin, Nina Ruchirat, Stephen Howard, Kevin Davis, and I'm sure many others I've forgotten. It has been fun working with you all during this process. Let's do it again sometime!

Thanks to the team at Wrox Press for giving us the opportunity to write this book. Jim Minatel, Mary James, Victoria Swider, San Dee Phillips (Apostrophe Editing Services), Lissa Auciello-Brogan, Kelly Henthorne, and many others I'm sure. Thanks for taking a chance on doing something different with a SharePoint book and helping us make it the best it can be.

To everyone at Rackspace, I'm so proud to work with the best SharePoint team in the universe! Thanks to Shane Young, Jeff DeVerter, and Walt Leddy for the support and encouragement throughout the entire process.

Last but certainly not least, I'd like to say a special thank you to all of my friends and family. To my lovely wife Vanessa, thanks for putting up with all the late nights, long weekends, and my general crankiness that goes along with the writing process. To my kids, Ben and Julia, thanks for all the hugs and smiles! And to all the rest of my friends and family, unfortunately you'll be seeing and hearing from me more often now!

—John Ross

Thanks to Randy Drisgill and John Ross, my coauthors, for driving this book and for asking me to join them in writing it. Working with Randy and John has been a great experience for me, and I have learned a lot about the design space from them. I also really appreciate their vision for this book to be more than just another reference book, but a book that can not only teach you, but inspire you. I also want to thank our project editor, Victoria Swider, for her infinite patience and understanding as we tried to balance the writing of the book with our day jobs, family, and SharePoint schedule. And finally, I would like to thank Mary James, our Acquisitions Editor, for making this book possible and enabling us to realize our vision.

—Paul Stubbs

Contents

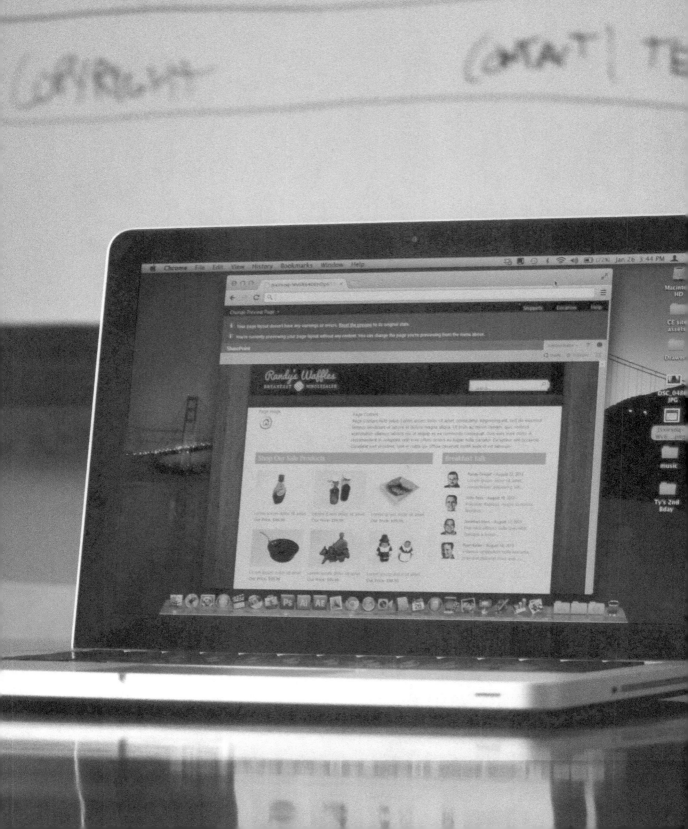

Foreword

I joined Microsoft at a time when the development of SharePoint 2013 was well underway. My first week there, I was told that I owned the Design Manager and Device Channel user experiences, which you'll learn about in just a matter of pages. As quickly and thoroughly as possible, I had to ramp up on a set of features that would later be part of the keynote demos at SharePoint Conference 2012 in Las Vegas. My starting point was the previous version of this book, written for SharePoint 2010. But the world changed significantly between these releases, and the authors went along for that ride, becoming my friends along the way as we worked together to make designing websites on SharePoint a great experience all around.

SharePoint has a rich history as a document management tool, but branding was often an afterthought. Although it was possible to create beautiful SharePoint sites, it wasn't a familiar process for designers. It was with this in mind that we created a new way to approach design in SharePoint Server 2013. We didn't want you to have to make the trade-off between an easy, gorgeous design and a SharePoint site. Whether you're a small business owner who can't afford to hire a designer, or a large enterprise with the ability to hire an entire design team, SharePoint Server 2013 provides a number of site design capabilities to match every customer.

People with no previous SharePoint experience should be pleased with the revamped and reenergized theming experience that gives you access to a swath of full-blown composed looks, which you should think of as a restaurant meal with whatever substitutions you'd like! From one place, you can mix and match fonts, color palettes, layouts, and background images to your heart's content. If that's not enough, you can also build your own set of composed looks for your company, using the existing ones as a template. More advanced users are able to break down the wall between HTML mockups and SharePoint implementation; with a couple of button clicks, you can convert your HTML design into something SharePoint understands while continuing to work in whatever code editor you like best. You'll find a set of common HTML controls you'll use to hook up SharePoint functionality, as well as the ability to easily create mobile- or tablet-specific designs.

All these improvements amount to an experience where you are no longer working from scratch or having to worry too much about how SharePoint works. Instead, you get to focus on adjusting and improving your design to make full use of the features and power SharePoint offers, and I can't wait to see what you do with it. The authors of this book will help get you there. They've been exploring these tools since we could first let them. They know the ins and outs of branding in SharePoint as well as, if not better than, anyone. In this book, they'll share with you their tips and tricks so you can go forth and build great sites!

—Alyssa Levitz, SharePoint Program Manager, Microsoft Corporation

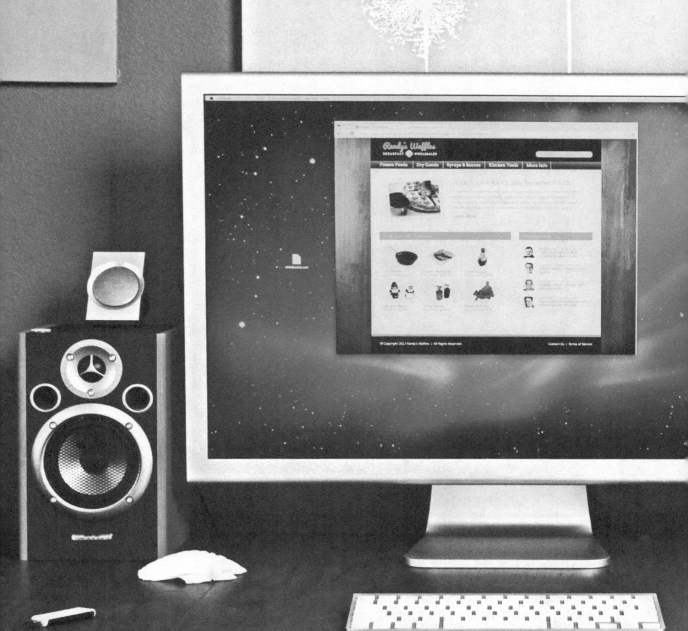

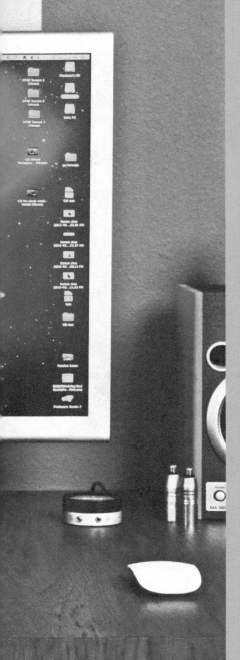

Introduction

Thank you for picking up this book!
We are truly experiencing an interesting step
in the evolution of SharePoint. For the first
time since SharePoint was invented, Microsoft is
embracing the idea that creating beautiful and engaging SharePoint sites should
be within reach of anyone from business users to developers, and of course,
traditional web designers. With the creation of new features such as the Design
Manager and composed looks, Microsoft has lowered the barriers to creating
branding in SharePoint.

This book is intended to explain the beginner features but also to provide knowledge of the underlying
SharePoint branding technology so that you can build a complete solution for branding your
SharePoint site, whether it is an internal intranet site or a public-facing Internet site. Making the
SharePoint user interface look good requires a designer that is comfortable with design theory and
traditional web technologies, as well as having the ability to deal with topics traditionally handled by
developers.

Not everyone who picks up this book is looking to become the next Picasso of SharePoint. For
these readers, the first two sections of the book are dedicated to understanding just enough about
SharePoint branding to plan, create, and apply custom designs to their sites. After you become
comfortable with the basics of SharePoint branding, the second two sections of the book take you on a
tour of creating custom SharePoint branding from scratch, providing the background knowledge
needed to understand how the new, easy branding features work behind the scenes.

HOW THIS BOOK IS ORGANIZED

The primary goal is to provide the best source of knowledge for SharePoint 2013 branding no matter
what your specific skill level is. Although you can certainly use the book as a reference for specific
topics, some of the examples throughout the book do build on each other. By the end of the book, you
will have learned how to work with all the technology needed to create a fully branded
SharePoint site.

The book is divided into four sections:

The Basics

Introductory topics are explored, such as understanding what SharePoint branding means, understanding the basics of how SharePoint works behind the scenes, and an overview of how the SharePoint user interface can be used to edit the page-level branding.

Planning a Design and Getting Started

After explaining the basics, the book dives into planning for branding and starting a design in SharePoint. This section includes topics such as requirements gathering, wireframes, using the new SharePoint 2013 Design Manager and composed looks features, and a deep discussion on how CSS works in SharePoint.

Advanced SharePoint Branding

The second half of the book goes into more intricate topics starting with advanced SharePoint branding. This includes a deep dive into creating master pages and page layouts from scratch, and a chapter that focuses on many of the common tasks associated with creating a fully branded Share-Point site. Rollup Web Parts such as the Content Query Web Part and the Content Search Web Part are covered as well as information on creating composed looks.

Other Branding Concepts

The final section of the book discusses using modern design techniques with SharePoint such as HTML5, CSS3, jQuery, web fonts, and responsive web design. Finally, you learn about using simple online tools to create and style SharePoint apps.

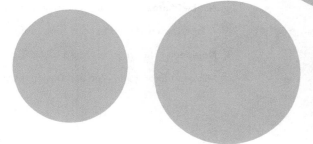

WHO SHOULD READ THIS BOOK

One of the most common SharePoint requests you might hear is to make a site "not look like SharePoint." In most organizations this request might be made to someone who wears many hats but isn't specifically a web designer. In other cases, the request might be made to a web designer or even a developer. To many of those users, SharePoint branding might simply mean that you want to change some colors and put your company header at the top of the page, whereas other users want to create a highly branded corporate intranet portal with a cutting-edge design.

This book is intended for a wide range of readers and skill levels. There is a basic assumption that you have some understanding of how modern websites are created. This includes knowledge of HTML, CSS, and some understanding of the creative design process.

TOOLS YOU NEED

Having a SharePoint 2013 installation available to follow along with the examples can definitely make a big difference when you read this book. If you don't have access to a dedicated SharePoint 2013 server, you can install SharePoint 2013 on a virtual machine to try it out locally, or you can look into cloud-based options such as Office 365's SharePoint Online.

You will also want to have a code-editing tool such as either Visual Studio, Adobe Dreamweaver, Expression Web (recently discontinued, but a free download), or even the free Notepad++. Along with these, you may also need to have some traditional web design programs, such as Adobe Photoshop or Microsoft Expression Design (also discontinued and free). The following list can get you started with software for following along with the book:

- **SharePoint 2013 Download:** http://technet.microsoft.com/en-us/evalcenter/hh973397.aspx

- **Install and Configure SharePoint 2013:** http://technet.microsoft.com/en-us/library/cc262957.aspx

- **Office 365 Trial:** http://www.microsoft.com/en-us/office365

- **Visual Studio 2012:** http://www.microsoft.com/visualstudio/eng/downloads

- **Adobe Photoshop:** http://www.adobe.com/products/photoshop.html

- **Adobe Dreamweaver:** http://www.adobe.com/products/dreamweaver.html

- **Notepad++:** http://notepad-plus-plus.org/

- **Microsoft Expression Web and Design:** http://www.microsoft.com/expression/

WHAT'S ON THE WEBSITE

As you work through the examples in this book, you may choose either to type in all the code manually or to use the source code files that accompany the book. All the source code used in this book is available for download at http://www.wrox.com. When at the site, simply locate the book's title (either by using the Search box or by using one of the title lists) and click the Download Code link on the book's detail page to obtain all the source code for the book.

THE ROAD AHEAD

As you start to learn about branding a SharePoint site, it's not uncommon to get frustrated. Designing for SharePoint is different than designing for your own website. It involves overriding and adjusting a design to fit within someone else's code base, in this case Microsoft's out-of-the-box SharePoint code. But don't get discouraged; with a little patience and the appropriate help, you can apply branding to SharePoint. This book aims to provide you with all the knowledge and techniques required to bridge this gap.

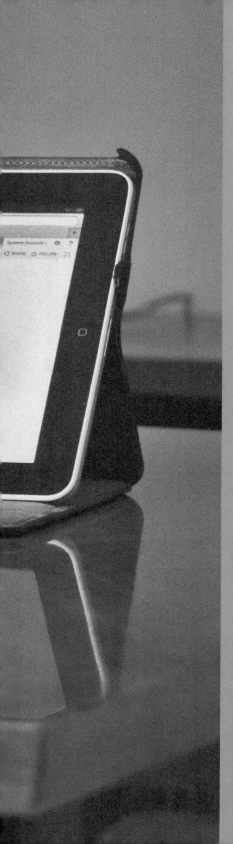

1

The Basics

1

WHAT IS SHAREPOINT BRANDING AND UI DESIGN?

What's in this Chapter

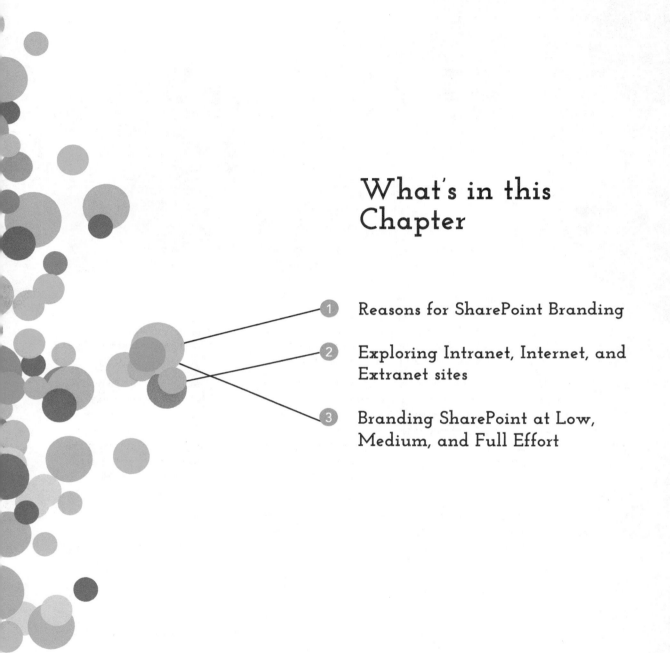

① Reasons for SharePoint Branding

② Exploring Intranet, Internet, and Extranet sites

③ Branding SharePoint at Low, Medium, and Full Effort

When most organizations think about SharePoint, style and design for the user interface (UI) traditionally hasn't been one of the first things to come to mind. But as SharePoint has evolved from its humble beginnings as a pure collaboration tool, the UI design has slowly moved up the list with every release. What was once a luxury for most SharePoint sites, custom branding and design are now an important part of every implementation. The old adage is, "You can't judge a book by its cover," and although that may be true, you can tell a lot by comparing the various versions of SharePoint to the earlier editions of this book. Beginning with the first edition of this book on SharePoint 2007 design, each edition has evolved from just another typical looking technical book to the full-color book you are reading today.

Chances are that if you are reading this book, you've already decided to take control of the way SharePoint looks. Perhaps you have a dated intranet that you want to replace with SharePoint 2013. Maybe you want to make your site look more modern and improve the function with better design. Or maybe you just want your site to not look like a SharePoint site.

There are plenty of reasons why people end up on the branding and UI design path, but no matter your reason, it can be difficult to know where to start. The goal of this book is to provide you with all the tools you need to brand your SharePoint sites. This book is structured into four sections, starting with easier concepts and moving to more advanced branding concepts. The first section is an overview of concepts that you must understand before diving into branding topics; as you progress through the book, the topics continue to become more granular. Whether you are new to design work, new to SharePoint design work, or someone who does SharePoint design full-time, there is something in this book for you.

This chapter starts at the highest level and discusses SharePoint branding: what it is and why it is important. You'll get an idea of exactly what branding means in the world of SharePoint. Later, the chapter discusses the branding features in SharePoint 2013 and explains what options are available.

INTRODUCING SHAREPOINT BRANDING

The textbook definition of *branding* is the act of building a specific image or identity that people recognize in relation to your company or product. That's quite a mouthful! In more simple terms, branding refers to the thoughts and feelings conveyed by a company or product. For example, one of the most iconic brands is Coca-Cola. When you simply see the logo, you can associate feelings or recall good times you've had in affiliation with the product—at least that's what the company hopes. There are plenty of other examples of companies with well-known brands such as Nike, McDonald's, UPS, Walt Disney, and others. These companies have chosen a marketing identity that enables the public to quickly and easily recognize them. This is branding and is one of the most important things to a company.

> **❝** A word is a word, and a picture is worth a thousand. . . but a brand is worth a million. **❞**
>
> —Tony Hsieh, CEO Zappos in Delivering Happiness

A company's branding is applied in many different ways, one of which typically includes a website. On the web, conveying a corporate brand usually involves the colors, fonts, logos, and supporting graphics all pulled together with HTML and CSS to provide the branded look and feel for a site.

You have likely visited a company's website before, so the idea of what it means to apply branding to a website shouldn't be a new concept. But when you start to think about SharePoint branding, additional elements are used to create the branding on the screen. The traditional aspects of branding on the web still apply; however, there are more moving parts in SharePoint. Master pages, page layouts, Web Parts, and other pieces are all involved. If you are a traditional web designer, you might be used to approaching a new site as if it were a blank canvas. SharePoint, however, was created to be used out of the box with no changes—applying branding and design essentially require an understanding of how to work with someone else's code, which in this case is the code generated by SharePoint. This can be a challenge for some who might be new to the world of SharePoint. For example, in an HTML site, if there's something on the page that you want to remove—say you want to hide the search box—the typical behavior might be to just remove it from the code. One of the most common stories told by designers who are new to SharePoint is just this: they want to remove something from the page and they try to just remove the code. In many cases this simple and familiar act creates an undesirable effect, such as the entire page failing to load and displaying an error message. The point here isn't to scare anyone, but rather to explain that branding in SharePoint is a little different. Most people don't consider driving to be too difficult, but you wouldn't advocate someone who has never driven just to hop behind the wheel without a little guidance.

Why Brand SharePoint?

If you are reading this book, it is likely that you don't need to be convinced to brand SharePoint. Organizations decide to brand SharePoint for a number of reasons, such as to match their corporate brand or even simply to make the new site "not look like SharePoint."

Consider that SharePoint wasn't created with a look and feel that necessarily works best for your organization. Branding isn't just about aesthetics; it also plays an important role in usability and user adoption. Part of the equation is helping users to feel comfortable using a site, which always seems to be an easier proposition when it feels familiar. In a corporate setting, users are inundated with corporate branding, so having a site that matches certainly helps. Branding also helps organizations that have employees geographically dispersed. If all employees log in to the same site, it helps if that corporate brand is reinforced, no matter where the user is located. All that might sound a bit touchy-feely but consider the alternative—a site with little or no branding that doesn't reflect your company's corporate image. In that case, the sky isn't going to fall; however, it isn't too difficult to see how a well-branded site can have a positive impact on its users. It is the same type of feeling you get walking into a well-designed and decorated room. You just get an extra welcoming and harmonious feeling.

As mentioned earlier, branding is a marketing term that has been also applied to SharePoint to refer to changing the look and feel of something. In a more complete sense, SharePoint branding is also often referred to as User Experience (UX) development. That term implies a deeper meaning than aesthetics and starts to show the complete value of why an organization might want to brand its SharePoint site. Although the value aesthetics bring is difficult to quantify, when you start to think about improving the UX for a site, there most definitely is measurable value. As a simple example, think about your company's current intranet or public website. It isn't uncommon for people to say that they think that it is difficult to find things on the current site or that it needs to be redesigned.

So why brand with SharePoint? The answer is going to be different for every organization, but the basic goal is to create a great user experience for anyone that visits the site. There's going to be many factors that ultimately determine what a "great user experience" means for your users. As you read through this book, you'll get a good idea of the options available and what is involved to deliver on those options to create the best possible experience for your users!

Is SharePoint Beautiful?

When you look at SharePoint, what do you think? When you create your first site, is what you see on the screen beautiful? Depending on what template you look at, you might see something different, but in general SharePoint has a distinct out-of-the-box look. Over the years, most would agree that the distinct SharePoint look has improved; although the most common branding request has remained unchanged: Can you make the site not look like SharePoint?

Companies spend lots of money developing their brand. Companies want to stand out in the crowd, which makes sense for many reasons. It isn't much different from how people feel about their personal "brand." Imagine if everyone in the world who worked with Microsoft technologies had to wear the same uniform. Some folks might be perfectly content, but many would prefer to wear whatever makes

sense to them. For some that might mean suits; for others it might mean a shirt, shorts, and flip-flops. Therefore, out-of-the-box SharePoint may be beautiful to you but not to others. However, one thing most can agree on is that it is nearly impossible to come up with a single look for a product that'll work for every organization on the planet using SharePoint. Customization is inevitable.

With the idea that custom branding is a common desire, it begs the question, "How much can I customize the design?" In truth, you'll most likely be more limited by time, budget, and technical resources than you would by SharePoint capabilities to customize a design.

COMMUNICATION VERSUS COLLABORATION

Although SharePoint sites are unique, they all fall into one of three categories: intranet, Internet, or extranet. Each of these SharePoint sites has a different audience and design considerations as part of the planning phase. It is important to note that the intended purpose for your site will have a major impact on your ultimate design.

The next few sections discuss the typical considerations for each of the three environments. At a higher level, each environment consists of many SharePoint sites, and each of these sites is usually designed to primarily facilitate either *communication* or *collaboration*. It is certainly possible to do a little bit of both, but for the core decisions made about branding, most sites favor one more than the other. For example, most of the sites on an organization's intranet fall under the category of a collaboration site because this is where most users store content and collaborate with others on their day-to-day tasks. The intranet home page for most companies is usually also designed as a place to convey information to employees, such as the latest company news, announcements, or events. When users first visit the site, they are taken to this homepage where they are presented with all this information, and from there they navigate to another area of the intranet to do work and collaborate. Effectively harnessing all SharePoint's capabilities into a seamless experience for users is part science and part art.

Branding projects often overlook the importance of determining whether the intended purpose of a site is either collaboration or communication. From a technical standpoint, sites designed primarily for communication or collaboration require different SharePoint templates, which require different approaches to branding. Consider that the approach for branding a SharePoint site based on the Publishing Portal template (which is designed for public-facing sites) is different from a branding site, which is designed purely for internal collaboration.

Considering who uses the site and how they are supposed to use it should be key in creating the design for your site. There's a distinct difference in the intended purpose of a site designed purely for communicating information in a one-way fashion verses a collaboration site designed for a two-way flow of information.

Intranet Sites

Intranet sites are typically available only to employees and partners who connect locally to the network or use a virtual private network (VPN). The focus of intranet sites is to facilitate information delivery and collaboration for specific sets of users. These sites often have multiple content authors, as well as many users who consume the content and collaborate on new content.

Unlike public Internet sites, the browsers and system capabilities of intranet sites are usually controlled by the IT department. This makes designing a SharePoint intranet easier because fewer variables need to be considered. For example, if your organization supports only one browser, your need to design and test is reduced to only that one browser.

As mentioned in the previous section, most intranets are designed to facilitate communication, but the vast majority of sites that are created are of the collaboration variety. Usually, this necessitates a highly customized homepage for the site with subsites that are focused on pure collaboration. Often, intranet sites must be customized to match the look and feel of a company's corporate branding. Following is an example of a custom-branded SharePoint intranet site that uses a custom master page, CSS, and images to create a new look and feel. Note that the version of SharePoint you use impacts the templates you can choose from (discussed more in Chapter 2, "SharePoint Overview").

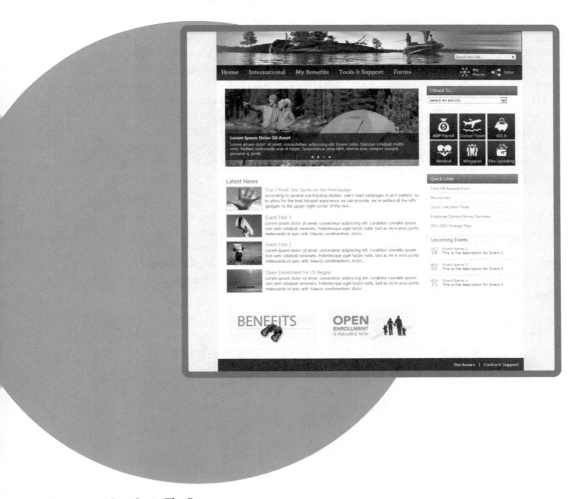

Internet Sites

Internet sites are public-facing and typically have anonymous users visiting them using a variety of Internet browsers and devices. These sites are usually driven by marketing, with only a few content authors and tightly controlled content.

Typically, public-facing Internet sites offer the opportunity to create highly stylized designs. They pose a greater design challenge than internal-facing sites because it is more difficult to control the technology being used by visitors who access the site. In other words, additional effort must be taken to ensure that the site displays properly across all types of browsers and conforms to whatever compliance standards need to be met for the given site. Not only is the creative effort usually greater for an Internet site than for an intranet site, but the actual implementation effort is also typically higher because of the added complexity.

One example of a corporate-branded Internet site that was built with SharePoint is Ferrari.com. It has a highly customized user interface, and without some poking around in the HTML source, it is hard to see any evidence that it uses SharePoint.

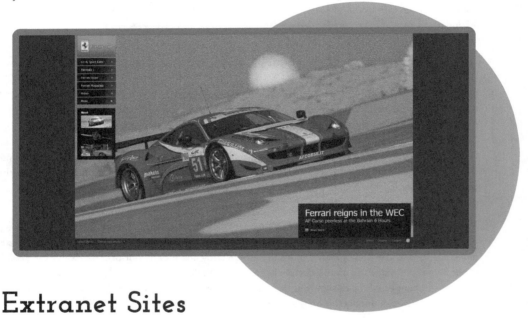

Extranet Sites

Extranet sites combine the security and collaboration of an intranet site with the more heavily emphasized branding found in Internet sites. The goal for most extranet sites is to enable external partners to collaborate with an organization. This is usually accomplished by having a public-facing Internet site that users can access initially. When on the site, users enter a username and password to access a secure site, where they can collaborate with users from inside the company. For example, a manufacturing organization might have an extranet site to enable distributors to log in and place orders or to obtain other information to help them sell the organization's products.

The biggest challenge with extranets is usually security. Most organizations want external users to log in to see what they need to see, but no more. Maintaining this balance of security can be tricky. From a branding perspective, it usually means that you must ensure that your branding is consistent across all areas of the site, especially those that extranet users will be accessing.

UNDERSTANDING THE LEVELS OF BRANDING

When you are thinking about your SharePoint branding project, understanding the environment you'll be customizing is the first step. As discussed in the previous section, each environment presents unique challenges. Another consideration is deciding what it is that you plan to actually implement. For instance, have you ever tried to do a home improvement project? Most people have no trouble changing a light bulb; a smaller number of people would be comfortable laying tile in a room; and even a smaller group would be comfortable adding on a new room to their house. The simplest tasks around the house can take a few minutes and are done by just about anyone, but other tasks take more time and require a more complex skillset. Customizing and branding SharePoint is similar. Depending on what you want to accomplish, some tasks require more skill or effort.

The various levels of branding for SharePoint have changed somewhat for SharePoint 2013 because the overall approach to branding has changed a bit more with this release than in previous versions. This section helps set expectations for some of the varied branding tasks in SharePoint and what's required for each level.

Following are three different approaches to create branding in SharePoint:

- **Low effort**—Typically, this approach includes all the branding tasks that an end user with limited training can perform. By using out-of-the-box branding, even someone with little knowledge of traditional website development and design can create a customized site. With out-of-the-box functionality, users can select master pages or composed looks. It is even possible to add a logo image to the top of every site by simply uploading an image and changing the reference in one of the menus (see the example "Replacing the Default Logo on a Composed Look" in Chapter 3, "Working with the SharePoint User Interface.") All these changes can be made through SharePoint menus and be completed in a matter of minutes.

- **Medium effort**—This approach is good to add some level of unique branding to a site. A medium level of effort would typically require users who have an understanding of CSS and HTML. These users can make changes to the CSS or HTML of a site or even copy and modify out-of-the-box master pages or other SharePoint pages to create custom branding for their site. Medium-effort users would typically make their changes with a design tool such as Dreamweaver or Expression Web. This approach usually takes days or weeks depending on the specific tasks.

- **Full effort**—If your design requirements are highly customized, your only option is the full-effort approach. This involves creating custom master pages, custom CSS, and potentially some custom page layouts. This approach is good for those who are experienced with traditional website design and have some knowledge of SharePoint or ASP.NET master pages. It is also well suited for public Internet sites and highly styled internal employee portals. These types of highly customized efforts can take weeks or months.

Which option you choose is likely going to depend on the skill set of the people doing the work and the budget for the project. Throughout this book you see different examples about what is possible for each of the approaches.

SUMMARY

- *Branding* is the act of building a specific image or identity that people recognize in relation to your company or product. It applies to both traditional websites as well as SharePoint.

- The basic goal for branding SharePoint is to create a great user experience for anyone that visits the site.

- Every site created in SharePoint is focused on either communication or collaboration. The types of sites you have impact the approach to branding you take.

- SharePoint 2013 has new options that have changed the ways that many approach branding. Whether you are a new SharePoint user or a seasoned SharePoint branding veteran, anyone can brand SharePoint!

2

SHAREPOINT
OVERVIEW

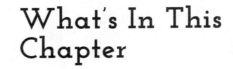

What's In This Chapter

For those of you who are familiar with SharePoint, much of this chapter might be a review. If you are new to SharePoint, however, this chapter is designed to give you a broad overview of the product—especially the elements relevant to the branding process. This chapter sets the stage for many of the concepts and terminology used throughout the book.

WHAT YOU NEED TO KNOW ABOUT SHAREPOINT

SharePoint is a vast product, and there are likely several dozen books written on a wide variety of topics pertaining to it. The focus of this book is obviously SharePoint branding and design—the cover probably gave that away. However, as a designer, you must have a fundamental understanding of SharePoint and the various pieces you'll be working with that can ultimately impact the type of work you create.

Versions

The most basic piece of information you need to understand is which version of SharePoint you'll be using. SharePoint 2013 is available at the time of this writing in a few different varieties:

- **SharePoint Foundation 2013**—Sometimes referred to as the free version of SharePoint. SharePoint Foundation provides the core collaboration and document management capabilities.

- **SharePoint Server 2013**—SharePoint Server is the licensed version of SharePoint and comes in two varieties: Standard and Enterprise.

- **Office 365 (SharePoint Online)**—SharePoint Online is the SharePoint component of the Office 365 suite. A number of plans are available, each with its own set of features and functionality.

For a more detailed comparison of the different versions of SharePoint, see `http://technet.microsoft.com/en-us/library/jj819267.aspx`.

Both SharePoint Server 2013 and SharePoint Online include the set of functionality referred to as publishing, which has several useful additions for branding projects:

- The Web Content Management (WCM) functionality provides users with a robust publishing platform. This means that users can author pages with rich and structured content and publish the pages in a controlled way using out-of-the-box workflows.

- Publishing provides more robust options for navigation. This gives users more control and provides greater flexibility than what is provided out-of-the-box by SharePoint Foundation.

- Publishing also enables site administrators to easily change a master page for any site, and all its subsites, from a SharePoint site's settings page.

NOTE

From a branding perspective, the publishing functionality in SharePoint Server 2013 and SharePoint Online provides many more options for creating highly styled sites than SharePoint Foundation 2013. Therefore, many of the examples throughout this book are geared toward sites with publishing enabled. However, in most cases the examples still apply to a nonpublishing site with minimal changes to the steps. The only exception to this would be when the examples cover functionality that is not available with SharePoint Foundation 2013. Where possible throughout the book, different approaches for achieving the same results in SharePoint Server, SharePoint Online, and SharePoint Foundation are highlighted.

Although the public site in SharePoint Online does use publishing, its features are slightly different from typical publishing sites. For more information on this, see Chapter 8, "Advanced SharePoint Branding Tasks."

Understanding the Site Structure in SharePoint

The version of SharePoint you use helps to determine what specific functionality is available to you, but some concepts in SharePoint are universal across every version. The overall structure of SharePoint objects is one of these concepts. The following list gives an extremely high-level overview of these major objects. These objects are listed in order of the biggest container to the smallest:

- **Web applications**—Essentially the same thing as a website in Internet Information Services (IIS). By default, each SharePoint web application has a unique URL and also a separate content database in SQL.

- **Site Collections**—Each web application contains one or more site collections. These are containers that define permissions and other functionality for the sites within the site collections.

- **Sites**—A site (developers sometimes refer to them as *webs*—short for website) is a collection of lists, libraries, and other content usually around a specific topic.

- **Lists and Document Libraries (Apps)**—Specific containers where content resides. Terminology for SharePoint 2013 had changed, so adding a new list or document library is under the **Add an App** menu of the Settings menu ⚙. Apps can also be added from the Site Contents page.

- **Items and Documents**—Individual pieces of content created in lists and libraries.

From a practical perspective, there are a few things to remember about the site structure. The first thing is that there are permissions at each level and how tightly (or loosely) controlled they are can cause unique challenges. This is usually something outside the realm of a typical SharePoint designer, but it is important to consider.

The second thing is that to create your branding in SharePoint you need to create things that interact with each of these objects to some degree. Which files need to be put where? What needs to be done at the site collection versus the site? The answers to these types of questions will become more obvious as you proceed through the book.

Master Page Gallery

The Master Page Gallery is a specialized document library. In SharePoint 2013, the Master Page Gallery has become the default location for all SharePoint branding assets. If you are used to creating websites with a technology that isn't SharePoint, this concept of all branding assets living under the same hierarchy is probably familiar. In previous versions of SharePoint, master pages and page layouts were stored in the Master Page Gallery, and this is still the case for SharePoint 2013. Other assets such as CSS, Images, and JavaScript were usually stored in a separate document library. The SharePoint 2013 approach is just simpler, which is often a good thing.

Every site has its own master page gallery that you can access by going to **Settings menu ➤ Site Settings** and then clicking on the **Master Pages and Page Layouts** link under the **Web Designer Galleries** section. At this point the details of the contents in the Master Page Gallery aren't too important, but you'll become familiar with this library as you progress.

HOW BRANDING WORKS IN SHAREPOINT

Before diving into the specifics of creating branding in SharePoint 2013, you must understand some of the key ways in which branding can be applied in SharePoint. The following sections examine these key concepts in detail.

Composed Looks

Imagine that you want to make some changes to spruce up your home that can be done relatively quickly and easily. Your budget is limited, so you decide to paint the walls with a brighter and more appealing color. In SharePoint terms, this would be equivalent to applying a *theme*. Technically speaking, themes can be thought of as changes that are applied to the existing look and feel through the use of CSS.

Over the past few versions of SharePoint, themes have evolved more than any other branding function. In SharePoint 2007, themes were stored on the file system of the SharePoint server and consisted of mostly XML, CSS, and images that were applied to a master page. The bigger issue was that although themes were considered to be one of the simplest approaches to branding, creating custom ones was actually quite complicated and required changes to files on the server, which required direct access to the file system. SharePoint Server Administrators aren't usually too fond of making changes to files on the file system, so to address this problem SharePoint 2010 took a new approach to themes and used the same mechanism used by Microsoft Office to create .THMX files that enabled users to select from twelve colors and two fonts. This could all be done through Office clients or through the SharePoint UI, which made custom theme creation much easier than with SharePoint 2007. When created, these files could be uploaded and applied to any site. This meant that themes could be applied without making any changes to the file system, but the downside here was that themes in SharePoint 2010 essentially just recolored sites. They didn't provide a way to modify CSS or add images. Many users felt this iteration of themes was almost too simplistic.

SharePoint 2013 introduces another approach to themes that is noninvasive like SharePoint 2010 but enables more flexibility to add background images and other customizations similar to the types of customization typically made with SharePoint 2007 themes. This new approach to themes is called *composed looks*. A composed look consists of a color palette, fonts, background image, and associated master page. When a user selects a composed look, all these associated design elements are applied to the site. There are several composed looks available to choose from out-of-the-box, but you can also customize these or even create your own.

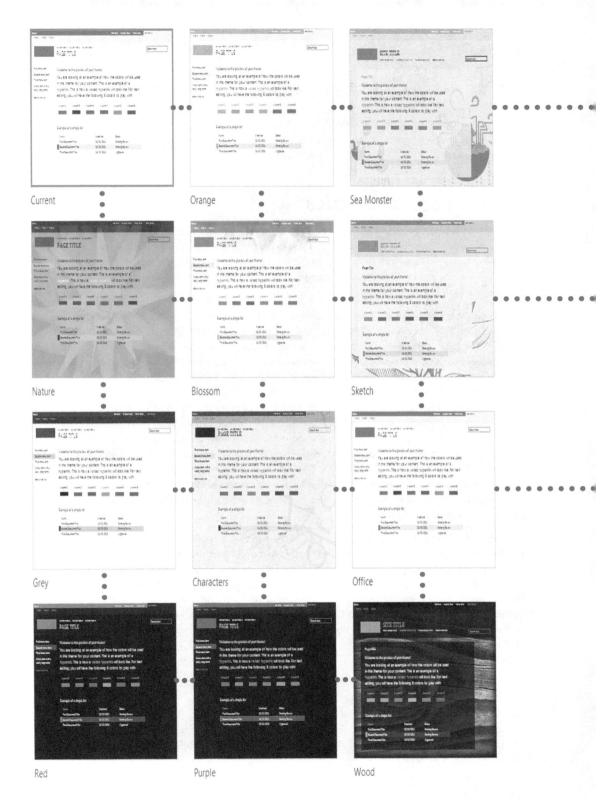

Current

Orange

Sea Monster

Nature

Blossom

Sketch

Grey

Characters

Office

Red

Purple

Wood

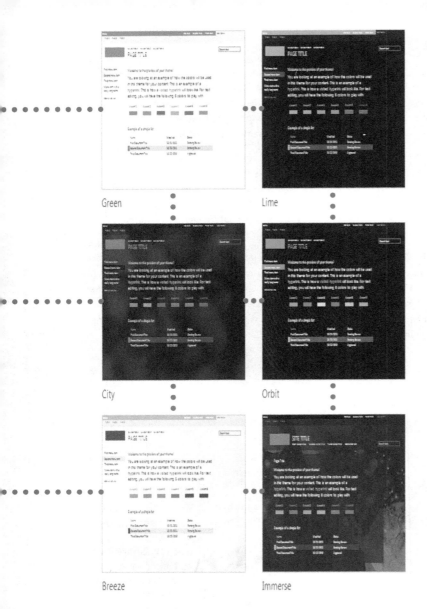

Green

Lime

City

Orbit

Breeze

Immerse

Composed looks are a simple way to brand your SharePoint sites, especially collaboration sites. Larger implementations will likely have both publishing and collaboration sites. In these cases a combination of approaches that include composed Looks and custom master pages could be used to present a unified look and feel.

NOTE

You can learn more about using composed looks in Chapter 3, "Working with the SharePoint User Interface," and about creating composed looks in Chapter 7, "Creating Custom Master Pages and Page Layout."

Master Pages

Revisiting the home improvements metaphor, if applying a composed look is comparable to painting the walls, then using master pages is comparable to altering the physical structure of the house. By changing the physical structure of your house, nearly anything is possible. Want to add a new room or knock down some walls? No problem. The sky is the limit as long as you have the right skills or can find a good general contractor to help you get the job done. The same is true with master pages in SharePoint.

Remember the good old days of classic web design, all the way back to the late 1990s and early 2000s, when web pages were created with the look and feel hard-coded in every page? Changing the footer, for example, typically required you to access every page in the site, repeating the same change on each one, and then uploading them back to the server. This tedious manual process created many opportunities to introduce errors.

With the advent of ASP.NET 2.0, master pages were introduced to alleviate this problem. Just like in a typical ASP.NET website, master pages enable designers and developers to create a consistent look and feel for all the pages in a SharePoint website. Every page on a SharePoint site references a master page. When a page is loaded in a browser, SharePoint merges the master page with the page, and the resulting styled page is returned to the user. Master pages enable organizations to create a consistent look and feel across all sites, which is a far better approach than was available in the past.

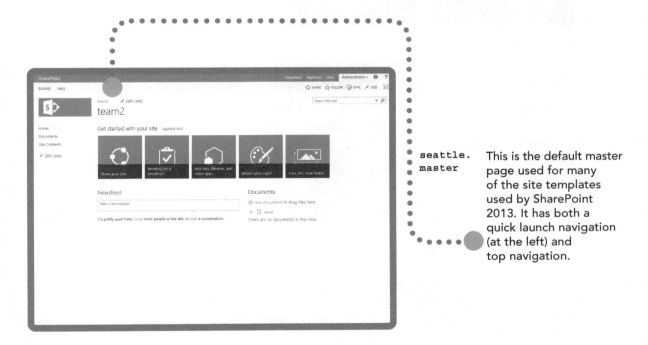

`seattle.master`

This is the default master page used for many of the site templates used by SharePoint 2013. It has both a quick launch navigation (at the left) and top navigation.

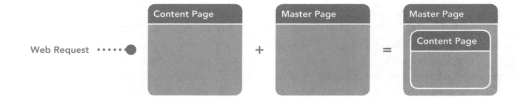

In the typical SharePoint site, master pages define the outer shell of the website. Sometimes called the *chrome*, this shell defines much of the overall look for every page loaded in the site. Master pages include HTML; SharePoint-specific controls (navigation, search, and so on); and *content placeholders*, containers used to load specific pieces of content from the referring content. A content placeholder is essentially a named container used to render various pieces of content. The most common example of this is `PlaceHolderMain`, which exists on every page layout. This is the content placeholder where field controls, Web Part zones, and anything else that is to be rendered in the central area of the page typically would exist.

SharePoint comes with a few out-of-the-box master pages that can be used for website branding right away. Unlike previous versions of SharePoint, the same out-of-the-box master pages are available for all versions:

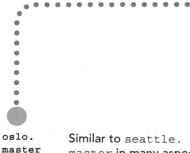

oslo.
master

Similar to `seattle.`
`master` in many aspects but displays the quick launch navigation horizontally at the top under the site title while the top navigation is hidden. Also, if you have a background image, this master page enables more of the image to come through.

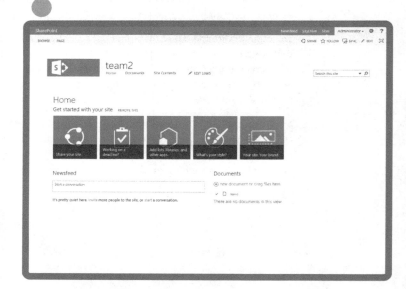

Content Pages

As discussed in the previous section, master pages define the outer shell of a SharePoint page, but the body of the page itself is also important. Depending on the purpose of your site (collaboration versus communication) and the site template you choose, you can have different types of content pages available to you. There are three main types of content pages in SharePoint 2013:

- Publishing pages
- Web Part pages
- Wiki pages

Each type of page has different options and a different intended use, so your functional requirements dictate which page is right for each scenario.

Publishing Pages

Publishing pages are available only in SharePoint on sites where the publishing feature is enabled. Publishing enables authors to create pages that have an approval workflow so that content can be reviewed and approved before being published. For example, you might create a page announcing a new policy, but the new page would need to be approved by your manager before it could be viewed by others on the website.

Publishing pages are created by using page templates called *page layouts*. If master pages create the outer shell of a SharePoint page, then page layouts define the body of a page. They enable content authors to create pages that contain text, HTML, graphics, rich media, and more.

To continue with the house metaphor used throughout the chapter, imagine a room with furniture in it—perhaps a couch and a few chairs and tables. The room would be similar in concept to a page in SharePoint; the pieces of furniture would be the various fields on the page. Applying a new page layout would be similar to rearranging the furniture in the room. The room is still the same and the pieces of furniture are still the same, but they are laid out differently and ultimately have a different look and feel.

Several out-of-the-box page layouts can be used right away in a SharePoint Server site, but also remember that designers and developers can always create their own custom page layouts. For example, when a user creates a new page in SharePoint Server, the same content can be arranged as a news article or as a welcome page, based on the page layout that is selected.

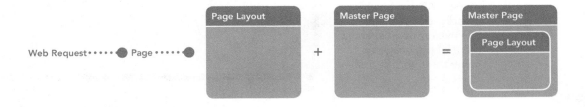

Chapter 7 discusses page layouts in greater detail.

Along with defining how content is arranged on a page, page layouts also define the location of editable fields and Web Parts. *Web Parts*, which can be thought of as self-contained widgets of functionality, can be arranged in pages through the use of *Web Part zones* that are defined in page layouts. Web Part zones enable content authors to add and arrange multiple Web Parts vertically or horizontally.

Publishing pages are the most highly structured of the SharePoint content pages. Not only do they use page layouts that provide a fairly strict template for creating content, but the approval workflow helps to prevent unwanted content from ever being seen. Because of the structure provided by publishing pages, they are best-suited for sites where communication is the primary goal. For situations that require a highly stylized layout, a publishing page with custom page layout is ideal.

Web Part Pages

The function of Web Part pages is fairly obvious by their name. They are pages that contain Web Part zones, where Web Parts can be placed that display things like list data, images, rich media, or other functionality. Any user with the proper permissions, usually a user with at least Contribute permissions, can create and edit Web Part pages.

Web Part pages are most appropriate when you simply need a page to display some information via Web Parts. Because the goal of Web Parts is to deliver functionality to the page, often by displaying content from lists and libraries, in most cases the Web Part page itself wouldn't be the place where actual collaboration occurs. In addition, it lacks the structure and formalized publishing process that you get with a publishing page. All versions of SharePoint 2013 support Web Part pages.

Wiki Pages

The goal of a wiki is to enable users to quickly create content and collaborate with other users; thus, wikis tend to be informal and unstructured.

One of the most commonly created types of site across most implementations is the Team site, which is intended to be a place where teams can collaborate. Beginning with SharePoint 2010, the Team site template came with wiki functionality. From a branding perspective this is important because Team sites will likely be the template used for the greatest number of sites across your organization—assuming you use SharePoint for your intranet.

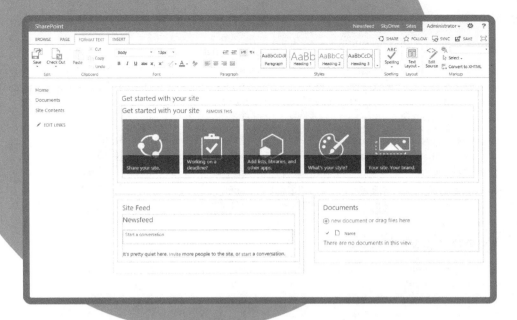

When you create a Team site, the first page you see when you go to the site is an example of a wiki page. In addition, every time you choose to **Add a New Page** from the Settings menu, a new wiki page is created. Wiki pages are unique because they have been designed to support this idea of quickly adding content to the page. For example, if you click the **Edit** button at the top right of a Team site, you see a few different areas that initially look like Web Part zones because they contain Web Parts. What you are actually looking at is a *Text Layout*, which arranges content areas on the page. In these content areas you can put text, HTML, rich media, or even Web Parts. You can also easily change the layout for the page by clicking the **Text Layout** button on the ribbon to choose from eight different options.

Wiki pages are available in all versions of SharePoint. Specifically for SharePoint versions with publishing available, the Enterprise Wiki template supports the capability to create and use page layouts with wiki pages.

Disabling Wiki Pages

Text Layouts are useful because of how they can be used to quickly create content. Designers, however, seem to have diverse opinions about wiki pages. Some love the flexibility, whereas others feel that because of the flexibility and unstructured nature of the wiki pages, it causes more problems than it solves. The purpose here isn't to pick one side or the other—but to point out the various opinions.

If you do find yourself in the camp that doesn't like wiki pages, the good news is that the functionality is easy to disable. All you need to do is click the Settings menu ➢ Site Settings and click Manage Site Features, which is found under the Site Actions heading (not to be confused with the old Site Actions menu). From here, click the Deactivate button next to the Wiki Page Home Page feature. Now when you go back to the homepage of your site, you'll notice that when you put the page into edit mode, you have a Web Part page instead of a text layout page. If you prefer this approach to the default Team site with the wiki, you could save your new site as a template, which would enable you to quickly create more non-wiki Team sites.

Cascading Style Sheets

CSS is pervasive in SharePoint branding. Almost every aspect of SharePoint is styled by CSS. All the SharePoint controls loaded by a master page are styled by CSS, as well as many Web Parts—even composed looks use CSS. Because of the importance of CSS in SharePoint, a sound understanding of it is crucial to becoming skilled at branding in SharePoint. Chapter 6, "Cascading Style Sheets and SharePoint," explains the typical SharePoint elements and what is involved with styling them using CSS.

SharePoint 2013 splits its default CSS across several smaller CSS files that are loaded according to what controls are available on a given page; however, much of the main CSS for SharePoint still resides in one CSS file named `corev15.css`. The intent of this division of labor is to load only the CSS that's necessary to render a given page. This approach reduces the total amount of data that needs to be downloaded with every page load compared to loading everything, regardless of whether it was needed.

WHAT'S NEW FOR BRANDING IN SHAREPOINT 2013

With more than 100 million SharePoint users worldwide, it is probably fair to assume that a good portion of those who are reading this book have at least some familiarity with SharePoint and its features. Whether you are a seasoned SharePoint design pro or someone who is just learning the ropes, there's been a large number of changes to branding and the processes related to branding in SharePoint 2013. Starting with SharePoint 2007, branding was something that started growing in importance, and by SharePoint 2010 custom branding seemed like it was a key part of every implementation project. Microsoft made a lot of investments in improving not only the features related to branding and design, but also around the process of creating custom branding.

New Approach to Branding

One of the most common perceptions people have about SharePoint branding is that it is a specialized skill that is difficult to master. One problem is that many traditional web designers struggle with some of the technical aspects of SharePoint. On the flip side, there are also plenty of developers who understand the technical aspects of branding but don't have design skills. This gap between designers and developers is an issue that Microsoft has attempted to address in SharePoint 2013 by looking at the way traditional web designers work and trying to adjust the way branding is created in SharePoint.

When you look at how websites are usually created, the design process across most platforms is the same. Most people start creating a design in whatever tool you are familiar with, such as Adobe Photoshop. From there the next step is to turn that design into HTML and CSS. However, turning your HTML and CSS into a SharePoint master page can be a tricky process, and this caused some confusion for traditional web designers. There are several tales of talented web designers who were brought to their knees the first time they tried to brand SharePoint. You'd usually hear them yelling things like "I don't understand why I can't make this work" or "[Other web technology] doesn't make me have to do it that way!"

To make the process of branding SharePoint 2013 sites less daunting, one of Microsoft's goals with this release was to create an experience that removed some of the technical hurdles many designers faced. Traditional web designers have no trouble creating working HTML and CSS-based mockups of a site design, but the process of converting that working mockup into a master page needed to be addressed.

Design Manager

The answer to this dilemma was to create a tool in SharePoint that did all the dirty work for you. The Design Manager is collectively a set of pages and functionality in SharePoint 2013 that can help guide you through the design process. Basically, the design manager gives you the ability to map a local drive to a site's Master Page Gallery and import HTML and CSS files into SharePoint. From there, SharePoint actually converts the HTML files into a master page. This helps to address one of the biggest pain points that designers had with SharePoint, but that is just scratching the surface of the possibilities. What if you don't have a designer? No worries. A quick search on the Internet can turn up a number of sites that offer various HTML design templates, many of which are free. You could even use one of these templates as the starting point for your SharePoint design.

NOTE

Chapter 5, "Using the Design Manager to Start a Design in SharePoint," offers details about the Design Manager.

HTML-based Master Pages and Page Layouts

The Design Manager has a number of other pages that give you the ability to further customize your design. One of the other important things to remember is that after you import your HTML and convert it into a SharePoint master page, there is still a corresponding HTML version of that master page. The same thing is true if you have any page layouts. Initially, this might seem strange—why would you want to have two versions of the same file?

The answer to that question is another big change to the branding approach for SharePoint 2013. Web designers usually have their favorite tools when it comes to building HTML and CSS, such as Adobe Dreamweaver, Microsoft Expression Web, or something else. In the past, the SharePoint design process would force them out of the tools that they were the most comfortable with and into others such as SharePoint Designer. So in SharePoint 2013, after HTML and CSS are imported, designers can still edit HTML and CSS files with the tools they are most familiar with, even after they've been converted into a master page. As designers make changes to the HTML files, SharePoint automatically makes the appropriate changes to the corresponding master page or page layout.

Cross-site Publishing

One of the more common complaints with previous versions of SharePoint was about the limited options for sharing content. For example, although it was possible to share content in SharePoint 2010,

there wasn't an out-of-the-box option to create content in one site collection and have it roll up to another site collection. The result was that often trade-offs were needed for certain scenarios.

A new feature of SharePoint 2013 is called *cross-site publishing*, which uses search to surface content—this is referred to as *search-driven content*. This concept might seem a little strange at first, but there are a number of examples across the web where search-driven content is already used. Perhaps you've been to a site such as Amazon.com and noticed that after buying a birthday present for your 4-year-old daughter the site is kind enough to show you other items it thought you might enjoy, such as various dolls and princesses. The site kept track of the items you had looked at in the past and, using search-driven content, displayed those items to you on the site's homepage the next time you visited. In a scenario like this, a lot of content that appears personalized to you is likely displayed via search-driven content.

A number of pieces work together to make the functionality known as cross-site publishing, which are discussed in this section. At the most basic level, this includes the site where the content is authored, the search piece that crawls and indexes the content, and a Web Part to query and display the content. It might all seem a bit complicated, but the goal for this section is to provide some basic information on the functionality; if your project needs cross-site publishing, you'll most certainly be interested to know how to brand and style it.

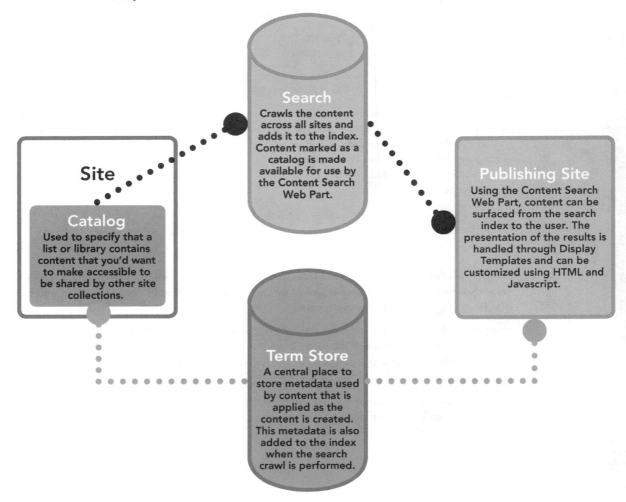

For more information about cross-site publishing, see the following articles:

- "SharePoint 2013 Cross-site Publishing Overview: Part 1" (http://sharepoint.microsoft.com/blog/Pages/BlogPost.aspx?pID=1038)

- "Plan for Cross-site Publishing in SharePoint Server 2013" (http://technet.microsoft.com/en-us/library/jj635876(v=office.15).aspx)

- "How to set up a Product-centric Website in SharePoint Server 2013" (http://blogs.technet.com/b/tothesharepoint/archive/2013/02/14/how-to-set-up-a-product-centric-web-site-in-sharepoint-2013.aspx).

Catalogs

A *catalog* is basically just an attribute that can be used to specify that a list or library contains content that you'd want to make accessible to be shared by other site collections. For example, imagine you have a public-facing product site. You might have all the information about your products in an internal site collection that only specific authors have access to. From there they can create, edit, and manage all the details of the products, which would be presented on your public-facing Internet site. This all might sound like an obvious scenario, but this wasn't easily possible in SharePoint before this version.

This new approach essentially enables the separation of content from the presentation. Content can be authored in a list as fields of data that are indexed by search and then presented to the user where they are needed and presented in a way that makes the most sense depending on the location. That means that the same content can be presented in different ways if needed. So if you consider the example of a product site, you might have a camera that has a corresponding page that provides all the usual details you might expect on a website. But if that camera goes on sale or you want to highlight it in a special way, you can present that same camera in a different way on a different page somewhere on the site—all you need to do is style the presentation accordingly. This is made possible through display templates, which are discussed later in this section.

You might want to use catalogs in several different ways. The following is a list of some common scenarios where this tool can be useful:

- **Intranet**—Authoring content in one site collection that is presented to another site collection. In this case, marketing or another department might be creating all the content in a central site that would then be displayed on the main intranet pages.

- **Internet**—Authoring content and products could be done in separate internal sites and syndicated to specific external sites as needed. This would be similar to the intranet scenario but would add a separate catalog for products in addition to the content. Content from multiple catalogs could be shared to one or more public-facing Internet sites.

- **Extranet**—Authoring for content could be done in internal sites and then shared with specific external sites. In this scenario, content could be shared from a single catalog to many external sites.

There is more involved with catalogs than just purely sharing content. The whole subject of catalogs could easily fill an entire chapter in this book. This section provided a high-level overview on the subject, but a deeper dive is needed to cover all the specific details. A good starting point is the Microsoft TechNet article, "Configure cross-site publishing in SharePoint 2013" (`http://technet.microsoft.com/en-us/library/jj656774(v=office.15).aspx`).

Content Search Web Part

In the past, the primary means of rolling up content was using the Content Query Web Part (CQWP), which basically sent out a query across all the objects in a site collection to find items that matched a specified set of criteria. Rolling up content using search is a more efficient way to do things because it pulls results from an index that is optimized for serving results. A more practical way to describe the difference between the two approaches is to do a search for a file on your computer. If the computer has been indexed, the results display almost immediately, but if the computer must search folder by folder, it takes significantly longer. In the case of SharePoint, that isn't to say using the CQWP was a bad thing; it just had limits to its scalability. The CQWP is still available in SharePoint 2013 and will remain an important way to roll up content for certain scenarios.

The Content Search Web Part is the primary mechanism for surfacing search-driven content to the page in SharePoint 2013. It can show any content as long as SharePoint search can crawl it and add it to the index. This is a huge change from the past because it means that not only is this approach far more scalable, but it also enables a tremendous amount of flexibility. From a planning perspective, this means that there are a number of new options available. For example, in the past you were limited to rolling up content within a site collection with the CQWP, but now with the Content Search Web Part, you can create content wherever you want and surface where it is needed.

Typically, when you type in a search query to try to find something, you enter a set of terms or criteria to make sure that your results are relevant to what you are looking for. The Content Search Web Part is no different, but instead of typing in a new set of search terms every time you go to the page, it uses a predefined query. To specify the query, the Content Search Web Part has a query builder that enables you to create a search query that can surface the results you're looking for. There are several queries that are predefined, or more advanced users can configure custom query parameters. There's even a results preview pane where you can see the items that are coming back to further refine the Web Part.

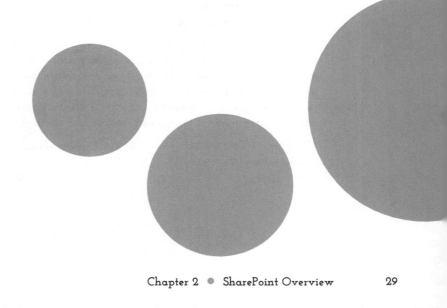

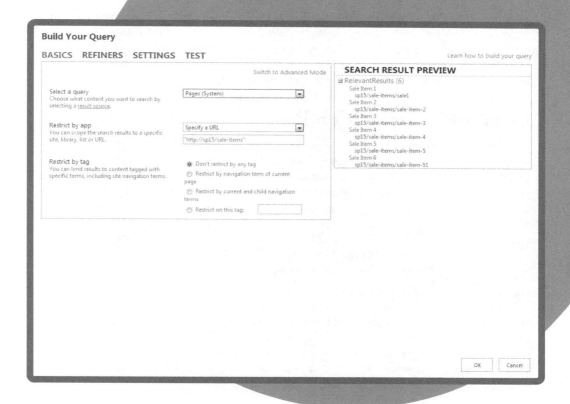

After the results come back from the Web Part, they are presented to the user, but by themselves those results would look quite rough. The Content Search Web Part uses a new mechanism called Display Templates to present the results to the user. Display templates are discussed in the next section.

There are a few things to keep in mind about the Content Search Web Part. The first thing is that content needs to be in the search index before it can be displayed by this Web Part. That means that your content won't display until the next search crawl happens. In most cases this won't be too big of an issue, but it is worth mentioning because you might be working on something and scratching your head when you aren't seeing a piece of content that you just know should be showing up.

Another consideration is that to take full advantage of this Web Part, you need to make sure that any content you want to surface has the right metadata associated with it. This is another case in which it doesn't sound like it is a big deal, but if your environment involves a large amount of content potentially spread across many site collections (or more), this can be a little more involved than it might initially seem. For any project that leverages the Content Search Web Part, you should take the time to carefully consider and plan accordingly for content and the metadata that's required.

Finally, the Content Search Web Part isn't available in all versions of SharePoint. As of this writing it is only available in SharePoint Server 2013 Enterprise. It is not currently available for SharePoint Online; however, Microsoft has stated that it is planned to be added in the future.

Display Templates

Display templates control the presentation of the results that come back from the Content Search Web Part as well as other search Web Parts, such as the Core Search Results and Refinement Panel. In the past, styling the results of Web Parts required XSL, which it seemed that no one was actually an expert with. The experience of trying to customize XSL to meet specific design requirements was often tedious and frustrating. For many it is probably good news that display templates use HTML and JavaScript as the way to customize results.

Display templates are stored in the Master Page Gallery of your site collection, and there are several available out-of -the-box. Even without making any changes to SharePoint, it is easy to understand the potential flexibility of display templates if you consider the different Web Parts, such as the Search Results and Refinement Web Parts that also use display templates in SharePoint 2013. At this point, the important thing to remember is that display templates should provide a more familiar way for designers to style rollups. They are extremely versatile and can be used for everything from styling simple search results all the way to dynamic animated rotators. Display templates are discussed in more detail in Chapter 9, "Creating Content Rollups with SharePoint WCM."

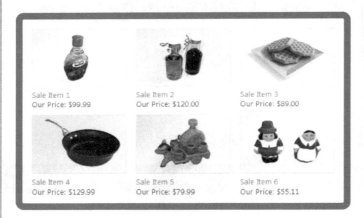

This shows a Content search Web Part using a custom display template.

Device Channels

Support for mobile devices, tablets, and other screen sizes have become an important design for modern websites. In previous versions of SharePoint, supporting different devices was possible, but building and customizing the experience for these devices wasn't as straightforward as many designers would have liked. SharePoint 2013 has addressed this need with a new feature of publishing called *device channels*. Device channels enable a site to be rendered in different ways depending on the type of device that is requesting the page. For example, if you browse to a website whatever browser you use can pass along some information called a *user agent string* that identifies the software making the web request. If you've never seen a user agent string, here are a few common ones:

```
Internet Explorer 9: Mozilla/5.0 (compatible; MSIE 9.0; Windows NT
6.1; WOW64; Trident/5.0)
iPhone 5: Mozilla/5.0 (iPhone; CPU iPhone OS 5_0 like Mac OS X)
AppleWebKit/534.46 (KHTML, like Gecko) Version/5.1 Mobile/9A334
Safari/7534.48.3
Lumia 920: Mozilla/5.0 (compatible; MSIE 10.0; Windows Phone 8.0;
Trident/6.0; IEMobile/10.0; ARM; Touch; NOKIA; Lumia 920)
```

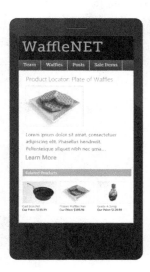
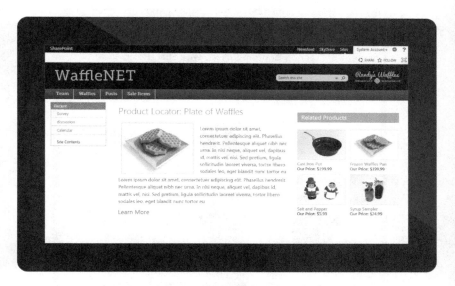

Device channels enable you to filter based on any piece of information that is available in the user agent string. From here you can assign a different master page to the respective channel. This enables you to create a master page with associated CSS that is more optimal for the targeted device.

SUMMARY

- The version of SharePoint you use determines the features and functions that you'll be able to use, which could impact your branding approach.

- Composed looks, master pages, page layouts, and pages are the major components used in SharePoint branding. Cascading Style Sheets (CSS) are used to style all the elements of the SharePoint pages that are rendered in the browser.

- SharePoint 2013 enables new approaches to branding. This includes the capability for users to import HTML and CSS, which get converted into a working SharePoint master page using the Design Manager.

- Designers are able to map the Master Page Gallery to a local drive and use familiar tools such as Dreamweaver to edit SharePoint branding.

- The addition of cross-site publishing and other improvements such as device channels make it easier to create custom-designed dynamic sites in SharePoint 2013.

3

WORKING WITH THE SHAREPOINT 2013 USER INTERFACE

What's In This Chapter

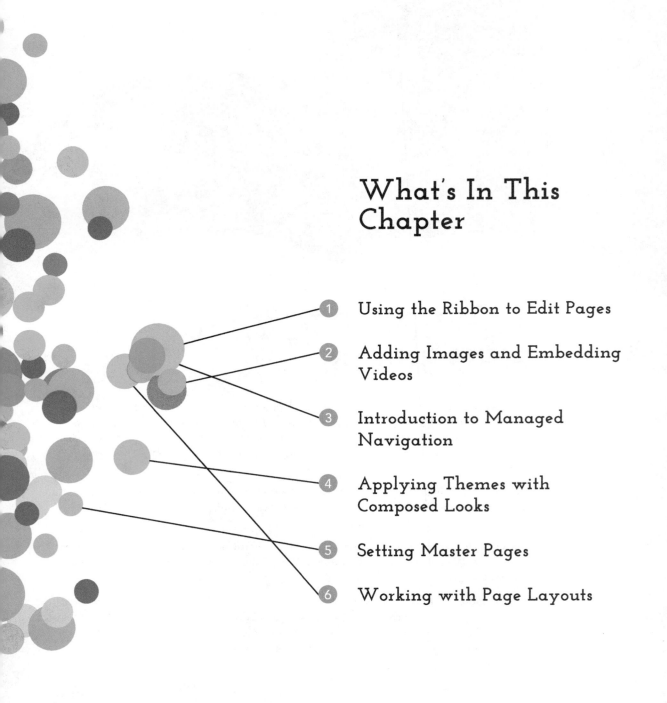

It's hard to create a design for SharePoint without at least a basic understanding of how it works from an end-user perspective. In this chapter, you will take a quick tour of the SharePoint 2013 user interface and learn how to work with content on a page, add apps and Web Parts, and modify the navigation. Then you'll take a look at the out-of-the-box ways to change the look and feel of your site with composed looks, master pages, and page layouts.

PAGE EDITING AND THE RIBBON

If you haven't heard of the ribbon by now, put this book down immediately and upgrade your old copy of Office 2003 to something from this decade—say, Office 2013. In short, the ribbon has been present in the Office suite of products since the 2007 release and found its way prominently into the SharePoint 2010 interface to make working with sites easier and more akin to its desktop counterparts such as Word and Excel.

The ribbon has made a triumphant return in SharePoint 2013 to continue on the legacy of its ancestors. It acts much in the same way that the ribbon acts in the Office desktop products and in SharePoint 2010, with a few refinements.

If you put a SharePoint page into edit mode you'll see the ribbon in all its glory—providing you with an interface similar to Word for formatting your text, adding pictures and other content, and even spell checking your web page.

The ribbon's contextual nature hides (or disables) options that don't apply to what you are working on at any given moment. For instance, if you click a picture you've added to a page, the Image Formatting and Design tabs appear. Otherwise, they are hidden because they don't apply to the immediate application. Likewise, you see a different set of ribbon options when you edit a page than when you work with a list.

The concept behind the ribbon is to put more options in front of the user rather than hide them in menus and dialogs. This enables you to accomplish more without changing screens or hunting for options; the most common tasks you need are right in front of you.

The behavior of the ribbon is similar to SharePoint 2010, but you may find that some items that you've been accustomed to have a new home. In addition, you'll notice that the ribbon is divided into two sections. The colored section at the top is called the Suite Bar. A closer look at the SharePoint 2013 ribbon's bits and pieces should clear up any inconsistencies between these two versions.

On the left you see the ribbon conveniently reminding you that you are using SharePoint with the text in the upper-left corner. In farm installations of SharePoint, the text says "SharePoint." If you're using Office 365, you'll see the Office 365 logo. It can't be changed or hidden from any site setting in the browser, but it could be removed on a custom master page or hidden with some custom CSS. Below that you see the available tabs that the ribbon offers at the moment. When you want to open different sections of the ribbon, this is where you click (just like in the Office clients). If you are used to SharePoint 2010 you may be wondering where the Site Actions button is; read on to solve the mystery.

Moving on, in the middle of the ribbon is where you can see additional links to commonly accessed areas in SharePoint. These include SkyDrive, Newsfeed, and Sites. If you use Office 365, you see a few extra links here including a link to Outlook. It's worth noting that you can create a custom delegate control to add additional links to the Suite Bar.

The right side of the ribbon is where things start to get interesting. On the top right of the ribbon, you see the name of the currently logged-in user, a gear icon, and a question mark icon. Below those icons is another row of icons and links, starting with Share, Follow, Sync, Edit, and a Full Screen toggle icon. These are described in the following table.

Although the ribbon sports a slightly updated look from its 2010 counterpart, you'll find that the functionality is largely the same. Sure, things have been moved around some, but you should find that the ribbon is intuitive and easy to use, especially after you start to use its functionality to edit pages.

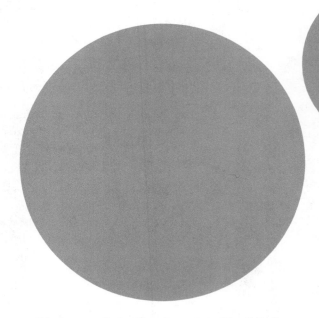

Newsfeed	**Newsfeed**	Opens a link to your My Site Newsfeed to see what's happening with your colleagues. The Newsfeed is one of the new features of SharePoint 2013's social capabilities. It's similar in nature to a discussion board. The Newsfeed in your My Site lets you follow discussions from many sites and colleagues in your organization in one convenient place.
SkyDrive	**SkyDrive**	Not to be confused with Microsoft's cloud storage option of the same name, this option takes you to your shared documents in the personal site in your My Site.
Sites	**Sites**	As the name implies, this takes you to your My Site again but shows you a list of all the sites you have access to and sites you have followed.
Administrator ▾	**User Name**	This shows the name of the logged-in user. Just like the welcome menu in SharePoint 2007 and 2010, you can click your name to open a menu. This time, because many links to your My Site have been moved onto the ribbon, there's not much here except a My Profile link and a link to Sign Out of the site.
⚙	**Settings menu (Gear icon)**	Remember when you read earlier that something familiar to SharePoint 2010 users was missing from the left side of the ribbon in SharePoint 2013? Well this is it. This gear icon is the new Site Actions button, now referred to as the Settings menu. If you upgrade to SharePoint 2013 from SharePoint 2007, you'll feel right at home because the SharePoint 2007 Site Actions button was on the right side of every page by default. However, those of you upgrading from SharePoint 2010 may find yourself moving the mouse to the left of the ribbon looking for the Site Actions menu the first few times you use SharePoint 2013.
?	**Help icon**	As you might suspect, this opens the SharePoint help menu, just as in past versions.
⟳ SHARE	**Share**	Opens a dialog for a quick way to add users to the site. You can pick which permission group your users should be added to by clicking the Show Options link in the dialog window.
☆ FOLLOW	**Follow**	You can "follow" sites in SharePoint 2013 in your My Site to see what new content is being added. A link is added to the Sites page of your My Site.
⬛ SYNC	**Sync**	You can sync the contents of document libraries with your local machine using SkyDrive Pro. Once you sync a library to your computer, you can drag and drop files into document libraries using Windows Explorer. (This option is available on collaboration sites.)
✎ EDIT	**Edit**	This button opens the current page in Edit mode, just like the Edit icon in SharePoint 2010. Like the Settings menu, this button has switched sides and now sits on the right side of the ribbon. When in Edit mode, this icon changes to a Save button (similar to SharePoint 2010).
⬚	**Focus on Content**	This button puts the focus of the page on the content by hiding the quick launch and header areas. Click again to show the page in its original state.

CREATING SITES AND SUBSITES

Throughout this chapter and the rest of the book you work with sites that are based on different templates such as team sites and publishing sites. If you have access to Central Administration on your SharePoint server you can create top-level site collections using the various site templates that are discussed in the book (to learn more about creating site collections see: `http://technet.microsoft.com/en-us/library/cc263094.aspx`). However, if you don't have access to Central Administration or you want to create subsites that are based on a template other than the root site collection, you can easily use the SharePoint web interface to create as many different types of subsites as you like.

If you have worked with SharePoint at all before you are probably comfortable creating many types of sites, but if you are new to SharePoint you should take a moment to review the following example.

EXAMPLE: CREATING A SUBSITE

1. From the homepage of your site, click the **Settings menu** ➤ **Site contents**.

2. Scroll to the bottom of the Site contents page to the Subsites section. Any existing subsites are listed here, with the option to create new subsites. Click the **new subsite** link.

3. Type a Title for the new subsite and optionally a description.

4. Type the end of the URL for the site you'll be creating. For example, if you are creating a Syrup subsite for Randy's Waffles, your URL might be `http://randyswaffles/syrup`.

5. Select the template to be used for the site. The type of site you choose will generally be dictated by the work done on it. For this example, click the **Collaboration** tab and choose the **Team Site** template.

6. Select whether you want to use the same permissions as the parent site (in which case the site will inherit the parent's permissions) or whether you want to use unique permissions for the site. For this example, select **Use same permissions as parent site**.

7. Choose whether the top link bar (top navigation) will be the same as the parent site. This setting also depends on what you are using the subsite for. If you are creating a site for a team to work together on a project, it might make sense for them to create a unique navigation structure that they can customize. If you're creating an Internet-facing site you would probably want to keep the navigation consistent throughout the site. For this example, select **Yes**.

8. Click the **Create** button to create your subsite.

Keep in mind that subsites can contain other subsites. The process is exactly the same, no matter if you are creating subsites from the root of the site collection or from within other subsites.

WARNING

If you notice that you are unable to create common types of sites there is a menu you can check: Site Settings ➤ Look and Feel ➤ Page layouts and site templates. Sometimes the Subsite Templates section is set to only allow you to create sites based on certain site templates. You can simply add back Site Templates here or you can change the setting to Subsites can use any site template.

THE PAGE EDITING EXPERIENCE IN SHAREPOINT 2013

Some minor editing differences exist between the various types of SharePoint sites, but there are a few basic concepts that apply to page editing no matter what type of site you use. These basics are important to know before getting into specifics.

To access the basic tools to begin editing your page, click the Edit link in the upper right of the ribbon. (If you're working on a publishing site and don't see the Edit icon, click the Settings menu, then click Show ribbon.) The page switches to Edit mode. This is where you can add and format text, add media (such as images and video), add apps and Web Parts, and generally lay out your page the way you want it to look.

NOTE

If you're familiar with SharePoint 2010's editing experience, rest assured that not a whole lot has changed this time around. A few buttons have been added or moved here and there, but overall if you knew the ribbon in SharePoint 2010, you aren't going to be in for much of a shock here.

Editing and Formatting Text

When SharePoint 2010 arrived, it drastically improved the page-editing experience for users. It was much easier to quickly add content to a page and format it because of the ribbon. It wasn't without its quirks, however, but overall the editing experience was a good one. SharePoint 2013 is no exception; it makes editing and formatting text on a SharePoint page easy and even improves the experience introduced in SharePoint 2010.

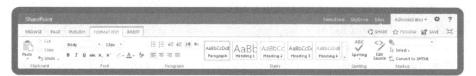

Editing a page in SharePoint 2013 is similar to editing a Word document. When you put your page into Edit mode, you'll be primarily working with the Format Text tab on the ribbon. In this tab, you have the ability to change fonts, change the font style (such as bold, italic, and underline), color your text, create bulleted and numbered lists, align your text, choose from predefined styles for page elements (such as Heading 1 and Heading 2), or choose between built-in text styles. This Styles section replaces the two drop-down options called Styles and Markup Styles from SharePoint 2010. You can also add custom styles to this section, which is detailed in Chapter 6, "Cascading Style Sheets and SharePoint."

No matter if you work on a collaboration site (such as a site built from the Team site template) or a publishing site (such as a site created using the publishing site template or a collaboration site with the publishing features enabled), the left side of the Format Text tab has Save and Check In buttons. If your site is a publishing site, you will find an additional Publish button under the Publish tab in the ribbon. More about these buttons and what they do is covered in the "Saving Your Page" section later in this chapter. For now, just remember where they are.

There are several other similarities between editing SharePoint pages using the ribbon and editing documents using Word. You can use the ribbon to check the spelling on your page (though this option is limited to sites with publishing features enabled). If you're so inclined, you can also edit the HTML source for your page's content if you need to fine-tune something. Also, just like in Word, you can copy, cut, and paste content, as well as undo any mistakes you make.

You may recall in past versions of SharePoint many users had a hard time copying content created in a Word document and pasting it into SharePoint. Often, content pasted into SharePoint from Word just didn't look right, especially if the Word document had numbered or bulleted lists, different fonts, or a stylized layout, and a lot of time and effort had to be spent cleaning up the look of the page. Sometimes users found it easier to manually re-create the contents of the Word document in SharePoint rather than spend the time cleaning up the look of the page. Fortunately, the copy-paste functionality from Word to SharePoint has been drastically improved and content now appears much cleaner in SharePoint 2013 than in previous versions.

To get a better feel for the page-editing experience in a couple of different site templates, try creating and editing a page in a site based on the Team Site template. (If you don't have a Team site created, refer to the "Creating Sites and Subsites" section of this chapter.) The following example applies to all collaboration sites (without publishing features enabled). Collaboration sites in SharePoint 2013 utilize text layouts for holding the text and content on a page. These are essentially templates that provide areas to add text on a page. You can choose from any of the eight available text layouts, but there isn't a way to add additional layouts. If your branding requires a layout that differs from what is available in the text layouts, you will need to look at enabling publishing features and creating custom page layouts for that.

EXAMPLE: GETTING STARTED EDITING A PAGE

1. Click the **Settings menu ➤ Add a page.**

2. In the New page name field, type **Why I Like Waffles.**

3. Click **Create**. The page opens in Edit mode. The default text layout is the One column layout that spans the entire body of the page.

4. In the Format Text tab of the ribbon, click the **Text Layout** drop-down and select **One column with sidebar**. The text layout changes so there are two areas for adding content now.

5. Click the cursor in the larger text area and type **Waffles are Delicious.**

6. Select the text with your mouse cursor, and click **Heading 1** in the Styles section of the ribbon. You see a live preview of what the text will look like as you hover over each option.

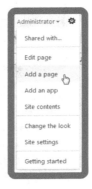

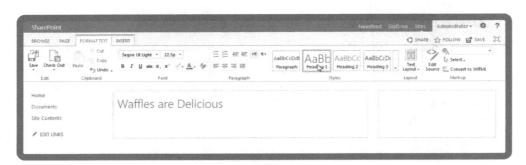

7 Click the mouse cursor after Waffles are Delicious, press **Enter** to go to a new line, and type the following text: **Here are three reasons I like waffles:**

8 **Select the text** you just typed and change the font by clicking the font drop-down (next to the font size drop-down) and selecting **Trebuchet MS**. Press **Enter** to go to a new line.

9 In the Paragraph section of the ribbon, click the **Bulleted List** button and type the following text (press **Enter** after each to go to a new line):

You can smother them in syrup and butter

They go well with bacon

They come in a variety of flavors

10 Click the **Save** button on the left side of the ribbon to see how the page looks.

11 On the right side of the ribbon, click the **Edit icon** to open the page in Edit mode again and on a new line below the bulleted items, type the following text: **I think I should go eat some waffles now!**

12 **Select the text** you just typed and make the text bold by clicking the **B** button under the font selection drop-down. Then click the **Save** button on the left side of the ribbon.

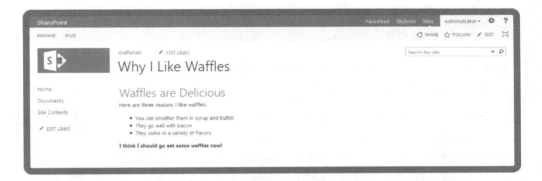

These steps are pretty basic to show a simple example of how page editing works in SharePoint 2013. When working with a site that has the publishing features enabled (such as a publishing site template) the editing experience is similar to editing pages on a collaboration site, except that publishing sites use page layouts instead of text layouts. Page layouts have different SharePoint field controls associated with them to store and display information. They are more flexible than text layouts in that designers can create custom page layouts to accommodate just about any design need. Page layouts can also utilize Web Part zones for storing Web Parts and apps.

EXAMPLE: EDITING A PAGE ON A PUBLISHING SITE TEMPLATE

1 From the homepage of the publishing site, click the **Settings menu ⯈ Add a page.**

2 In the Give it a name field, type **Why I Like Waffles**, then click **Create**. Your new page layout opens in Edit mode. By default, SharePoint publishing sites use a page layout that has a page content field control that spans the width of the page (you'll learn how to change this setting later in the section "Working with Page Layouts.")

You might notice that the Format Text tab in a publishing site is identical to the Format Text tab in a collaboration site with one exception: the Text Layouts button has been replaced with a Check Spelling button.

3 Click within the Page Content field control and type **Why I Like Waffles**.

4 In the ribbon, click the **Page** tab, and then click the **Page Layout drop-down**. In the Article Page section, choose the **Image on left** layout.

5 Your page's content remains the same, but now you can see extra fields built in to the page that you can fill out, such as an image field, an article date field, and a byline field. You won't be doing anything with these fields at the moment; for now, just note that this is one of the differences between page layouts and text layouts. You'll learn more about fields on page layouts later in the chapter.

6 Select the **Why I Like Waffles** text you just typed, and then select the **Heading 1** style from the ribbon.

7 Click the mouse cursor after Why I Like Waffles, press **Enter** to go to a new line, and type the following text: **Here are three reasons I like waffles:**

8 Select the text you just typed and change the font by clicking the font drop-down (next to the font size drop-down) and selecting **Trebuchet MS**. Press **Enter** to go to a new line.

9 In the Paragraph section of the ribbon, click the **Bulleted List** button. Type the following text (press Enter after each to go to a new line):

> **Waffles are delicious**
>
> **They go well with bacon**
>
> **They come in a variety of flavors**

10 Click the **Save** button on the left side of the ribbon to see how the page looks.

11 On the right side of the ribbon, click the **Edit icon** to open the page in Edit mode again and on a new line below the bulleted items, type the following text: **I think I should go eat some waffles now!**

12 Select the text you just typed and make the text bold by clicking the **B** button under the font selection drop-down. Then click the **Save** button on the left side of the ribbon.

As you can see, the processes for editing pages in a collaboration site and a publishing site are virtually identical. The major difference is the fact that publishing sites utilize page layouts, which can feature additional fields and Web Part zones, on the page that you can take advantage of.

Working with Images

If you spend any amount of time browsing the web, you have probably noticed that almost all websites use some sort of imagery on their pages. So it's likely that you'll want to add images to your page as well. There are several ways to add images to a page.

● **In a Page Content control or text field on a Wiki page**—The Page Content control found on page layouts in publishing sites and the wiki page text areas in collaboration sites not only enables you to insert text, but also enables you to insert images. You can choose to insert an image in SharePoint from your computer or from another URL.

● **Using an Image Viewer Web Part**—You can use a Content Editor Web Part or Image Viewer Web Part to add images to your page in a zone or in a page content area. This option is more limiting (and cumbersome to work with) than using other methods. You need to have your image uploaded to SharePoint and know the URL (or at least have the URL copied to the clipboard) before you use the Image Viewer Web Part; it curiously doesn't have a Browse feature to let you find the image. In addition, you can't take advantage of the new image renditions feature or resize the image in any way, so you are stuck using the original image size. In other words, if you need to add an image to your page, there aren't many compelling reasons to use the Image Viewer Web Part from a branding perspective.

● **Using a Content Editor Web Part**—The Content Editor Web Part is sometimes referred to as the Swiss army knife of Web Parts, and with good reason. It enables you to add text, images, scripts, and styles to your page. Content Editor Web Parts are kind of like mini-page content field controls. You can add images, select where the image comes from, and format the image to fit your needs.

● **In an image control on a publishing page**—Some page layouts have a built-in image field control that enables you to add an image. Although the link in the control says to **Click Here to Insert an Image from SharePoint**, you can also upload an image file from your computer as you browse the site's contents.

Each of these ways follows the same basic steps to get an image on your page. Generally, you can choose to add an image that's already been uploaded to your site somewhere, or you can browse your computer for an image you want to upload and add. These steps can apply to either a collaboration site or a site with publishing enabled.

EXAMPLE: ADDING AN IMAGE TO A PAGE

1 Click the **Settings menu** ➤ **Add a page**.

2 In the **New page name** field (or **Give it a name** field if you're on a publishing site), type **Waffle Picture**.

3 Click **Create**. The page opens in Edit mode.

4 On the ribbon, click the **Insert** tab; then click the **Picture drop-down**.

5 In the Picture drop-down, select **From Computer**.

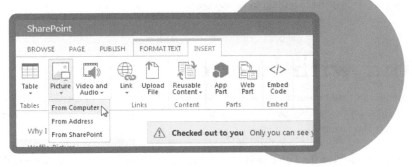

6 Click the **Browse** button to browse your computer for an image. If you have downloaded the files for this chapter, look for **WaffleWithSyrup.jpg**, and click **Open**.

7 Select the Destination Library you'd like your image to go in (Images for publishing sites or Site Assets for collaboration sites are the default locations, but you can change this if you wish). If your site has publishing enabled, optionally type some comments in the Version Comments field.

8 Click **OK**. If your site has publishing enabled, you'll be prompted to fill in additional metadata about the image. Optionally do so, and click the **Check In** button in the ribbon in the dialog, or the **Save** button at the bottom of the dialog. Your image is added to the page. .

9 Click the image to select it. In the ribbon, click the Image tab that has appeared.

10 In the Horizontal Size field in the ribbon, type **500px** and press **Enter**. The image is resized.

11 Click the **Image Styles** drop-down and select **Light border**.

12 Toward the left side of the ribbon, change the Alt Text field value to **A Picture of a Waffle and Syrup**. This text will appear when the mouse cursor is hovered over the image.

13 Click the **Save** button on the right side of the ribbon.

You'll also notice in the Image tab on the ribbon that there are a few other options you can take advantage of when working with images, such as changing out the image with the Change Picture button, changing the position of the image in relation to the text with the Position drop-down, and increasing the horizontal and vertical spacing between the image and text with the Vertical Space and Horizontal Space options. Finally, if your site has publishing features enabled, you can use image renditions to resize/crop your images.

Image Renditions

A new concept to SharePoint 2013 is image renditions. The basic purpose of image renditions is to offer differently sized versions of images uploaded into SharePoint. To take advantage of this useful feature, you need to be working on a site with publishing features enabled, and also have BLOB caching enabled for your web application.

EXAMPLE: ENABLING THE BLOB CACHE

1 Log in to your SharePoint server as an administrator.

2 Click **Start** ➤ **Computer** and navigate to the following directory: `C:\inetpub\wwwroot\wss\VirtualDirectories`.

3 Open the folder of the web application in which BLOB caching will be enabled. For instance, if your site's URL is `http://wafflenet/` the folder you want is most likely called `wafflenet80`.

4 Create a backup copy of the `web.config` file. This is always recommended if you ever need to edit or modify this file, so you can always revert back in the event that something happens.

5 Open the `web.config` file in Notepad or another editor.

6 Press **Ctrl+F** to open the Find dialog and type **<BlobCache**.

7 Press **Enter** to perform the search, which brings up the following line:

```
<BlobCache location="C:\BlobCache\14" path="\.(gif|jpg|jpeg|jpe|jfif|bmp|dib|
tif|tiff|themedbmp|themedcss|themedgif|themedjpg|themedpng|ico|png|wdp|hdp|cs
s|js|asf|avi|flv|m4v|mov|mp3|mp4|mpeg|mpg|rm|rmvb|wma|wmv|ogg|ogv|oga|webm|x
ap)$" maxSize="10" enabled="false" />
```

8 At the end of the line, change `enabled="false"` to `enabled="true"`.

9 **Save** the `web.config` file. You can log out of the server now.

When using image renditions, your image will be cropped and resized according to a handful of preset sizes, including any custom sizes you create. You can then further customize how each image is cropped and resized for each rendition, and add those versions of the image to the page. In past versions of SharePoint, it was possible to resize an image on a page; however, the image's file size remained the same no matter how large or small the image actually displayed on the page. Image renditions aren't just the original image displayed smaller or larger. They are entirely unique image files stored on the SharePoint server's hard drive. When image renditions are configured, SharePoint automatically crops and sizes the original image to the specified dimensions and saves those files as individual images on the hard drive. Those newly created images are then referenced back to the original image.

When you add an image onto a page, you can click the **Pick Rendition** button in the Image tab on the ribbon to choose the size (or image rendition) of the image. SharePoint swaps out your original image with its image rendition version, which can reduce the overall size of the page weight. Image renditions are also useful when leveraged in Device Channels, so the same image can be used on mobile sites without having to resize everything manually. The other major benefit of image renditions is that you can use it to enforce consistency among the images on a site.

If one of the renditions of a particular image doesn't look right, you can adjust how the image displays in each rendition. Keep in mind that editing the renditions for an image affects all instances of that image rendition throughout the site.

EXAMPLE: CREATING AND USING AN IMAGE RENDITION

1 Click the **Settings menu** ➤ **Site Contents.**

2 Click the **Images** library. (If you don't have an Images library, click the **Add an App** link, select the **Picture Library** app, and name it **Images.**)

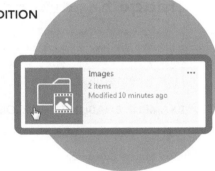

3 Click the **+ New item** link to browse your computer for an image to upload, or you can simply drag an image from your desktop to the image library to quickly upload it. (This example uses **EggsAndBacon.jpg** from the chapter downloads.)

4 Click the **Settings menu** ➤ **Add a page.**

5 In the Give it a name field, type **Image Rendition Page** and click **Create.**

6 Click the **Insert** tab in the ribbon, click the **Picture drop-down,** and select **From SharePoint.**

7 In the left pane, click the **Images** library, click the **EggsAndBacon** image to select it, and click **Insert** at the bottom of the Select an Asset dialog.

8 Click the **Save** button on the right side of the ribbon. The image you just added is pretty big and a little busy. Your image rendition would be better if it was smaller and focused on a specific part of the image; namely, the delicious-looking plate of food.

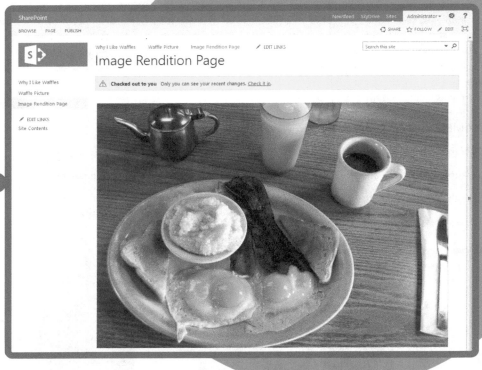

Photo Credit: Tom Drisgill

9. Click the **Settings menu ➤ Site Settings**.

10. Under the Look and Feel header, click **Image renditions**. (If you don't have the BLOB cache enabled, you'll see an error on this page, so make sure it is enabled.)

11. Above the existing image renditions, click the **Add new item** link.

12. In the Name field, type **WaffleNet Image Rendition**. This is what will show up in the Pick Rendition drop-down, so be descriptive. Here you can also specify the width and/or the height of the image, in pixels. In this example, type **500** in the Width field. This results in a 500-pixel-wide image. You must specify either the width or height of an image rendition, or both.

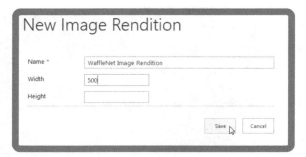

13. Click **Save**.

When specifying both a height and width for an image rendition, SharePoint crops images down to the specified size. You might lose part of your pictures, which is why it's a good idea to preview your images and adjust the rendition for an image as needed. This is explained in greater detail in the next example. If you specify only the width or height, the image rendition resizes the image and shows the entire image at the specified width or height, keeping the image proportions the same. No cropping occurs here, unless you manually crop the image when you edit the rendition for a particular image. After you set up your image rendition, you can try it out.

EXAMPLE: EDITING AN IMAGE RENDITION

1. Click the **Settings menu ➤ Site contents**.

2. Click the **Images** app and hover the mouse cursor over the **EggsAndBacon.jpg** image preview.

3. Click the **...** (ellipsis) in the lower-right corner of the thumbnail.

4. In the pop-out menu, click **Edit Renditions**.

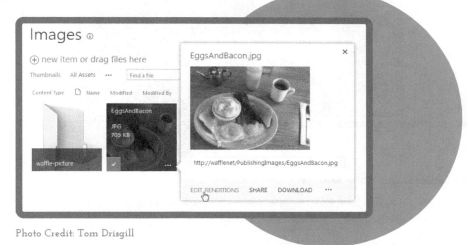

Photo Credit: Tom Drisgill

5. On the Edit Renditions page, look at the various renditions that SharePoint has put together. The various renditions are ordered by size. Chances are some of the cropping doesn't look great on some of them, which is why it's not a bad idea to preview the image renditions when you upload an image to the site. Click the **Click to change** link under the image preview for the WaffleNet image rendition you created.

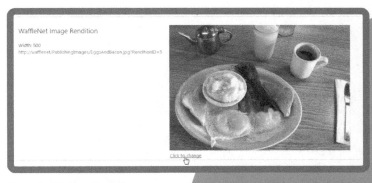

Photo Credit: Tom Drisgill

6. If you are prompted to check out the image, click **OK**; otherwise continue to the next step.

7. In the Crop Rendition window, click and drag the corner handles of the image to change the cropping area. Crop the image so only the plate of food is visible. You can also click and drag the highlighted section around on the image to change what area of the image will show in the image rendition. A preview of your rendition appears at the bottom of the dialog window.

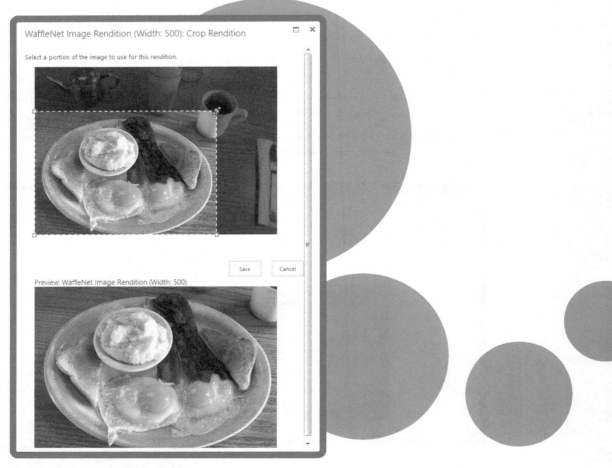

Photo Credit: Tom Drisgill

8. Above the image rendition preview, click **Save**.

9. Scroll to the bottom of the Edit Rendition page and click **OK** to save your changes to the image renditions.

10. If you checked out the image, be sure to check it in so other users can use the image renditions you set up.

Now that you've created and edited your rendition, it's time to put it to use.

EXAMPLE: ADDING AN IMAGE RENDITION

1 Return to the image rendition page you created earlier. (SharePoint added a link to the page on the top and left navigation areas of the site, or you could view the site contents and find the page in the Pages library.)

2 On the right side of the ribbon, click the **Edit** button.

3 With the page in Edit mode, click the image you added earlier.

4 Click the **Image tab** that appears on the ribbon.

5 Click the **Pick Rendition** drop-down. (Note that this drop-down will not show if BLOB Cache is not enabled.)

6 Select the **WaffleNet** image rendition you created and your image will be resized and cropped to the dimensions specified in the image rendition.

7 Click the **Save** button in the ribbon to save your page. As you can see, the image is much smaller on the page and has been cropped to show only a specific area of the overall image.

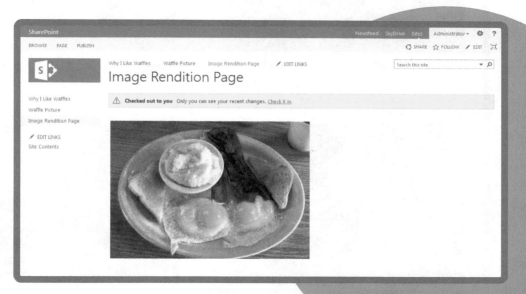

Photo Credit: Tom Drisgill

Working with Videos

Video has now become an almost essential part of many websites and you will likely want to add one to your site one day. There are two ways you can add video to your site: You can use the built-in Media Web Part to play videos stored on the site, or you can embed a video from an external video provider

(such as YouTube or Vimeo). Both ways work well, although there is some consideration to be made when storing videos in the SharePoint site because videos tend to take up a lot of disk space. Storing on an external video hosting site can save you a lot of disk space, but the downside is that the video needs to load from an external site, which can potentially cause a slight increase in page load times.

The Media Web Part was introduced in SharePoint 2010, and it's largely the same in SharePoint 2013. Embedding a video is a different story, however. Although you could technically embed externally hosted videos in previous versions of SharePoint using the Content Editor Web Part to edit the HTML source, it was always more trouble than it felt like it should have been and it wasn't a very intuitive process for many users. Luckily, Microsoft has made the process much easier by adding functionality to embedded code. When you want to embed a video (or other code, for that matter), you simply paste in the embed code provided from the video provider site, and SharePoint does the rest. Just like that, you have added a video to your page.

EXAMPLE: UPLOADING A VIDEO USING MEDIA WEB PART

1. Click the **Settings menu ➤ Site contents**.

2. Click the **Documents** library to open it. You'll upload the video here.

3. Drag a video file from your computer to the document library to upload it. If you're using the file downloads for this chapter, you'll be using **WaffleTower.mp4**.

4. Click the **Settings menu ➤ Add a page**.

5. Give the page a name, such as **Waffle Video**, and click **Create**.

6. When the new page opens, it is in Edit mode. Click the **Insert** tab on the ribbon.

7. Click the **Video and Audio** drop-down and select **From SharePoint**. (Note that there is also a From Computer option in this drop-down. You can use this to upload and add videos on-the-fly without leaving your page.)

8. In the **Select an Asset** dialog window, click the **Documents** library where you uploaded your video, and click **WaffleTower.mp4** so that its URL appears in the Location (URL) field at the bottom of the dialog window.

9. Click **Insert**. The Web Part is added to your page. Click the **Play** button or anywhere in the Web Part to view the video.

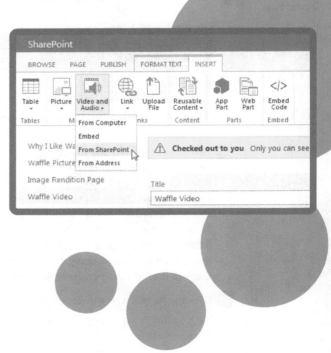

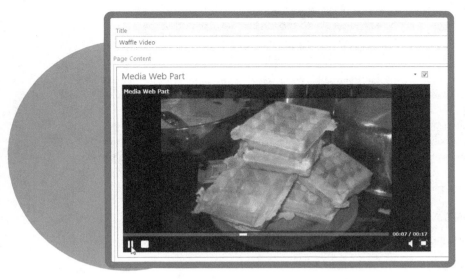

Photo Credit: Tom Drisgill

10 Click the **Media Web Part** title to open the Web Part tab on the ribbon. (Note that two titles appear: the Web Part title only appears in Edit mode by default, and the video title appears on the video itself when you hover the mouse over the video.).

11 On the Media tab, change the **Title** field from Media Web Part to **Waffle Tower Video**.

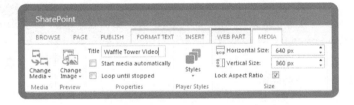

12 Take note of the options you have in the Web Part tab of the ribbon for the Media Web Part. These include the ability to change the video, set basic playback options such as automatically starting the video on page load, looping the video continuously until it is stopped by the user, changing the style of the video player (you can choose between a dark or light player), and how large (in pixels) the video should display on the screen. For example, if you wanted to increase the video size to take more horizontal space than the default size, you could increase the horizontal width to your desired size. Below the sizing fields is a check box that allows you to preserve the aspect ratio of the video, meaning that SharePoint automatically adjusts the height as you adjust the video's width (and vice versa) in order to maintain the same proportions of the video in the Web Part.

13 Click the **Page** tab on the ribbon, and click **Save**.

The Media Web Part's default look is a little bland, but you can choose a different image to display as the preview image of the video. The bad news is that if you want it to be a still frame from the video, you need to capture that still frame, save it as an image, and upload it to SharePoint. The process is a little complicated.

EXAMPLE: ADDING A PREVIEW IMAGE TO A MEDIA WEB PART

1. Start playing the video and pause it on the scene you want to capture.

2. Open a screen capture tool such as the built-in Snipping tool in Windows 7 and 8.

3. Grab the frame from the video and save it to your computer. If you're following along using the files for this chapter, you can use the **WaffleTowerPreview.jpg** image instead of getting a screenshot yourself.

4. On the Waffle Video page, click the **Edit** button on the ribbon.

5. Click the **Waffle Tower Video Web Part** title to open the Media tab on the ribbon.

6. Click the **Change Image drop-down** and select **From Computer**.

7. Browse your computer for the image you captured from your video (or **WaffleTowerPreview.jpg** if you are using the files for this chapter).

8. Select the destination library to which you want to upload the image and click **OK**. If you're on a publishing site, you can use the **Images** library. If you are using a collaboration site, you can use the **Site Assets** library.

9. If necessary, fill in any of the metadata information about the image, and click the **Save** or **Check In** button. (Depending on your site type or library settings, you may not be prompted for this step.)

10. Click the **Save** button in the ribbon to preview your page.

The Web Part now displays your preview image and looks much nicer than the default. Users will have a better idea of what they can expect from the video.

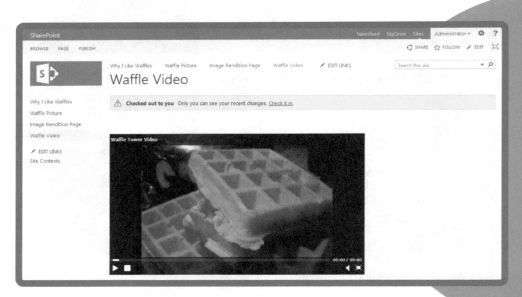

Photo Credit: Tom Drisgill

Now that you know how to use the built-in Media Web Part, take a look at embedding external videos onto your page.

EXAMPLE: EMBEDDING EXTERNAL VIDEOS

1. On your favorite video site, find the video you want to add.

2. Many video sites provide you with a code snippet to embed the video on another site. In YouTube and Vimeo, you can click the **Share** button. (At the time of this writing, you can find these buttons below the video or to the right of the video, respectively.)

3. **Copy** the embed code provided by the video site.

4. Return to your Waffle Video page in SharePoint, and make sure it's in **Edit mode**.

5. Click the **Insert** tab on the ribbon.

6. Click the **Embed Code** button.

NOTE

You may have noticed earlier that the Video and Audio drop-down also contains an Embed option for adding video to the site. These two options open the same dialog.

7. On the Embed dialog, paste your copied code into the input field. SharePoint gives you a preview of your embedded object.

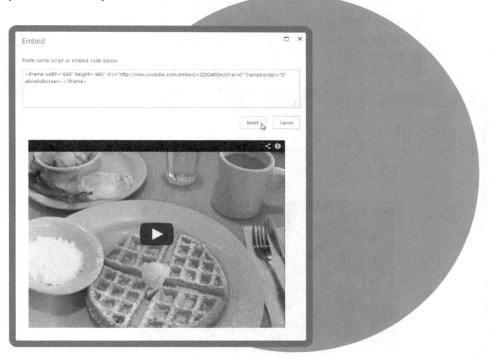

Photo Credit: Tom Drisgill

8. Click the **Insert** button to add the video to the page and click **Save**.

You can now play the video pulled in from an external site directly on your page with minimal effort required to set it up.

Adding Web Parts and Apps

Web Parts and apps can be thought of as blocks of functionality that can be added to the page to accomplish a certain task. You just learned how to add images and video to your page using various Web Parts. The only difference between adding regular Web Parts and adding those for pictures or videos is that the Web Parts for pictures and videos get their own special shortcut buttons in the Insert tab on the ribbon. Web Parts and apps can also be views of the contents in a list or library, a rollup Web Part for aggregating content from across your site, and other collaborative components.

NOTE

Many places in SharePoint 2013 the term "app" is sometimes used generically to describe a Web Part for a list or library. There are also actual apps (similar to the type of app that can be purchased on a mobile device) that can be downloaded and installed to SharePoint 2013 to be used on their own or surfaced on a page with an App Part.

Web Parts and apps can be added just about anywhere on a SharePoint page:

- In a text layout column (on collaboration sites)
- In a page content control (on publishing sites)
- In a Web Part zone (on publishing sites)

Text layouts, used by the wiki features, enable users to quickly insert text, images, and Web Parts/apps. Publishing sites feature page layouts that can have control blocks for specific types of content. One of these content controls is called the Page Content control and is similar to a text layout because it enables users to insert text, images, and Web Parts/apps. Finally, page layouts can also contain Web Part zones, which are sections of the page specifically for adding Web Parts and Apps.

NOTE

You can also add some Web Parts to a custom page layout outside of the areas previously mentioned; however, the Web Part needs to be configured directly on the page layout in these instances because its properties won't be editable in the browser. Working with page layouts is covered in more detail in Chapter 5, "Using the Design Manager to Start a Design In SharePoint" and Chapter 7, "Creating SharePoint Branding"; this chapter is all about what you can do in the user interface of SharePoint 2013.

If you're working in a content field or text layout, position the cursor where you want the Web Part to be added. On the ribbon, click the **Insert** tab ➢ **Web Part**. (You can also click **App Part** on the ribbon to insert existing lists or libraries, now called Apps in SharePoint 2013, to your page.)

If you want to add a Web Part to a Web Part Zone on the page, simply click the **Add a Web Part** link in the zone.

When you start adding a Web Part, the first thing you see is a big Web Part menu appear at the top of your page. On the left of this menu is a Categories section, which divides up the Web Parts into groupings. Select a category and you can see all the different Web Parts that it contains. Then select the Web Part you want, click the Add button, and you're on your way. (This process is identical to Share-Point 2010, so if you've upgraded to SharePoint 2013 you'll feel at home here.)

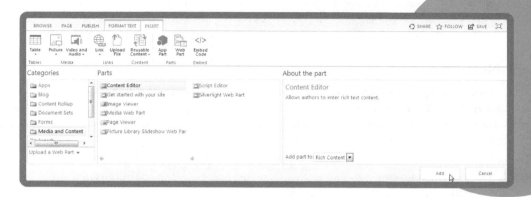

You can click through the various categories to see the different types of Web Parts available. Depending on your needs, chances are there's a Web Part that can help you. For branding purposes, here are some of the most common Web Parts you're likely to encounter:

Content Editor Web Part—Similar to a text box in Word. You can add a CEWP to a zone for an extra area of content that you can format and edit, or even add styles and scripts to. The CEWP can be found in the Media and Content category in the Web Part picker menu.

Content Query Web Part—Aggregates content (such as news articles or items in a list) and displays them in predefined styles. You can also create custom styles to use for the CQWP, which is covered in Chapter 9, "Creating Content Rollups with SharePoint WCM." The CQWP is found in the Content Rollup category, and is only available on sites with publishing enabled.

Content Search Web Part—New to SharePoint 2013, this is similar to the CQWP but more powerful because it can show content from search results based on a query you specify. Like the CQWP, the Content Search Web Part is found in the Content Rollup category and is also only available on publishing sites. As of this writing, the CSWP is not available on SharePoint Online sites; however, Microsoft has indicated it may become available at some point. You can find more information on the CSWP in Chapter 9.

Script Editor Web Part—You can insert snippets of HTML or scripts in this Web Part. This Web Part is found in the Media and Content category.

Of course, this list barely scratches the surface of the available Web Parts in SharePoint 2013, but these are the most common ones you'll likely encounter.

Saving Your Page

Earlier you were introduced to the Save, Check In, and Publish buttons found on the ribbon. These buttons are your way of saving and sharing your formatted page with your team or the world. The Save and Check In buttons appear in the Format Text tab in the ribbon, as well as in the Page tab. The Publish button, unique to publishing sites, appears in its own publishing tab.

When you put a publishing page into Edit mode, it is automatically checked out to you, but to share the page with others, it needs to be checked in and/or published, depending on the type of site you work with. Collaboration sites don't automatically check out the page to you unless you specifically click the Check Out button. Checking out a page prevents someone else from editing the page at the same time as you. When you have a page checked out, you can see the latest changes you've made, but other users still see the page as it appeared before you checked it out.

To exit Edit mode and save your changes, you can click **Save**. In collaboration sites, simply saving your changes without having the page checked out enables others to see the changes you've made. If you have the page checked out, clicking Save enables you to save your latest changes while retaining your check out. Only you can see the latest changes on the page as long as you have it checked out. If you finish making changes you can click the **Check In** button. This saves your edits and allows others to see your new content and make their own edits.

On a site with publishing features enabled, checking in pages allows users with certain edit rights to see your latest changes, but everyone else will still see the previously published version of a page. If the page has never been published, users without edit rights won't be able to see the page at all. Not all users can see changes unless a page has been published, which gives you a buffer between making changes and sharing the final version with your team or the world. The Publish button is found within the Publish tab on the ribbon. As you might guess, it's only available on sites with publishing features enabled.

NOTE

If you are using the Publishing Site with Workflow site template (or have enabled content approval requirements in the site's Pages library), your Publish tab won't have a Publish option. Instead, you'll see various buttons such as Submit, Schedule, Approve, Reject, and Start a Workflow. These enable you to control approval for a page to be published and to schedule when that publication will happen. For more information on publishing workflows, visit http://office.microsoft.com/en-us/sharepoint-server-help/work-with-a-publishing-approval-workflow-HA102891575.aspx

WORKING WITH NAVIGATION IN SHAREPOINT 2013

One of the most important parts of any website is how users can find their way around. A common way they do this is using the site's navigation, which either organizes the various areas of the site into categories or displays the site structure in an easy-to-follow format. Some navigation may be simple, whereas other sites may sport more complex navigation. Although users will spend plenty of time admiring the beautiful branding on your site, eventually they are going to want to dig in and find some content, which is what they'll be using the navigation for. You'll likely want to set up a navigation that makes sense for your site; therefore, you must understand how navigation in SharePoint 2013 works. If you already know this, and are just looking for information on how to style the navigation, you can find that topic detailed in the "Styling Key Areas of SharePoint" and "Putting CSS to Work in SharePoint" sections of Chapter 6.

Types of Navigation

Among the other improvements and changes in SharePoint 2013 is navigation. Now, there are two distinct types of navigation in SharePoint:

Structured Navigation

Structural navigation is the same navigation structure that SharePoint 2007 and SharePoint 2010 used and is sometimes referred to as *classic navigation*. This navigation structure can be automatically or manually built out by accessing the Navigation page from the Site Settings screen. Basically, you can have SharePoint automatically build out the site's navigation to match the site hierarchy, or you can manually add headers and links to replace or supplement the automatically built navigation.

Managed Navigation

Managed navigation is a new concept in SharePoint 2013 that enables you to build navigation based on managed metadata. Your site's navigation can be derived from a managed term set in the metadata term store. There are a few major benefits to using managed navigation. You can structure the navigation to give your SharePoint pages and sites "friendly URLs," which are easier to remember than the more traditional URLs SharePoint generally creates. For example, where you would normally see the URL `http://www.randyswaffles.com/marketing/pages/About-Us.aspx`, you could use managed navigation to create a friendly URL of `http://www.randyswaffles.com/AboutUs`. Another benefit of managed navigation is that friendly URLs are easily read and ranked by search engines, so if you run a public-facing site in SharePoint 2013, using managed navigation may make more sense than traditional navigation. When setting up managed navigation, you also have several options for further refining the search engine optimization. Managed navigation is also used by the new product catalog feature in SharePoint 2013.

It's worth noting that you can use both types of navigation in your site at the same time. You can set up the global navigation (also known as top navigation or main navigation) to use managed metadata navigation and have the current navigation (also known as left navigation or contextual navigation) be built using the structural navigation. You might consider this type of approach if you wanted to maintain a consistent navigation across the top of your site with the benefits of managed metadata navigation but with the ease of updating and adding additional links to the current navigation using the structural navigation.

Modifying the Navigation

SharePoint 2013 gives you quite a bit of flexibility to modify the navigation. You can sit back and let SharePoint handle building out the navigation for you, or you can take a more hands-on approach and build the whole thing out yourself. You can even take a hybrid approach in which you let SharePoint handle most of the heavy lifting while you add a few links here and there to suit your needs. An example of this approach in an intranet scenario would be allowing SharePoint to automatically list all of the subsites in a site collection in the navigation as they are built, while you manually add a navigation header with links to other non-SharePoint internal systems within your organization.

Because there are two styles of navigation this time, you need to decide which method you want to use and how you want the navigation to be structured. Using the classic structural navigation takes a more straightforward approach to the site's navigation, whereas the managed navigation offers some additional flexibility but requires more work up front to configure, mainly due to the many options that are available, such as the ability to specify friendly URLs.

One of the first things you'll notice on your site is that in the navigation areas, you get a distinct Edit Links option. This enables you to edit the navigation inline by adding, removing, or editing links on-the-fly. Editing this navigation ties directly into the method of navigation you use.

EXAMPLE: EDITING NAVIGATION

1. On the homepage of your site, click **Edit Links** in the top navigation area. The Edit Links link is replaced with a + link option, as well as Save and Cancel buttons and an area for dragging and dropping links.

2. Click **+ link**, which opens an Add a link dialog.

3. In the Text to display field, type **WaffleNet Home**. In the Address field, type / and click **OK**. This creates a link back to the home of the current site. The link is added to your navigation.

NOTE

The address field accepts absolute hyperlinks, such as `http://wafflenet/`, as well as relative hyperlinks, such as `/pages/default.aspx`.

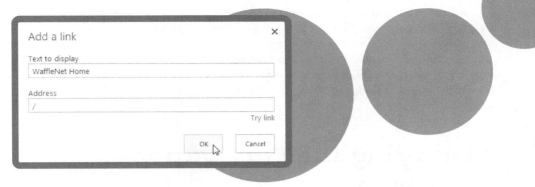

4. Click the **WaffleNet Home** link and drag it to the first position in the row of navigation items, just to the right of the SharePoint site logo.

5. When you finish working with the navigation, click the **Save** button to the right of your navigation (depending on your browser window's size you may need to scroll to the right to see the button).

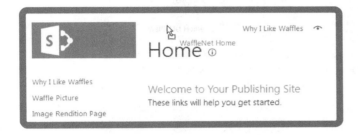

If you are working on a collaboration site without publishing features enabled, there is another way you can add and manage the links in your site's navigation; however, your options for creating a robust navigation are somewhat limited compared to sites with the publishing features enabled.

Working with Navigation Items

Depending on the type of site you're working with and that site's navigation settings, you'll see one of two icons next to each navigation item. In a collaboration site, you'll see an X to the right of each navigation item. Clicking this X removes the item from the navigation. If you're working on a publishing site, you'll see an icon that looks like a stylized eye to the right of each navigation item. Clicking this icon hides the item from appearing in the navigation (but doesn't delete it). In a publishing site, you might also see navigation items with an X next to them, which lets you delete the item. The difference is that on sites with publishing enabled, SharePoint can automatically build out a navigation structure as you add sites and/or pages. On these automatically added links, you have the ability to show or hide them without completely deleting the item from the navigation. If you have set up your navigation to have drop-down items, you can click the drop-down and hide or show links in the drop-down by clicking the icon next to each navigation item. (How to build out drop-down items is covered in the next section.)

EXERCISE: EDITING NAVIGATION IN A COLLABORATION SITE WITHOUT PUBLISHING FEATURES

1. From the site's homepage, click the **Settings menu** ➤ **Site settings**.

2. Under the Look and Feel header, you'll see two links related to the navigation: Quick launch, which lets you manage the navigation elements along the left of the page, and Top link bar, which lets you manage the links at the top of the page. Click **Top link** bar.

3. On this page, you can edit the properties of the existing links by clicking the **Edit** icon next to each item. You can also add a new link by clicking on **New Navigation** link and reorder the links by clicking **Change Order**. These options are pretty self-explanatory.

4. Return to the Site Settings page and click **Quick Launch.**

5. Managing the navigation for the quick launch is nearly identical to the Top link bar, except you have the ability to add heading links to group your navigation items. Click the **New Heading** link to do so. Headings need a URL and a description. When you add a new item to your navigation, you have the option to select the heading it will appear under.

As you can see, it's pretty easy to set up a basic navigation structure on a collaboration site. If your navigation needs are more robust than what is available in a collaboration site, you'll need to consider using a publishing site template or enable the SharePoint Publishing Infrastructure feature in your site.

Using the inline editing feature on a publishing site lets you set up a basic navigation quickly, but you need to put in a little more effort if you want your navigation to have drop-down menus or non-linked headers. This example is designed to give a quick overview of the navigation options available on the Navigation Settings page.

EXAMPLE: ADDING DROP-DOWN MENUS TO NAVIGATION

1. Click the **Settings menu** ➤ **Site settings.**

2. Under the Look and Feel header, click **Navigation.** (If you don't see a link for Navigation, but instead see links for Quick Launch and Top Link Bar, you aren't on a site with publishing enabled.)

3. Begin by selecting which type of navigation you want to use for the global navigation: structural or managed. If you are on a subsite, you can also select to use the same navigation as the parent site.

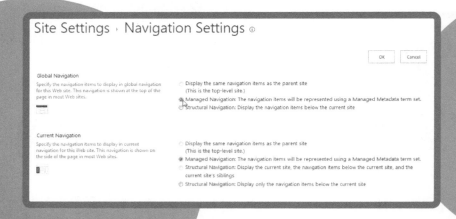

4 Next, select the type of navigation you want to use for the current navigation: structural or managed.

There are two types of structural navigation to choose from here: You can have the navigation show the current site, the contents of the current site, and the site's siblings, or you can show only the contents of the current site. If you choose structural navigation for either the global or current navigation areas, you have the additional options of showing only subsites, only pages, or both. In addition, you can specify how many dynamic items the navigation should be limited to showing.

NOTE

Depending on your master page selection, the current navigation may be positioned toward the top of your page instead of its usual position on the left. Oddly, Oslo.master, one of the master pages included out-of-the-box, moves the current navigation into the position of the top navigation area. This is something to keep an eye out for as you build out your navigation.

If you use managed navigation for either the global navigation or current navigation, a section called Managed Navigation: Term Set appears. This is where you choose an existing term set that has been created on the site or in Central Administration, or you can create a new term set in the term store for your current site collection. Take a look at the next section, "Creating a Term Set," for details on how to create a new navigation term set.

WARNING

By default, SharePoint 2013 should automatically create a term set named Site Navigation for use with managed navigation. There are instances, however, where SharePoint fails to automatically create this term set. In these cases, SharePoint may also prevent you from creating new term sets, responding with an error that says: "Failed to create term set. A default managed metadata service connection hasn't been specified."

While it may seem like the service application wasn't set up at all, there is actually a simple change that can be applied from Central Administration to fix this issue.

To learn more about this fix, see the following blog post on the subject by Todd Klindt: http://www.toddklindt.com/SP2013ManagedNav.

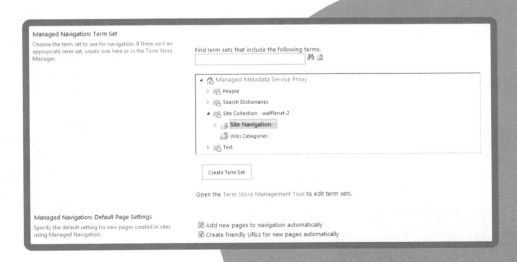

5. In the Managed Navigation: Default Page Settings section, select whether you want to add newly created pages to the navigation automatically (which is why the pages you have created thus far in the chapter have been appearing automatically in the navigation). Also choose whether the navigation should create friendly URLs automatically. If you select this option, SharePoint creates pages in the default Pages library, however, instead of a URL like `http://wafflenet/pages/WaffleOfTheMonth.aspx`, it will be `http://wafflenet/WaffleOfTheMonth`. This is known as a friendly URL (or FURL).

6. If you use structural navigation, you see the Structural Navigation section near the bottom of the Navigation settings page. Set options for whether you want to manually sort the navigation items or have SharePoint automatically sort them for you, choose how the items should be automatically sorted, and edit the existing navigation structure.

7. To edit the structural navigation, use the Editing and Sorting section. You can move links around in the global navigation or current navigation by clicking the **Move Up** and **Move Down** buttons on the tool bar. You can hide and show links that SharePoint has automatically created in your navigation for you by clicking the **Show** or **Hide** buttons. You can manually add, delete, and edit headings and links by clicking the **Add Heading** and **Add Link** buttons. Headings are top-level items in your navigation that can be used to group links under.

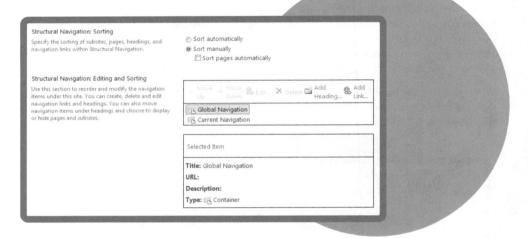

8. To add a heading, click the **Add Heading** button on the tool bar. In the dialog window, give the heading a title, optionally give it a URL, select whether the link should open in a new window, and optionally provide a description, which is used as alternative text when a user hovers the mouse over the navigation item. You can also use audience targeting on a link, which shows or hides the heading and anything under it based on the audience that a user is a part of. Click **OK** to create your header.

9. Click the **Add Link** button to create links to content in your SharePoint site or to external websites. Adding a link is exactly the same process as adding a header. The main difference is that a link can be moved under a header for grouping.

10. Finally, at the bottom of the Navigation settings page, choose whether the Show ribbon and Hide ribbon commands are available on the Settings menu.

11 When you have made your changes to the navigation, click **OK** to commit your changes. This step is important. None of the changes will be applied until you click OK, so make sure you don't navigate away from this page while building your navigation, otherwise you will lose your changes.

Although the Navigation setting screen is straightforward, you need to spend some time thinking about how your navigation will be set up on your site. Think about how your audience will use your site and whether the navigation should actually mimic the physical hierarchy of your site, be completely separate from the physical hierarchy of the site, or follow a kind of hybrid approach where you add or remove some items to the automatically created navigation. In reality, any of these scenarios are perfectly valid, though one will likely make the most sense based on knowledge of your requirements, your site, and your site's audience. Chapter 4, "Planning for Branding," discusses many other topics to consider when planning out your SharePoint site.

If you decide that you want to use managed navigation for either the global or current navigation, there are some additional configurations that need to be made for each navigation item. Read on to find out how to set up and configure a navigation term set.

Creating a Navigation Term Set

There are a couple ways you can open up your term store to edit the navigation. On the Navigation settings page, you can click the **Term Store Management Tool** link under the Managed Navigation Term Set section. Or from the Site Settings page, you can click the **Term Store Management** link under the Site Administration header. Alternatively, if you are in Central Administration, you can open your Managed Metadata service application and create your term set there.

When you're in the Term Store Management Tool, use the tree on the left to navigate the various term sets. On the right side of the Term Store page is a tabbed interface for modifying the settings of the item you have selected.

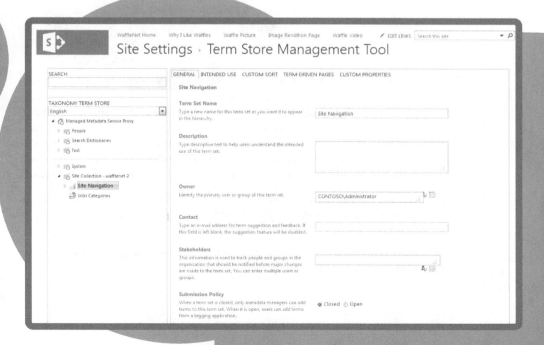

NOTE

To create term sets in the term store, you may need to set up as a term store administrator in the Managed Metadata service application. For more information on this, you can visit http://office.microsoft .com/en-us/office365-sharepoint-online-enterprise-help/assign-roles-and-permissions-to-manage-term-sets-HA102771983.aspx.

Also, be sure to check the warning in the previous section for information on a problem that could affect your ability to create new term sets.

Keep in mind that this is a chapter covering the basics of the SharePoint 2013 UI in a branding book and not a deep-dive into setting up an advanced, complex metadata navigation structure, so every item and option isn't covered in detail.

As you learned earlier, when configured properly, SharePoint automatically creates a term store named Site Navigation, which is also the default setting for managed navigation. SharePoint automatically adds new terms to this Site Navigation term store for every publishing page that is created. If you want to create your own pre-configured managed navigation hierarchy, you can follow this example, which walks you through the basics of creating a new navigation term store.

EXAMPLE: CREATING A TERM SET

1. Click the **Settings menu ➤ Site settings**, and then click the **Term store management** link under the Site Administration header.

2. Click the drop-down on the right side of the **Site Collection - <your site collection>** node to open the menu, and select **New Term Set.** A new term set is created and is waiting for you to enter a name. Type **WaffleNet Nav** for the name of your term set, and then press **Enter.**

3. With the WaffleNet Nav Term Set selected, click the **Intended Use** tab at the top of the right pane.

4. Check the box next to **Use This Term Set for Site Navigation,** and click **Save.** This (as you might suspect) enables you to use the term set you are about to create as your site's navigation. Optionally, you can uncheck the Available for Tagging check box if you don't want your navigation items to also be available as terms for tagging content. For this example, you can just leave the item checked.

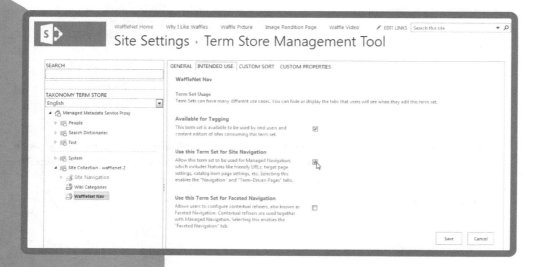

5 Click the drop-down on the right side of the WaffleNet Nav term set, and select **Create Term**. If you don't see your term set, just click the arrow to the left of the **Site Collection - <your site collection>** node to expand it and show the tem sets on the site collection, including the WaffleNet Nav term set.

6 Now you'll begin building out the top level of your navigation. Type **WaffleNet Home** and press **Enter**. After each navigation item, press **Enter** to automatically create a new term, which is used as an item in the navigation. After each term is created, you can start typing the next term. Create the following terms in the term set:

Waffle Departments

Waffle News

Waffle Projects

When you have entered the last term, press **Enter** twice to stop entering terms.

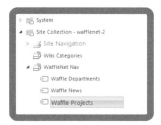

7 Terms can have child terms nested below them, which appear as drop-down items in your navigation. Click the drop-down arrow to the right of the Waffle Departments term and select **Create Term**. Then build out the following subterms exactly as you did the top-level terms:

Waffle Baking

Food Tasting

Syrup Engineering

8 Repeat this same process to build out the following terms under the Waffle Projects term:

    Bacon Flavored Syrup

    Giant Waffle Oven

    Waffle Food Truck

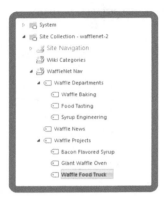

9 When you finish building out your navigation, click the **WaffleNet Nav** Term Set name.

10 In the right pane, click the **Custom Sort tab**. This is where you can either have the navigation items sort alphabetically or choose a custom order for your navigation items. Click the **Use custom sort order** option. Change the sort order drop-down of the **Waffle Projects** term to number **2**, then click **Save**.

11 Click the **Term-Driven Pages** tab in the right pane. If your site is going to feature dynamically driven content on templates or if you are designing a navigation for a catalog of items, you can set the target page for term set items or catalog item page items. For this example, you won't be utilizing dynamic page content, so leave these items unchecked.

12 Click the **Waffle Departments** term and then click the **Custom Sort** tab. Notice that you can change the sort order of all the child tags underneath a tag.

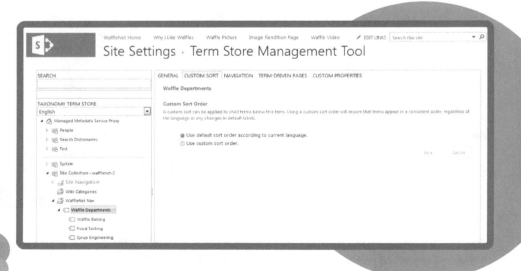

13 With the Waffle Departments term still selected, click the **Navigation** tab at the top of the right pane and in the Navigation Node section, click the check box next to **Customize**, then in the field change the navigation node title to **Waffle Depts**. This enables individual navigation items to display differently than when you set it up in the term set. In this case, the term "Waffle Departments" will actually display as "Waffle Depts" in the navigation.

14 Next click the **Term-Driven Page** tab and in the **Configure Friendly URL** settings for child terms section, click the check box next to **Customize** and change the field from waffle-departments to **depts**.

15 Click **Save** to save the changes to your navigation.

Because the Waffle Departments term was set to display as a link header, step 14's setting affects the child items under the navigation. Items under the Waffle Depts header in the navigation appear in the navigation as `/depts/<nav item>` due to changing the friendly URL setting here. For instance, your navigation URL might display as `http://wafflenet/depts/bacon-flavored-syrup`. If your navigation item was set on the previous tab to be a term-driven page with a friendly URL instead of a header, you could configure the page's friendly URL here. As another example, your page could be physically located at `www.randyswaffles.com/pages/waffle-recipes.aspx`, but you can configure the URL to appear as `www.randyswaffles.com/recipes`, which is much easier to remember and type.

The Term-Driven Pages tab also lets you specify a target page for a navigation item if necessary. In other words, you can specify which page each navigation item is supposed to go to on this tab.

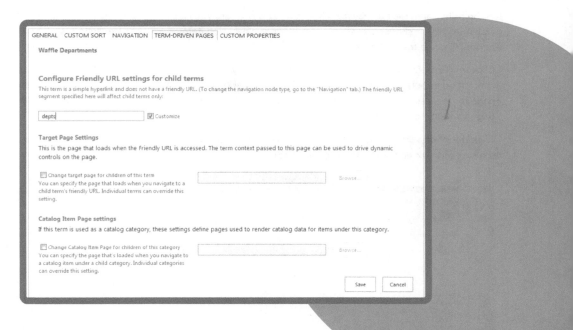

EXERCISE: ADDING CUSTOM NAVIGATION

1 Click the **Settings menu ➤ Site settings**.

2 Under the Look and Feel header, click **Navigation.**

3 In the Global Navigation section, make sure the navigation type selected is **Managed Navigation**. The navigation items will be represented using a Managed Metadata Term Set.

4 In the Managed Navigation: Term Set section, click the **WaffleNet Nav** term set. Scroll to the bottom of the Navigation Settings page and click **OK**. Your custom navigation now shows up at the top of the site.

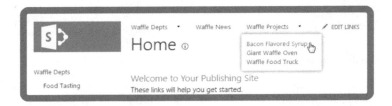

The example you just worked through was meant to serve as an introduction to setting up a managed navigation term set. As you probably noticed during the exercise, there are many other settings that can be changed and utilized to create a far more complex navigation scheme than what you just set up. None of these navigation items actually takes you anywhere other than a page not found error though. This is because although you created the navigation itself, it's not directly tied to any existing pages or sites yet.

One important thing to note is that although it seems that creating a central, out-of-the-box cross-site collection navigation is possible with managed navigation (something that has long been on many SharePoint site collection admins' wish lists), sadly this isn't the case. A managed navigation term set is "owned" by the site collection it's being used by, and trying to use it on another site collection results in the ownership of the term set being transferred to the other site collection. This breaks the navigation for the original site collection until the term set is associated with the original site collection again or a new navigation scheme is used.

Each type of navigation has its benefits and drawbacks, and although managed navigation took more effort to set up, you can see there is a lot of potential benefit and customization that can be achieved if you want to take the time to work through setting up all the various properties for each navigation item. To really get familiar with managed navigation and all it has to offer, spend some time building corresponding pages and subsites within your site, and use the skills you have learned so far, associating them with your navigation terms. Experiment with the various options available in the managed navigation settings.

USING COMPOSED LOOKS

As you learned in Chapter 2, the idea of applying themes to a SharePoint site isn't exactly a new concept. It actually dates all the way back to SharePoint 2003. SharePoint 2007 offered theming capabilities to change the look of your site through the use of images and CSS. This approach offered more flexibility but it required access to the file system of the SharePoint server and changes to system files, which many admins had reservations about. SharePoint 2010 changed course for how themes behaved and how they were applied to a site, but creating and applying themes in the browser was considered too simplistic by many users. Now, in SharePoint 2013, the idea of changing the look of the site through a theme-type engine is quite different from the themes of yesteryear. This version introduces a concept called composed looks, which takes theming to a new, modern level. The approach here is a happy medium between the 2007 and 2010 approaches to themes.

Chapter 2 compared the use of themes to decorating a house. Another way to think of composed looks is in their similarity to how WordPress themes work. If you run a blog in WordPress, you may have used

custom WordPress themes to change the look of your site to set it apart from others on the web. Even if you aren't a blogger using WordPress, you likely have come across WordPress blogs online. Composed looks are similar; they can take a default SharePoint 2013 site and give it a customized look and feel with minimal effort.

As noted in Chapter 2, composed looks consist of a background image, a master page selection, a color palette, and a font set. When you choose a composed look, SharePoint applies the styles and master page associated with the composed look, and with minimal effort you have created a customized site.

Out-of-the-box, you get 14 prebuilt composed looks to choose from in SharePoint 2013. At the time of this writing, public sites running in Office 365 have several more options than an on-premise SharePoint installation has. You can use the included composed looks as-is, customize them a little to put your own twist on your site, or create your own custom composed look. You learn more about creating a completely custom composed look in Chapter 10, "Composed Looks and Custom Branding." We could talk all day (okay, maybe not all day, but at least for a few hours) about composed looks, but they'll make more sense if you actually try it out for yourself.

Choosing a Composed Look

Like many things in SharePoint, there is more than one way to get to the Composed Look settings page. If you use a SharePoint Team site template, the Getting Started app includes a helpful tile called **What's Your Style?** that can take you to the Composed Look screen. If you're on a publishing site, in the set of links for Visual Designers, the link **Design Your Site** takes you to the Design Manager where you can click the **Pick a Pre-Installed Look** link. Alternatively, you can click the **Settings menu ➤ Site settings ➤ Change the look**. No matter how you get there, the Change the Look screen is where the real fun begins.

EXAMPLE: SETTING UP A COMPOSED LOOK

1 Browse through the available composed looks.

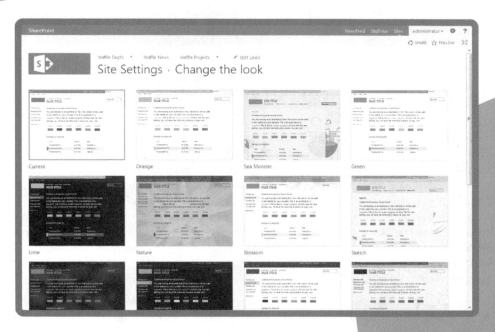

2 Select the **Immerse** composed look to see a sample preview of the look.

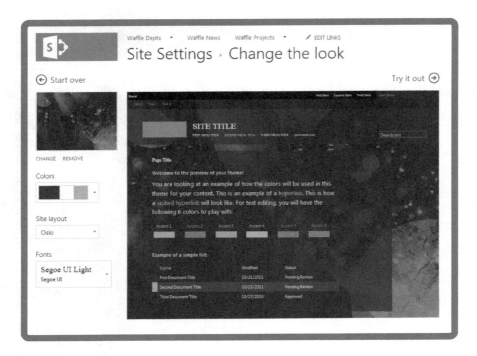

3 Click the **Try It Out** link to see a preview of your site with your site's actual content. This look might be too dark for what you're after, so you can change it up.

4 Click the **No, Not Quite There** link to go back to the sample preview screen.

5 Click the **Start Over** link on the left to return to the selection screen.

6 Select the **Sketch** composed look.

7 Click the **Try It Out** link.

8 Click the **Yes, Keep It** link to apply the composed look to the site.

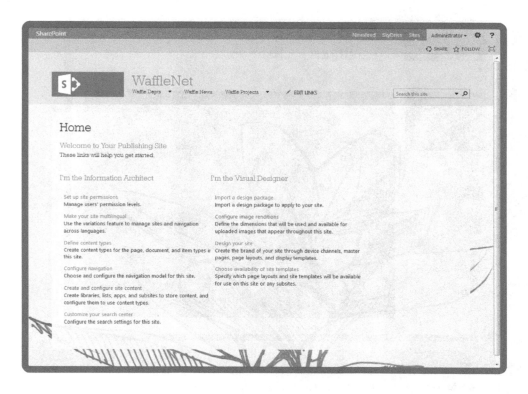

Changing a Composed Look

The composed look you've chosen isn't bad, but it's not close to your company's colors or overall corporate branding. You'll likely want to modify this composed look to get the site to look more personalized to the company.

EXAMPLE: MODIFYING A COMPOSED LOOK

1 Return to the composed look screen. The currently applied Composed Look appears first in the grid of available composed looks. Click the **Current** composed look (or you could select Sketch again if you want) to open the quick preview of the composed look.

2 On the left, click the **Change** link underneath the thumbnail of the background image; then browse your computer for an image to use as a background image. If you're following along with the files for this chapter, use **WafflesIntranetBG.jpg**. The preview sample updates with your new background.

NOTE

You can also drag-and-drop an image file from Windows Explorer to the thumbnail area of the composed look to swap out the background image faster. It's also important to note that if you want to use a .png or .gif file for the background, the file size needs to be 150 kilobytes or less.

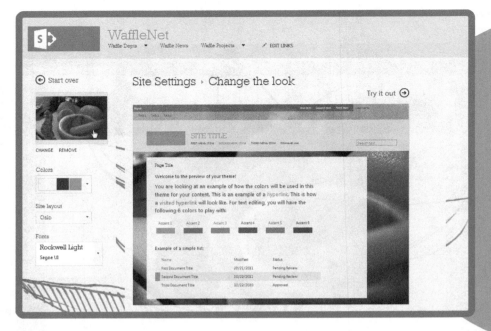

Photo Credit: Robert S. Donovan

③ The color palette needs to be changed, too. In the Colors drop-down, hover over the colors for a brief description of the palette. Select the color palette that is Primarily White with Grey-80% and Black. It's the last option in the Colors list.

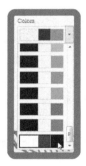

④ Leave the site layout as **Oslo** (the master page setting) and leave the Font drop-down set to **Rockwell Light/Segoe UI**.

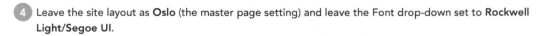

NOTE

The fonts that are set here apply to the headers and default body font for the site. The first listed font in the pair is applied to headers in the site, whereas the second font is used as the body font.

⑤ Click the **Try It Out** link for a preview of the actual site.

6 Click **Yes, Keep It** to apply the revised composed look to the site.

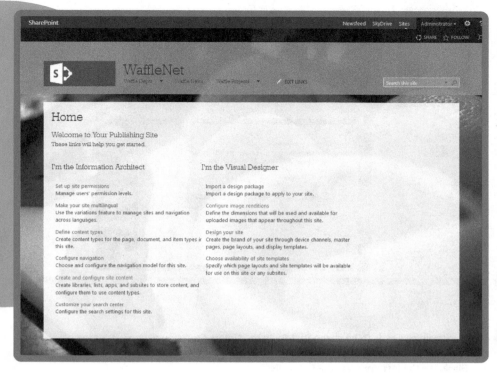

Photo Credit: Robert S. Donovan

If you want to give the site an even more complete, customized look, upload the company logo to replace the out-of-the-box site icon.

EXAMPLE: REPLACING THE DEFAULT LOGO ON A COMPOSED LOOK

1 From the site homepage, click the **Settings menu** ➤ **Site Settings**.

2 Under the Look and Feel header, click **Title, description, and logo**.

3 In the Logo and Description section, you can choose to upload a logo file from your computer or browse for one already in your SharePoint site. For now, click **From Computer**.

4 Browse your computer for a logo file and click **OK**. If you're using the file downloads for this chapter, use the **WafflesIntranetLogo.png** image file.

5 The logo is placed in the Site Assets folder by default. If you don't want to use this location upload the logo to a different location first. If you decide to change the logo later, click in the Insert Logo field, delete the path, and start again.

6 Type a description of the logo that will be used as alternative text for the logo and click **OK**.

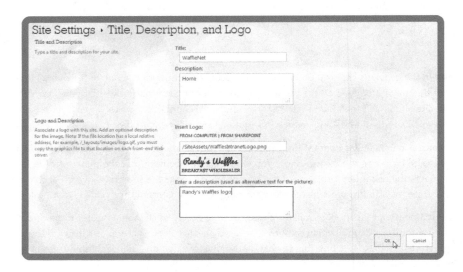

7 Pat yourself on the back. Your site is now branded with a custom background, color palette, and now a custom logo!

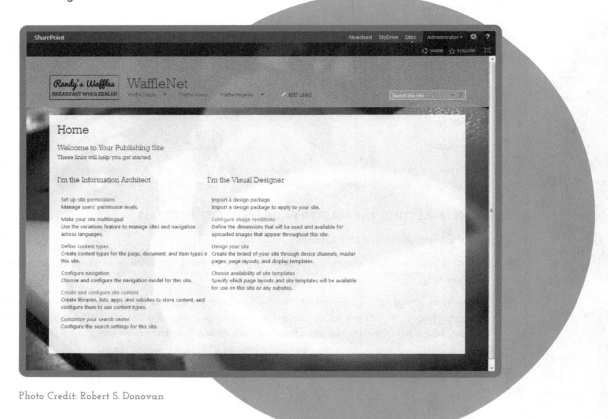

Photo Credit: Robert S. Donovan

SHAREPOINT MASTER PAGES

As discussed in the previous chapter, SharePoint 2013 uses master pages to control the overall look and placement of the major elements on the page. You can think of master pages as the overall template of a SharePoint site's look and feel. Elements that are common throughout the site will be found on a master page, such as the site heading, search, navigation, and maybe a footer.

SharePoint master pages utilize content placeholders for most of these elements. For example, instead of coding a search box onto the master page, you would insert a content placeholder control, and SharePoint injects the necessary code into the placeholder to render the search box when each page is loaded. Master pages also include a placeholder for rendering the content on a page layout.

All versions of SharePoint 2013 utilize master pages, but the ability to change a master page directly (without using a composed look) within the browser is only available on SharePoint sites with the publishing features enabled. It is possible to change the master page on a non-publishing site using SharePoint Designer 2013 or PowerShell.

SharePoint 2013 comes with a couple master pages to get you started:

- Seattle.master

- Oslo.master

As of this writing, SharePoint Online includes a couple extra master pages not available in stand-alone installations of SharePoint 2013, although this could change at any point:

- Berlin.master

- Lyon.master

- Tokyo.master

There are a few ways to set the master page on your site. If you work on a publishing site (or a site with the publishing features enabled), you can set the master page from the Site Settings page.

EXAMPLE: SETTING THE MASTER PAGE FROM SITE SETTINGS

1. Click the **Settings menu** ➤ **Site Settings**.

2. Under the Look and Feel header, click **Master Page**. (This link is not available on sites without publishing enabled.)

3. On the Master Page settings screen, choose the Site master page (the master page that will be used on all content pages). If you have set up device channels for your site to utilize alternative master pages, you can choose which master page is applied to each device channel here as well.

4. In the System master page section, choose the master page you want to use on non-content pages (generally pages served from the _layouts directory such as Site Settings pages).

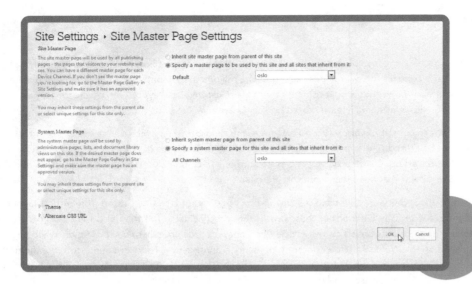

5. Two other options are available toward the bottom of the Site Settings page: Theme and Alternate CSS URL. These options are collapsed by default, but to expand their respective sections click the arrow to the left of the section titles. Theme enables you to control whether your current site inherits the parent site's composed look and enables you to apply the composed look of the current site to all child sites. Alternate CSS URL enables you to apply a custom CSS file to override the out-of-the-box SharePoint styles.

6. Click **OK** to set your master page.

If you work on a site without publishing enabled, you can still set a different master page, but it can be done only through SharePoint Designer or a custom SharePoint feature. You'll learn more about creating branding features in Chapter 7.

EXAMPLE: SETTING THE MASTER PAGE FROM SHAREPOINT DESIGNER 2013

1. Open **SharePoint Designer 2013** (SPD).

2. If you haven't opened your site in SPD before, click the **Open Site** button. If you have, look for your site in the Recent Sites list, and click it.

3. If you clicked the **Open Site** button, type the full URL of your site, and click **Open**.

4. If prompted, log in with your credentials.

5. When the site opens, click **Master Pages** in the navigation pane in SPD.

6. In the main window, right-click the master page you want to set, and select **Set as Default Master Page**.

7. Repeat step 6, but select **Set as Custom Master Page**.

8. Return to your browser and refresh the page to see your new master page applied to the site.

WORKING WITH PAGE LAYOUTS

In a publishing site, page layouts are essentially the templates that contain the page content. Although the master page controls the overall positioning of the major site elements, a page layout controls the overall look of each page that is built using its template. Custom page layouts can be created and applied to your site, which you'll learn more about in Chapter 7.

A page layout can consist of various Web Part zones and field controls, which define the areas of the page that can be edited. The availability of the various field controls are defined by the content type the page layout is based on. Content types are a collection of site columns used to store information about an item in SharePoint that describes what that item is.

In SharePoint 2013, there are two main out-of-the-box page layout types to choose from: article layouts and welcome layouts. The functions of these layouts are pretty similar, but the fields they each contain vary because page layouts based on the Article Page content type contain one set of fields, while page layouts based on the Welcome Page content type contain another set. There are some common field controls between the two content types, such as the Page Content field control you learned about earlier in the chapter. You'll learn more about content types in Chapter 7.

In Chapter 2, page layouts were compared to a room in your house, where the content fields in the page layout were represented by the furniture in the room. Rearranging the furniture makes the room look different, but it ultimately contains the same furniture. Similarly, changing a page layout rearranges the content on the page, which makes it look different. In some instances (such as changing from an article page layout to a welcome page layout) you might see additional fields that you didn't see before. This is like rearranging the furniture in your room and replacing an ottoman with a coffee table.

Page layouts also provide the strictest control over page editing. As discussed earlier in the "Saving Your Page" section, one of the benefits of using page layouts is that you have a buffer between your edits and the audience for your page. When editing a page created using a page layout, you can make changes and check the page in, providing only a small set of users with edit rights to see the page. When you are ready to share your page, you can publish it. Although page layouts give site owners strict control over the look of pages, they also provide designers with the most flexibility because they can create completely custom page layouts for a site using additional fields, custom content types, additional HTML, CSS, and images. For instance, a site could have a completely customized landing page layout that sets it apart from the rest of the site.

On publishing sites, you can change the page layout of your page with just a couple clicks. The availability of page layouts depends on what settings you have selected for your site. You can choose to make all page layouts available or restrict the available page layouts to a select few for consistency throughout your site.

EXAMPLE: SETTING AVAILABLE PAGE LAYOUTS

1. Click the **Settings menu** ➤ **Site Settings**.

2. On the **Site Settings** page, under the **Look and Feel** header, click **Page layouts and site templates**.

3. Scroll down to the Page Layouts section of the page. Notice that you have three options for controlling which page layouts are available: You can inherit the available page layout settings from the parent site; you can make all page layouts available; or you can choose which specific page layouts you want to make available to use on the site.

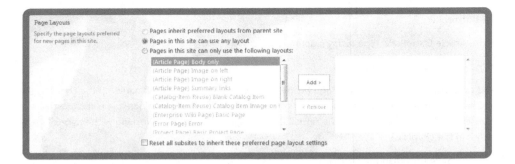

4. Select the option **Pages in this site can only use the following layouts**, then select the following layouts to be available on your site (you can select multiple items at once by holding down Ctrl and clicking the items in the list). When you've selected all the items, click the **Add >** button.

- (Article Page) Body only
- (Article Page) Image on left
- (Article Page) Image on Right
- (Article Page) Summary Links
- (Welcome Page) Blank Web Part page
- (Welcome Page) Splash
- (Welcome Page) Summary Links

5. Scroll down to the **New Page Default Settings** section. This section allows you to change the default page layout for the site, which is the page layout that is used when you create a new page from the Settings menu. Select **(Article Page) Image on Left**.

6. When you finish, click **OK**.

EXAMPLE: USING THE DEFAULT PAGE LAYOUT

1. Navigate to the homepage of your site.

2. Click the **Settings menu ➢ Add a page**.

3. In the Add a page dialog, type **Types of Waffles**, then click **Create**. Your new page is created using the (Article Page) Image on Left layout you specified.

4. On the new page, type **Here are my favorite kinds of waffles.** Select this text and click the **Heading 2** style in the ribbon. Then place the cursor after the Types of Waffles text, and press **Enter**.

5. Type the following on your page:
   - **Original**
   - **Belgian**
   - **Blueberry**
   - **Buttermilk**

6. In the Article Date field, type today's date.

7. In the Byline field, type your name.

8. Add an image to the page in the Page Image field control, as you learned earlier in the chapter. Don't forget about image renditions! If you are working with the chapter downloads, you can use the **WaffleBreakfast.jpg** image. (Need a refresher on images? Revisit the "Working with Images" section earlier in the chapter.)

9. Click the **Save** button in the ribbon.

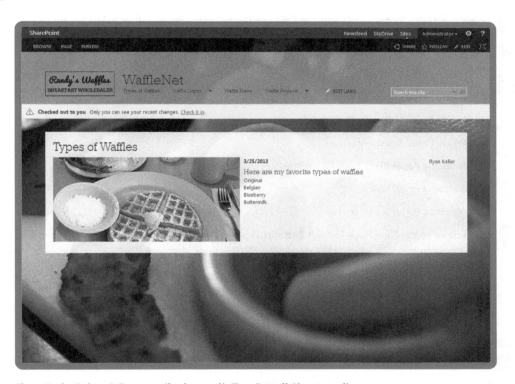

Photo Credit: Robert S. Donovan (background); Tom Drisgill (foreground)

Of course, it is also possible to change the layout of a page after it has been created, as you know from working with page layouts earlier in the chapter. Here's a refresher on how that's done. You'll also take a look at the various properties of the page you just created so you can see how page layouts reference columns to store information.

EXAMPLE: CHANGING AN EXISTING PAGE LAYOUT

1. Put your page into Edit mode. (Remember, you can click the **Edit** icon on the ribbon or click the **Settings menu ➤ Edit Page**.)

2. Click the **Page** tab on the ribbon.

3. Click the **Page Layout** drop-down.

4. Notice that only the page layouts that you selected earlier (the article page layouts and welcome page layouts) are available to choose from now. Select the **Summary Links** layout in the Welcome Page section.

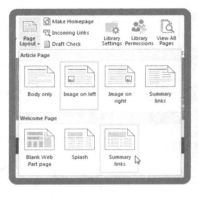

5. Notice that your text and image are still preserved in the field controls on the page, but the Article Date and Byline fields are gone. Click the **Page** tab in the ribbon and change the Page Layout to the **Image on Right** page layout. Your Article Date and Byline fields return, and they still contain the same information you populated them with.

6. Save the page, then click the **Settings menu ➤ Site contents ➤ Pages** library.

7. Click the ... (ellipses) to the right of the Types-of-Waffles page, then in the pop-up menu that appears, click the ... (ellipses) on that menu. Finally, click the **View Properties** option.

8. Scroll through the various properties associated with this page. Because the page is currently set to use an article page layout, all the available columns are coming from the article page content type. Note that all the fields that appeared on your page, such as Article Date and Byline, display here. These fields are all stored in the Pages library as columns from the site content types added to the library. Page layouts reference these columns and can display them as field controls that users can fill out. Click the **Close** button to return to the Pages library.

9. Click **Types-of-Waffles** to return to this page. Switch the page layout back to **Image on Left**.

10. Click the **Publish** tab in the ribbon, then click the **Publish** button to publish your page. In the Publish dialog, click **Continue** to finish the publish process. (If you don't see a Publish button, you are probably working on a publishing site with workflow site template. In this case, just click the **Save** or **Check In** button on the Page tab in the ribbon.)

This exercise shows you how the content that you have on your page remains associated with your page, even if the corresponding field or Web Part zones do not appear on the new layout. This is because the information is stored in the columns of the Pages library, even if those fields aren't actively being displayed. Another thing to note, if your page contains Web Parts in Web Part zones, and the layout you change the page to doesn't have the same zones, your Web Parts will all be preserved on the page, but will likely all appear in the same zone, so you probably need to reorder them on your page.

Before continuing on to the next chapter, you should change the page layout options to use any available page layout again. That way you won't run into any issues completing the exercises in the rest of the book.

EXERCISE: REVERTING PAGE LAYOUT OPTIONS TO DEFAULT

1. Click the **Settings menu** ➢ **Site settings**.

2. Under the Look and Feel header, click **Page layouts and site templates**.

3. In the Page Layouts section, select the option **Pages in this site can use any layout**.

4. Scroll down and click **OK**.

SUMMARY

- The page-editing experience in SharePoint 2013 is similar to SharePoint 2010. The ribbon has a new look and some items such as the Settings menu (formerly known as the Site Actions menu) and some buttons have moved around, but the experience is largely the same as SharePoint 2010.

- Adding images, videos, and other Web Parts can add to the functionality of your page. Image renditions should save SharePoint administrators (and end-users) some headaches by displaying physically smaller, resized, and/or cropped versions of images on pages in the site.

- The new embed functionality also makes embedding code and external videos on a page much easier than in past versions of SharePoint.

- SharePoint 2013 introduces managed navigation to go along with the traditional structural navigation. This new navigation type introduces much more robust features, such as the ability to utilize friendly URLs, but also takes some extra effort to set up.

- Composed looks are one of the most noticeable changes on the branding front in SharePoint 2013. This is the new way of applying a theme to your site and allows you to apply a custom look and feel with minimal effort.

- SharePoint 2013 still makes use of master pages and page layouts, with many of the same concepts found in past versions. The two out-of-the-box master pages, `Seattle.master` and `Oslo.master`, are similar but each has some unique characteristics. Master pages can also be applied using composed looks.

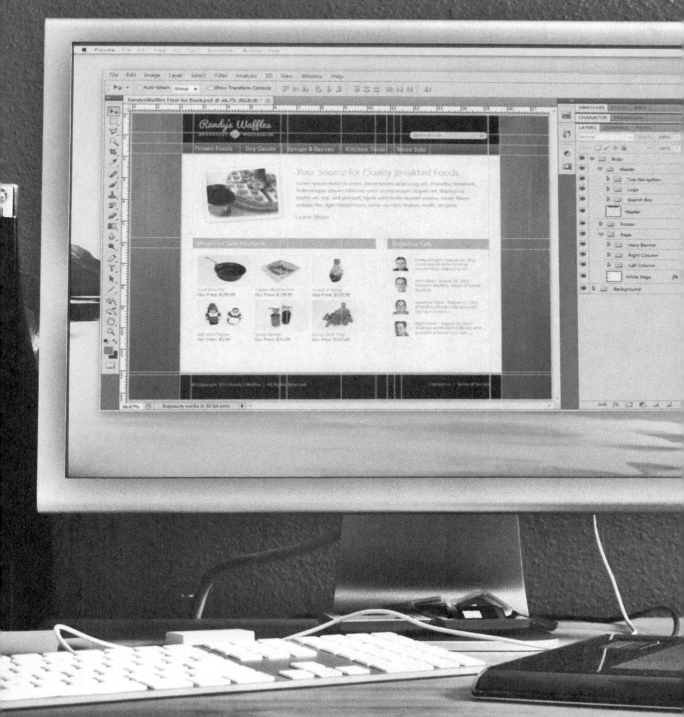

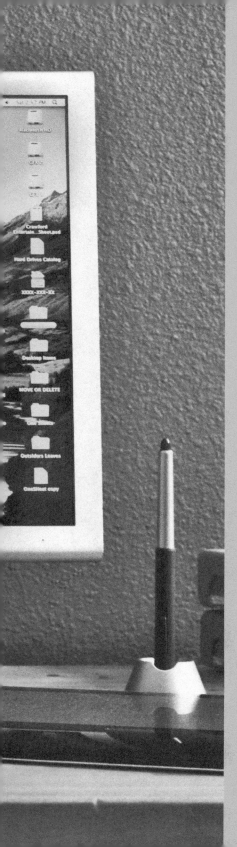

2

Planning a Design and Getting Started

4

PLANNING FOR BRANDING

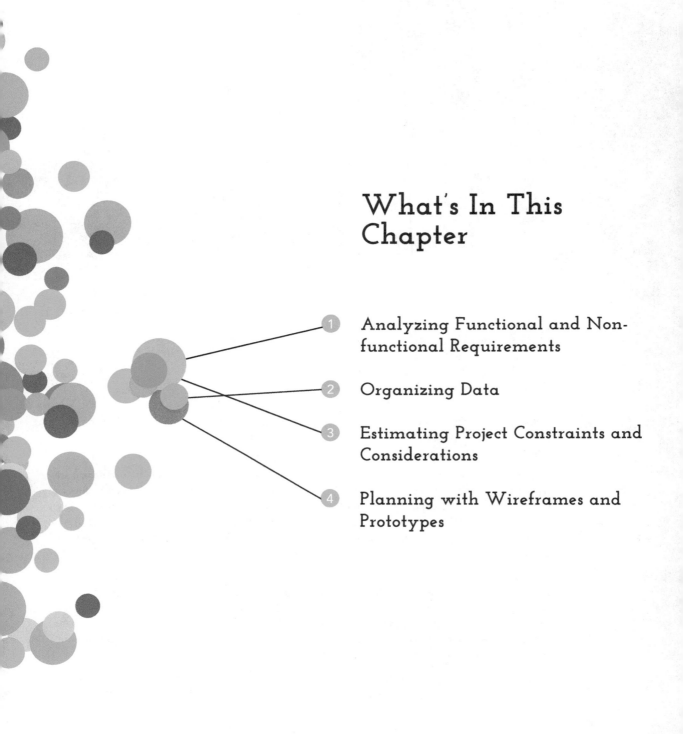

What's In This Chapter

This chapter discusses the process of properly planning for SharePoint branding. In many ways, this topic is similar to the planning that goes into any creative project, but some of the steps are unique for SharePoint. Even if you are experienced with planning typical design projects, this chapter provides an overview for what it takes to get your SharePoint branding project started.

WHY PLAN FOR BRANDING?

Planning is important for just about any type of project, regardless if it is technical. But all too often people and organizations fail to do proper planning. Most seem to be eager to start and decide to figure out specific details along the way.

The value of planning seems to be easier to understand when the context is personal. Imagine you are renovating your house and you want to convert a den into a bedroom, but you have a fixed budget and want to make sure you are adding the most value to your home for the money you are spending. Given those parameters it should seem more logical to talk with a designer or architect to get a sense of what you want to accomplish instead of just sending in a construction crew to start knocking down walls and building things in hopes that the final product is good.

By skipping the planning, you run the risk of putting a wall in the wrong place, so a door won't open properly, or maybe you end up with a project that instead of adding value becomes an eyesore in the rest of your house. Mistakes like that tend to be expensive to fix. In the digital world, many times people take this type of situation for granted because they usually deal in pixels or other digital assets that seem less permanent than the physical walls of a home. But just because you don't live in the websites you create doesn't mean that you shouldn't plan.

Whether your project is a construction project or a new SharePoint site, the first part of the process should be to put together a plan. Making mistakes on paper (or whatever your medium of choice is)

will always be less expensive to address compared to making those same mistakes during construction.

Given that upfront planning clearly makes a lot of sense for most SharePoint websites, how much planning is needed? Do you need to spend months and months of daylong meetings? Not necessarily. Depending on the size of the project, the intricacy of the SharePoint site, and the amount of decision makers involved (often known as *stakeholders*), planning for branding could take months, just a few days, or even hours. The next few sections discuss some of the key steps you should take when planning for branding. Although it may seem like a lot, keep in mind that smaller projects can get away with doing only a portion of them. For example, if your branding project requires only small changes to the out-of-the-box user interface, there is probably no need to go through the full process of making design comps. In many ways, the decision for how much planning is needed for a project will be unique for every project. The key to this process is to carefully consider your branding before actually executing it in SharePoint.

PERFORMING REQUIREMENTS ANALYSIS

Whether your SharePoint branding project is a site for 10 users or 10,000 users, before the project can be considered complete, certain requirements must be met. This is why the first step of almost any project, regardless if it is a SharePoint branding project, should include some amount of requirements analysis. Requirements analysis involves gathering and understanding the specific needs of a project.

If you look back on the construction example in the previous section, you can imagine that as homeowners who want some new changes to your house, there are some basic preferences about what you'd be looking for. For example, what is the intended use for the room? How much storage is required? What are the power and lighting needs? These are just a few of the questions that need to be asked before designing what the project will ultimately look like. In a sense, these questions help to define the functional requirements for the project. *Functional requirements* define what the project is supposed to accomplish but not necessarily how those things will be achieved.

NOTE

Functional requirements are usually defined as something specific to the way the site will look or behave. *Nonfunctional requirements* refer to the more overarching requirements, such as cost and reliability.

Requirements analysis involves gathering and understanding the specific needs of a project. Typically, this process includes asking a lot of questions and breaking larger problems into more manageable pieces to gain a better understanding of them. Requirements should not be vague or lofty ideas; instead, they should be both measurable and actionable. To put it another way, for a requirement to be useful, you should be able to tell when it has been accomplished successfully. If the requirement has no success criteria, it should be broken down into smaller, more discrete requirements that do.

Consider the following two example requirements. The first is ambiguous and not measurable, which makes it difficult to know when the task is accomplished; whereas the second can easily be measured for successful completion:

● **Requirement #1**— The design shouldn't have horizontal scroll bars for most users.

● **Requirement #2**— The site will support a resolution of 1280 x 720 without horizontal scroll bars.

In general, gathering requirements isn't too difficult. The challenge is determining which of the requirements are the most important and which ones should take the highest priority. Because every project and organization is different, there isn't one sure-fire answer to this dilemma, but here are a few tips that can help you choose:

● For each requirement, consider the overall value to the business and the cost to implement. You could even create a spreadsheet and assign scores to each requirement based on each attribute. For example, a requirement could have a high business value and be rated a 9 on that dimension but be costly to implement and therefore be rated a 3. The total "score" for this requirement would be 12. This approach is a more unbiased way of determining priority.

● Be realistic about what is possible given timelines and the skillset of your team. It is always easier to add items when a project is ahead of schedule rather than trying to remove items that are too complex.

● Using a phased implementation is a great way to break up a more complex project. Stakeholders tend to prefer seeing smaller pieces sooner as compared to waiting a long time to see the "perfect" solution. A phased implementation also enables minor course corrections along the way, which ultimately leads to a better solution.

When gathering project requirements, you must involve all the project stakeholders. Stakeholders are people or groups that have a vested interest in the project's success. They may be affected by the project directly, such as an executive or manager, or indirectly, such as users who will depend on the final product.

Owners	Developers	Content Authors
Management	Designers	Find Users
Marketing Department	IT Department	Partner Users
	Project Managers	

Adding stakeholders to the requirements gathering process can mean more time to complete the process and increased complexity. In fact, depending on the project, some stakeholders can actually be detrimental to successful requirements analysis. For example, the owner of a company may be too abstracted from day-to-day operations to give meaningful feedback, or certain employees, such as those recently hired, may not offer a valuable opinion regarding the project. Determining the right stakeholders can be a difficult task, but at the end of the day, if someone has enough influence to change the project in later stages, it's a good idea to include that person early. The reason is obvious: By involving the appropriate stakeholders early in the requirements analysis process, you can avoid making those dreaded, and costly, last-minute changes to a project to meet a critical need.

The following sections discuss the most important aspects of the requirements gathering that are necessary before starting any SharePoint branding project.

SharePoint Version

One of the first decisions to make is which version of SharePoint to use for the project. The major decision for most is choosing between SharePoint Server 2013 and SharePoint Foundation 2013. Many organizations also choose to use SharePoint Online as part of Office 365 from Microsoft. From a branding standpoint, the biggest difference between these products is the availability to use a set of features called *publishing*. Both SharePoint Server 2013 and Office 365 provide the ability to use publishing.

For highly customized sites, publishing is preferred because it has several useful additions for branding projects:

- Enabling publishing gives the ability to use Design Manager, which is a central hub to manage most aspects of a custom design. It provides the ability to import HTML and CSS, which can then be converted into a SharePoint master page. Additional tasks such as creating and editing page layouts, managing device channels, and importing/exporting design packages can also be managed through the Design Manager. For more information on the Design Manager see Chapter 5, "Using the Design Manager to Start a Design in SharePoint."

- Publishing sites enable you to select a new master page by using the web user interface in Site Settings. Although you could use custom code to perform this task in SharePoint Foundation, it is not included out-of-the-box.

- Publishing sites enable developers and designers to create page-level templates by using page layouts.

- Advanced Web Content Management functionality is available with publishing. This includes Web Parts such as the Content Query Web Part (CQWP) and Content Search Web Part (CSWP), which can be used for delivering a large amount of content to highly customized sites.

Although it is still possible to create a custom look and feel to your website if you don't have access to a version of SharePoint with publishing available, it does limit your options, and from a planning perspective, it makes the overall design process more challenging. Some tasks that are simple otherwise become more difficult without publishing. A good example of this is switching master pages—in a site with publishing, there is a menu where you can just choose a master page. In a non-publishing site there is no menu so you must set the master page with either SharePoint Designer

or PowerShell. Not impossible, but not preferable. There are a number of similar examples to this, along with the fact that some functionality just isn't available without Publishing. The key is just to understand what version you are working with and align your plan accordingly. You can make a beautiful and engaging site with any version of SharePoint!

Type of SharePoint Website

Typically, SharePoint sites are set up as one of three types of websites: public-facing Internet sites, internal-facing intranet sites, and extranet sites, which have aspects of both Internet and intranet sites. The users of each of these types of websites differ vastly. Here is a quick breakdown of some of the differences between them:

- **Internet sites**—These sites are usually marketing-driven and typically have tightly controlled content with few content authors. They tend to be more stylistic than intranet sites and are targeting a much wider spectrum of users. Because Internet sites are public-facing, developers have no control over the type of browser, device, or the screen resolution that will be used to visit the site.

- **Intranet sites**—These sites typically sit behind a corporate firewall and are specifically tailored to help internal users work in a more collaborative and efficient manner. Intranet sites usually have many content authors and numerous employees who are consuming documents and collaborating. Because these sites are internal-facing, companies can control browser and screen-resolution requirements if wanted.

- **Extranet sites**—These sites are a hybrid of the previous two. They are typically intranet sites that have a separate area for external users to authenticate into. From a branding perspective, the extranet area can be similar to an Internet site or an intranet site, depending on the particular objective for the extranet. Sometimes, an extranet can be collaborative, and sometimes it can be simply information published to external users. For example, a company may work with external partners and want a place to securely collaborate without giving these partners access to the internal network. An extranet is the ideal place to do this.

Targeted Browsers

Another important decision to make is which browsers will be targeted by your branding. Although many people may say that a website should support all browsers equally, it is often impractical to test each browser for pixel-perfect display. This is why it's a good idea to decide early what browsers and operating systems will be supported by your SharePoint site. As mentioned earlier, this decision is typically more important for public-facing Internet sites, for which you have no control over which browser is used to access the site. Conversely, corporations can dictate strict browser requirements for intranet sites and prohibit unsupported browsers from accessing the system.

One typical way of choosing a level of supported browser is to consult industry websites that track this information across extremely large usage statistics. One such site is W3Counter.com; here are its published browser statistics as of January 2013 (http://w3counter.com/globalstats.php):

BROWSER VERSION	MARKET SHARE
Chrome 24	17.37%
Internet Explorer 9	11.14%
Firefox 18	9.35%
Chrome 23	8.71%
Internet Explorer 8	8.08%
Safari 6	7.82%
Internet Explorer 7	5.79%
Firefox 17	4.32%
Safari 5.1	3.35%
Android 4	2.95%

In a perfect world scenario, determining which browsers to target would be as simple as checking the current statistics for what browsers visit your site. Or if you have an internal site, perhaps you only need to account for whatever browsers are supported by your IT department. But if you're looking for more general information, the preceding statistics for usage among Internet sites can be a helpful guideline when determining which browsers to target for your project, even if it is for an internal site. Especially considering that an increasing number of companies use SharePoint to collaborate with others outside of their organization.

Screen Resolution

You also need to decide what screen resolution will be targeted for your SharePoint branding. Until a few years ago, computer monitors supported only a limited number of screen resolutions, mostly 800 x 600 or even 640 x 480. Nowadays, it's not uncommon to see website visitors browsing at resolutions of 1920 x 1200 or higher. Most web designers currently consider 1366 x 768 to be the most common screen resolution. According to the most recent survey on W3Counter.com (January 2013), more than 55 percent of users are running a resolution of 1280 x 800 or higher.

As you create your branded SharePoint website, you must balance the desire to display large amounts of information with common user screen resolutions. This can be even more challenging depending on how you choose to support mobile devices. For more information on mobile support in SharePoint see Chapter 8, "Advanced SharePoint Branding Tasks" and Chapter 11, "Modern Web Design and SharePoint."

Information Architecture and Organization

When you think of any of the iconic buildings of the world such as the Sydney Opera House, Taj Mahal, or the Pyramids, it is usually the physical appearance that is so memorable. However, those buildings also required proper engineering and architecture to achieve their respective greatness.

A SharePoint site is similar in that it requires a good foundational architecture and organization system to make that memorable physical appearance possible. There are few examples of web design on any platform in which you talk only about pure design. Most SharePoint projects include functional requirements beyond simply looking good. The way that you achieve these requirements is to create a well-organized information architecture that gives you the ability to create a site that functions as good as it looks.

Information Architecture

Information architecture is a general term that describes the organization of data in a website. From a SharePoint perspective, information architecture refers to the structure of the various SharePoint objects in a farm, which could include web applications, content databases, service applications, site collections, lists and document libraries, metadata, permissions, and so on. Based on the requirements for a given effort, an information architecture is created that supports the overall business goals. For example, the information architecture needed for a public-facing Internet site to sell products is fundamentally different than one for an internal corporate site focused on collaboration.

As a rule of thumb, it is a good idea as you create your mockups and creative designs to look at the elements on a given page and ask, "What is that and where does it come from?" For example, if you have a creative design and show news items, you need to determine where that content was created? How was it created? Is it intended to be shown on the page via a web part? If so, which one and what customizations are needed to display the web part on the page? As you start thinking about your SharePoint design in this way, it becomes easier to see the relationship that information architecture plays in relation to SharePoint branding and design.

Taxonomy

Taxonomy is the science of classifying and organizing things and is a core component of a site's architecture. In science it is often used to organize, or classify, plants and animals in a hierarchy based on their relationships. You may remember a famous taxonomy from science class: kingdom, phylum, class, order, family, genus, and species.

From a web perspective you can think of taxonomy in two different ways. Developers think about the structure of the data, and designers typically think of the visual aspect of the taxonomy and how users would navigate through a site. Both are correct, and for planning your site, you must consider both approaches.

SharePoint can understand only one structure for how things are organized, but that structure might not be the most intuitive for visitors to your site. The good news is that you can present whatever view of the taxonomy you want to your users to help make the site as usable as possible.

There are a number of books and theories for creating taxonomies, and this text just scratches the surface. When creating a taxonomy, think about the website's audience. How will they use the site? Are they familiar with your internal organizational structure, or will they be expecting information to be organized differently? People with different roles inside of an organization may use information differently. Executives may look for strategic information, whereas workers on the floor may need specific information to do their job.

This structure can eventually manifest itself in the SharePoint site's navigation. Chapter 3's section, "Working with Navigation in SharePoint 2013," looks at SharePoint navigation in detail. Providing multiple forms of navigation could be beneficial. Some users may feel comfortable using the primary navigation, whereas others may prefer to search. Your site may even contain information that is so important it should "roll-up" to a top-level page from where the content is located. In these cases, a SharePoint Web Part would be perfect.

Usability

Architecture and taxonomy are both key parts in creating SharePoint sites, but by themselves the greatest information architecture, taxonomy, or creative design cannot guarantee a successful project. The ultimate measure of success for any project is user adoption and whether those users feel like they are benefiting from the site. The most technically complex effort or most innovative creative design won't be appreciated if no one wants to use it.

The best sites strike a balance between form and function. Again, every site is going to be different, but as long as you've been listening to your users' needs, you'll have a good understanding of the problems that need to be solved. After you've determined these problems, the next step in the design process is to design a site that enables those same users to get to what they need in an efficient way:

- **Keep your design clean and simple**—There is plenty of research that shows that people become less efficient when presented with too many options. A clean and simple design with clear options can make it easier for users to get where they are going. This is often one of the most challenging usability rules for an organization to follow.

- **The mythical three-click rule**—In web design you often hear people say that you need to access more than 80 percent of content in a website within three clicks. This is a good rule of thumb, but more than three clicks is okay as long as users still feel they know where they are and where to go next. This relates to the clean and simple design rule, too. For example, every piece of content doesn't need to be linked directly from the homepage as long as users know where to look.

- **Navigating your site shouldn't take special training**—This might seem like an obvious rule, but if you take users and sit them down in front of your design, would they know where to go to find common pieces of content? Whether you do something basic such as ask the opinion of co-workers, or perform formal usability testing, this is a good way to check if your new site is as easy to use as you think it is.

- **Users seek content in different ways**—There are four primary ways that users find content in a website. Every user has a different preference, but an effective usability strategy should consider these different approaches:

  - Using the site's navigation

  - Clicking on the content on the page

  - Searching for content

  - Using a site map or other direct link

The topic of usability is another deep topic. Large complex implementations will probably go through a more formal exercise of usability planning. But for most projects just being aware of some basic usability principles can provide massive benefits. One of the simple things you can do is when you design your site, imagine people that you know who aren't as computer savvy as the users. Consider how difficult it would be for them to find things in your design. All usability theory aside, that is usually a good place to start with a design of any size.

ASKING THE RIGHT SHAREPOINT BRANDING QUESTIONS

It is often helpful to start the planning process with a set of simple standard questions. These questions are best answered by those who are familiar with business need driving a new implementation. This section provides some common questions that are a good starting point for most projects:

NOTE

In practice, you may not proceed through your requirements gathering and analysis process in the order listed. The order is less important than making sure that you capture enough information to help you make the correct decisions during the design process.

- Is there an existing website or SharePoint site that the new SharePoint site will replace? If so, will the content need to be migrated?

- Will this be a new design or will it be based on some existing branding?

- Is there an existing corporate style guide that needs to be followed?

- What is the time frame to deliver the new branding?

- Is there any existing branding or marketing material that can or should be used, such as corporate logos?

- Are there any stylistic requirements, such as preferred or disliked colors, fonts, or imagery? (Example: "Our competitor's website is red, so we'd prefer to avoid red for ours.")

- Who will the audience be? What will they be looking for in the website? Are they corporate users? Are they teenagers? Would a cutting-edge, modern design speak to them or would a tried-and-true corporate layout be better?

- Will the site be primarily used for communication? Collaboration? Both?

- Who will approve the new branding? Is it a single person or committee?

- How will the branding files be deployed to the server? What is the plan for deploying updates and maintenance of the branding files?

- Will master pages or composed looks be used to create the branding? Will both be required?

- How will the pages of the site be created? Is there a person or team responsible for creating the content and entering data?

- Are there different requirements for displaying the site on different devices such as tablets or mobile phones?

- According to what criteria will the branding be judged a success? What goals does it need to address?

- What sort of navigation is required? Horizontal navigation? Vertical navigation? Both? Are dynamic drop-downs or fly-outs wanted for submenu items?

- Are there any specific types of content that require company-specific information that needs to be accounted for? (Example: Internal news item with metadata to identify which products it is related to).

- Are there any specific requirements for Web Parts to roll up content? Will they require custom development or just styling?

- Will any third-party Web Parts or controls be needed? Will any of the third-party Web Parts need to be migrated to the new site?

Requirements analysis can be a formal process, involving scheduled meetings and full documentation, or a brief process, involving just a few key stakeholders and some quick decisions. Either way, the result should be a better understanding of what will actually be built—in this case, how SharePoint will look and behave.

PROJECT ESTIMATION

In many ways, project estimation for SharePoint is the same as any other IT project. Constraints such as due date, feature scope, and budget impact the estimation process greatly. These three common constraints are often interconnected; when one becomes more aggressive, it could affect the other two.

For instance, the budget could be too low to accommodate all the wanted requirements. This would indicate that the scope needs to decrease. Alternatively, the timeline for delivery could be aggressive, which could translate into more hours or workers assigned to the project.

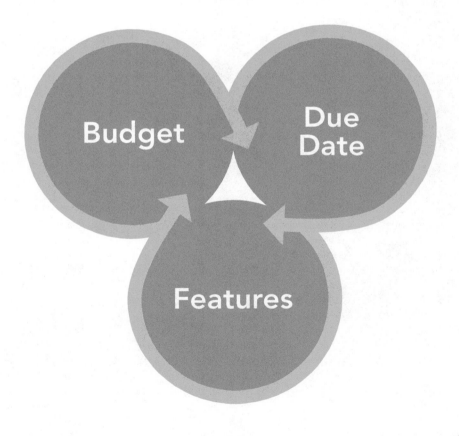

The topic of project estimation, in theory and in practice, could fill an entire book. A comprehensive discussion is therefore impossible within one chapter. Your organization may follow a particular development approach such as Waterfall or Agile. But regardless of your approach the process should generally involve the following steps:

1. Decide on a high-level project timeline. When will the project start and when do you estimate it will end?

2. Break down the requirements into specific tasks.

3. Estimate the amount of time each of those tasks will take.

4. Determine which resources will work on each task. Will certain tasks require specialized skills? If so, be sure to account for the availability of someone with those skills.

5. To the extent possible, determine any roadblocks or risks you might face, and attempt to troubleshoot them proactively.

6. Allow enough time to include all phases of traditional development, including any necessary extra planning, building the branding and the SharePoint site, testing and review, making any necessary adjustments, and deploying the project to a production environment.

SharePoint projects have specific factors that could impact project estimation. The following is a list of some things that should be considered:

- Will the project involve creating custom master pages and page layouts, or will it just use a composed look?

- What is the skill level of the designers and developers involved in the project? Do they have experience with SharePoint?

- How will the project be deployed to a production environment, and how will updates be applied?

- How complex is the design that is being attempted?

- How many different areas of SharePoint will be branded?

- How many Web Parts will need custom styling?

- How flexible is the due date and budget?

- How many different browsers will you be targeting?

- Will mobile devices be considered?

- Will any third-party Web Parts or apps need to be branded?

- Will the effort require custom development work?

Even after thinking through all of this, estimates can still be off. SharePoint projects tend to have a lot of moving parts, and it is almost impossible to anticipate every minor detail. Team members are often dependent on each other's specific skill sets. Rarely in a SharePoint project will every task be accomplished by the same person; the server administrator who installs SharePoint will most likely not be the same person who designs the branding. Whether this is your first SharePoint project or your fiftieth, be

sure to assume extra time in your estimate to account for the unknown. It is usually advisable to plan for potential variance to both the effort level as well as the duration of the project. In the event that everything goes exactly as planned, then you can use any extra planned variance to do even more great things!

CREATING WIREFRAMES

There are many different aspects of planning a branding project. So far you've seen the technical, architectural, and organizational sides of planning, but there is still a side remaining: creative planning. The creative planning process for larger websites often begins with the creation of several black-and-white wireframes. *Wireframes* are skeletal page designs; they capture the layout and flow of a website without focusing on colors and graphics.

The major reason for creating wireframes before full-color comps is to ensure that all the stakeholders and decision makers focus on the content, layout, and page flow, rather than get hung up on whether emerald green is better than mint green. This allows for quicker iteration between ideas because creating black-and-white wireframes is faster than creating full-color designs. In some cases, wireframes should be built for every page on a website, whereas in other cases you can get by with just making wireframes for the major sections of the site. The decision for whether wireframes should be made for every page will be different for every project, but it generally is based on how different all the pages will be and how granular you want to get with the planning process.

Before delving into the process of creating a wireframe, however, take a look at a sample wireframe for Randy's Waffles (the fictitious company used in several examples throughout this book).

Notice that the focus of a wireframe is the placement of page content, user behavior, and functionality, not stylistic colors or fonts. By creating wireframes such as this, you enable the project's stakeholders to quickly visualize, and hopefully approve, the site's general layout. This gives designers a lot of latitude to create a branded SharePoint design using whatever styles they like because as long as it matches the approved wireframes, the design will meet the project's needs.

Wireframes can be created in a number of ways, from simple pen and paper diagrams to dedicated software programs such as Microsoft Visio, Adobe Illustrator, or Balsamiq Mockups. Several of these tools have prebuilt shapes or stencils that can be used to piece together typical web user interfaces.

When creating a brand for SharePoint, a key consideration is what pieces of SharePoint functionality will be supported by the design. A typical SharePoint page is made up of several controls and other pieces of functionality. Some of these functional controls are required for SharePoint to be used, but others are purely optional, based on your own project requirements. This is particularly true for public-facing Internet sites; several pieces of SharePoint functionality are not appropriate to show to anonymous public website viewers. For instance, by default, the help button in the top-right corner of the typical SharePoint user interface contains help for SharePoint itself, not the website that users are currently viewing.

Here you can see the default SharePoint user interface (based on `seattle.master`), with each of the major areas of functionality labeled.

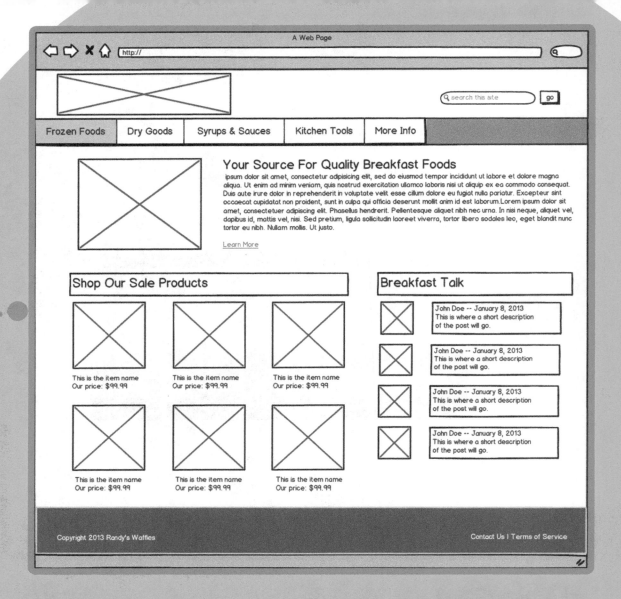

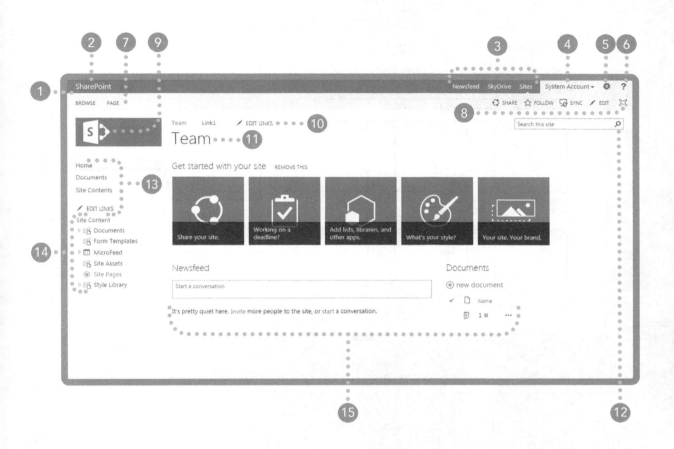

1 The Ribbon	The ribbon is the contextual menu at the top of the page used to interact with the current page or activity. Technically the blue bar at the top is actually the suite navigation, but the two are grouped together in this diagram because visually they form the ribbon area that "sticks" to the top of the browser window and does not scroll with the page content.	
2 Suite Navigation	Also known in code as the suite bar, this provides consistent navigation across the suite of applications available in Office 365 as well as surfacing branding and links for traditional farm installs of SharePoint. On the left it includes Microsoft branding for either SharePoint or Office 365. On the right it includes several of the other links labeled here.	
3 Suite Links	This includes links to My Sites functionality and, depending on how the server is configured and whether it is living in Office 365, there may be several links to other applications like Outlook and Calendar.	
4 Welcome Menu	This control shows the current username and has a drop-down menu to go to the About Me page (which links to your My Site) and a Sign Out button. When there is no authenticated user, this control shows the Sign In link.	
5 Settings Menu or Gear	Formerly known as the Site Actions button, this drop-down menu displays options for managing many aspects of the SharePoint site.	
6 Help	This links to the SharePoint help pop-up window.	
7 Ribbon Contextual Tabs	These tabs enable the user to switch between major sections of the ribbon. They are contextual based on what activity the user is currently performing on the site.	
8 Quick Access Toolbar	This toolbar is a selection of quickly accessible menu items for performing various tasks on your SharePoint site. The items vary by the type of SharePoint site and what activity the user is currently performing on the site. For instance, you can quickly edit and save the pages from the quick access toolbar. This section also includes the Focus on the Content button, which shows a minimal view of just the main areas of the SharePoint site.	
9 Site Logo	The site logo shows by default in SharePoint. The logo can be changed by clicking Site Settings ➢ Look and Feel ➢ Title, description, and logo.	
10 Top Navigation	Also known as the top link bar or global navigation, this is the primary horizontal navigation for the SharePoint site.	
11 Page Title	This shows the page title, as well as other related page information, sometimes including an icon that shows the description in a pop-up.	
12 Search Box	Here you see a search box and button that will launch SharePoint site searches. It can be configured to show more options such as a drop-down of search scopes.	
13 Left Navigation	Also known as the Quick Launch or current navigation, it is typically used for vertical secondary navigation to show pages related to the current location.	
14 Tree View	This displays a Windows Explorer style tree view representation of the current site. It also shows metadata navigation and filtering if the appropriate feature is activated.	
15 Page Content	This is the main content placeholder for SharePoint. It is required for rendering the actual content of pages.	

When creating wireframes for your SharePoint site, you must remember all the different types of content that are supported in SharePoint. It is easy to forget that content authors could be creating community sites, wiki sites, meeting workspaces, and many other types of content other than just the traditional content pages.

> **NOTE**
>
> Looking back at the wireframes for Randy's Waffles, note that not every single piece of SharePoint functionality is going to be included on this site.

You can see that some of the functionality that won't be included in this design is the left navigation and the Tree View. Because this wireframe is diagramming the public Internet site for Randy's Waffles, this functionality would probably confuse anonymous Internet visitors who are not familiar with SharePoint. Conversely, if you were to create wireframes for Randy's Waffles intranet pages, they would probably include most of these functional elements because intranet users may need them to collaborate more efficiently with each other.

Another thing to notice in these wireframes is that the body content areas are filled with fake text. This technique is known as *greeking* because it uses text in Greek or Latin (as shown in the figure) in a pseudorandom pattern to fill in the blocks of text. Much like other aspects of the wireframes, the goal here is to get stakeholders to focus on the general layout, rather than the actual text in the document. Greeking works better than just filling in the text blocks with "Content goes here" because it more accurately mimics the size and spacing of actual body content. Rather than make up greeked text by hand, resources such as Lorem2 (`http://lorem2.com`) provide stock greeked passages of varying size for anyone to copy and paste into wireframes and design comps.

By creating wireframes early in a SharePoint branding project, decisions about what should be on the page and how it should be generally arranged on the screen can be discussed and agreed upon. When it's time to actually create the user interface, the designer can focus purely on the creative aspects of the design rather than get mired in functional requirements.

CREATING REALISTIC DESIGN COMPS

Creating wireframes is certainly a valuable process for planning a new SharePoint website; however, for any serious branding effort, you need to make decisions based on creative concepts such as colors, font, and images as well. Before actually creating a brand in SharePoint, much like with wireframes, it would be good to have a way of creating realistic mockups of what the final website will look like. This is where *design comps* (sometimes known as *prototypes*) come into play. Unlike wireframes, design comps are intended to mimic the final branding of the actual SharePoint site as closely as possible without actually creating any code. Design comps should include all the things that make up a final design, such as colors, fonts, form elements, photos, and anything else that will appear on the final rendered website page.

Many programs are available to create realistic design comps. For instance, you could use something such as Microsoft Paint, which has been included with every copy of Windows since version 1.0. You

could even use a pencil and paper if you want a sense of nostalgia. However, there are some compelling reasons to seek out a more advanced solution. Design programs such as Microsoft Expression Design and Adobe Photoshop are shining examples of modern software that is geared toward creating design comps (among many other things). Both programs provide capabilities that aid in creating and maintaining reusable, realistic design comps.

With all the amazing things you can do in Expression Design and Photoshop, it's tempting to go crazy creating the world's most uniquely branded website. However, remember that the design comp is meant to imitate what can actually be created in a SharePoint website. Ultimately, learning whether something is easily creatable in SharePoint will take some time to get the hang of. One good method for learning this is to look at the functionality provided in the out-of-the-box master pages, both `seattle.master` and `oslo.master`. For example, if you plan to use SharePoint's top navigation functionality, it will be difficult to support long navigation item titles. This is because the horizontal navigation rendering in SharePoint does not wrap multiple lines of text per item by default.

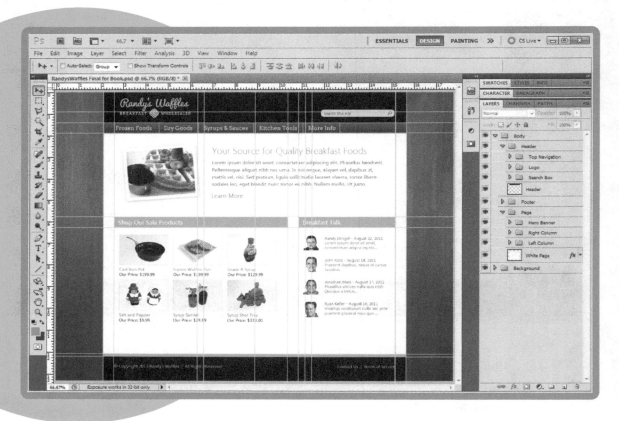

As you create your design comp, it's a good idea to consider how the various elements in your design will be created in SharePoint. Will the elements use out-of-the-box SharePoint functionality with some styles applied to them, or will they require some amount of custom code? If they can be accomplished with Web Parts, will they require custom styling? All the answers to these questions aren't needed immediately while creating the design comp, but the project's schedule and budget should be considered, and the design's complexity may need to be scaled back to accommodate these factors.

As the design comps are completed, key stakeholders may need to be engaged again to sign off on the final look and feel. Are the colors and the design in line with what they were hoping for? If not, you might need a few iterations of the design comps before they are fully agreed upon and finalized. Although this can certainly be time consuming, ultimately it's much better to work these issues out earlier in a design tool than try to adjust master pages and CSS later.

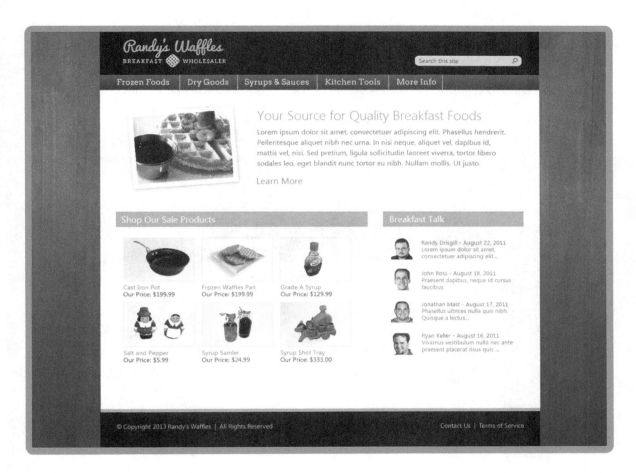

NOTE

The layered Photoshop design comp for Randy's Waffles is available for download with the rest of the examples in this book at Wrox.com.

The design comp shown here is highly stylized relative to the out-of-the-box SharePoint branding. If your project needs to make only minor changes to the seattle.master master page styling, you could create a design comp by starting with a screen shot of an existing SharePoint page. From there, you could use a design program to replace only the areas that are going to change. This technique could be used to quickly and easily create realistic design comps for the kind of simple branding discussed in Chapter 5.

SUMMARY

- Planning for any project is all about clarifying your goals and mitigating changes and problems early before they become more difficult to deal with during implementation.

- Ask questions up front to gather requirements early in the process.

- Based on the purpose of your site, create an information architecture that is functional and highly usable.

- Wireframes enable you to plan by focusing on the page structure and user behavior before creative elements are applied.

- Create realistic design comps based on the wireframe, which can then be used as you implement your design.

- In the following chapters you start with more basic SharePoint branding and work toward fully branded SharePoint sites with custom master pages and page layouts.

5

USING THE DESIGN MANAGER TO START A DESIGN IN SHAREPOINT

What's In This Chapter

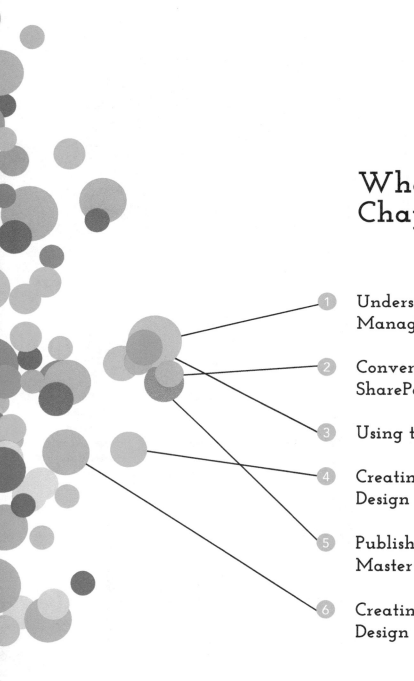

The reason you picked up this book and have made it this far is to learn how to make SharePoint look, well, not like SharePoint. You've learned what it means to brand SharePoint, some of the basics of SharePoint branding, and how to actually use SharePoint. You've gone through the planning process and created your design. This is where things get interesting! In this chapter, you will learn how to turn all your hard work, planning, and HTML design into a SharePoint site using the Design Manager.

INTRODUCING DESIGN MANAGER

First things first: What exactly is the Design Manager? If you skipped over Chapter 2, "SharePoint Overview," here's a brief refresher. The Design Manager is a new addition to SharePoint 2013 publishing sites. At its most basic level, the Design Manager is essentially a central hub for helping designers create and apply SharePoint branding. This can be accomplished by creating a blank master page that can be edited later or by converting an existing HTML file into a master page. There's a little more to it than that, which you learn as you dig deeper into each step in the process, but that is the main purpose.

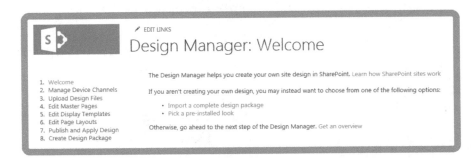

NOTE

A SharePoint Online Public Site in Office 365 has different Design Manager steps, but they are similar to those in publishing sites.

The Design Manager consists of eight easy steps, and step 1 barely counts because it is just a quick Welcome screen with a couple useful links to import a design package (covered in the "Creating a Design Package" section of this chapter) or to change the composed look of the site. You walk through these steps as the chapter progresses.

One of the most significant changes to SharePoint 2013's approach to branding is that the Design Manager facilitates the use of any HTML editor for maintaining your page layouts and master pages, such as Dreamweaver, Notepad++, Expression Web, and even SharePoint Designer 2013 if you're so inclined. After you run your HTML page through the Design Manager to convert it to a master page, SharePoint creates a corresponding `.master` file and syncs it with the `.htm` or `.html` file that you started from. This is a big change from previous versions in that you edit the HTML file directly and let SharePoint automatically make the changes to the master page or page layout files.

Another thing to consider is that the Design Manager is only available on sites with the publishing features enabled. Branding created with the Design Manager will work on team/collaboration sites, but there could be modifications that are needed for the branding to fully support all of the site features. Check out Chapter 7, "Creating SharePoint Branding," for the lowdown on creating SharePoint branding from scratch. Once you have the Design Manager there are several ways to start using it on publishing sites: From the homepage of a freshly created publishing site, you can click the **Design Your Site** link under the **I'm the Visual Designer** header. Alternatively, you can click **Settings menu ➤ Design Manager**. Finally, if you are on the Site Settings page, under the Look and Feel header, you can click the **Design Manager** link. However you get there, the first thing you see is the helpful welcome page. There's not that much going on here, so just click on **Manage Device Channels** on the left to move onto the next step.

Step 2 of the Design Manager is very similar to the Device Channels page that you can access from the Site Settings page.

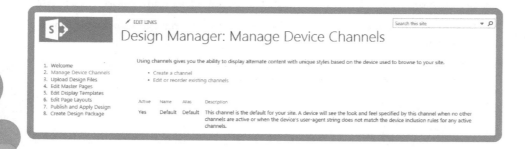

It shows the device channels already set up on your site and gives you the option to set up additional device channels. By using device channels, you can opt to apply different master pages for different devices or browsers through the use of keywords that SharePoint looks for in a requesting browser's user agent string. For instance, a mobile device may receive a master page optimized for mobile viewing, whereas a desktop browser would get the site's default master page. If you'd like more information on building and using device channels, see Chapter 8, "Advanced SharePoint Branding Tasks."

UPLOADING DESIGN FILES

In many cases, step 3 is actually the first step used in Design Manager. This is where you'll map a network drive to your Master Page Gallery and move your branding assets into the SharePoint site. Once you map a network drive to this URL, you can lay the foundation for working with your SharePoint branding going forward.

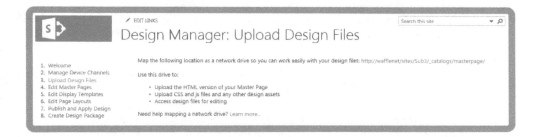

EXAMPLE: MAPPING A NETWORK DRIVE TO THE MASTER PAGE GALLERY

1. If you're not already in the Design Manager, click the **Settings menu** ➤ **Design Manager** ➤ **Upload Design Files.**

2. Copy the URL provided in step 3 of the Design Manager. (Note: If you use Internet Explorer, don't right-click the link and select Copy Shortcut. This copies the URL in a format that drive mapping can't read. Instead, simply select the text and press **Ctrl+C** to copy it.)

3. Depending on your version of Windows, the steps to start mapping a drive are slightly different:

    - In Windows 7 or Windows Server 2008/2008 R2, click **Start** ➤ right-click **Computer** ➤ **map network drive.**

    - In Windows 8 or Windows Server 2012, open the **Start Screen**, type **Computer**. Right-click **Computer** and select **Map Network Drive** at the bottom of the screen.

4. Choose your drive letter.

⑤ Paste the URL you copied from the Design Manager into the **Folder** field.

⑥ Select whether you want the drive to reconnect at logon, and also whether you would like to connect to the drive using different credentials than what you are currently logged into the machine with. You need to log on to the server with an account that has at least the Design permission level to work with the Design Manager and files in the Master Page Gallery. Click **Finish** when done and Windows Explorer opens and displays the contents of the Master Page Gallery in all its glory.

NOTE

You can find out more about the drive mapping process at http://support.microsoft.com/kb/2616712.

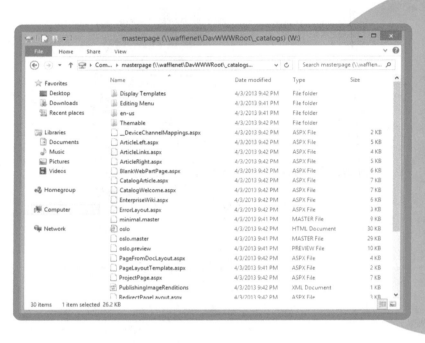

When building custom branding for previous versions of SharePoint, you would have put your master pages and page layouts in the Master Page Gallery and store all your custom CSS, images, and scripts in the Style Library or other document library. Things have changed slightly in the latest version. In SharePoint 2013, you can put your CSS, images, scripts, master pages, and page layouts all in the Master Page Gallery. The Style Library is still available, but now that you can map a drive directly to the Master Page Gallery to manage your branding assets from one location, it makes more sense to keep everything together.

Because you have just mapped a drive to the Master Page Gallery, uploading all your design assets is as simple as dragging and dropping from one window to another. The following steps walk you through uploading your branding assets to the Master Page Gallery:

EXAMPLE: UPLOADING YOUR BRANDING ASSETS TO THE MASTER PAGE GALLERY

1. If your drive isn't already open, navigate to your newly mapped drive. In Windows 7/Server 2008/2008 R2, click **Start** ➢ **Computer**. In Windows 8/Server 2012, open the **Start screen** ➢ type **Computer** and click **Computer** to open it. In the list of drives, open your mapped drive.

2. Create a folder within the mapped Master Page Gallery to hold all your images and styles. Because you're working with the Randy's Waffles site, call the folder **Waffles**.

3. Open the Chapter 5 HTML folder on your computer, select all the files, and drag them into the Waffles folder in the Master Page Gallery. This should include the Assets folder and all its contents, the Font folder and all its contents, the Products folder and all its contents, seven image files, `favicon.ico`, `style.css`, and `Waffles2013.html`.

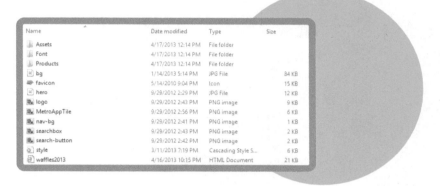

At this point, you're ready to convert your master page and start editing.

EDITING MASTER PAGES

Now that you've uploaded your design files to the Master Page Gallery, the next step is to convert your HTML to a SharePoint master page. SharePoint does all the heavy lifting here, so all you need to do is point it in the right direction and sit back and relax. The next sections walk you through this process and the basics of working with the Snippet Gallery to create your master page masterpiece.

NOTE

One thing that's strongly recommended here is creating a backup of your original HTML file. After you go through the conversion process, you may notice that SharePoint added a number of commented blocks of code in it. It may initially cause some concern, but this is all expected. By making a backup of your original file, you can rest easy if something goes horribly wrong later in the process, knowing that you can do another conversion process from your original HTML file and start over.

Converting an HTML Design into a Master Page

The process of converting HTML to a SharePoint master page is the cornerstone of the Design Manager. Everything you've done up to this point has led to this moment—it's time to turn your plain HTML into something more: a SharePoint master page.

Click step 4 of the Design Manager, **Edit Master Pages**.

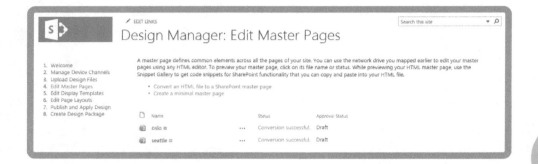

What you see here are options for converting an HTML file to a master page, or creating a blank starter master page. Below that, there are two master page files (`oslo.master` and `seattle.master`, SharePoint 2013's out-of-the-box master pages) that have been successfully converted.

NOTE

Because you're interested in converting your `Waffles2013.html` file into a SharePoint master page, you can ignore the Create a Minimal Master Page link. Just know that clicking it opens a dialog window where you can give your minimal master page a name, and it'll create a corresponding HTML version for you to edit using your web design tool of choice.

EXAMPLE: CONVERTING AN HTML FILE TO A MASTER PAGE

1. Click **Convert an HTML file to a SharePoint master page**.

2. In the Select an Asset dialog, browse to your **Waffles** folder within the Master Page Gallery, and select the `Waffles2013.html` file. The Location (URL) field at the bottom of the Select an Asset dialog shows the filename of the selected file.

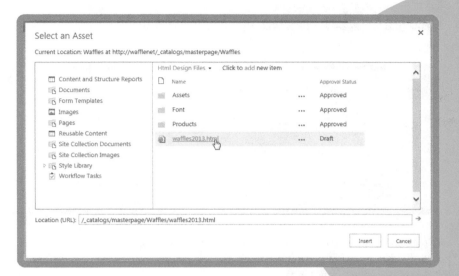

3. Click the **Insert** button.

4. After a few seconds the Design Manager refreshes, your Waffles2013 file is listed, and its status reads **Conversion Successful**.

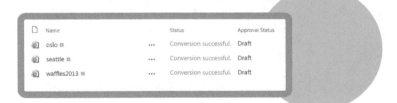

That's it! Not overly exciting, but that's actually a good thing—an uneventful conversion generally means a successful conversion. What actually happened in the background was impressive. SharePoint parsed through your HTML file, adding commented code blocks and snippets throughout, turning it from a simple HTML file into a master page file that it can read and understand.

If for some reason your conversion is unsuccessful, you'll receive a status of Warnings and Errors. If you click the **Warnings and Errors** link, SharePoint will try to point out where you went wrong. Generally, it's due to malformed HTML. Because SharePoint parses through the document, your HTML needs to be XML compliant—make sure you have no stray, unclosed tags; make sure your tags are closed in the proper order and tag properties are properly enclosed in quotes; and just generally make sure your HTML has the correct syntax.

A few other things you'll need to check as you go through the conversion process:

● Your DOCTYPE needs to be listed in all uppercase letters.

● Don't include any `<form>` tags in your HTML document; SharePoint adds a form automatically during the conversion.

● If you decide to use a modern template such as the HTML5 Boilerplate, there are some "gotchas" to be aware of. These are covered in detail in Chapter 11, "Modern Web Design and SharePoint."

● The Design Manager has a bug where apps cannot be added to sites using custom branding. As of this writing the issue has not been corrected, although Microsoft has indicated it will address the issue in a future patch. For more information on the issue and a fix, see `http://blog.drisgill .com/2012/12/design-manager-bug-sharepoint-2013-rtm.html`.

After the conversion process has been completed, **click the Waffles2013 filename** and you can see a preview of your master page.

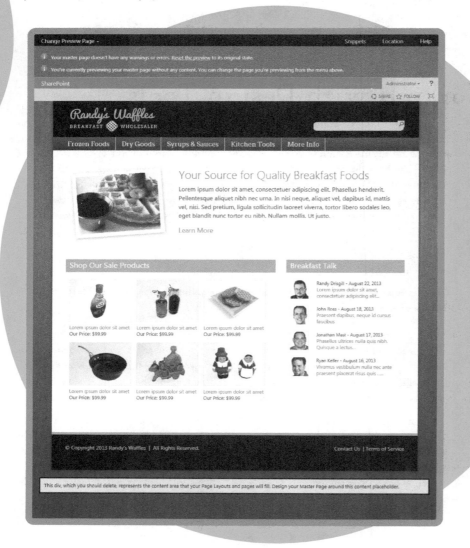

If your design has a background image applied to the <body> tag with CSS, there are some potential "gotchas" that you may need to look out for. SharePoint 2013 can be picky about how it displays background images on the <body> tag. If your background image isn't showing, you might try applying the background to another element on the page. Microsoft has added a CSS class called .ms-backgroundImage to the <body> tag that you can add properties to, including the background-image property. Or, you can try applying the background image to the .s4-workspace div. In the case of this design, the background image displays on the <body> tag without using any of these other methods.

As you can see from the screen shot there are a couple things that just don't quite look right. For one, the search box isn't lined up correctly. (This is OK for now; you'll replace the placeholder HTML search box with a SharePoint search box code snippet in the next section and style it in the next chapter.) The other important thing to point out is that at the bottom of the page, below the footer, a yellow box has been added, containing the text "This Div, Which You Should Delete, Represents the Content Area That Your Page Layouts and Pages Will Fill. Design Your Master Page Around This Content Placeholder." This yellow box is important; it represents the area in which SharePoint displays page content within the master page. You eventually want to move this yellow div to its proper place within the master page, which you learn to do in the next section.

Working with Design Tools

Now that the conversion process is finished, it's time to look at the converted HTML. Earlier the chapter mentioned that with the new approach to branding SharePoint 2013, virtually any web design tool can be used, and there are several design tools of the trade that are available to you. In SharePoint 2010, just about the only program you could use for working with master pages was SharePoint Designer 2010. You can still work with master pages in SharePoint Designer 2013, but you must use the Code view; the WYSIWYG Design view has been removed. Otherwise, the interface is nearly identical, so if you're familiar and comfortable working with SharePoint Designer, you certainly can.

NOTE

SharePoint Designer can't access mapped drives, but it has the ability to browse to the Master Page Gallery within the program.

Many designers may prefer something more traditional though, such as Dreamweaver or Expression Web. Even a text editor such as Notepad++ (http://notepad-plus-plus.org) can be used if you don't need a design preview. This was the idea of changing how SharePoint branding works in 2013: By expanding the available tools for creating and maintaining branding for SharePoint, it is easier to create branding because designers can use familiar tools.

Because you've mapped a drive to the Master Page Gallery, you can browse to that location, open the Waffles2013.html file, and begin the editing process, just as you would with any other HTML file. The HTML is a bit different than the last time you looked at it. Because of the conversion process, it looks at first glance like you sent your HTML through a digital meat grinder. SharePoint added all sorts of commented code blocks and snippets, increasing the 160-line HTML file to a 344-line file. Initially, you might be a little lost and disoriented among all the clutter. After all, it was easy to find your way

through your nice clean HTML file. But if you look through everything SharePoint has added, you'll actually find your original HTML, largely intact, and you'll see that the converted file isn't so scary.

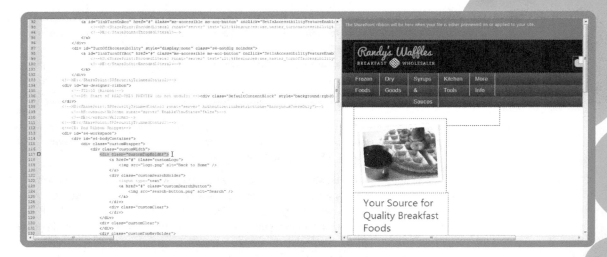

Many web design tools such as Dreamweaver and Expression Web have preview modes that give you an idea of what your site will look like in the browser. If you're using one of these kinds of web design tools you've probably noticed that things look a little off. Part of it may be the way the program renders the preview, but some of it has to do with the fact that SharePoint branding relies on a lot of moving parts, which make rendering a challenge. You can see the preview of the `Waffles2013.html` file in Dreamweaver in the following figure. You will also notice that in the preview of your site, SharePoint has added some snippet blocks for some elements of the UI—notably the block where the ribbon will be positioned, and the aforementioned yellow block below your main content.

A good starting point for editing your converted master page is moving the yellow block of content to the correct location. Right now it's sitting below the content of your page, which means that all page layout content will appear here as well if you apply this master page to your site. It needs to be moved into the main body area of the page.

Consider that your initial HTML design includes all elements you will see on the page including what will eventually become a master page and a page layout. Your job at this point is to start figuring out which part of the overall page layout is related to page content.

NOTE

When creating your own HTML design, you might find it helpful to add a comment to the beginning of the content that will be a page layout and another comment at the end, so it's easy to discern where you will move the placeholder at this point.

In the `Waffles2013.html` file, the area you want to replace is the content within the `<div class="customBodyHolder">` tag. Complete the following steps to remove the HTML mockup and move the page content placeholder to its correct location. These steps were created

using Adobe Dreamweaver CS5.5. They are as generic as possible, but you may find some slight difference in your editing program:

EXAMPLE: MOVING A CONTENT PLACEHOLDER

1. If you haven't opened `Waffles2013.html` from the mapped drive in your web design program, do so now. You should also see a corresponding `Waffles2013.master` file, but you'll only be working with the HTML file. SharePoint automatically updates the master page file with any changes you make in the HTML file. If you don't see the master page file, you may just need to refresh the Windows Explorer window by pressing **F5**.

2. In the HTML, find the `<div class="customBodyHolder">` tag. It should start around line 158.

3. Select all the content inside the `customBodyHolder` div tag; there are two comment tags to help you find the areas you should select. Select all of the content from `<!-- START Page Content -->` to `<!-- END Page Content -->`, which should be near lines 159–306.

4. Cut (Ctrl+X) these lines from the HTML file. (Don't delete them!) Create a new page in your web editing program (usually, pressing Ctrl+N will do this, though your program may differ) and paste (Ctrl+V) the lines in the HTML for later. If your web design program adds starter HTML such as a DOCTYPE and `<head>` and `<body>` tags, you can delete everything and simply paste your block of cut code. If you want, you can save this HTML page somewhere easily accessible, such as your desktop. It's just a temporary page that you're using to keep this HTML set aside for the time being.

5. Save the `Waffles2013.html` file, and switch back to the preview of your master page in the browser. Refresh the page to see your progress. You should see the master page with the now-empty main body. The yellow div block is still positioned below the footer.

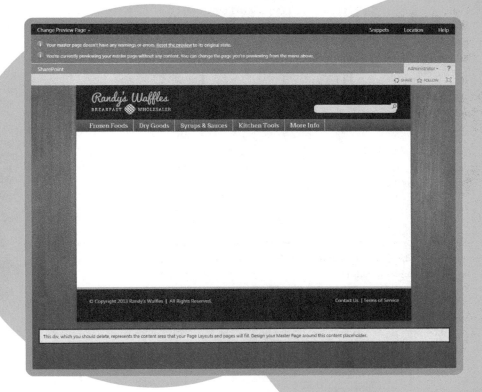

6 Now you're ready to move the placeholder into the main body area of the page. Switch back to your web design program. Scroll to the bottom of the HTML and find the following block of code (approximately lines 182–194, though your line numbers may differ if you left any empty lines when you cut the body content in step 4).

```
<div data-name="ContentPlaceHolderMain">
 <!--CS: Start PlaceHolderMain Snippet-->
 <!--SPM:<%@Register Tagprefix="SharePoint" Namespace="Microsoft.
SharePoint.WebControls"
  Assembly="Microsoft.SharePoint, Version=15.0.0.0, Culture=neutral,
  PublicKeyToken=71e9bce111e9429c"%>-->
 <!--MS:<SharePoint:AjaxDelta ID="DeltaPlaceHolderMain"
IsMainContent="true" runat="server">-->
  <!--MS:<asp:ContentPlaceHolder ID="PlaceHolderMain"
  runat="server">-->
  <div class="DefaultContentBlock" style="border:medium black solid;
  background:yellow; color:black; margin:20px; padding:10px;">
   This div, which you should delete, represents the content area
   that your Page Layouts and pages will fill. Design your Master
   Page around this content placeholder.
  </div>
  <!--ME:</asp:ContentPlaceHolder>-->
 <!--ME:</SharePoint:AjaxDelta>-->
 <!--CE: End PlaceHolderMain Snippet-->
</div>
```

7 Cut this code from the HTML (**Ctrl+X**) and place the cursor within the
`<div class="customBodyHolder"></div>` tags. Press **Enter** to create an empty
line between the opening `<div>` and closing `</div>`.

8 Paste the code snippet (**Ctrl+V**) in the empty line between the `customBodyHolder` div tags. If you use a design tool with a preview window, the preview should update with the yellow block in the body area of the HTML file. Save `Waffles2013.html`.

9 Switch back to the browser, and refresh the preview window. The yellow block is correctly positioned in the body area. (There is now a gap between the navigation and the white body of the page. Don't worry about this. It goes away when you clean up the yellow div tag in the next couple steps.)

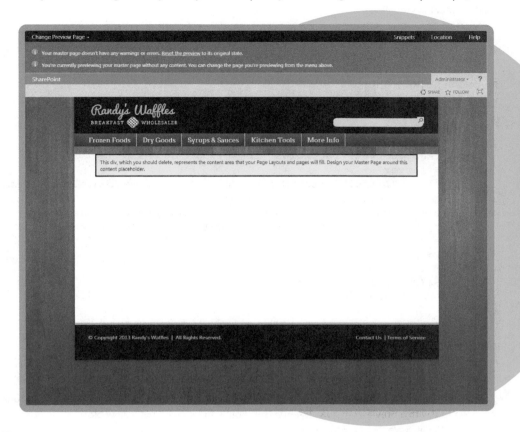

10 Within the placeholder code you just pasted is a `<div>` tag that needs to be deleted. The text and yellow box simply help you locate the div to position it properly; it is not needed for any other purpose, so you can safely delete it. Switch back to your design program and in the code you just pasted, select and delete the following content (approximately lines 164-167):

```
<div class="DefaultContentBlock" style="border:medium black solid;
background:yellow; color:black; margin:20px; padding:10px;">
            This div, which you should delete, represents the content
area that your Page Layouts and pages will fill. Design your Master
Page around this content placeholder.

    </div>
```

11 Save `Waffles2013.html`.

12 Return to the browser and refresh the master page preview. You should see your master page with an empty body area, which is exactly what you would like to see at this point. You now see what the master page should look like after the yellow div block is removed. (The gap between the body area and the navigation is fixed, too.)

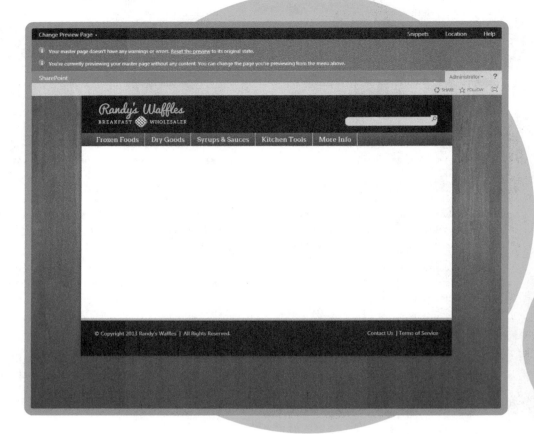

At this point you've mapped a drive to the Master Page Gallery, uploaded your design files, converted your HTML file into a SharePoint master page, and have moved the page content placeholder to its correct location. Not bad, but there's still more to come.

In the next few examples, you'll use the Snippet Gallery to put actual SharePoint controls onto the page, such as the search box and top navigation. When doing so you will be copying and pasting code around your HTML file. If you get lost along the way you can download the completed HTML master page and page layout examples from the downloadable code for this chapter.

Using the Snippet Gallery

Up to now you've made your changes to the `Waffles2013.html` file using the design tool of your choice. When SharePoint converted the HTML file into a master page, it added a placeholder for the main content of the site to the file, albeit not where you would have liked it to end up. In the previous section you walked through the process of working with the HTML file in your web design tool to make some changes to the HTML file and moving the placeholder to its correct location.

But what about other areas of the site? As you may know, SharePoint uses a number of content placeholders for various elements that you see on the site, such as the navigation, search box, header, and a host of other content. When a page is requested by a browser, SharePoint injects the proper code into each placeholder, which shows up as the HTML in the final rendered version that you see. In the `Waffles2013.html` file, several areas of the page need the placeholder HTML you used for your design purposes to be replaced with SharePoint placeholders. Two of the areas are the search box and top navigation. You can find the SharePoint placeholders used for these areas in the Snippet Gallery.

The Snippet Gallery is a collection of code snippets for various pieces of SharePoint functionality that you can use in your master page. Each snippet is found on the gallery's ribbon. Clicking a snippet button on the ribbon presents you with a preview window of what that snippet will look like when it's rendered, the actual snippet of code that you can copy and paste into your master page, and an expanding accordion set of options that you can use to make changes to the code snippet if you want.

There are actually two versions of the Snippet Gallery: one for master pages and one for page layouts. Because you're working with a master page here, you're presented only with those code snippets that can be added to a master page.

WARNING

Several of the examples in this chapter include approximate line numbers to look for in your HTML file. Your line numbers may differ some based on how your editor works, and if you have published the file in SharePoint. When HTML master pages and page layouts are published, some of the snippet code is expanded automatically from single long lines of code to several tabbed out lines.

EXAMPLE: ADDING SNIPPETS TO A MASTER PAGE

1. You should have the master page preview opened in your browser from the previous section. If you closed your browser or navigated away from the preview, simply open Design Manager and click **Edit Master Pages** and click **Waffles2013.html**.

2. Toward the upper-right corner of the page, above the ribbon preview, click the **Snippets** link to open the Snippet Gallery. The Snippet Gallery opens in a new browser tab, so you can easily switch back and forth between the gallery and the master page preview.

3. In the Snippet Gallery, click the **Search Box** button in the Navigation section on the ribbon. The Preview window shows what the default search box looks like, and you see a code snippet in the area directly below the preview.

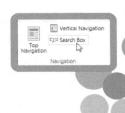

4 On the right in the Customization - Search Box `SearchBoxScriptWebPart` section, click some of the various headers to explore the options you can set on the search box. You won't make any changes here, so just leave the fields blank, but if you were making changes, you must click the **Update** button for them to be reflected in the code snippet. If you accidentally make a change, simply click the **Reset** button above the Customization section. This resets the code snippet back to its default state.

5 In the HTML Snippet section, select and copy all the text in the scrolling window. (If you use Internet Explorer, you have a **Copy to Clipboard** button below the HTML snippet window that can be used to easily copy the snippet to the clipboard. If IE asks if you want to allow the webpage to copy the code after you've clicked this button, just click **Allow**).

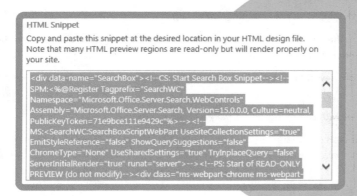

6 Return to your design program and find the `<div class="customSearchHolder">` tag (around line 121).

7 Select and delete the contents within the `customSearchHolder` div, which should be the `<input>`, `<a>`, and `<img>` tags. The highlighted text in the screenshot shows the content that should be deleted.

```
<div class="customSearchHolder">
    <input type="text" />
    <a href="#" class="customSearchButton">
        <img src="search-button.png" alt="Search" />
    </a>
</div>
```

8 Place the cursor inside the `<div class="customSearchHolder"></div>` tags, press **Enter** to create a blank line, and paste in the snippet you copied from the Snippet Gallery onto the blank line between the `customSearchHolder` divs.

9 Save the `Waffles2013.html` file, return to the master page Preview tab in your browser, and refresh the page to see your change.

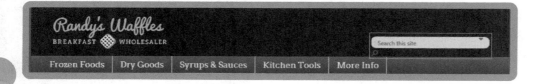

When you started with your HTML design, some items were essentially HTML placeholders that were going to be replaced with SharePoint controls. The search box is one of them. The original HTML file used a simple HTML `<input>` field to represent the search box. SharePoint's search control is more complex than that and as such requires a bit of extra work to style to match the original design. You'll learn more about that in Chapter 6, "Cascading Style Sheets and SharePoint."

As for the code snippets, there is actually some logic to how they are laid out, despite looking like a bunch of gibberish at first glance. You'll notice that every snippet is made up of commented blocks of code. Each comment begins with a set of letters, which helps you figure out what each line means. The general structure of a code snippet is as follows:

- **Snippet Start**—Starts the code snippet with an opening `<div>` tag and comments.
- **SharePoint markup**—The code that contains the namespace registration tag (if one is required) and the corresponding control that renders the item in SharePoint.
- **HTML Preview**—A read-only preview that web design programs can read and generate an approximate look for the control.
- **Snippet End**—Ends the snippet with comments and usually a closing `</div>`.

Some snippets may have more than one section of SharePoint markup and HTML Preview sections, but the preceding list provides the basic structure. Each of the comments that appear in each section begin with various abbreviations and have specific meaning to help you understand the markup a little better. These abbreviations represent the following:

- **CS/CE (Comment Start/Comment End)**—Starts and ends the code snippet.
- **SPM (SharePoint markup)**—Denotes a single line of code and in some cases is used as registration for a namespace.
- **MS/ME (Markup start/Markup end)**—Starts and ends a SharePoint control snippet.
- **PS/PE (Preview Start/Preview End)**—The code inside these comment blocks is the HTML preview file that help design tools render the look of the SharePoint control.

Generally speaking, you shouldn't need to modify anything in the code snippets outside of the Snippet Gallery. Any styling you need to do can generally be done by overriding the out-of-the-box styles. Again, this will be covered in the next chapter.

Now you can return to the Snippet Gallery to replace your static HTML navigation with a dynamic SharePoint navigation control.

EXAMPLE: REPLACE NAVIGATION PLACEHOLDER WITH SHAREPOINT NAVIGATION SNIPPET

1. Return to the Snippet Gallery in the browser. If it's no longer open, you can get there by opening **Design Manager** ➤ **Edit Master Pages** ➤ **Waffles2013.html** ➤ **Snippets**.

2. On the ribbon, click the **Top Navigation** button on the left. In some snippet previews, the preview window renders a live preview of the control. For example, if you have already built your site's navigation, your navigation structure displays in the preview window instead of a generic preview.

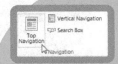

③ By default, the navigation snippet doesn't show drop-downs, so you need to adjust its properties. Scroll down the page to the **Customization - Top Navigation (AspMenu)** section. Change the **Static-DisplayLevels** value to **1**. In this same section, click the **Behavior** section to expand it, and change the **MaximumDynamicDisplayLevels** value to **1**.

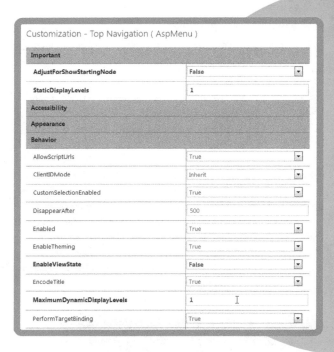

④ Scroll up the page and click the **Update** button to update the HTML snippet.

⑤ In the HTML Snippet section, select and copy all the text from the scrolling text field.

⑥ Switch to your web design program with `Waffles2013.html` open and find `<div class="customTopNavHolder">` (around line 130). Within that tag, select and delete the entire `<ul class="customTopNav">` tag and all its contents (around lines 131-152).

⑦ Place the cursor within the `<div class="customTopNavHolder"></div>` tags, and paste in the Top Navigation snippet you just copied from the Snippet Gallery.

⑧ Save `waffles2013.html`.

One last thing you'll want to do to make navigating the site a little easier is to replace the site logo link and image with the Site Logo snippet, which makes the logo a link back to the homepage of the site.

EXAMPLE: REPLACING PLACEHOLDER SITE LOGO WITH SHAREPOINT SITE LOGO SNIPPET

① Switch to the Snippet Gallery and click the **Site Logo** snippet in the ribbon.

② Scroll down the page to the **Customization - Site Logo (SPSimpleSiteLink)** section and click the **Appearance** header to expand it. In the **CssClass** properties, replace the default text, ms-siteicon-a, with **customLogo**.

③ Still in the **Customization - Site Logo (SPSimpleSiteLink)** section, expand the **Navigation** section and in the **NavigateUrl** field, type `~sitecollection/`.

④ In the **Customization - Site Logo (SiteLogoImage)** section, expand the **Appearance** section and delete the default text from the CssClass field. Then expand the **Misc** section, and in the **LogoImageUrl** field, replace the default URL in the field with **/_catalogs/masterpage/waffles/logo.png**. Be sure to change the path if your site collection is not at the root of your web application (Example: /sites/SubSiteCollection/_catalogs/masterpage/waffles/logo.png).

⑤ Scroll up and click the **Update** button, then select and copy the HTML snippet.

⑥ Switch to your web editing program and replace the following HTML with the Site Logo snippet you just copied, which should be around lines 118-120:

```
<a href="#" class="customLogo">
  <img src="logo.png" alt="Back to Home" />
</a>
```

NOTE

You also could have left the original HTML for the logo and simply changed the <a href="#"... to <a href="/"... to link back to the root of the site. However, using the Site Logo control gives you the ability to easily switch out the site's logo in the SharePoint UI by clicking the **Settings menu** ➤ **Site settings** ➤ **Title, description, and logo**. In the Logo and Description section, you can add a new logo image from your computer or from within SharePoint, which replaces the logo currently displaying in the header area. This can be helpful if your design utilizes variations of the same logo, such as for different department sites or sites for different branches of the same company.

⑦ Save **Waffles2013.html**, return to the master page preview in the browser, and refresh the page to see your changes. The site logo should look exactly the same as it did before. You can see the SharePoint navigation in place of the HTML navigation. If you don't have any navigation links created, you only see an Edit Links link in the navigation. The link is highlighted in the screenshot.

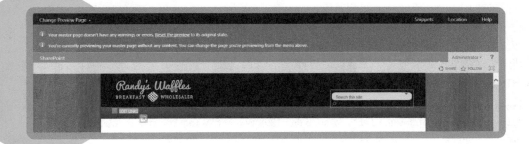

The search box, top navigation, and site logo are just three of the many snippets available in the Snippet Gallery to add to your custom master page. In addition to these, you can add a variety of other controls and Web Parts to your page. The following table details the available controls you can add via the Snippet Gallery.

The process for adding these snippets is exactly the same as the process for the ones you just added to the Waffles2013 file. When you work with your own design, select the snippet from the ribbon, copy the code, and paste it into the appropriate location in the HTML within your design tool.

In the **Waffles2013.html** file, the <div> tags you selected were conveniently named to make it as easy as possible to find the blocks of code you needed to work with. This is a fine option as you build out your own HTML file, or you could add comment blocks around the various elements on your HTML page so it's easier to find what you need to replace after your file is converted.

One last important thing to note is that if you were to apply this master page to the site as the system master page and open a SharePoint dialog box, many of the branding elements will show in the dialog, which isn't always desirable. This issue discussed in more depth and remedied in Chapter 7 in the section "Using a Starter Master Page."

SNIPPET OR GROUP	FUNCTIONALITY
Top Navigation	Add a top navigation to your site.
Vertical Navigation	Add vertical navigation (sometimes called left navigation or contextual navigation) to your site.
Search Box	Add a search box to your site.
Site Title	Add a control to display the site's title.
Site Logo	A placeholder for a site logo that can be changed out with the SharePoint interface.
Sign In	Adds a sign-in link to the site. Useful for anonymously accessible sites that still need a login link because the ribbon is only accessible to authenticated viewers.
Edit Mode Panel	A panel whose contents display only in Edit mode.
Security Trim	A panel whose contents will display only to users with the correct permission level. There are three preconfigured options to select from as well under the Security Trim drop-down: Show to Authors, Show to Authenticated Users, and Show to Administrators. Clicking the Security Trim button selects the Show to Authors option by default.
Device Channel Panel	A panel similar in approach to Device Channels. Instead of targeting an entire master page, a Device Channel Panel can show or hide a specific block of content based on the browser's user agent string.
Media and Content	Web Parts in this group enable you to add video, pictures, scripts, and other media directly to the master page. These options also include a Page Viewer Web Part, a Content Editor Web Part, a Silverlight Web Part, and the Get Started Web Part that displays by default on sites created from the Team site template.
Dynamic Content	Web Parts in this group enable you to dynamically display content from your site in a variety of formats, including the Content Query Web Part, a Summary Links Web Part, a Table of Contents Web Part, and several other Web Parts.
Other Web Parts	Most other Web Parts are available in this grouping.
Custom ASP.NET Markup	Enables you to paste in custom ASP.NET markup to generate a SharePoint 2013 code snippet that you can add to your page.

EDITING PAGE LAYOUTS

You'll recall from Chapter 2, "SharePoint Overview," that page layouts are basically layout templates for displaying content on each page in SharePoint. All publishing pages are based on a page layout, and each page layout is based on a content type. Microsoft has a handful of page layouts you can use when building your sites, but you also have the option to create custom page layouts. Just like the out-of-the-box page layouts, your custom page layouts need to be based on a content type. A content type is simply a collection of site columns that SharePoint uses to hold information about a particular item. There are a couple kinds of content types that are applied to page layouts, including Article Page and Welcome Page. These two content types share some similarities, but differ in some of the columns that they contain. Page layouts based on the Article Page content type are generally used for creating content pages, whereas page layouts based on the Welcome Page content type are often used for site or subsite homepages. There's no hard rule that says you have to use one or the other, but the different fields that appear on each page layout may help influence your preference depending on your needs.

On step 6 of the Design Manager you see a **Create a Page Layout** link and a list of all the page layouts available in the site. If you are just starting out and haven't created any page layouts yet, this list will be blank, letting you know that there are no HTML Page Layouts to show. You can also see which content type each page layout is associated with. In the last section, you worked with your web design tool to make some changes to the `Waffles2013.html` file and turn it into a useable master page. One of those changes was to remove the content from the body of the design because it would normally appear as a page layout. This section walks through adding that content back as a page layout, stripping out some of the extra placeholder content and replacing it with Web Part zones for adding SharePoint Web Parts.

EXAMPLE: CREATING A PAGE LAYOUT AND ADDING PLACEHOLDER CONTENT

1. In step 6 of the Design Manager, click the **Create a Page Layout** link. You may need to open Design Manager again because the preview page doesn't provide any link to head back to the Design Manager.

2. In the Create a Page Layout dialog, type `WafflesHome` in the Name field. This becomes the filename that appears in the Master Page Gallery when editing the page layout.

3. Select **Waffles/Waffles2013** in the Master Page drop-down to associate this page layout with your custom master page.

4. Select **Welcome Page** in the Content Type drop-down. Because you're going to be creating the page layout that you'll use for the homepage of your site, it makes sense to use the Welcome Page content type. Click **OK** to create your new page layout. The Edit Page Layouts page refreshes and lists the newly created WafflesHome page layout.

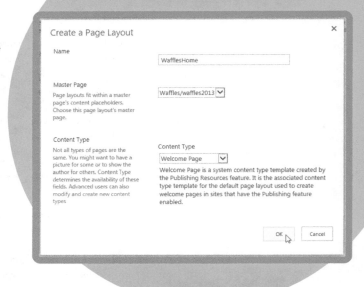

5. Switch to your mapped drive. When SharePoint creates a new page layout, it puts it in the root of the Master Page Gallery. You can leave it there, or if you'd like to keep all your related files together, you can move the HTML file into the Waffles folder with your custom master page. Open the drive mapped to the Master Page Gallery, and find `WafflesHome.html`. Drag and drop this file into the Waffles folder. (If you receive a warning that the file might be harmful, you can safely click OK.) You don't need to move the associated `WafflesHome.aspx` page because after the HTML file is moved, SharePoint moves the .aspx file automatically, although you may need to refresh your mapped drive by pressing F5 to see the change right away.

6. Return to the Design Manager in the browser and refresh the step 6 page. Click **WafflesHome** to open a preview of the page layout within your custom master page.

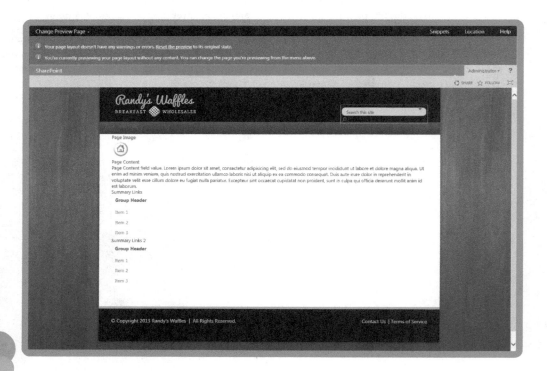

NOTE

On the preview page for the custom page layout, SharePoint has already added some sample content. This set of controls appears because you are basing your layout on the Welcome Page content type. If you had selected the Article Page content type, you would have seen a different set of controls. Some fields are common among the various content types, including the Page Image and Page Content fields.

7. Near the upper right of the page, click the **Location** link. A dialog opens telling you the location of the file you're previewing. Verify that it appears as `[YourMappedDrive]:\Waffles\ WafflesHome.html`.

8. Switch to your web editor, and open the `WafflesHome.html` file from within the Waffles directory in the mapped drive.

9. Look at the HTML code and find the line `<!--MS:<asp:ContentPlaceHolder ID="PlaceHolderMain" runat="server">-->` (line 70). There are several lines that begin with `<asp:ContentPlaceHolder`, so make sure you find the correct one with the ID of `PlaceHolderMain`. This is the placeholder for the main body of the page layout. All the controls and content that appear on the page should be within this tag. Look through the various `<div>` tags within the `PlaceHolderMain` control to familiarize yourself with how the page layout is built. Each `<div>` contains a snippet for the various components on the page that SharePoint added for you.

10. Select all the content within the `PlaceHolderMain` control (all the divs and code snippets) and delete it (approximately lines 71–112). You will add some of these controls back in the coming steps. For now, it's just easier to start from a blank slate.

11. Position the cursor at the end of the line `<!--MS:<asp:ContentPlaceHolder ID="PlaceHolderMain" runat="server">-->` and press **Enter** to create a new line below.

12. Switch to the document where you pasted the HTML of the body of the mockup from the last section. Select all of the HTML and copy it. (If you didn't do this step or closed the new page without saving the content, you can just open your original unconverted Waffles2013 file and copy the HTML between `<!-- START Page Content -->` and `<!-- END Page Content -->`.)

13. Return to your editor, and paste in the HTML you just copied within the empty `PlaceHolderMain` control. **Save** the file. Return to the page layout preview in the browser and refresh the page.

Right now things look a lot like the original file you converted, but you've only completed moving the SharePoint placeholder for the main content area of the page.

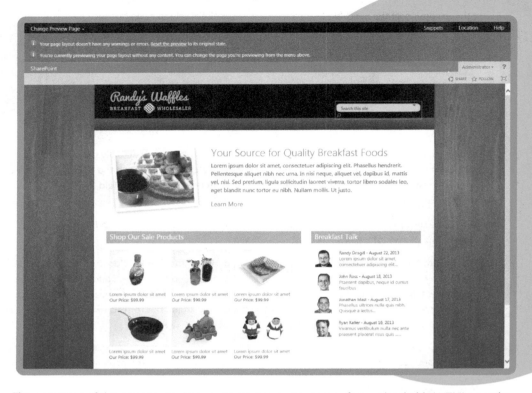

The next stage of this process requires you to start removing some of your placeholder HTML to make room for Web Part zones and other SharePoint control snippets.

EXAMPLE: REPLACING PAGE LAYOUT PLACEHOLDER CONTENT WITH SNIPPETS

1. Switch back to your design program. In the WafflesHome.html file, find the following block of code:

```
<div class="customHeroLeft">
  <a href="#" class="customHeroPhoto"><img src="hero.jpg" alt="" />
  </a>
</div>
```

2. Delete the lines `<a href="#" class="customHeroPhoto"><img src="hero.jpg" alt="" /></a>`. The highlighted code shown in the screenshot is what should be removed from the page.

```
<div class="customHeroLeft">
    <a href="#" class="customHeroPhoto"><img src="hero.jpg" alt="" /></a>
</div>
```

3. A couple lines down, find the `<div class="customHeroRight">` tag and delete all the contents within the tag (which should include the `<h1>`, `<p>`, and `<a>` tag). The `customHeroRight` div should be empty. Go ahead and **save** your page now.

4. Switch back to the preview page in the browser, and click the **Snippets** link near the upper right of the page. This opens the Snippet Gallery for page layouts in a new Browser tab. The page layout Snippet Gallery looks and behaves identically to the master page Snippet Gallery, with the exception of the available controls. These are specific only to page layouts.

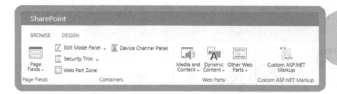

5. By default, the Snippet Gallery opens to the Page Image control, which is actually the snippet you're going to add first. This snippet is located under the Page Fields drop-down on the ribbon. Just like you did in the master page Snippet Gallery, select all the text in the scrolling text field in the HTML Snippet section and copy it.

6. Return to the design program, and paste the snippet within the `<div class="customHeroLeft">` tag, where the picture of the waffles used to be. **Save** your page.

7. Switch back to the Snippet Gallery tab in the browser, and click the **Page Fields** drop-down; then select and copy the **Page Content** snippet from the HTML Snippet section. (This field and the Page Image field are ones that were already included on the page layout by default when you created it. You could have simply moved these snippets around instead of deleting them, but for this example it was easier to delete everything and add the fields back in.)

8. In your design program, paste the snippet code inside the `<div class="customHeroRight">` tag. **Save** the file and return to the page layout preview in the browser. Refresh the page and see your changes.

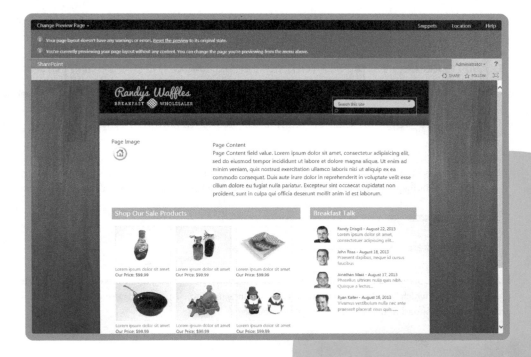

9   Switch back to the design program, and delete the content within the `<div class="customColLeft">` and `<div class="customColRight">` tags because this was simply placeholder HTML for the design. You are going to replace the content with Web Part zones, which can allow you to add in Web Parts later to fill in the content.

10 Return to the Snippet Gallery, and click the **Web Part Zone** button in the Containers section on the ribbon.

11 In the Customization area on the snippet page, the Important section is expanded, showing the ID field. By default SharePoint generates a unique ID for each Web Part zone. You can change the long string of random numbers and letters to something more digestible. Delete the text from the ID field, and type **LeftCol** as the ID.

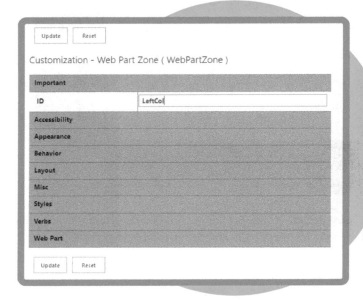

12 Click the **Update** button above the Customization area to update the code snippet. Look at the snippet and notice that your new ID of LeftCol appears in the tag that begins `<!--MS:<WebPartPages:WebPartZone...`.

13 Just like before, select and copy the HTML snippet code, and in your design program, paste in the copied snippet within the `<div class="customLeftCol">` tag.

14 Switch back to the Snippet Gallery. Change the ID of the Web Part zone to **RightCol**, click the **Update** button to update the code snippet with the new ID, and select and copy the HTML snippet.

15 In your design program, paste the snippet in the `<div class="CustomRightCol">` tag. **Save** your changes.

16 Return to the page layout preview and refresh the page. You can't see the zones because you're not in edit mode, but if you've followed these steps, rest assured they are there.

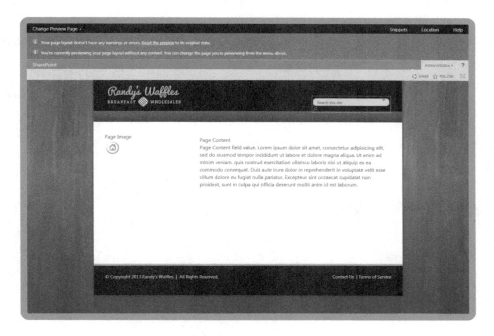

In the next section you will look at publishing and applying your custom master page, and you also see how to apply your custom page layout so that you can see the results of your hard work.

PUBLISHING AND APPLYING A MASTER PAGE

Now it's time to actually publish your master page, page layout, and your design elements so that you can apply them and see how it looks and behaves on the site, outside of a preview page. In a real-world scenario, you'd probably want to spend some more time tweaking the look and feel of some of the SharePoint controls before getting to this point, although you can still make changes to your files even after they've been published. When you publish your files, you are checking them in and making them available to anyone who has read access to the site. In the next chapter, you'll learn about styling the SharePoint controls to match the original design.

When you click on step 7 in the Design Manager, you're presented with some rudimentary instructions for publishing your custom designs and a couple links: one for opening the Master Page Gallery and another for opening the master page settings. You can also get to either of these places from the Site Settings page under the Galleries heading and the Look and Feel heading, respectively.

Now you'll walk through the process of publishing your design assets, page layout, and master page. Then you'll apply the master page to the site.

EXAMPLE: PUBLISHING YOUR DESIGN FILES

1. Click on **Publish and Apply Design** on the left side of the Design Manager.

2. Click the link **Go to the Master Page Gallery**. The Master Page Gallery opens in a new browser tab. (Alternatively, if you were outside the Design Manager, you could simply click the **Settings menu ➤ Site settings ➤ Master pages and page layouts**.)

3. Click the **Waffles** folder to display its contents and put a check in the box that appears next to the `Waffles2013.html` file when you hover over the filename.

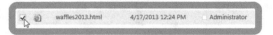

4. On the ribbon, click the **Files** tab; then click the **Publish** button toward the right side.

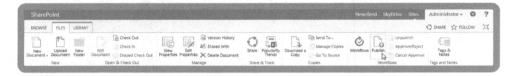

5. In the dialog that opens, optionally type a comment in the Comments field; then click **OK** to publish your master page. SharePoint automatically publishes the corresponding `Waffles2013.master` file.

6. In the column headings, check the box in the leftmost column to select all the items in the Waffles folder. Notice that the Publish button isn't available to click. That's because there's no way to mass publish all the items in this folder from within the Master Page Gallery. (Okay, technically there is; you *can* actually mass check out every file in the Waffles folder, with the exception of folders, and then check in all the files at once, electing to publish a major version of each. But for now you're going to take a different approach.)

7. Click the **Settings menu ➤ Site settings**.

8. Under the Site Administration header, click **Content and Structure** to open the Content and Structure manager. This page, which has been present in SharePoint since the 2007 release, still retains the same basic look and feel it had in SharePoint 2007.

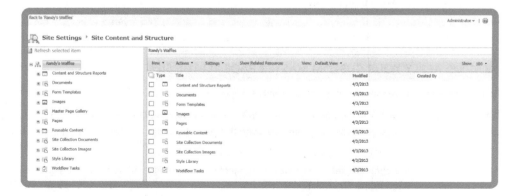

9. In the left pane of the Content and Structure page, click the **+** next to Master Page Gallery. Then click the **Waffles** folder to display its contents in the main window of the page.

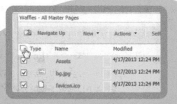

10 At the top of the main body, click the icon of stacked check boxes to select all items in the folder.

11 Click the **Actions** drop-down in the toolbar, and select **Publish**. In the dialog that appears, optionally type a comment, and then click **OK**. This publishes all items in the Waffles folder.

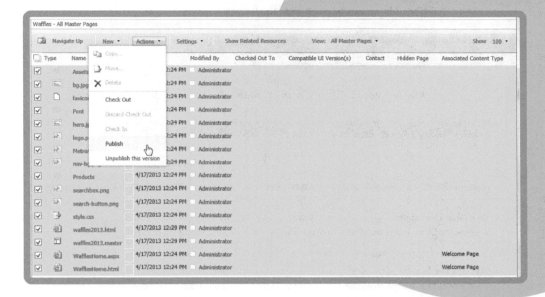

12 Click the **Assets** folder within the Waffles folder to open it up. Then repeat steps 10 and 11 to publish the items inside this folder.

13 In the toolbar, click the **Navigate Up** button to return to the Waffles directory.

14 Repeat the publish process for the items in the remaining folders (Font and Products).

15 When everything is published, click the **Back to '[*Site name*]'** link in the upper left of the Content and Structure window to return to your site.

Now that your custom master page, custom page layout, and all associated styles and images have been published, you can apply the master page to the site.

EXAMPLE: APPLY YOUR CUSTOM MASTER PAGE TO THE SITE

1 Return to the Design Manager tab in the browser.

2 Still on step 7, click the link **Assign Master Pages to Your Site Based on Device Channels**. This opens the Master Page Settings in a dialog. (When you open this page from the Site Settings page, it doesn't display in a dialog.)

3 If you have any device channels set up, the device channel name appears with a drop-down to select an alternative master page in the Site Master Page settings section, so set whatever master page you'd like for your device channels, or set it to **Follow Default Channel**. For the Default drop-down, select **Waffles/Waffles2013**. (If you don't have any device channels set up, just apply the **Waffles/Waffles2013** master page to the only drop-down that appears.)

4 Change the System Master Page setting drop-down to **Waffles/Waffles2013**.

NOTE

In case you are wondering what the difference is between the two master page settings, the Site master page setting applies the selected master page to all publishing pages, while the System master page setting applies the selected master page to all other page types, including settings pages.

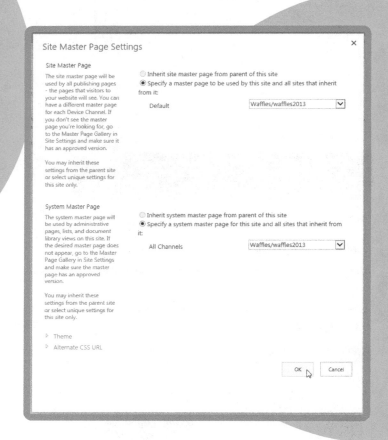

5 Click **OK** to apply your custom master page to your site. If you are changing the master page from within the Design Manager, you need to refresh the page to see the newly applied master page. This is because the master page settings opened in a modal dialog and didn't refresh the original page when it closed. When you access the master page settings from the Site Settings page, the branding is applied as soon as you click OK because you'll be redirected back to the Site Settings page immediately after.

And *voilà!* Just like that, you're looking at your master page on a live SharePoint site! You can see the Design Manager with your custom design applied.

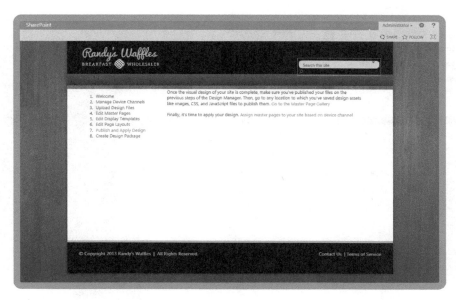

Now it's time to try out your custom page layout:

EXAMPLE: APPLYING YOUR CUSTOM PAGE LAYOUT

1. Click the **Settings menu ➤ Add a Page**. In the Add a page dialog, type **Home** in the Give It a Name field and click **Create**.

2. Your page opens up in Edit mode. Click the **Page** tab on the ribbon; then click the **Page Layout** drop-down. Scroll to the bottom of the Page Layout drop-down, and select your custom page layout, **WafflesHome**.

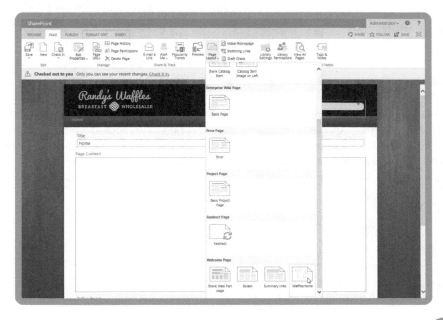

3 Your custom page layout displays, with the fields and Web Part zones you added in. The page may look a little "off" at first, but once you start adding some content it will display correctly. In the Page Content field control, click the text **Click here to add new content.** Use the Format Text tab on the ribbon to make some text changes if you want. Alternatively, you can edit the HTML source for this field control by clicking the **Edit Source** button in the Format Text tab of the ribbon. If you are so inclined, you could add in the HTML from the original design:

```
<h1>Your Source for Quality Breakfast Foods</h1>
<p>
Lorem ipsum dolor sit amet, consectetuer adipiscing elit. Phasellus
hendrerit. Pellentesque aliquet nibh nec urna. In nisi neque, aliquet
vel, dapibus id, mattis vel, nisi. Sed pretium, ligula sollicitudin
aoreet viverra, tortor libero sodales leo, eget blandit nunc tortor eu
nibh. Nullam ollis. Ut justo.
</p>
<a class="customLearnMore" href="#">Learn More</a>
```

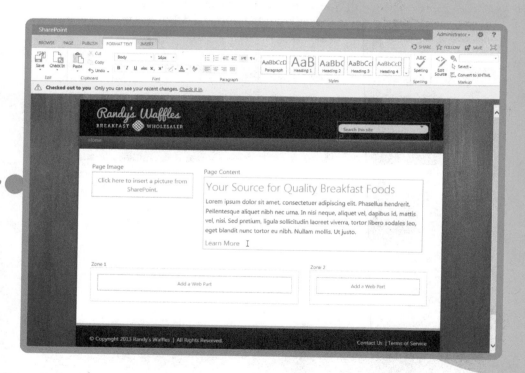

4 In the Page Image field control, click the link **Click here to insert a picture from SharePoint.**

5 In the Edit Image properties dialog that opens, click the **Browse** button next to the Selected Image field.

6 At the bottom of the Select an Asset dialog, type **/_catalogs/masterpage** in the Location (URL) field, and press **Enter** to open the Master Page Gallery.

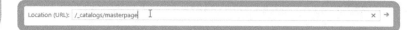

7 In the Master Page Gallery, click the **Waffles** folder to open it up; then click the `hero.jpg` file to select it. Its URL should appear in the Location (URL) field. Click **Insert** to close the Select an Asset dialog.

8 Optionally fill in the rest of the fields on the Edit Image Properties dialog, such as selecting an Image Rendition, adding Alternate text (which shows up when you hover the mouse over the image and is also used by screen readers as a description of the image), and a hyperlink to go to a different page if you'd like. In addition, you have the option to set some layout properties and resize the image if you want. For now, you can just click **OK** to add the image to the page and then click the **Save** button on the right side of the ribbon to see how your page is coming along.

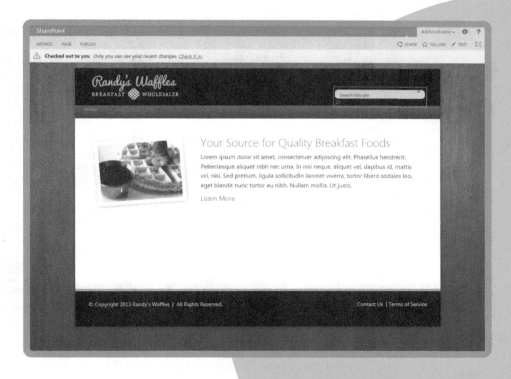

9. Open the page in Edit mode again by clicking the **Edit** button on the right side of the ribbon, where the Save button was previously.

10. In Zone 1 on the page, click the **Add a Web Part** link. The Web Part menu opens.

11. In the Categories section, scroll through the categories, and click **Media and Content**.

12. In the Parts section, **Content Editor** should be selected. (If not, click it.) Click **Add** to add this Web Part to Zone 1. This Web Part will be used as a placeholder for now; you'll replace it later when you go through the examples in Chapter 9, "Creating Content Rollups with SharePoint WCM."

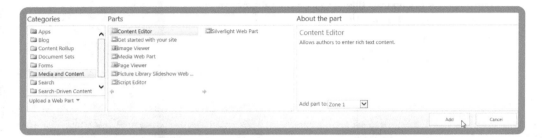

13. Hover over the Web Part's title, and click the **drop-down arrow** that appears at the far-right side of the Web Part. Select **Edit Web Part** from the menu.

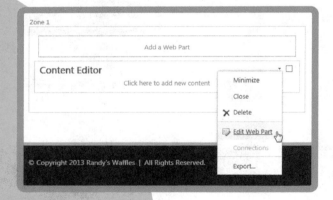

14　In the tool pane that opens on the right side of the page, expand the Appearance section, and change the Title field to **Shop Our Sale Products**. Click **OK** at the bottom of the tool pane.

15　In the newly added Content Editor, click the link **Click here to add new content** and type some text in the Web Part.

16　Repeat steps 10 to 15 to add a Content Editor Web part to Zone 2. Change the title of this Content Editor to **Breakfast Talk**. (This Web Part is also just a place-holder for now.)

17　Click the **Save** button on the ribbon.

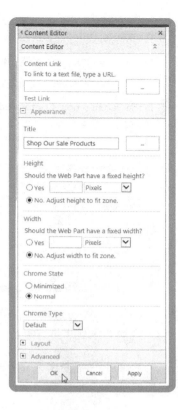

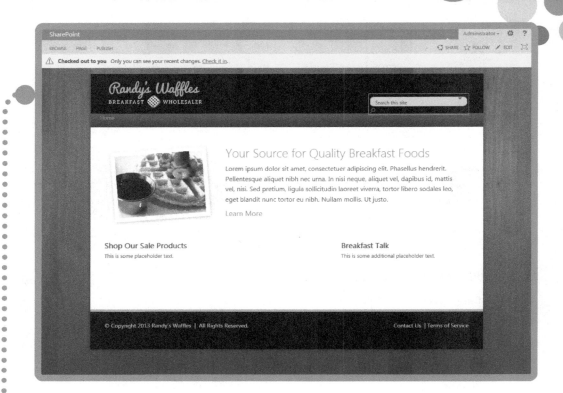

In a real-world scenario, you'd probably want to change the page layout of your site's actual home page (`default.aspx`) and just delete the Web Parts Microsoft has added to help you start. For this example, you may still want to keep the original home page intact for now if you're still new to SharePoint 2013 because it provides some useful links.

NOTE

When you are finished with the default links Microsoft has provided on the publishing site's default homepage, you can delete them all at once instead of one by one. To do this, simply append `?contents=1` to the end of the URL in the browser's address bar to open the Web Part maintenance for the current page. Then you can check the Select All check box to select all the Web Parts on the page, and click Delete to remove them.

The page layout now works as expected, and the master page looks decent. It's not perfect, but that will be fixed in the next chapter. It's now time to finish using the Design Manager by creating a design package.

CREATING A DESIGN PACKAGE

Now that you've (mostly) completed the design for your site, you can package up your changes into a design package using the Design Manager. A *design package* is a Windows Solution Package (WSP), sometimes called a SharePoint Solution, which contains your custom branding assets from the site and instructions on where those assets should be deployed. When a design is packaged up in a WSP, it can be imported to other SharePoint sites or farms, and the custom branding you've built can be applied to other sites. Generally, you wouldn't want to package up your design until it's complete and free of some of the style issues you're seeing. Although you won't be fixing some of the style issues (such as the search box and top navigation) until the next chapter, you can still walk through the process of packaging your design now so that you'll be familiar with it later.

EXAMPLE: CREATING A DESIGN PACKAGE

1. In the Design Manager, click **Create Design Package**.

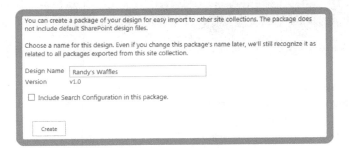

2. In the Design Name field, SharePoint has provided a name for you; it uses the site's name by default. You can change it if you want. This becomes part of the filename for the design package. The other part is the version number of the design that appears directly under the name field. As SharePoint points out, you can always change this filename later, and it will still be recognized as the same design package. This is due to the unique identifiers included in the package.

3. You have the option to include the site's search configuration in the design package. This can be useful if you've spent some time customizing the search experience in the site with custom query rules, result types, result sources, and other search-related assets. For this example, leave the box next to **Include Search Configuration in This Package** unchecked.

4. Click **Create** to create your design package. You see a message that SharePoint is working on creating the package, and after a few moments, the Design Manager reappears with a link underneath the Create button.

5. Click the **Your package is ready. Click here to download** link to save your WSP to your computer for importing into another site. Save your WSP file to a location on your computer, such as your desktop.

Key Facts about the WSP

There are several things worth noting about the WSP. First, the WSP includes your custom assets only if they have been published. If a file is checked out to you, it won't be included in the WSP. In addition, any file that has been published but checked out again to be modified won't have the latest version. Only the last major published version of a file is included. For example, if your master page is checked in as version 2, and you check it out to make a few additional changes and check it in as minor version 2.1, the Design Manager includes only version 2.0 in the WSP.

The other thing you should know about creating a design package is that it includes all files that have been customized. This means that if you've created a page layout that uses a custom content type it will get the content type and all custom site columns. If you had previously applied a composed look to your site, the Design Manager includes several files related to that as well. This is just something to keep in mind as you create design packages so that you don't mistakenly package files that shouldn't be deployed.

You can actually open the WSP file in a few steps because it's really just a Windows cabinet file (.cab) with a different extension.

EXAMPLE: EXPLORING THE CONTENTS OF A WSP FILE

1. Find the WSP file you just saved on your computer.

2. Right-click the file and select **Rename**.

3. Replace `.wsp` with `.cab` as the file's extension. (Alternatively, you could juts append `.cab` after `.wsp`.) If you receive a warning about changing the file's extension, you can click **Yes**. The file's icon should change to the `.cab` file icon.

4. Double-click the file to open it, and browse its contents. Scrolling through you can notice files and images related to your branding. You may also notice quite a few files with file extensions such as `.themedcss` and `.themedpng`. The Design Manager actually collects files related to composed looks and includes them as well if you applied a composed look to the site before starting your custom branding. If you've uploaded any files to a site assets library, the style library, and anything else you've included in the Master Page Gallery, they are in here as well.

You have little control over what the Design Manager includes in the WSP. However, you also had to do little to create the WSP. If you'd prefer to have more control over which files get deployed or to add custom behaviors when the branding is applied to the site (such as automatically switching the master page), it is possible to manually create a WSP using Visual Studio. You will learn more about creating custom branding packages in Chapter 7.

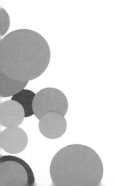

Limitations of Design Packages

There are some things you need to consider when using the Design Manager to create a design package. For starters, the Design Manager only creates sandbox solutions. This is perfect for deploying code to Office 365 (where sandbox solutions are the only option), or between site collections, but for larger implementations that have more complex requirements, it might be limiting. Chapter 7 covers the differences between sandbox solutions and the other type, farm solutions.

Another thing to consider is that Design Manager is only available in sites with publishing enabled. It works well to create a design package and import it into another publishing site, but it can be a bit trickier if the intent is to use that branding in a site that doesn't have publishing. Although it is possible, some extra work needs to be done to make sure the design is compatible, and different steps need to be taken to apply the branding to the new site.

The design export functionality of Design Manager is a great way to quickly move a custom design to another site, but it isn't a silver bullet for every scenario. Chapter 7 provides alternatives, including creating a SharePoint design package from scratch. It is good to understand both approaches to determine which way is right for you.

Final Steps

You might be wondering what happens now that you've packaged up your design into a WSP. Well, for starters, you can import it to another site collection to apply your branding. If you want to try it out, you can try creating a new site collection based on the Publishing Site template to import the branding package.

EXAMPLE: IMPORTING YOUR DESIGN PACKAGE

1. If you've just created a fresh publishing site collection, you can click the **Import a design package** link on the home page. If your site is already established and you've removed the default content from the home page, click the **Settings menu ➤ Site settings ➤ Import Design Package** (found under the Look and Feel header). Or if you remember all the way back to step 1 of the Design Manager, there's a link there to import a package as well.

2. On the Import Design Package page, click the **Browse** button. Then browse your computer for your WSP file that you saved, and click **OK**.

3. Click the **Import** button to begin importing your design package. SharePoint lets you know that it's working on it, and after it's finished, the page reappears with the design applied, just like magic.

When you imported the design package, SharePoint added the WSP to the Solutions gallery, which you can access by clicking the **Settings menu ➤ Site settings ➤ Solutions** (found under the Web Designer Galleries header). In here, you can see your solution name and notice that its status is listed as Activated. Part of the import process is the automatic activation of the feature.

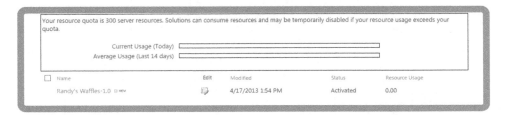

SUMMARY

- The new SharePoint 2013 Design Manager was introduced to lower the bar of entry for SharePoint designers. The Design Manager can be used to convert static HTML files into SharePoint master pages.

- You now have the ability to map a drive to access the HTML file and make changes to the look and feel of the master page. When you save the HTML file, SharePoint automatically updates the corresponding .master file. Just about any web design tool can be used to edit SharePoint 2013 master pages because you are editing an HTML file.

- The Snippet Gallery enables you to add in snippets of SharePoint code for elements on SharePoint master pages and page layouts, such as the top navigation, left navigation, search box, and site image, among others.

- The Design Manager can be used to create custom page layouts, which can also be edited in the web design tool of your choice.

- SharePoint 2013 can export design files as a sandbox solution that can be imported and applied to other SharePoint locations.

6

CASCADING
STYLE SHEETS
AND
SHAREPOINT

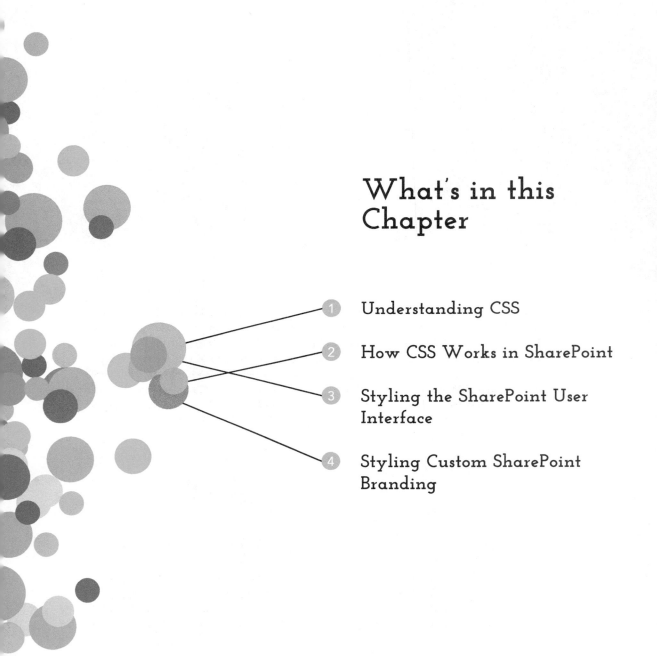

What's in this Chapter

In the last chapter you learned about features that Microsoft created to help with arranging and styling SharePoint sites, such as the Design Manager, master pages, page layouts, and composed looks. Unlike those features, Cascading Style Sheets (CSS) is one key area in which Microsoft has leveraged existing industry technology to provide you with a lot of power to change the look of a page. Behind the scenes SharePoint relies on a lot of CSS to make the user interface look like it does; there are more than 13,000 lines of uncommented CSS in SharePoint 2013 (up from 7000+ in SharePoint 2010). Being good at SharePoint branding often means having a thorough understanding of CSS; there is no other technology that makes a more profound impact on the rendered interface.

This chapter is not intended as a reference manual for coding CSS—to do so would take too many pages. Instead, you get a brief overview of some of the key CSS concepts. If you are experienced with CSS, you may want to still review this chapter because SharePoint tends to push the limits of normal CSS expertise. Unlike when you work on your own websites, in many cases with SharePoint branding you need to override HTML and CSS written by engineers at Microsoft whose first priority is performance, not your ability to easily restyle their markup. If you are new to CSS or feel your skills aren't as strong as they need to be, be sure to study this section carefully. There is a list of more in-depth resources for learning CSS at the end of the following section; read through them to learn more about CSS before diving into more intricate SharePoint styling.

A BRIEF CSS PRIMER

CSS is a style sheet language that tells web browsers how to present a document, whether that document is HTML or any technology based on XML. CSS was created as a way to separate the presentation from the content or data in a document. This split allows for much greater reuse of styles and permits an easier and more maintainable editing process than the old way of adding presentation directly to each page's HTML markup. In many ways CSS is used in SharePoint exactly the same as any other website; this is because SharePoint uses ASP.net to ultimately render HTML, which displays when a page is visited.

NOTE

CSS has gone through a few iterations since it was introduced more than 15 years ago. Modern browsers (as of this writing) primarily support CSS3 and all versions prior, although many times browser manufacturers disagree on the appropriate response for a given CSS3 code snippet. Because of this, it's a good idea to test all your CSS in a few different browsers. SharePoint 2013 makes use of several newer CSS3 concepts, which is likely the reason why versions of Internet Explorer prior to IE8 are not fully supported for SharePoint 2013.

To understand CSS properly, you must start with the basic CSS rule syntax. Rules control how specific HTML elements will be styled by CSS. At first glance CSS seems simple; the rules are based on only two things: a selector and a declaration. Don't be fooled by this simplicity; creating pixel-perfect web design with CSS can be challenging.

Selector { Declarations }

SELECTORS

Define the HTML element to which the rule applies. Rules can apply to one selector, or multiple selectors can be grouped together, separated by commas.

DECLARATIONS

Define how the selected element is styled.

Declarations are surrounded by braces (or curly brackets) and are divided into two parts, *Properties* and *Values*, which are separated by a colon. Multiple declarations are separated by a semicolon. *Properties* represent the visual attribute of the element that you want to style based on the setting specified by the *Value*.

Selector { Property: Value; Property: Value; }

NOTE

You can omit the final semicolon after the last declaration in a rule, but many designers include it for ease of maintenance. Adding the last semicolon is helpful when you make quick additions to CSS; this way you don't need to remember to add one back before adding new declarations.

Keep in mind that the examples in this section of the chapter are specifically talking about traditional web pages, not CSS as it would apply in an actual SharePoint site where there are other factors that would affect the results.

CSS

```css
p, h1        { font-family:
               "Segoe UI";
               color: Red;
             }
```

HTML

```html
<div>
 <h1>Waffles</h1>
 <p>Sweet delicious waffles</p>
 I would eat them every day if I
could.
</div>
```

The CSS rule can cause all <p> and <h1> tags to render in the Segoe UI font with a red color. Note that font family values that include more than one word, like Segoe UI here, should be surrounded by quote marks.

RESULT

Waffles

Sweet delicious waffles

I would eat them everyday if I could.

WARNING

A quick word about case-sensitivity and CSS: The W3C says: "The case-sensitivity of document language element names in selectors depends on the document language. For example, in HTML, element names are case-insensitive, but in XML they are case-sensitive." Because of this inconsistency, it's often a good idea to code your CSS with case-sensitivity in mind.

For more information on this topic see SitePoint's article on case-sensitivity: http://reference. sitepoint.com/css/casesensitivity.

Selectors

When deciding how to style your HTML elements, you can use several different types of CSS selectors. This table describes each type of selector and the HTML elements it matches, followed on the next page by a visual of how the concepts would look in a modern web browser:

SELECTOR	EXAMPLE	MATCHES
Type	h1	Basic HTML elements like H1, P, and DIV.
Class	.myClass	HTML elements with a corresponding class attribute.
ID	#header	HTML elements with the corresponding id attribute.
Child	div>a	HTML elements that are a direct child of the first element.
Descendant	div a	HTML elements that are a descendant of the first element (doesn't need to be a direct child).
Adjacent Sibling	div+P	HTML elements only when the second element is the next element at the same level as the first in the HTML document tree.
General Sibling	div~P	Any of the second elements at the same level as the first element in the document tree. Similar to the previous except they don't need to be immediately following each other.
Universal	*	Any element. Often implied by the previous selectors, so this is usually omitted.

```css
span { color: red; }
.myClass { color: green; }
#myID { color: purple; }
.myClass2 a { color: orange; }
.myClass2 > a { color: lightblue; }
.myClass3 + div { color: blue; }
.myClass4 ~ div { color: lime; }
* { color: silver; }
```

```html
<span>This Type selector will be Red</span>

<div class="myClass">
 This Class selector will be Green
</div>

<div id="myID">
 This ID selector will be Purple
</div>

<div class="myClass2">
 <a href="#">This is a Child of myClass2, it will be Light Blue</a>
 <div>
  <a href="#">This is a Descendent of myClass2 but not a direct child,
it will be Orange</a>
 </div>
</div>

<div class="myClass3"></div>
<div>This is Adjacent to myClass3 so it will be Blue</div>
<div>This is not Adjacent to myClass3. It is nothing but it will be
styled with the Universal selector, it will be Silver</div>

<div class="myClass4"></div>
<div>This is a General Sibling of myClass4 so it will be Lime</div>
<div>This is also a General Sibling of myClass4 so it will be Lime
</div>
```

This Type selector will be Red
This Class selector will be Green
This ID selector will be Purple
This is a Child of myClass2, it will be Light Blue
This is a Descendent of myClass2 but not a direct child, it will be Orange
This is Adjacent to myClass3 so it will be Blue
This is not Adjacent to myClass3. It is nothing but it will be styled with the Universal selector, it will be Silver
This is a General Sibling of myClass4 so it will be Lime
This is also a General Sibling of myClass4 so it will be Lime

Pseudo Classes

You can expand upon the basic set of selectors by using pseudo classes to apply styles based on the state of specific elements. For example, with pseudo classes you can apply style based on whether a link has been visited previously or if the mouse hovers over an element. This table shows some of the most common pseudo classes you can find in SharePoint.

SELECTOR	MATCHES
:link	Links that haven't been visited
:visited	Links that have been visited
:focus	An input element that has focus
:hover	A link that the mouse is hovering over
:active	A link being clicked
:first-child	Only the initial child element of a specific parent element

Attribute Selectors

Attribute Selectors were added with CSS2 and expanded in CSS3. They enable rules to match HTML elements that have specific attributes defined. For example, an attribute selector could match a specific type of <input> element such as <input type="submit">.

ATTRIBUTE SELECTOR EXAMPLE	MATCHES	CSS VERSION
a[href]	Elements with a specific attribute regardless of the attribute value	CSS2
input[title="submit"]	Elements with an attribute with a specific value	CSS2
div[title~="myClass2"]	Elements with an attribute value that contains a space-delimited list of words where one word exactly matches a specific value	CSS2
div[lang|="en"]	Elements with an attribute whose value contains a string directly followed by a dash (useful for matching language codes such as "en-us")	CSS2
div[title*="my"]	Elements with an attribute that contains a specific string anywhere in the value	CSS3
div[title^="m"]	Elements with an attribute whose value begins with a specific string	CSS3
div[title$="Class"]	Elements with an attribute whose value ends with a specific string	CSS3

CSS

```
div[title] { color: red; }
div[title="myTitle"] { color: green; }
div[title~="myTitle2"] { color: purple; }
div[lang|="en"] { color: orange; }
div[title*="waffle"] { color: lightblue; }
div[title^="waffles"] { color: blue; }
div[title$="waffles"] { color: lime; }
```

This shows how the concepts from the preceding table would look in a modern web browser.

HTML

```
<div title="">This will be Red</div>
<div title="myTitle">This will be Green</div>
<div title="myTitle2 myTitle3">This will be Purple</div>
<div lang="en-us">This will be Orange</div>
<div title="I like waffles too much">This will be Light Blue</div>
<div title="waffles are great">This will be Blue</div>
<div title="My favorite meal is waffles">This will be Lime</div>
```

Understanding CSS Specificity

If more than one rule applies to an element, a set of guidelines decides which style to apply. This concept is important in SharePoint because you often need to override existing out-of-the-box CSS rules to apply your own style to SharePoint.

Typically, if a selector has more than one rule applied to it, the most specific rule takes precedence and has its styles applied to the selector. This concept is known as *specificity* and is probably one of the most challenging things to understand in CSS. The following details all the different rules and lists them in order of specificity.

- The universal selector * is the least specific.

- Elements such as H1 are more specific.

- If a rule has more than one selector, it is more specific.

- Class selectors are more specific than elements.

- ID selectors are more specific than class selectors.

- *Inline styles* are styles applied directly to an HTML element (rather than assigned from an internal or external style sheet) and are the highest normal specificity.

- Applying !important to the end of an attribute trumps everything else, always taking precedence unless a later !important attribute overrides it.

If you want to dig into the specifics of specificity (try saying that ten times fast) you can use the following equation to calculate specificity:

(If there is an inline style applied add 1000)

+

(The number of ID selectors) x 100

+

(The number of Class selectors) x 10

+

(The number of HTML element selectors) x 1

This gives you the specificity of a given selector; the selector that is most specific applies its style. If two selectors are otherwise equivalently specific, the selector that comes last has its style applied to the element. Adding !important to an attribute immediately changes this equation, making that attribute the most important style to apply. For example, in the following CSS, the first style takes precedence because it has a specificity of 11, whereas the second has a specificity of 1.

CSS:

```
<style type="text/css">
.myClass div { color: blue; }
div { color: red }
</style>
```

HTML:

```
<div class="myClass">
 <div>What color will this be?</div>
</div>
```

RESULT:

What color will this be?

NOTE

Often when working with CSS and SharePoint, you run into instances in which a simple CSS rule won't apply the style you want to an element. Typically in these cases, the solution is to try to make your CSS rule more specific by adding parent classes or an !important to the end of the declaration.

Inheritance

Certain CSS properties (like fonts and colors) pass on their value to child elements. This process is known as inheritance, and it allows for smaller CSS files because you don't need to manually call out simple settings for every element in your HTML file. For example, you can set the font-family for the body tag, and it is passed on to all the child elements automatically.

Not all CSS properties pass on inherited values to their children. For a full list of which CSS properties have inheritance, see the W3C article, "Cascading Style Sheets Level 2 Revision 1 (CSS 2.1) Specification – Appendix F" at http://www.w3.org/TR/CSS2/propidx.html. If a property doesn't have inheritance though, you can often force specific child elements to inherit the value of the parent by adding the inherit value in CSS.

CSS

```css
div {border: 1px solid red;}
p {border: inherit;}
```

HTML

```html
<div>
 <p> Help, I'm trapped inside a box inside another box!</p>
</div>
```

RESULT

Help, I'm trapped inside a box inside another box!

Applying CSS to a Web Page

In standard web development you can apply CSS to an HTML page in three ways:

- **Inline Styles**—CSS is applied to elements with the style attribute defined inside individual HTML elements. This option should be avoided in most scenarios because of the specificity rules described earlier; inline styles remove the ability to easily override styles without using the `!important` tag.
  ```html
  <div style="color: red;">Hey I'm going to be red</div>
  ```

- **Internal Style Sheet**—CSS is added directly to the HTML file via the `<style>` tag, typically in the `<head>` of a document. This is a good option for adding styles to individual pages, but ultimately this method lacks the benefit of reuse and ease of maintenance. To reuse these styles you would have multiple versions of the internal style sheets applied to multiple pages.
  ```html
  <head>
   <style type="text/css">
    div {color: red;}
   </style>
  </head>
  ```

- **External Style Sheet**—CSS lives in its own file and is loaded into an HTML page with the `<link>` tag in the `<head>` section of the HTML. This is the best option for applying a lot of styles across an entire site.
  ```html
  <head>
   <link rel="stylesheet" type="text/css" href="style.css" />
  </head>
  ```

CSS INSIDE OF SHAREPOINT

If you are comfortable with CSS as it applies to traditional web design, you may wonder how CSS is different in SharePoint. It was mentioned earlier that SharePoint has a lot of CSS applied to it by default. You can learn a lot about how to style SharePoint just by looking at the default SharePoint CSS. Take a moment and view the source of the main SharePoint CSS file COREV15.CSS by opening it in a text editor (from the server in the SharePoint 15 folder under \TEMPLATE\LAYOUTS\1033\STYLES\Themable\COREV15.CSS).

When you open COREV15.CSS in a text editor such as Notepad++, you can quickly see that there are a lot of lines of CSS with few helpful comments. You can also notice that a large portion of the CSS rules apply to classes that start with .ms-. Although there are some other class prefixes such as .s4-, they are in the minority. These prefixes can be helpful when you inspect the CSS of a page because you can scan for .ms- classes quickly and see styles that you know were created by Microsoft. You will also notice that there are many child and descendent selectors used. When you try to override a style rule, you want to make sure your rule is at least as specific as the original, or it won't apply to these elements.

Another thing that jumps out immediately when looking at COREV15.CSS is that there are many comments that look like this:

```
/* [ReplaceFont( themeFont:"body")] */
```

As you may have guessed, these aren't your typical CSS comments; instead, they are related to composed looks, which is the new version of SharePoint 2010 themes. When a composed look is applied, these comments tell SharePoint to change the attribute of the CSS that immediately follows the comment. You can see more about creating composed looks and using these comments in your own custom CSS in Chapter 10, "Composed Looks and Custom Branding," but for now just know that when

a composed look is applied to SharePoint, many of the default colors, fonts, and even background images will change from how they are defined in the SharePoint CSS file.

Modern CSS in SharePoint

SharePoint 2013 takes advantage of some modern CSS techniques, including CSS3, vendor prefixes, and media types. Some common CSS3 techniques that you see in SharePoint 2013 include: box-shadow to apply a shadow behind elements; border-radius to round the corners of elements; word-wrap to break long words onto a new line; text-overflow to show ellipses when text would overflow out of its container; and RGBa colors, which define the red, green, and blue values (0-255) and also a decimal number (0-1) to apply alpha transparency to the color, like this:

```
background-color:rgba( 255,255,255,0.85 )
```

Microsoft also uses vendor prefixes in its CSS to push the envelope of web design and take advantage of features that some modern browsers support beyond the agreed upon CSS specification. You can see vendor prefixes that start with specific prefixes, for example: Microsoft (-ms-), Mozilla browsers (-moz-), WebKit browsers (-webkit-), and Opera (-o-). Some common uses for vendor prefixes in SharePoint 2013 are for gradient fills, alpha fills, and rotation.

NOTE

For more information on these advanced techniques, check out these resources:

CSS3.Info—CSS3 Previews at http://www.css3.info/preview/

WC3—Media types at http://www.w3.org/TR/CSS2/media.html

About.com—CSS Vendor Prefixes at http://webdesign.about.com/od/css/a/css-vendor-prefixes.htm

TOOLS FOR WORKING WITH CSS

Besides using dedicated web design tools such as Dreamweaver and Expression Web, browser-based CSS tools are some of the most powerful ways to work with large amounts of CSS. The following tools can help you analyze a SharePoint site and identify the CSS classes so that you can override them. In general, these tools can often be launched via the F12 key when browsing a website:

- **Internet Explorer F12 Developer Tools**—Named after the key combination that opens it, this plug-in was previously a separate download for IE7 called IE Developer Toolkit. Now it is included with every Internet Explorer.

- **Firebug for Firefox**—A third-party add-on for Firefox that can be downloaded from www.getfirebug.com.

- **Chrome Developer Tools**—Included with modern versions of the Chrome browser.

One useful feature of these tools is the capability to point to an area of the rendered page inside the browser to see a breakdown of what CSS is being applied to that area and how CSS rules are being overridden. Because of minor differences between the ways that different browsers render pages, you may need to use each tool to truly understand all the styles applied to a SharePoint site. After your selected style overrides are identified, you can add them into a custom CSS file and apply them to SharePoint to make the overrides permanent.

EXAMPLE: USING FIREBUG TO WORK WITH CSS

For this example you use Firebug for Firefox to change the header of the team site with the out-of-the-box `seattle.master` applied to it. The concept is similar for the other browser-based CSS tools.

1. Ensure that the Firebug add-on has been installed in Firefox.

2. Open Firefox and browse to your SharePoint site.

3. Press **F12** or click **Tools ➤ Web Developer ➤ Firebug ➤ Open Firebug** to open Firebug.

4. Click the inspect icon at the top of the Firebug panel or right-click on an element inside your page and select **Inspect Element with Firebug**.

5. Try to highlight the entire header portion of the page (the horizontal area below the ribbon that contains the site icon, navigation, and site name). One easy way to select the entire header is to click the mouse to the left of the SharePoint site icon. After clicking the area, you can see (on the right side of the Firebug window) that the CSS class `#s4-titlerow` has no background-color applied yet.

6. Firebug enables you to manipulate the CSS values to immediately see the results. To try this, make sure `#s4-titlerow` is still selected, and on the right panel, click 64px next to `height`. Press the up and down arrows on your keyboard to see the height changes in real time in the browser.

7. To add a new CSS declaration, double-click the selector's closing bracket and a new row will be added. Then type a new rule, such as `background-color: silver;`. Notice that as you type values Firebug tries to guess what you are going to type based on the available options.

Any changes made here are only temporary; they disappear when the browser is refreshed. You can, however, select classes in the right panel and copy and paste them into your own custom CSS to make them permanent.

APPLYING CUSTOM CSS TO SHAREPOINT

In SharePoint 2013 applying custom CSS to a page works similarly to how you would do it for traditional HTML pages (discussed earlier in the "Applying CSS to a Web Page" section). If you want to include any of these types of CSS, you can add them manually to master pages and page layouts, and in some cases

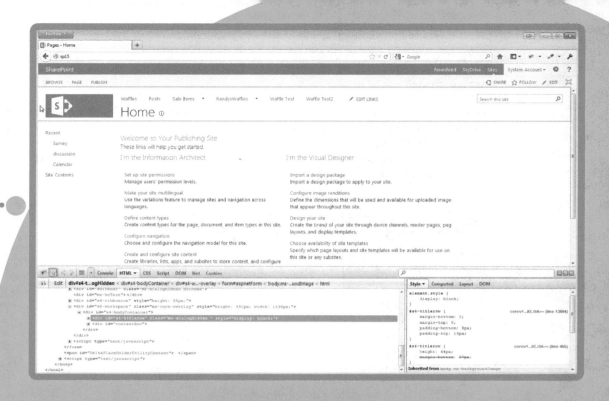

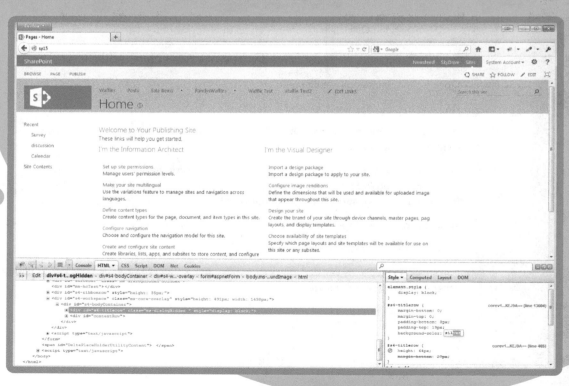

you can even add references to them within the page content. However, SharePoint also provides its own mechanisms for adding CSS that you can see in the next few sections.

WARNING

One common mistake is to just log in to the server and find and edit the core SharePoint CSS file in the SharePoint root. This should be avoided because it is problematic for supportability. If Microsoft releases an update for SharePoint (which is inevitable), the COREV15.CSS file in the SharePoint root is likely to be overwritten. Also, changes to this file will apply branding to all web applications on the server, which is probably not desirable.

Adding CSS to Page Content

If you need to add an internal style sheet to a single page in SharePoint, it would be tempting to put the page in edit mode and, from the ribbon, click **Format Text** ➢ **Edit Source**, or even to use a Content Editor Web Part. However, SharePoint's handling of both of these is quirky, depending on which edition of SharePoint you have (Server or Foundation) and whether you have a publishing or team site.

SharePoint 2013 includes some more elegant solutions for adding CSS to a rich text field or a Web Part zone. Adding CSS to a rich text field is as simple as putting the page in edit mode and, from the ribbon, clicking **Insert** ➢ **Embed Code**. This opens a dialog box where you can add CSS that will be applied to the page when you click **Insert**. For Web Part zones you can use the new Script Editor Web Part (SEWP), which enables content authors to add HTML snippets or scripts to the page, and it's also a good option to add internal style sheets easily. One common page level CSS change that people find useful with the SEWP is hiding the Quick Launch navigation on the left side of the default SharePoint UI.

EXAMPLE: HIDING THE QUICK LAUNCH WITH THE SCRIPT EDITOR WEB PART

1. Open a SharePoint page in Edit mode.

2. Find a Web Part Zone and click **Add a Web Part**.

3. When the Web Part menu opens at the top of the page, click **Categories** ➢ **Media** and **Content** ➢ **Script Editor** ➢ **Add**.

4. When the Script Editor Web Part is added to the page, click the link on the right side called **Edit Snippet**. Sometimes the link won't show until you first click **Edit Web Part** from the drop-down at the top right of the Web Part.

5. When the dialog box opens, add the following code:

6. Click the **Insert** button on the right of the dialog box.

7. You should immediately see that Quick Launch is hidden. You can save the page and publish so that other users can see the change.

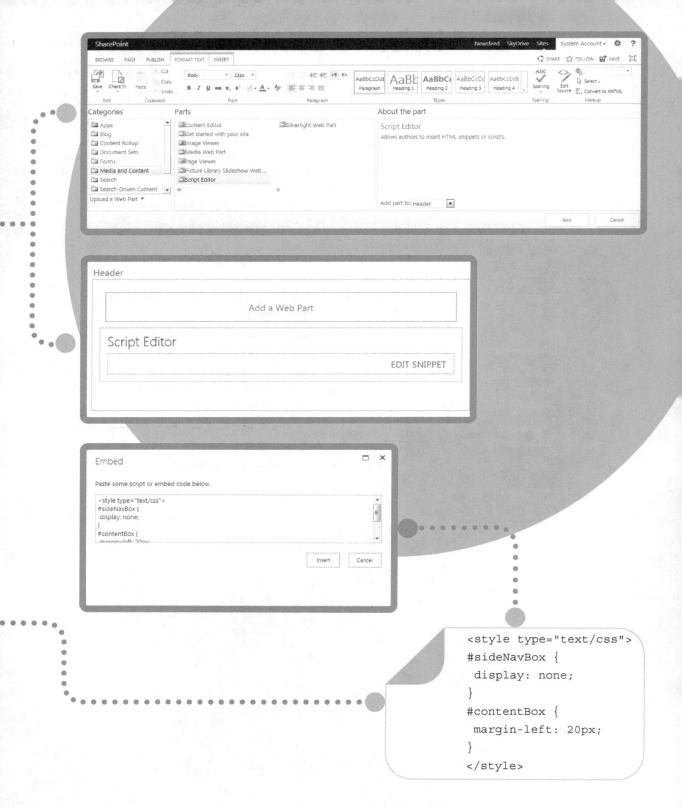

Using Alternate CSS

Alternate CSS is a feature that enables you to quickly and easily apply custom CSS to a particular site and all its subsites. Alternate CSS is available only from the SharePoint web user interface in a SharePoint Server site with publishing activated. That said, the same techniques could be used in a nonpublishing site with custom code or a Windows PowerShell command.

The following steps describe how to add an external style sheet to a SharePoint Server 2013 publishing site using Alternate CSS. Before trying these steps, be sure you have a custom CSS file added to your SharePoint site in a subfolder under the master page gallery. If you need a refresher on adding a CSS file, see the "Uploading Design Files" section in Chapter 5, "Using the Design Manager to Start a Design in SharePoint."

EXAMPLE: USING ALTERNATE CSS

1. Load the SharePoint 2013 site in your web browser and navigate to **Site Settings ➢ Look and Feel ➢ Master Page**.

2. To test with the default SharePoint UI, make sure Site and System master pages are both set to `seattle.master`; then expand the section titled **Alternate CSS URL**.

3. Next, choose **Specify a CSS file to be used by this site and all sites that inherit from it**, and then click the **Browse** button.

4. From the **Select an Asset** dialog box, navigate to your custom CSS file, and select it and click **Insert**. If you placed your CSS in the master page gallery you may have to type **/_catalogs/masterpage** in the **Location (URL)** box and press Enter to start browsing in the correct location.

5. If you want to apply the style sheet to all subsites, you can check **Reset all subsites to inherit this alternate CSS URL**.

6. From the master page menu, click **OK**, and the site refreshes with the CSS styles applied to it.

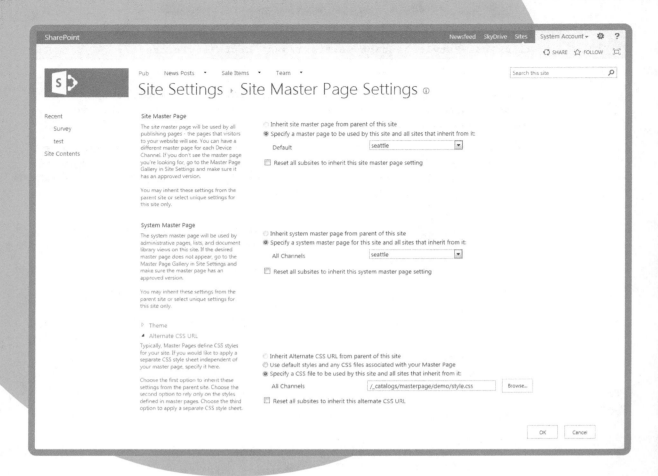

Adding External Style Sheets with CssRegistration

If you view the source of the default SharePoint 2013 master page `seattle.master`, you can see a reference to `<SharePoint:CssRegistration>` that points to `COREV15.CSS`. This is how SharePoint loads the primary CSS that is applied to most of the default user interface. The same control is used to add your own custom CSS to override `COREV15.CSS`.

When you use the Design Manager to make an HTML master page like you did in the previous chapter, SharePoint converts your external CSS links behind the scenes into valid `<SharePoint:CssRegistration>` controls that point to the custom CSS files in the Master Page Gallery.

For example, if your HTML file has the following reference:

```
<link rel="stylesheet" type="text/css" href="style.css" />
```

The corresponding master page would look like this:

```
<SharePoint:CssRegistration name="&lt;% $SPUrl:~sitecollection/
  _catalogs/masterpage/DemoBranding/style.css %&gt;" runat="server"
  after="SharepointCssFile" />
```

SharePoint knows where the CSS file is located in the master page gallery (_catalogs/masterpage/DemoBranding) and makes a site collection relative reference. The After property is used to add the CSS link after the COREV15.CSS file to ensure your custom CSS always loads after the out-of-the-box CSS. By applying the CSS with CssRegistration, the master page and CSS are always applied together.

You will learn more about using the CssRegistration control in master pages in Chapter 7, "Creating SharePoint Branding."

EDITOR STYLES

Much like the previous version, SharePoint 2013 enables you to add specific styles to your custom CSS that can be accessed through the ribbon and used by content authors on your site. In this section, you learn about adding styles to the following areas of the Format Text tab on the ribbon:

- **Font Face**—The font face used on the selected text.
- **Font Size**—The size of the selected text.
- **Highlight Color**—Background color behind the selected text.
- **Font Color**—The selection text color.
- **Styles ➢ Page Element**—An HTML element will be injected around the selection and a style will be applied to that element.
- **Styles ➢ Text Style**—A specific style will be applied to the selection.

For these styles, the selector always begins with .ms-rte (for Rich Text Editor), then the ribbon area that is being updated (like FontFace), followed by a dash and a custom name that you provide. For example, .ms-rteFontFace-WafflesFontFace adds a new FontFace to the ribbon. The declaration often includes a special Microsoft code such as -ms-name to tell the ribbon how the item should be named when the user hovers over visual options, such as -ms-name:"Custom Comic Sans";.

The following CSS shows some example editor styles. If this CSS were added to your SharePoint site, the rich text editor in the ribbon would update to include these new style options.
The table that follows the code shows how the CSS would work and look, from top to bottom.

```css
/*--Font Face--*/
.ms-rteFontFace-WafflesFontFace {
  -ms-name:"Custom Comic Sans";
  font-family: 'Comic Sans MS';
}

/*--Font Size--*/
.ms-rteFontSize-WafflesFontSize {
  font-size: 50px;
}

/*--Highlight Color--*/
.ms-rteBackColor-WafflesBackColor {
  background-color: purple;
  -ms-name: "";
  -ms-color:"CustomPurple";
}

/*--Font Color--*/
.ms-rteForeColor-WafflesForeColor {
  color: lime;
  -ms-name: "";
  -ms-color:"CustomLime";
}

/*--Styles - Page Element--*/
DIV.ms-rteElement-WafflesElement {
  -ms-name:"My Custom Element";
}
.ms-rteElement-WafflesElement {
  border: 1px solid red;
}

/*--Styles - Text Styles--*/
.ms-rteStyle-WafflesStyle {
  -ms-name:"CustomStyle";
  color: lime;
  font-size: 50px;
}
```

Font

Selector

`.ms-rteFontFace-WafflesFontFace`

Declaration Description

`-ms-name:"Custom Comic Sans";`

The name that shows in the font options in the ribbon.

`font-family: 'Comic Sans MS';`

The font applied to the selection.

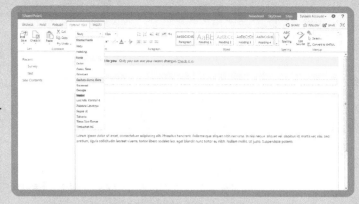

Font Size

Selector

`.ms-rteFontSize-WafflesFontSize`

Declaration Description

`font-size: 50px;`

The font size applied to the selection.

NOTE

No `-ms-name` is used for this because the ribbon just shows the option.

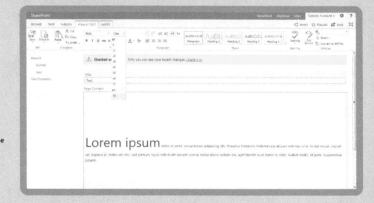

Highlight Color

Selector

`.ms-rteBackColor-WafflesBackColor`

Declaration Description

`background-color: purple;`

The background color applied to the selected text.

`-ms-color:"CustomPurple";`

The name that shows when the user hovers over the option on the ribbon.

`-ms-name: "";`

Whatever text is listed here shows after the `-ms-color` name. Behind the scenes Microsoft uses this to tell you how the color relates to the theme option it might represent.

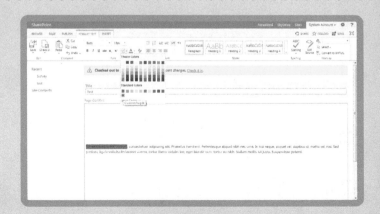

Font Color

Selector

`.ms-rteForeColor-WafflesForeColor`

Declaration Description

`color: lime;`

The color applied to the selected text.

`-ms-color:"CustomLime";`

The name that shows when the user hovers over the option on the ribbon.

`-ms-name: "";`

Whatever text is listed here shows after the `-ms-color` name. Behind the scenes Microsoft uses this to tell you how the color relates to the theme option it might represent.

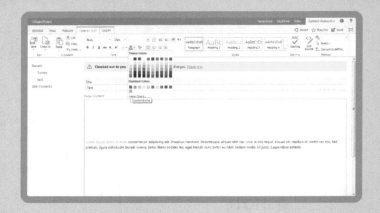

Page Element Style

Selector

`DIV.ms-rteElement-WafflesElement`

Declaration Description

`-ms-name:"My Custom Element";`

The name that shows in the option on the ribbon.

NOTE

This one works a little differently than the others: The first selector has an HTML element before it. (In the example this is DIV.) When this option is selected from the ribbon, SharePoint injects this HTML element around the selected text and then applies the style declared next to that element.

Selector

`.ms-rteElement-WafflesElement`
`border: 1px solid red;`

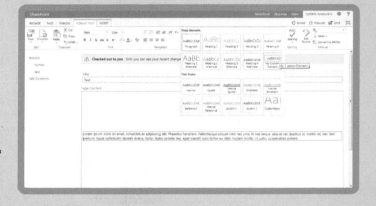

Declaration Description

This is the style applied to the element defined in the previous item.

Text Style

Selector

`.ms-rteStyle-WafflesStyle`

Declaration Description

`-ms-name:"CustomStyle";`

The name that shows in the option on the ribbon.
`color: lime;`
`font-size: 50px;`

Any styles listed are applied to the selected element.

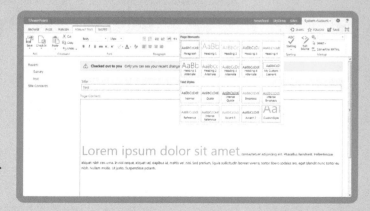

STYLING KEY AREAS OF SHAREPOINT

It's been said before, there is a lot of CSS in SharePoint 2013, and because of that, there are a lot of elements that need to be styled in any given SharePoint branding project. The following sections describe the most common areas you might want to style with CSS. Think of this section as an X-ray that shows you the underlying CSS behind what appears on the page.

NOTE

Many styles have several selectors and are specific. It is impossible to cover all the styles in SharePoint 2013, but you can use tools such as Firebug for Firefox, which was discussed earlier in this chapter, to figure out any complex styling challenge with some effort and a good bit of patience.

Body and Ribbon

NOTE

The body of a SharePoint page can be confusing. You can certainly apply styling to the body element tag and have it show for the entire page. However, because of how the ribbon applies to SharePoint, you can also think of the area below the ribbon as the "body" of the page because it is the main scrollable container for all non-ribbon content. This area has an ID of `s4-workspace` applied to it.

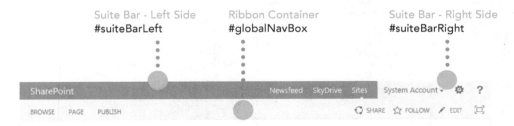

Suite Bar - Left Side
#suiteBarLeft

Ribbon Container
#globalNavBox

Suite Bar - Right Side
#suiteBarRight

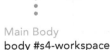

Main Body
body #s4-workspace

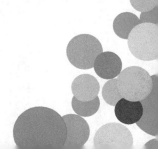

Search Box

Search Box Border
.ms-srch-sb-border

Search Box Border Hover
.ms-srch-sb-border:hover

Search Box Border when clicked
.ms-srch-sb-borderFocused

Search Box Body
.ms-srch-sb

Search Box Submit Button
.ms-srch-sb-searchImg

Search Box Submit HREF
.ms-srch-sb > .ms-srch-sb-searchLink

Search this site

Search Box Drop Down Arrow
.ms-srch-sb-navImg

Search Box Dropdown Arrow HREF
.ms-srch-sb > .ms-srch-sb-navLink

Search Box Input Text Box
.ms-srch-sb > input

Top Navigation

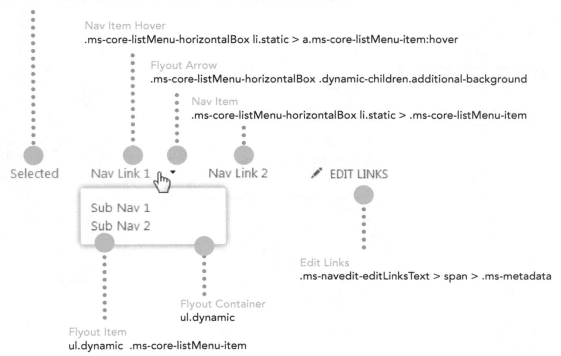

Nav Item Selected
.ms-core-listMenu-horizontalBox li.static > .ms-core-listMenu-selected

Nav Item Hover
.ms-core-listMenu-horizontalBox li.static > a.ms-core-listMenu-item:hover

Flyout Arrow
.ms-core-listMenu-horizontalBox .dynamic-children.additional-background

Nav Item
.ms-core-listMenu-horizontalBox li.static > .ms-core-listMenu-item

Selected   Nav Link 1   Nav Link 2   EDIT LINKS

Sub Nav 1
Sub Nav 2

Edit Links
.ms-navedit-editLinksText > span > .ms-metadata

Flyout Container
ul.dynamic

Flyout Item
ul.dynamic .ms-core-listMenu-item

Top Navigation in Edit Mode

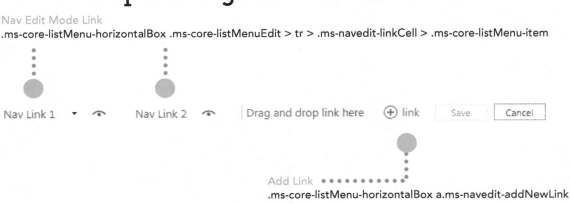

Nav Edit Mode Link
.ms-core-listMenu-horizontalBox .ms-core-listMenuEdit > tr > .ms-navedit-linkCell > .ms-core-listMenu-item

Nav Link 1   ⌄   👁   Nav Link 2   👁 | Drag and drop link here   ⊕ link   Save   Cancel

Add Link
.ms-core-listMenu-horizontalBox a.ms-navedit-addNewLink

Quick Launch or Left Navigation

NOTE

Quick Launch navigation works essentially the same as Top Navigation but instead of being prefixed with `.ms-core-listMenu-horizontalBox`, it is prefixed with `.ms-core-listMenu-verticalBox`.

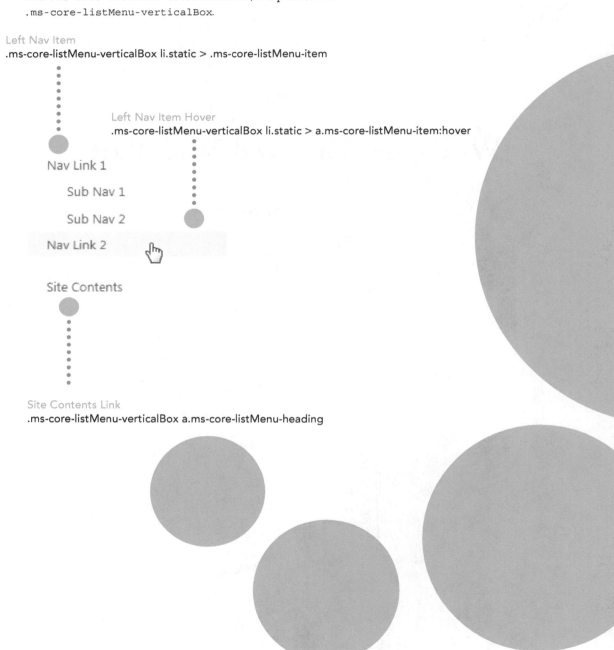

Left Nav Item
.ms-core-listMenu-verticalBox li.static > .ms-core-listMenu-item

Left Nav Item Hover
.ms-core-listMenu-verticalBox li.static > a.ms-core-listMenu-item:hover

Nav Link 1

Sub Nav 1

Sub Nav 2

Nav Link 2

Site Contents

Site Contents Link
.ms-core-listMenu-verticalBox a.ms-core-listMenu-heading

Site Logo, Title, and Description

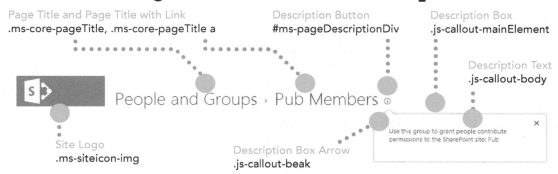

Page Title and Page Title with Link
.ms-core-pageTitle, .ms-core-pageTitle a

Description Button
#ms-pageDescriptionDiv

Description Box
.js-callout-mainElement

Description Text
.js-callout-body

People and Groups › Pub Members ⓘ

Site Logo
.ms-siteicon-img

Description Box Arrow
.js-callout-beak

Use this group to grant people contribute
permissions to the SharePoint site: Pub

Web Part Zone and Web Part

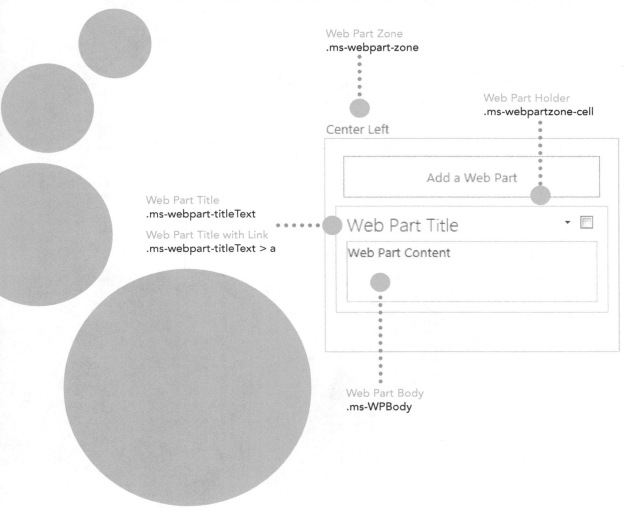

Web Part Zone
.ms-webpart-zone

Web Part Holder
.ms-webpartzone-cell

Center Left

Add a Web Part

Web Part Title
.ms-webpart-titleText

Web Part Title with Link
.ms-webpart-titleText > a

Web Part Title

Web Part Content

Web Part Body
.ms-WPBody

PUTTING CSS TO WORK IN SHAREPOINT

Now that you have a better understanding of how the out-of-the-box styles work in SharePoint 2013, you can apply this knowledge to an actual SharePoint site. If you have worked through the examples in Chapter 5, you remember converting the Randy's Waffles HTML design into a functioning master page using the Design Manager and snippets.

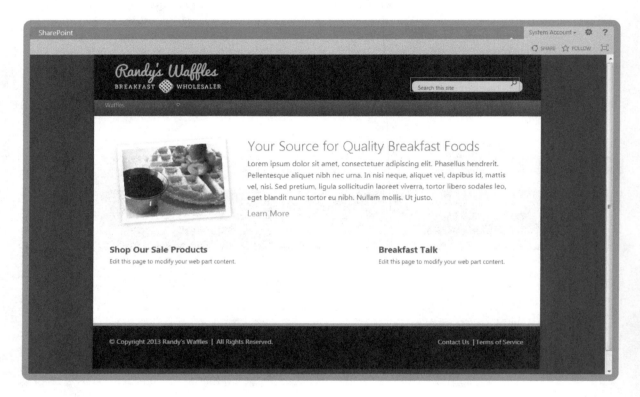

WARNING

If you haven't finished the Randy's Waffles example from the previous chapter, the following examples may not make a lot of sense. If you want to jump directly into the examples anyway, you can download the finished files for Chapter 5 from the companion website for this book on Wrox.com. But be sure to see the section "Uploading Design Files" in Chapter 5 to learn how to upload the files into the Master Page Gallery. If you'd rather not type each of these examples, you can copy them from the finished code included with this chapter's download files.

This master page was functional, but it wasn't very pretty. You can update the Randy's Waffles CSS to appear more aesthetically pleasing in SharePoint. To make the necessary updates, use a mapped drive to your master page gallery and open the Randy's Waffles style sheet at `/_catalogs/masterpage/waffles/style.css` in your editor. The following sections guide you through which changes to make and how. After each CSS listing, a screenshot is shown of how each change would affect the result in a browser.

Background Image

The first thing you might notice about the converted HTML master page is that the background image isn't showing properly. This has to do with a unique style that SharePoint adds to the markup for use with composed looks. By default, without a composed look applied, CSS is set to override the body background with a blank image. To add the wood grain background image back, add the following line below the body styles in the style sheet:

```css
.ms-backgroundImage {
  background-image: url(bg.jpg) !important;
}
```

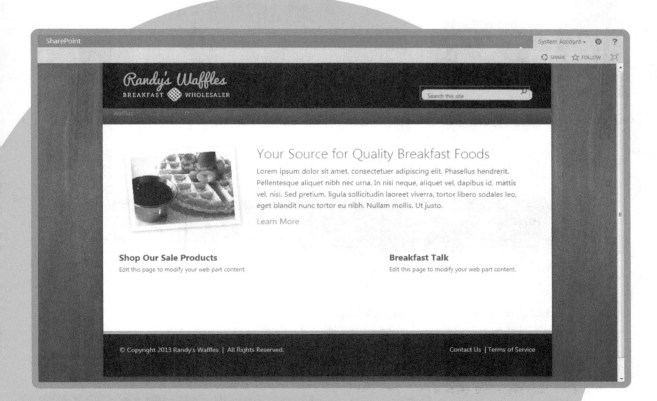

Search Box

To make the search box look like the original design, you need to add the rounded box background image behind it, hide the borders and background color of the input box, and hide and replace the original search button. You can replace the entire search section of the style sheet with this code.

```css
/* add rounded background behind search box */
.customSearchHolder {
background: url("searchbox.png") no-repeat scroll center
top transparent;
float: right;
height: 38px;
position: relative;
right: 0;
top: 50px;
width: 246px;
}
/* style input box */
.customSearchHolder input {
background: none repeat scroll 0 0 transparent;
border: medium none;
color: #585858;
margin: 0 0 0 16px;
padding-top: 10px;
width: 173px;
font-weight:normal;
}
/* box around search */
.customSearchHolder .ms-srch-sb {
background: none no-repeat scroll 0 0 transparent;
margin-top: 0px;
width: 226px;
}
/* search box border */
.customSearchHolder .ms-srch-sb-border, .customSearchHolder
.ms-srch-sb-borderFocused {
border-style: none;
}
/* add new search button image */
.customSearchHolder .ms-srch-sb > .ms-srch-sb-searchLink {
background: url("search-button.png") no-repeat scroll left
top transparent;
```

continues

continued

```css
 height: 18px;
 left: 5px;
 margin: 0;
 padding: 0;
 position: relative;
 top: 10px;
 width: 18px;
 float: right;
}
/* hide the original search button */
.customSearchHolder .ms-srch-sb-searchImg {
 display: none;
}
/* hide search dropdown */
.customSearchHolder .ms-srch-sb > .ms-srch-sb-navLink {
 top: 10px;
 display: none;
}
```

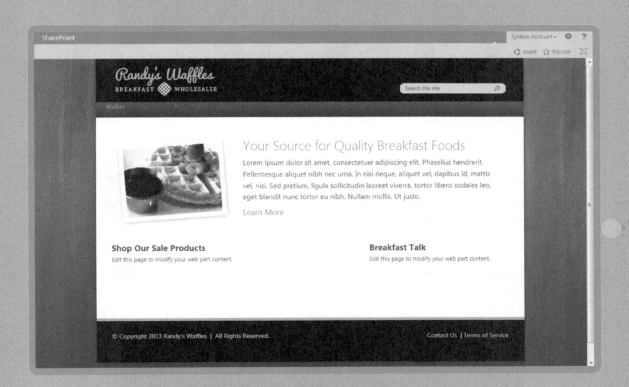

Top Navigation

The top navigation consists of a few different states; you can start with the main navigation holder and items. You must style the holder, UL, LIs, links, the link selected state, and the link hover state, and you also need to hide the drop-down arrow that shows for items that have subnavigation flyouts.

Like the previous section, just replace the entire top navigation section of the style sheet with this new CSS:

```css
/* add style behind top navigation */
.customTopNavHolder {
 height: 35px;
 background-image: url('nav-bg.png');
 background-repeat: repeat;
 padding-left: 23px;
}
/* top nav ul */
.customTopNavHolder ul {
 margin: 0px;
 list-style-type: none;
 padding: 0px;
}
/* blue divider */
.customTopNavHolder .root > li {
 border-right: 2px solid #66a2c4;
}
/* no border on edit link */
.ms-listMenu-editLink {
 border-right: 0px none !important;
}
/* top nav item */
.customTopNavHolder .static > li  > .ms-core-listMenu-item {
 font-family: 'ArvoRegular',arial,sans-serif;
 font-size: 15px;
 height: 33px;
 line-height: 31px;
 padding: 0 15px;
 margin-right: 0px !important;
 color: white;
}
/* selected */
.customTopNavHolder .root > li  > .ms-core-listMenu-selected  {
 color: #403a35;
 background-color: white;
}
/* top nav hover */
.customTopNavHolder a.ms-core-listMenu-item:hover {
 text-decoration: none;
 background-color: white;
 color: #403a35;
```

continues

continued

```
}
/* top nav selected hover */
.customTopNavHolder  .ms-core-listMenu-selected:hover  {
 color: #403a35 !important;
 background-color: white !important;
}
```

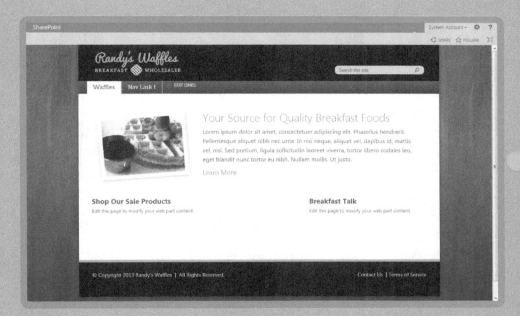

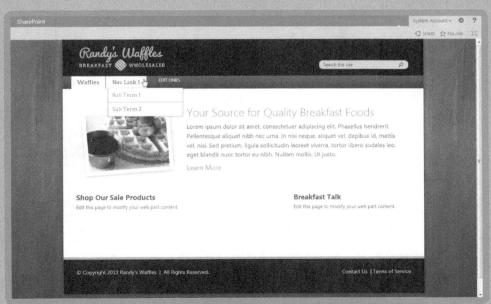

*Next, style the flyout holder, flyout items, and their hover state. You
see these only if you have subnavigation flyout items for your site. Add
the following lines to the previously added navigation styles:*

```
/* flyout arrow */
.customTopNavHolder .additional-background {
 padding-right: 0px !important;
 background-image: none !important;
}
/* flyout holder */
.customTopNavHolder ul.dynamic {
 min-width: 200px;
 border:0px none;
 padding-top:1px;
 margin-left: 0px;
 margin-top: 1px;
}
/* flyout item */
.customTopNavHolder ul.dynamic  .ms-core-listMenu-item {
 display: block;
 border: 1px solid #bbbbbb;
 border-top: 0px;
 color: #827C70;
 font-family: 'ArvoRegular',arial,sans-serif;
 font-size: 14px;
 padding: 10px;
}
/* flyout item hover */
.customTopNavHolder li.dynamic > a:hover {
 text-decoration:none;
 background-color: #EEEEEE;
 color: #827C70;
}
```

Lastly, you may find that the navigation looks bad when a user clicks on the Edit Links button. The following style forces the navigation items and background colors to match the nonedited styles:

```css
/* edit and edit mode links */
.ms-navedit-linkCell a,
.ms-navedit-linkCell .ms-core-listMenu-selected:hover,
.customTopNavHolder .ms-navedit-editLinksText > span > .ms-metadata,
.ms-core-listMenuEdit:hover > tr >
.ms-navedit-linkCell > .ms-core-listMenu-item,
.ms-core-listMenu-horizontalBox div.ms-navedit-hiddenAppendArea,
.ms-navedit-addLinkText  {
 color: white !important;
 background-color: transparent !important;
 height: 33px;
 border: 0px none;
}
```

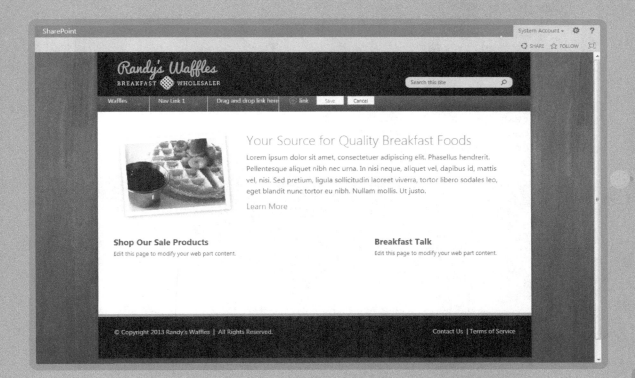

Page Content

For the page content the big change that needs to be made is how SharePoint styles the title text "Your Source for Quality Breakfast Foods." You need to add some default styles that override the H1 and H2 elements. For this and the remaining sections, you can place the new code at the end of the style sheet.

```css
/* main page title colors */
.customHeroHolder h1, .customHeroHolder h2{
 color: #535353;
 font-weight: normal;
}
```

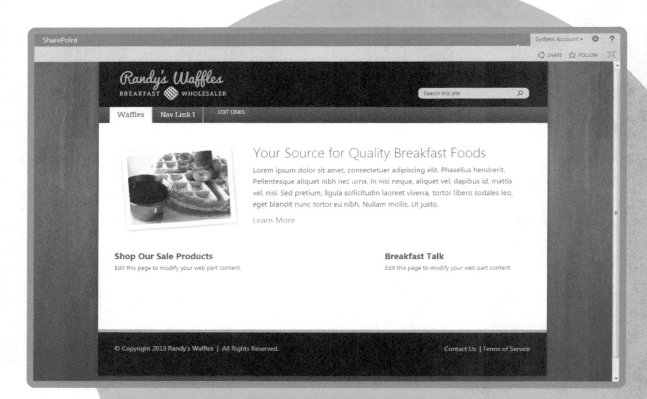

Web Parts

Because SharePoint uses Web Parts for a lot of the user interface, you must be careful here. You can decide to apply custom styles to all these instances, but if you make a big change, it might be better to limit the styling to only Web Parts displayed on your custom publishing pages. This can be achieved by adding a parent `DIV` around content in a custom page layout and then prefixing all your CSS styles with the class assigned to this `DIV`. In the Randy's Waffles example, the Web Part Zone already had a parent `DIV` with a class of `customColumns` that can be used for these styles.

To finish the styles for the Web Parts, style the Web Part title text, URLs in these titles, padding around the Web Part zones, and padding on the actual Web Part body.

```
/* web part title color on custom page layout */
.customColumns .ms-webpart-titleText.ms-webpart-titleText,
.customColumns .ms-webpart-titleText > a {
 background-color: #80AFCB;
 font-size: 20px;
 padding: 5px 15px;
 font-weight: normal;
 color: white;
}
/* web part zone on custom page layout */
.customColumns .ms-webpart-zone {
 padding: 0px 0px 10px;
}
/* web part zone on custom page layout */
.customColumns .ms-WPBody {
 padding: 15px;
}
```

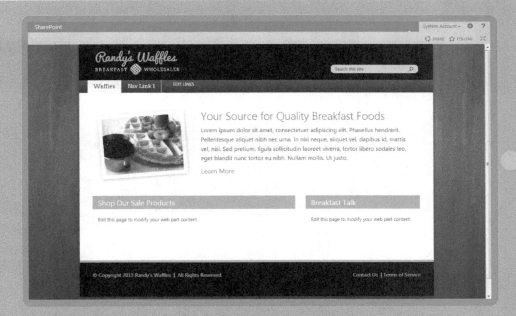

The Ribbon

The ribbon at the top of the page is best left in its default arrangement, but there is no reason why you can't change some of the colors that clash with the new look and feel. You can change the links on the top right to white, the top bar to black, and the bottom bar to white. You must also make changes for IE8 because it uses special CSS prefixed with `.ms-core-needIEFilter`.

```css
/* suitebar link color */
.ms-core-suiteLink a {
 color: white;
}
/* suitebar left */
#suiteBarLeft {
 background-color: black;
}
/* handle ie8 */
.ms-core-needIEFilter #suiteBarLeft{
 filter: none;
 background-color: black;
}
/* ribbon bar and suite bar right */
#globalNavBox, #suiteBarRight {
 background-color: white;
}
/* handle ie8 */
.ms-core-needIEFilter #suiteBarRight {
 background-color: white;
}
```

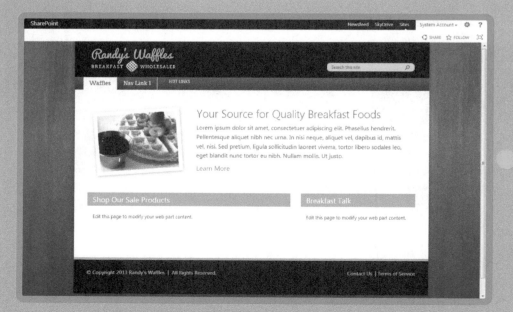

Dialogs

The dialog boxes that SharePoint presents for activities such as creating a new page can pose unique styling challenges. For instance, if you went through the example in the previous chapter, you know that your master page needs to have `.ms-dialogHidden` added to any container elements that you don't want to show in a dialog box.

That works easy enough, but there may be times when you have parent HTML elements that pass down inherited styles to child elements (specifically the main page content area) that don't look nice in a dialog box. This typically happens with container elements that apply decorative styles like backgrounds, padding, margin, width, height, and so on. In these instances, you can't just hide the parent element because it would also hide the page content of the dialog box.

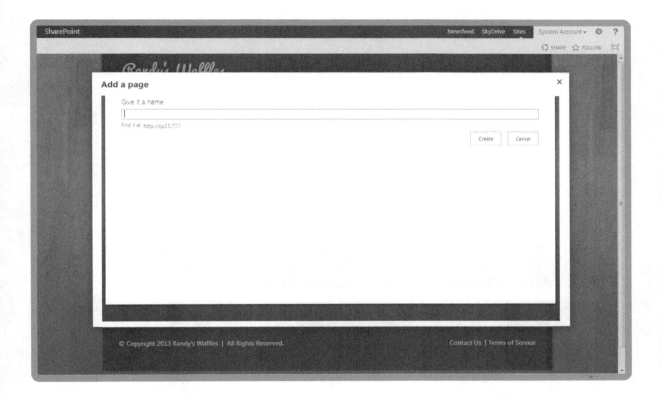

You can knock out these rogue styles by resetting the parent element's CSS only when it shows inside of a dialog box. By including `.ms-dialog` before the CSS declaration, the CSS rules apply their style only when the elements are in a dialog.

```
/* fix margins when dialog is up */
.ms-dialog .customWidth, .ms-dialog .customBodyHolder, .ms-dialog body {
  margin:0 !important;
  min-height:0 !important;
  min-width:0 !important;
  width:auto !important;
  height:auto !important;
  background-color: white !important;
  background-image: none !important;
  padding: 0px !important;
  overflow:inherit;
  box-shadow: none;
}
```

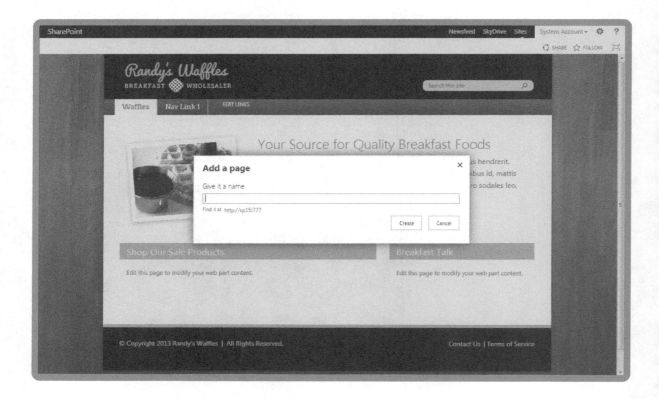

At this point the CSS is complete for the Randy's Waffles example. Save the file and refresh your browser to see the results. Don't forget that you need to publish the CSS file if you want anonymous users to see the changes. In Chapter 9, "Creating Content Rollups with SharePoint WCM," you learn more about creating rollup Web Parts to complete the bottom half of the original design.

SUMMARY

- The role of CSS is significant in the understanding of how branding and styles are applied to SharePoint. A strong understanding of CSS helps you create custom SharePoint branding.

- CSS is made up of rules that have selectors for matching HTML elements and declarations that define how the elements will be styled.

- When multiple CSS rules are applied to an HTML element, the most specific rule overrides other less specific styles.

- Inheritance causes some CSS properties to pass their style along from parent elements to their children.

- CSS can be applied to a web page in three different ways. Inline styles are applied directly to HTML elements, internal style sheets are embedded inside of an HTML page, and external style sheets are separate CSS files that are linked from the HTML page.

- Tools like Internet Explorer's F12 Developer Tools, Firebug for Firefox, and Chrome Developer Tools are helpful for determining how CSS is applied to complex HTML like you find in SharePoint 2013.

- CSS can be applied to SharePoint on pages themselves using rich text fields or Web Parts; applied via the Alternate CSS feature in publishing sites or with code; or directly linked from a custom master page using the `CssRegistration` tag.

- Applying branding to SharePoint can involve overriding many default SharePoint styles. Take your time and work through each section of the page including the page body, navigation, search, Web Parts, and more until you have SharePoint branding that achieves your design goals.

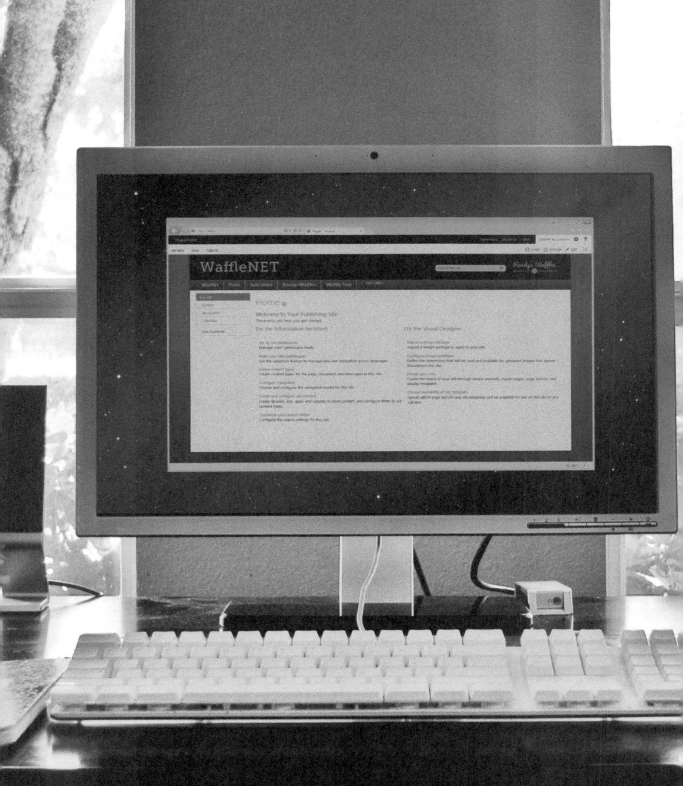

3

Advanced SharePoint Branding

7

CREATING CUSTOM MASTER PAGES AND PAGE LAYOUTS

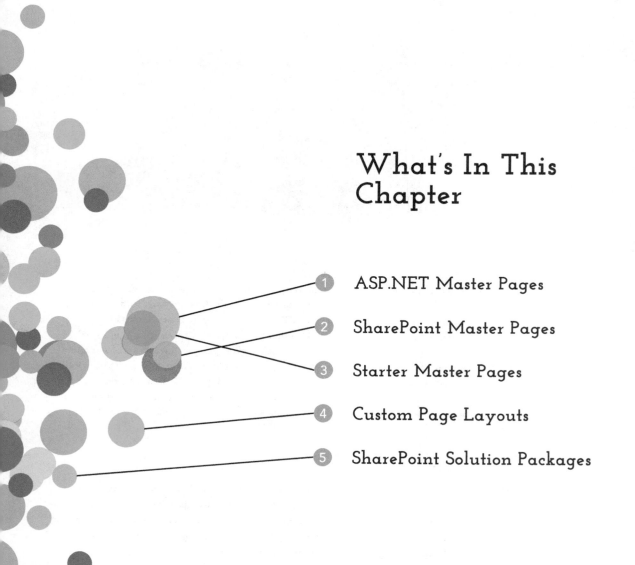

What's In This Chapter

In Chapter 5, "Using the Design Manager to Start a Design in SharePoint," you learned about how the SharePoint 2013 Design Manager can help you easily create master pages and page layouts from standard HTML and CSS designs. Although this option is fine for many scenarios, there may be times when creating SharePoint branding from scratch is a better option. One major reason for this alternative might be if you have SharePoint Foundation or don't have access to a SharePoint Server Publishing site. (The Design Manager feature is only available in sites with the Publishing feature activated.)

Even if you do have access to the Design Manager feature, after you become accustomed to how master pages and page layouts work, you may find it easier to skip the Design Manager and go right to creating custom branding by hand. Think of it like this: if you want to create an iPhone or Windows Phone app, you could use a code generator to make a simple app, but this approach is limited. When you feel comfortable coding for the phone, you would probably find that you have more power and control when coding the app by hand in the native coding language for the device. SharePoint branding is similar; if you are building a highly stylized website, you could build it with Design Manager, but you will likely find it easier to just learn the underlying technology and code it with master pages and page layouts. This is especially true if you already have experience branding in a previous version of SharePoint.

NOTE

SharePoint 2013 can use branding created from HTML by using the Design Manager features or custom branding that has been created by hand, like in previous versions of SharePoint. There isn't really a good word to describe these handmade master pages and page layouts; some people call them custom branding and others call them classic branding. In this chapter, any master page or page layout that is not created from HTML with the Design Manager is referred to as a *custom* master page.

Another reason why you might decide to code master pages by hand is that the Design Manager master pages were not built with SharePoint collaboration sites in mind (such as Team and Blog sites), and as such, there may be issues that crop up. For example, there is a SharePoint Feature activated on many collaboration sites called the Minimal Download Strategy (MDS). The MDS feature enables collaboration sites to load pages a lot faster than SharePoint 2010. The feature accomplishes this by running all page requests through a single page, /_layouts/15/start.aspx, which looks for visual differences

between new page requests and the previously loaded page, and it refreshes only the content that is different between the two pages.

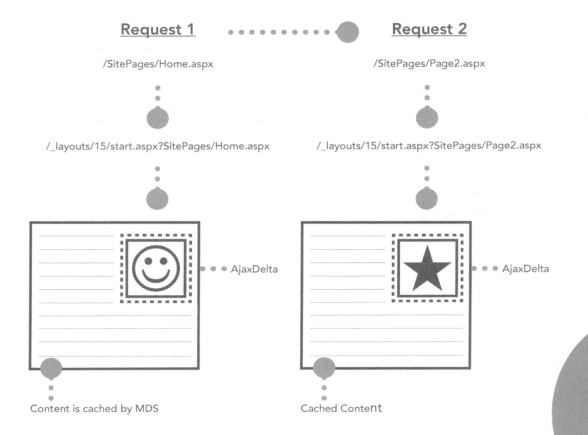

The problem here is that Design Manager master pages were designed to work with publishing sites, and the master pages have code that turns off the MDS caching behavior. When the MDS functions are turned off, you end up with every page on your site loading twice; first loading start.aspx and then a second time just loading the normal non-MDS URL. This double page load is not a great user experience, so you have two options to mitigate this issue when creating collaboration sites. You can either deactivate the MDS feature from **Site Settings ➢ Site Actions ➢ Manage site features** and lose that performance gain, or you can code your master page by hand with the MDS feature in mind.

The following chart gives a breakdown of when the Design Manager is appropriate and when custom master pages should be made. Of course, not everything is cut and dry, and there are situations in

which you could use one or the other. These instances are indicated with a solid dot in the recommended column, and a lightly shaded dot in the acceptable column.

	Design Manager	Custom Master Page
You have Foundation or non-Publishing site.		●
You have SP Server or O365 Ent.	●	●
You need quick nice looking branding.	●	
You need highly stylized/complex branding.	○	●
Existing SharePoint Branding.	○	●
You need to apply branding to Team/Collab sites with MDS.		●
You are experienced with HTML and CSS.	●	
You are experienced with Pre-SP 2013 branding.	○	●

In this chapter, you learn how master pages work in traditional ASP.NET applications and, more importantly how they work in SharePoint 2013. You will learn how to create custom master pages and page layouts by hand and to work with the MDS feature. Lastly, you learn about the process for deploying branding files to a production environment with a SharePoint Solution.

UNDERSTANDING TRADITIONAL ASP.NET MASTER PAGES

If you remember back to Chapter 2, you learned about how master pages were introduced in ASP.NET 2.0 to solve the problem of web pages having styling, content, and code commingled on every page. Master pages made the process of maintaining websites much easier and less error-prone by separating the styling and layout from content and code.

Master pages are used to create a template that controls many aspects of the overall layout of multiple pages in an ASP.NET website. They are typically used as a shell to hold all the common HTML content, such as the DOCTYPE, meta information, CSS, navigation, footers, and the general layout of the chrome of the site. A website may have one master page that controls all the pages, or it could have several master pages that apply different layouts to different areas of the site. In addition to enabling easier website maintenance, master pages are especially helpful for creating a consistent look for large websites with many content authors of varying skill levels.

The next few sections discuss traditional ASP.NET master pages before you dive into the deep end to see how master pages work in SharePoint.

Master Page Structure

From a coding perspective, a master page is a type of ASP.NET page written in either Visual Basic (VB) or C# and has a file extension of `.master`. Although you can use either language to create traditional ASP.NET applications, SharePoint uses only C# master pages. The following example illustrates a simple master page:

```
<%@ Master language="C#"%>
<!DOCTYPE HTML>
<html>
<head>
 <meta charset="utf-8">
 <title>Demo Title</title>
</head>

<body>
<form runat="server">
 <div class="mainbody">
  <asp:ContentPlaceHolder ID="MainBody" runat="server" />
 </div>
 <div class="footer">
  <asp:ContentPlaceHolder id="Footer" runat="server">
   Copyright 2013 - Randy's Waffles
  </asp:ContentPlaceHolder>
 </div>
</form>
</body>
</html>
```

You can see that master pages begin with the `@ Master` directive that declares the language in which the master page will be written. In this case the master page is written in C#. There is a `<form>` tag with the `runat="server"` property, which is a common attribute that tells ASP.NET that it needs to do some server processing on this control. There are also two content placeholders in the body of the master page: One has no content and is closed immediately but the other has some default footer content. Otherwise, the rest of the master page code is composed of standard HTML used to lay out the page.

Content Pages

Master pages on their own don't actually produce anything useful; browsing to a master page's URL directly can cause the web server, in this case Internet Information Services (IIS), to display an error. In traditional ASP.NET websites, content pages (files with an .ASPX extension) can refer to a master page for their layout. When users browse these pages, IIS merges the page content with the master page, and the resulting web page displays to the user.

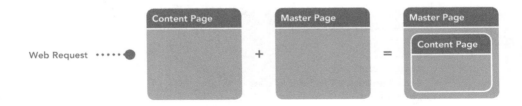

Content pages declare a master page via an @ Page directive at the top of their code. Following is a simple content page:

```
<%@ Page Language="C#" MasterPageFile="demo.master" %>

<asp:Content ContentPlaceHolderID="MainBody" Runat="Server" >
 Hello World
</asp:content>

<asp:Content ContentPlaceHolderID="Footer" Runat="Server" >
</asp:content>
```

Notice that the @ Page directive MasterPageFile property defines this page's master page as demo. master. Assuming the master page shown earlier was named demo.master, this content page would load that master page and use it to display its content.

Content Placeholders

Content placeholders define areas of a master page that can be replaced by information located on a content page. The master page's content placeholders receive their content from controls placed on content pages. The content pages can override content in as many or as few of the master page's content placeholders as desired; this means that not every content placeholder in a master page needs to be overridden by content pages. Because of this, content placeholders can define some default content to show whenever a content page does not override them. In the "Master Page Structure" section example the Footer content placeholder provided the default content Copyright 2013 - Randy's Waffles.

Content pages that use master pages, like the one in the preceding "Content Pages" section, require all content after the @ Page directive be located inside of content controls that start with <asp:Content>. If anything is placed outside a content control, an error occurs.

The content controls are tied to specific content placeholders by a matching ContentPlaceHolderID. In the "Content Pages" section's example, the content page would add the text Hello World where the MainBody content placeholder is located in the master page, and it would override the default text in the Footer content placeholder with nothing. When loaded in the browser, the resulting page would have the following HTML source:

```
<!DOCTYPE HTML>
<html>
<head>
 <meta charset="utf-8">
 <title>Demo Title</title>
</head>

<body>
<form>
 <div class="mainbody">
  Hello World
 </div>
 <div class="footer">
 </div>
</form>
</body>
</html>
```

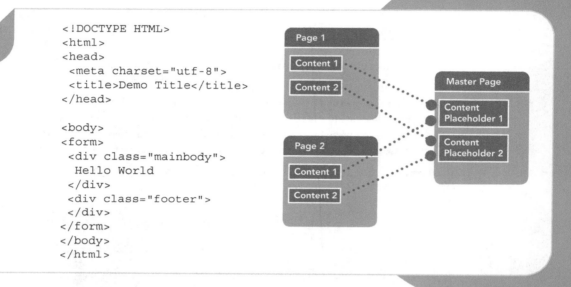

User Controls and Server Controls

Another important concept related to master pages is how controls are used to take complex code functionality and reduce it down to a few lines of code. Developers use controls to bundle HTML, existing ASP.NET server controls, and custom functionality into reusable components that can be added to master pages and content pages. User controls have a file extension of .ascx and perform more simple tasks than server controls. Server controls are coded and compiled into DLLs to be loaded on the web server. These controls enable master pages to provide large amounts of custom functionality while containing a relatively small amount of code for maintainability.

To use a control, you must first register it at the top of a content page or master page. This assigns a TagPrefix and a TagName, both of which are used to refer to the control in the page, as well as an src that points to the .ASCX control on the web server, or both a Namespace and an Assembly to point to a compiled DLL. Imagine that you had some search functionality prebuilt as a custom user control named searchbox.ascx. To include this functionality on a master page or content page, you would first register the control near the top of the page, below the language declaration, as shown here:

```
<%@ Master language="C#"%>
<%@ Register TagPrefix="Custom" TagName="Search"
src="searchbox.ascx" %>
```

To actually use the registered control in the master page, you use a combination of the TagPrefix and the TagName. The following example shows the control added to the page inside of a <div> tag:

```
<div id="header">
 <Custom:Search ID="mySearchControl" runat="server" />
</div>
```

When the page is loaded in a browser, whatever content the control is programmed to display will be added to the page inside of the <div> tags. Also, if the control was set up to receive custom properties, they could be applied when the control is added to the page. For example, if the search control has a property named ButtonImage to set the search button image, it could be added like this:

```
<Custom:Search ID="mySearchControl" ButtonImage="go.png"
runat="server" />
```

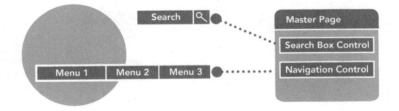

SharePoint leverages the concept of controls heavily to encapsulate much of the functionality in a SharePoint site. In the next section, you look at SharePoint master pages; you can probably notice that many controls are used.

MASTER PAGES IN SHAREPOINT

Master pages in SharePoint 2013 work much the same way that they do in traditional ASP.NET applications because SharePoint is essentially one big ASP.NET application. Every page browsed in a SharePoint site uses a master page to lay out its content. One striking difference with master pages in SharePoint is that master page references aren't hard-coded in pages. Instead, SharePoint pages point dynamically to either the Site or System master page applied to the SharePoint site that contains the page. The site master page is used by publishing pages while the system master page is generally

applied to all nonpublishing pages such as forms, views, and settings pages. By pointing dynamically to these two master pages, SharePoint sites can have their master page easily switched for all their pages via the web interface.

Applying Master Pages in SharePoint

Besides using custom code or PowerShell, there are two primary ways to apply master pages in SharePoint 2013: by using the SharePoint Server master page setting screen or using SharePoint Designer 2013.

Using SharePoint Server Publishing to Apply Master Pages

If you have a SharePoint Server publishing site, the web interface provides an easy method for applying master pages. With publishing enabled on the root site collection, you can apply master pages to all subsites in the site collection, including subsites that do not have publishing enabled. To change the master pages in the web interface navigate to **Site Settings ➤ Look and Feel ➤ Master page**. From this page you can change both the **Site Master Page** and **System Master Page**, and you can also apply these selections to any subsites below the current site. Remember that the Site master page is used primarily by publishing pages, whereas the System master page is used throughout SharePoint, including nonpublishing pages and the application pages, such as Site Settings.

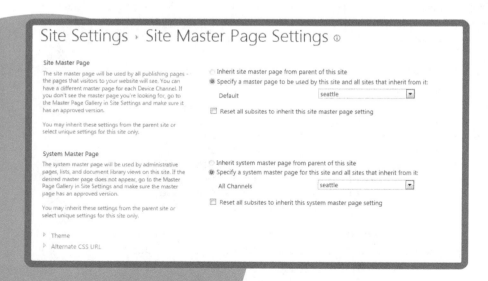

Using SharePoint Designer 2013 to Apply Master Pages

If you don't have SharePoint Server or don't have access to a publishing site, the next easiest option for applying master pages is to use SharePoint Designer 2013.

EXERCISE: APPLYING MASTER PAGES WITH SHAREPOINT DESIGNER 2013

1. Open SharePoint Designer 2013, and load a SharePoint Server 2013 site.

2. From the **Site Objects** menu on the left, click **Master Pages**.

3. In the main area of SharePoint Designer, click next to the name of a master page.

4. On the ribbon in the **Actions** group, you can click either **Set as Default** or **Set as Custom**. These options correspond to the System and Site master pages, respectively. If the master page is currently set as either of these options, the icon will be grayed out for setting the master page on the ribbon.

In SharePoint Designer, you can also right-click on the master page name in the **Site Objects** menu and select either **Set as Default Master Page** or **Set as Custom Master Page**. After setting the master page as either Default or Custom, you can browse back to your SharePoint site and see that the master page has changed.

SharePoint Master Page Structure

Earlier you saw a sample ASP.NET master page; you can compare this to a SharePoint master page to better understand the differences. To do so, map a drive to your Master Page Gallery and open `seattle.master` in your editor of choice. In the interest of space, the following is a portion of `seattle.master` with some of the lines of code truncated to fit better on the pages:

```
<%@Master language="C#"%>
<%@ Register Tagprefix="SharePoint" Namespace="Microsoft …
<%@ Register Tagprefix="Utilities" Namespace="Microsoft …
<%@ Import Namespace="Microsoft.SharePoint" %>
<%@ Assembly Name="Microsoft.Web.CommandUI …
<%@ Import Namespace="Microsoft.SharePoint.ApplicationPages" %>
<%@ Register Tagprefix="WebPartPages" Namespace="Microsoft …
<%@ Register TagPrefix="wssuc" TagName="Welcome"
 src="~/_controltemplates/15/Welcome.ascx" %>

<!DOCTYPE html PUBLIC "-//W3C//DTD XHTML 1.0 Strict//EN"
 "http://www.w3.org/TR/xhtml1/DTD/xhtml1-strict.dtd">
```

```
<SharePoint:SPHtmlTag
 dir="<%$Resources:wss,multipages_direction_dir_value%>"
 ID="SPHtmlTag" runat="server" >

<head runat="server">
 <meta name="GENERATOR" content="Microsoft SharePoint" />
 <meta http-equiv="Content-type" content="text/html;
  charset=utf-8" />
 <meta http-equiv="X-UA-Compatible" content="IE=10"/>
 <meta http-equiv="Expires" content="0" />

 <SharePoint:SPPinnedSiteTile runat="server"
  TileUrl="/_layouts/15/images/SharePointMetroAppTile.png"
  TileColor="#0072C6" />
 <SharePoint:RobotsMetaTag runat="server"/>

 <SharePoint:PageTitle runat="server">
  <asp:ContentPlaceHolder id="PlaceHolderPageTitle" runat="server">
   <SharePoint:ProjectProperty Property="Title" runat="server" />
  </asp:ContentPlaceHolder>
 </SharePoint:PageTitle>

 . . .
```

The first thing you may notice looking at the SharePoint master page is that it is generally much larger than the simple ASP.NET master page listed earlier. Like ASP.NET, it begins with an @ Master directive that declares the language as C#, and then several controls and assemblies are registered or imported. These controls and assemblies are what make SharePoint work, and they are sprinkled throughout the master page and arranged with HTML and ASP.NET to create all the SharePoint functionality that appears on the page. After the controls and assemblies you see the Document Type Declaration or DOCTYPE, which tells the browser how to render the HTML markup. SharePoint 2013 can use a variety of DOCTYPEs, but it has been tuned to work best with either XHTML 1.0 Strict or HTML5 DOCTYPES. The previous example uses the XHTML 1.0 Strict DOCTYPE.

One prevalent control is registered as SharePoint, and you can see tags throughout the master page listed as <SharePoint:XYZ>, where XYZ describes the control's functionality. The <SharePoint:SPHtmlTag> is one of those controls; it injects the page's HTML tag dynamically based on various page criteria. Along with controls like this, you see that a lot of standard HTML, JavaScript, and CSS are also declared, such as the four meta tags at the top. The other major feature of the master page is a series of content placeholders, such as PlaceHolderPageTitle, which injects the title of the SharePoint pages into the HTML <title> tag. Many of these content placeholders are required by SharePoint and you can see an error if you simply remove them.

The following content placeholders are required in SharePoint 2013. Their names provide a fairly accurate description of what they are typically used for, but SharePoint pages can use them for anything, and they may not always contain the content you would expect.

PlaceHolderAdditionalPageHead	PlaceHolderPageDescription
PlaceHolderBodyAreaClass	PlaceHolderPageImage
PlaceHolderBodyLeftBorder	PlaceHolderPageTitle
PlaceHolderBodyRightMargin	PlaceHolderPageTitleInTitleArea
PlaceHolderCalendarNavigator	PlaceHolderQuickLaunchBottom
PlaceHolderFormDigest	PlaceHolderQuickLaunchTop
PlaceHolderGlobalNavigation	PlaceHolderSearchArea
PlaceHolderGlobalNavigationSiteMap	PlaceHolderSiteName
PlaceHolderHorizontalNav	PlaceHolderTitleAreaClass
PlaceHolderLeftActions	PlaceHolderTitleAreaSeparator
PlaceHolderLeftNavBar	PlaceHolderTitleBreadcrumb
PlaceHolderLeftNavBarBorder	PlaceHolderTitleLeftBorder
PlaceHolderLeftNavBarDataSource	PlaceHolderTitleRightMargin
PlaceHolderLeftNavBarTop	PlaceHolderTopNavBar
PlaceHolderMain	PlaceHolderUtilityContent
PlaceHolderMiniConsole	SPNavigation
PlaceHolderNavSpacer	WSSDesignConsole

NOTE

When you use the Design Manager to create HTML-based master pages, the required content placeholders are handled for you. This is not the case when creating a custom master page by hand.

The Ribbon

Another major aspect of SharePoint master pages is the inclusion of the ribbon. The ribbon is the area at the top of the page that includes all the contextual buttons that help content authors and site owners use SharePoint.

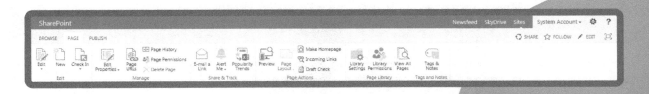

If you look at the source of a Design Manager-created master page, you see that Microsoft uses a one-line control to include the ribbon:

```
<PublishingRibbon:PublishingRibbon runat="server" />
```

Although this control is extremely helpful, it is specific to SharePoint Server publishing and is not intended to be used with SharePoint Foundation sites. If you need to create a master page that will be used in one of these scenarios you can actually use the full ribbon, which can be seen by opening `seattle.master`. The ribbon actually includes all the code from line 72 through 343...a good portion of the 616-line master page. Luckily, for the most part you don't need to worry about the actual ribbon code in a custom master page; you can just copy the code as it's provided in one of the out-of-the-box master pages. This is also true for creating master pages for special SharePoint features like My Sites, which require a special ribbon like the one in `mysite.master` that is created automatically with My Sites.

WARNING

The way the ribbon is implemented in SharePoint can often give designers grief. This is because the SharePoint master page turns off the normal browser scrollbars. SharePoint then uses JavaScript to calculate the remaining browser height and adds the scrollbars back manually in a way that enables the ribbon to stay "pinned" to the top of the browser.

AjaxDelta Controls and Minimal Download Strategy

You can also see a lot of instances of a specific control, `<SharePoint:AjaxDelta>`, in SharePoint master pages. The AjaxDelta control is directly related to how the Minimal Download Strategy (MDS) knows which parts of the layout to refresh before the page is rendered. More specifically, anything not wrapped in an AjaxDelta control will *not* refresh between pages of a site with the MDS feature activated.

For example, if you have some dynamic page element, such as the page title, and it is not wrapped in an AjaxDelta control, every page on a site with MDS enabled will show the same title from page to page. This is because the first page routed through `start.aspx` causes MDS to cache everything on the page that isn't wrapped in an AjaxDelta; every other page will show the same title. On the other hand, if it were wrapped in an AjaxDelta control, MDS would know it needs to render any differences from the previously loaded page.

Here is an example of a control wrapped in an AjaxDelta control:

```
<SharePoint:AjaxDelta ID="DeltaSearch" BlockElement="true"
runat="server">
 <asp:ContentPlaceHolder id="PlaceHolderSearchArea" runat="server">
  <SearchWC:SearchBoxScriptWebPart
   UseSiteCollectionSettings="true"
   EmitStyleReference="false"
   ShowQuerySuggestions="true"
   ChromeType="None"
   UseSharedSettings="true"
   TryInplaceQuery="false"
   ServerInitialRender="true"
   runat="server" />
 </asp:ContentPlaceHolder>
</SharePoint:AjaxDelta>
```

Each AjaxDelta control has a unique ID and an optional attribute BlockElement. When BlockElement is true the AjaxDelta wraps the control in an HTML <div>; otherwise it uses a <span>.

NOTE

At some point in your SharePoint branding life, chances are good that you will forget to put an AjaxDelta around something important on your master page. If you see an issue in which something isn't updating from page to page or notice that some users are experiencing different rendering than you would expect for the same control, it's a good idea to double-check that the control is wrapped in an AjaxDelta.

Editing Custom Master Pages

To edit a custom master page, you can still use a mapped drive to the site collection master page gallery much like you do with the Design Manager. The major difference is that because you are working directly with a .master file, WYSIWYG editors such as Dreamweaver and Expression Web cannot show a design preview. This isn't a big problem if you are comfortable editing code; you can easily have your favorite web browser open in another window and just refresh every time you make a change. Because your changes are saved directly to the server, you can see the updates immediately if you are authenticated as the same user to browse the site as you are to edit with. If for some reason you need to test with a different user, you need to publish and approve a major version of your .master file before the user can see the changes. Some common tools for working with custom master pages are Notepad++, Adobe Dreamweaver, Microsoft Expression Web, Microsoft Visual Studio, or even SharePoint Designer 2013.

Although you can work on custom master pages with SharePoint Designer 2013, you cannot edit files from the mapped drive. SharePoint Designer is limited to connecting directly to the site collection using its own methods. The Site Objects pane on the left side of the screen is a view of your site collection much like you would see in a mapped drive.

This is probably a great time to remind you not to make edits like this directly on your production server. Best practice dictates that you should have a development environment, whether it is a cloud-based server, local server, or even a virtual machine, as long as it closely replicates the intended production environment. Later in the "Understanding SharePoint Solution Packages" section you learn about packaging your changes into a SharePoint Solution (WSP) with Visual Studio for deploying to production environments.

Creating a Custom Master Page

Because of all the required content placeholders and other functionality that is loaded by default in SharePoint master pages, it is often impractical to just start a custom master page from a blank file. Instead, you can choose between a few different options when starting a new custom master page that includes much of this required code.

Design Manager

You could create a master page with the Design Manager and then decouple the `.html` and `.master` file and just start editing the `.master` file. To do this, follow these steps:

1. From the **Design Manager** click **Edit Master Pages**.

2. Find the master page, and click the **Ellipsis** menu.

3. In the pop-up menu, click the next **Ellipsis** menu, and in that pop-up menu, click **Edit Properties**.

4. From there you can uncheck **Associate File**, and click **Save**.

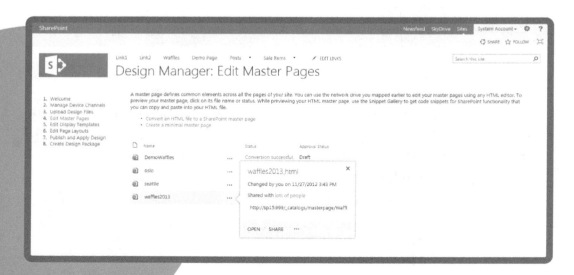

Although this is a tempting and easy way to start, there are some downsides to this method. First, the master page created from the Design Manager is often tabbed and spaced poorly, and not easy to read. Perhaps more important though, as mentioned earlier, master pages created with this method are not intended to be used with collaboration sites with MDS activated.

Editing an Existing Master Page

If you want to make a custom master page that is only slightly different from the out-of-the-box master pages, you can make a copy of `seattle.master` or `oslo.master` and make any changes you would like. This method is also easy, but it is only appropriate for making lightly branded master pages. Anything more stylized would require a lot of work to undo the layout that is already created. Also, these master pages are fairly lengthy and are not commented to help you with the process.

The easiest way to try this method is to open a mapped drive to your Master Page Gallery and simply copy, paste, and rename `seattle.master`. From there you can edit away to your heart's content.

Starter Master Page

Probably the best way to start a new custom master page is to use a *starter master page*. The concept of starter master pages has been around since SharePoint 2007, although they were known as *minimal master pages* back then. A starter master page is a community-based solution that is freely download-able and includes only the bare minimum of code to make SharePoint work properly, with nice comments and tabbing. Otherwise, it is just a blank canvas for you to build branding around. You can download my starter master pages from `http://startermasterpages.codeplex.com`.

Using a Starter Master Page

The process of implementing a starter master page is quite similar to using the Design Manager to create one. Here is a quick overview of the steps:

1. Create a traditional HTML and CSS design.
2. Map a drive to the site collection's Master Page Gallery.
3. Copy the HTML design's images and CSS to a folder in the Master Page Gallery.
4. Download and copy a starter master page to the Master Page Gallery.
5. Edit the starter master page with your editor of choice, and add the HTML from the original design to the starter master page. Arrange it around the key areas of the starter master page.
6. Instead of adding snippets, add and arrange the SharePoint controls and content placeholders that the Design Manger would have created.
7. Reference the custom CSS, and modify it to adjust for how SharePoint is showing the page.
8. Create page layouts with SharePoint Designer 2013.
9. Package as SharePoint Solution WSP with Visual Studio and deploy to production.

As you can see, many of these steps are similar to using the Design Manager except you aren't relying on it to generate much of the code for you. The upside to this is that you have maximum control over the readability and functionality of the master page.

Now take a look at an example of using a starter master page to create a branded intranet design for your friends at Randy's Waffles. The following example uses a predesigned HTML site for Randy's Waffles intranet known as WaffleNET. Because this design will be used in a collaborative intranet, the body content wasn't mocked up in the HTML; instead, you can just use the page content that Share-Point creates and style it as needed.

The design for this example is similar to the design for Randy's Waffles used in Chapter 5, but there are some notable differences. Obviously, there is the addition of an intranet logo, in this case WaffleNET. The public-facing Randy's Waffles logo has been made smaller and moved to the right. Also the width of the page has been changed to a variable size that will expand to 90 percent of the browser screen width. A subtle background was added to the header area to make it more interesting at this larger size, and the footer has been removed to allow for more content. Lastly, the font for the top navigation has been decreased in size because intranets often have a lot of navigation. There are also some important concepts that are not shown in the HTML design: the intranet site will include Quick Launch navigation on the left and the out-of-the-box SharePoint site title, page, and description information will be added above the body content.

You can download the HTML for this example from the downloadable code for this chapter. For this example you use a SharePoint Server site with publishing turned on. If you don't have SharePoint Server or the ability to activate the publishing feature, you can still follow along, but there will be some differences.

EXAMPLE: CREATING A CUSTOM MASTER PAGE WITH A STARTER MASTER PAGE

1. Start by downloading the starter master pages from `http://startermasterpages.codeplex.com`. This includes several starter master pages, but for this example you want `Starter PubCollab. master`. If you don't have publishing, you can follow along instead with `Starter Foundation. master`.

2. Like in previous chapters, map a drive to your SharePoint site collection, and navigate to your Master Page Gallery. Make a subfolder here called WaffleNET, and drag in the starter master page and all the files from the WaffleNET HTML (from the chapter downloads) except `WaffleNet.html`. You don't need the HTML file because you'll be merging the contents with the starter master page.

3. Rename the starter master page to `WaffleNet.master`, and open it and the `WaffleNet.html` file in your editor of choice.

4. Next, you need to begin merging the layout of the HTML design with the functions of the starter master page. Start by editing a few key areas in the `<head>` section of the starter master page. In the Favicon section, update the `SPShortcutIcon`'s `IconUrl` and `SPPinnedSiteTile`'s `TileUrl` to match the corresponding folder and filename. Be sure to change the path if your site collection is not at the root of your web application (Example: `/sites/SubSiteCollection/_catalogs/masterpage/WaffleNet/favicon.ico`):

```
<SharePoint:SPShortcutIcon runat="server"
 IconUrl="/_catalogs/masterpage/WaffleNet/favicon.ico" />
<SharePoint:SPPinnedSiteTile runat="server"
 TileUrl="/_catalogs/masterpage/WaffleNet/MetroAppTile.png"
 TileColor="#2184bc" />
```

5. Update the preconfigured `CssRegistration` at the bottom of the `<head>` to match the branding CSS. The `CssRegistration` tag is smart enough to allow `$SPUrl`, which uses the `~sitecollection` token to point to the root of the current site collection. This was not usable in the previous step.

```
<SharePoint:CssRegistration ID="CssRegistration1" name="&lt;%
 $SPUrl:~sitecollection/_catalogs/masterpage/WaffleNet/style.css
 %&gt;" runat="server" after="SharepointCssFile" />
```

6. You've now completed the head section; of course, more complicated designs might require more work in the preceding steps. Next, you look at using the body of the HTML design to lay out SharePoint functionality: copy all the content of `WaffleNet.html` between the opening and closing `<body>` tags. Paste this into the `WaffleNet.master` after `<div id="s4-bodyContainer">`. This is the main container for the scrolling area of the page below the ribbon.

7. Replace the static HTML logo with the actual SharePoint `SiteLogoImage`. Scroll down to `<SharePoint:AjaxDelta ID="Custom_Logo"...>` and cut it out along with all the included controls, and replace the static HTML image. You will be replacing this:

```
<a href="#" class="customLogo"><img src="wafflenet.png"
 alt="Back to Home" /></a>
```

with:

```
<SharePoint:AjaxDelta ID="Custom_Logo" BlockElement="true"
 runat="server">
 <SharePoint:SPLinkButton runat="server"
  NavigateUrl="~sitecollection/">
  <SharePoint:SiteLogoImage ID="x63829de2201a4365a3904788f682d0a3"
   LogoImageUrl="&lt;% $SPUrl:~sitecollection/_catalogs/masterpage/
    StarterBranding/logo.png %&gt;" AlternateText="Back to Home"
   runat="server" />
 </SharePoint:SPLinkButton>
</SharePoint:AjaxDelta>
```

8. In the section you just replaced, update the placeholder logo with the actual branding logo:

```
<SharePoint:SiteLogoImage ID="x63829de2201a4365a3904788f682d0a3"
 LogoImageUrl="&lt;%
 $SPUrl:~sitecollection/_catalogs/masterpage/WaffleNet/wafflenet.png
 %&gt;" AlternateText="Back to Home" runat="server" />
```

9. Replace the static HTML search with the SharePoint search control. This requires you to replace this line

```
<input type="text" />
<a href="#" class="customSearchButton">
 <img src="search-button.png" alt="Search" />
</a>
```

with:

```
<SharePoint:AjaxDelta ID="DeltaSearch" BlockElement="true"
 runat="server">
 <asp:ContentPlaceHolder id="PlaceHolderSearchArea" runat="server">
  <SearchWC:SearchBoxScriptWebPart UseSiteCollectionSettings="true"
   EmitStyleReference="true" ShowQuerySuggestions="true"
   ChromeType="None" UseSharedSettings="true"
   TryInplaceQuery="false" ServerInitialRender="true"
   runat="server" />
 </asp:ContentPlaceHolder>
</SharePoint:AjaxDelta>
```

10. Replace the entire static HTML top navigation with the SharePoint top navigation. You will be replacing this

```
<ul id="customTopNav">
 <li><a href="#" class="customTopNavItem">Home</a></li>
 <li><a href="#" class="customTopNavItem">Sales</a></li>
 <li><a href="#" class="customTopNavItem">Marketing</a></li>
 <li><a href="#" class="customTopNavItem">HR</a></li>
 <li><a href="#" class="customTopNavItem">IT</a></li>
 <li><a href="#" class="customTopNavItem">Help</a></li>
</ul>
```

with this:

```
<SharePoint:AjaxDelta ID="DeltaTopNavigation" BlockElement="true"
 CssClass="ms-displayInline ms-core-navigation ms-dialogHidden"
 runat="server">
 <SharePoint:DelegateControl runat="server"
  ControlId="TopNavigationDataSource" Id="topNavigationDelegate">
  <Template_Controls>
   <asp:SiteMapDataSource ShowStartingNode="False"
   SiteMapProvider="SPNavigationProvider" id="topSiteMap"
   runat="server" StartingNodeUrl="sid:1002"/>
  </Template_Controls>
 </SharePoint:DelegateControl>
 <SharePoint:AspMenu ID="TopNavigationMenu" Runat="server"
  EnableViewState="false" DataSourceID="topSiteMap"
  AccessKey="<%$Resources:wss,navigation_accesskey%>"
  UseSimpleRendering="true" UseSeparateCss="false"
  Orientation="Horizontal" StaticDisplayLevels="2"
  AdjustForShowStartingNode="true" MaximumDynamicDisplayLevels="2"
  SkipLinkText="" />
</SharePoint:AjaxDelta>
```

11 You now move the major body functions from the starter master page up into the `customBodyHolder` of the HTML design. This starts with the `sideNavBox`, which holds the Quick Launch menu and the `contentBox`, which holds the main body content placeholder `PlaceHolderMain`: Select `<div id="sideNavBox"… >` and everything inside of it, as well as `<div id="contentBox">` and everything inside of it. Cut and paste this code between the starting `<div class="customBodyHolder">` tag and closing `</div>` tag.

12 Now you need to move the page title, breadcrumbs, and description to the area at the top of the `<div id="contentBox">`. First, however, you must remove some extra markup that is left over from all your previous cutting and pasting. Inside of `<div id="s4-titlerow">`, you can see three extra sets of comments and `<div class="ms-dialogHidden"></div>` tags. These won't be needed, so you can remove them.

13 Now all that remains inside of `<div id="s4-titlerow">` is the out-of-the-box page title, bread-crumbs, and description. You can select the entire section including the start and end tags for `<div id="s4-titlerow">` and paste that right below `<div id="contentBox">`.

At this point the basic master page structure is complete, but if you applied this master page now, you would notice that all the SharePoint dialogs (such as the **Settings menu ➢ Add a page**) include parts of the branding that are unwanted.

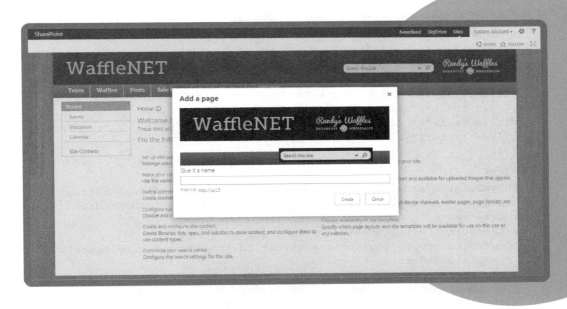

This is because SharePoint uses the System master page for the chrome of all dialogs. To remove the extra branding inside of dialogs, you can add the CSS class `ms-dialogHidden` to a few of the existing tags. Any element with this CSS class is not rendered inside of a dialog but shows fine in a normal page. To do so simply update both the `customTopHolder` and `customTopNavHolder` `<div>` tags to include `ms-dialogHidden` like so:

```
<div class="customTopHolder ms-dialogHidden">
<div class="customTopNavHolder ms-dialogHidden">
```

That's all that needs to happen for the WaffleNET master page. At this point none of the CSS changes have been applied to handle SharePoint styling, but the process for updating the CSS is similar to what

you saw in the previous chapter. The final CSS is actually quite similar to the Randy's Waffles CSS with just a few subtle tweaks to make the design more intranet-friendly. You can download the final master page and CSS from the downloadable code for this chapter.

NOTE

As you were moving SharePoint functionality around in the master page, did you notice that most of the controls and content placeholders in the starter master page are surrounded by AjaxDelta controls? This is meant to handle the Minimal Download Strategy feature that was discussed earlier. Any control or content placeholder that can have dynamic content needs to be wrapped in a unique AjaxDelta control.

Taking the Master Page Further

Before you can apply the master page to your site, you first need to publish a major version. In Chapter 5, you learned how to publish an HTML-based Design Manager master page; the process for publishing a custom master page is only slightly different.

EXAMPLE: PUBLISHING A CUSTOM MASTER PAGE

1. Navigate to **Site Settings**, and under **Web Designer Galleries**, click **Master pages and page layouts**.
2. Click the `WaffleNet` subfolder, and then click `WaffleNet.master`.
3. You see an arrow appear to the right of the filename; expand that and then click **Publish a Major Version**.
4. When the Publish a Major Version dialog opens, click **OK**.

To apply this master page to your site, you can follow the steps shown earlier in the "Applying Master Pages in SharePoint" section.

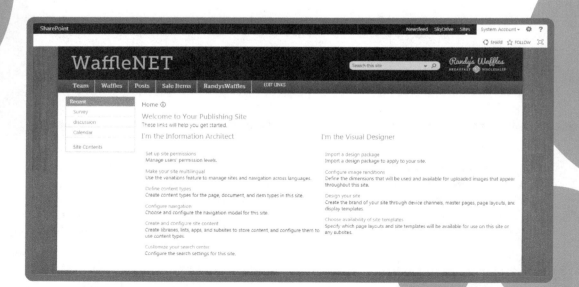

If you intend to use this branding on a public-facing site, all the assets including master pages, page layouts, CSS, images, and JavaScript need to be checked in as major versions and published before anonymous users can load the site. This can take a long time if you use the same method that you published the master page with earlier. Instead, an easier way to publish a lot of files is to use the old Content and Structure page. This is one area of SharePoint that has had little enhancement since SharePoint 2007, which is a shame because there are some useful features hidden in here.

EXAMPLE: PUBLISHING FILES USING THE CONTENT AND STRUCTURE PAGE

1. From **Site Settings** under **Site Administration**, click **Content and structure**.

2. On the left side of the screen, you see a view of your site collection. Expand **Master Page Gallery**, and then click the `WaffleNet` folder.

3. Now on the right side of the screen, you can see the contents of the WaffleNet folder. You can click the check boxes next to each item, or you can click the **Select All** box at the top of the grid.

4. With all the files selected, click the **Actions** menu, and select **Publish**.

5. From the Publish dialog, simply click **OK**.

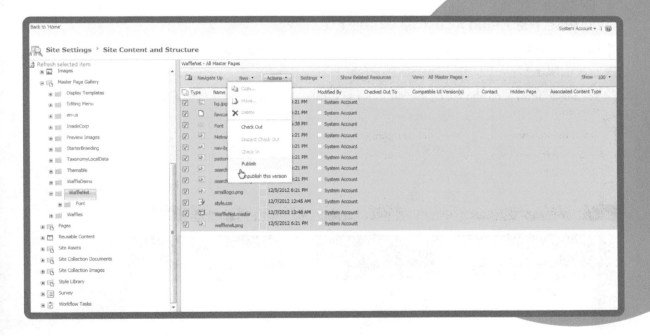

If you want to add more out-of-the-box SharePoint functionality to the master page, one way to find out what code to add is to make a quick HTML-based master page with the Design Manager, and use the Snippet gallery to see what the resulting SharePoint code looks like in the related master page. You learn some more advanced tips and tricks for working with specific master page tasks in the next chapter. If you want to remove functionality from the master page, see the next section to learn how to remove required content placeholders.

Working with Required Content Placeholders

With all these required content placeholders, you are likely wondering how you can remove areas of functionality that aren't required for a specific branding project. Rather than delete required content placeholders (which causes an error), you can hide them on the master page. If you look at the code for either a Design Manager master page or one of the starter master pages, you see that unused content placeholders are relegated to the bottom of the master page and they are hidden by using the attribute `Visible="False"`. Content placeholders with the visibility turned off can still function properly in SharePoint, but any content they generate will be omitted from the HTML source seen by browsers.

The following code shows an example of some hidden content placeholders:

```
<asp:ContentPlaceHolder id="PlaceHolderBodyAreaClass" Visible="False"
runat="server" />
<asp:ContentPlaceHolder id="PlaceHolderTitleAreaClass" Visible="False"
runat="server" />
```

Dealing with Errors

One of the first things you will realize when working on your custom master page is that when you make a mistake, SharePoint's default error messages are rather unhelpful. If you omit one of the required content placeholders and browse a site that uses your master page, SharePoint replies with simply Sorry, Something Went Wrong. An Unexpected Error Has Occurred.

Although newer versions of SharePoint include a correlation ID that can be looked up on the server, that process can be daunting. For more information on looking up correlation IDs, see `http://zimmergren.net/technical/sp-2010-find-error-messages-with-a-correlation-id-token-in-sharepoint-2010`.

For a more useful solution, SharePoint can actually return descriptive error messages, but for security reasons they are turned off by default. If you work in a development environment, though, it can be quite helpful to enable these full error messages.

EXAMPLE: TURNING ON THE FULL ERROR MESSAGES

1. Log in to the physical SharePoint Server machine, and navigate to the IIS directory that holds your SharePoint website. It will most likely be located at `C:\inetpub\wwwroot\wss\VirtualDirectories\` and will be in a subdirectory with the port number of your SharePoint site. If you have trouble finding it, you can open IIS, and in the **Sites** folder, right-click your SharePoint site, and then select **Explore**. This takes you directly to the directory that holds your SharePoint website.

2. Locate the file named `web.config`, and open it in a file editor such as Notepad++.

3. Press **Ctrl+F**, and find the line of code that contains the word `callstack`. You should find a line that looks like this:

```
<SafeMode MaxControls="200" CallStack="false" DirectFileDependen-
    cies="10"
  TotalFileDependencies="250" AllowPageLevelTrace="false">
```

Change both the `CallStack` and `AllowPageLevelTrace` attributes from `false` to `true`.

4. Press **Ctrl+F** again, and this time search for the word `errors`. You should find a line that looks like this:

```
<customErrors mode="On" />
```

5. Change the mode from `On` to `Off`. This tells IIS not to show its customary basic error messages and to instead display the raw detailed error messages.

6. Save and close `web.config`. This change causes IIS to restart the web application in which your SharePoint site resides. Be careful when making edits to this file in production or shared development environments.

With these changes in place, browsing a page with an error will now reveal the complete error message.

Server Error in '/' Application.

Cannot find ContentPlaceHolder 'PlaceHolderMain' in the master page '/_catalogs/masterpage/WaffleNet/WaffleNet.master', verify content control's ContentPlaceHolderID attribute in the content page.

Description: An unhandled exception occurred during the execution of the current web request. Please review the stack trace for more information about the error and where it originated in the code.

Exception Details: System.Web.HttpException: Cannot find ContentPlaceHolder 'PlaceHolderMain' in the master page '/_catalogs/masterpage/WaffleNet/WaffleNet.master', verify content control's ContentPlaceHolderID attribute in the content page.

Source Error:

An unhandled exception was generated during the execution of the current web request. Information regarding the origin and location of the exception can be identified using the exception stack trace below.

Stack Trace:

```
[HttpException (0x80004005): Cannot find ContentPlaceHolder 'PlaceHolderMain' in the master page '/_catalogs/masterpage/WaffleNet/WaffleNet.master', verify content c
   System.Web.UI.MasterPage.CreateMaster(TemplateControl owner, HttpContext context, VirtualPath masterPageFile, IDictionary contentTemplateCollection) +1090
   System.Web.UI.Page.ApplyMasterPage() +74
   System.Web.UI.Page.PerformPreInit() +208
   System.Web.UI.Page.ProcessRequestMain(Boolean includeStagesBeforeAsyncPoint, Boolean includeStagesAfterAsyncPoint) +1571
```

Version Information: Microsoft .NET Framework Version:4.0.30319; ASP.NET Version:4.0.30319.17929

CREATING CUSTOM PAGE LAYOUTS

Page layouts are critical to web content management because they enable content authors to create pages with specific editable fields and predefined HTML for content arrangement. Compared to traditional ASP.NET, you can think of page layouts as templates for creating content pages with specific layouts. This section focuses on providing a deep understanding of how page layouts work and how you can create your own page layouts for use in SharePoint 2013. To follow along with the examples in the chapter, you need to have SharePoint Server 2013 with a publishing site; SharePoint Foundation and Team sites without publishing activated do not include the capability to use page layouts.

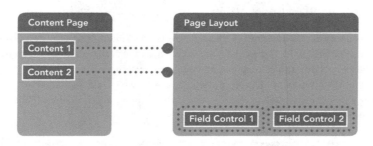

Understanding Content Types and Site Columns

Although content types are certainly used for many other things in SharePoint, such as lists, they are critical to the creation of page layouts as well. One particularly tricky concept to understand with page layouts is that they are always based on exactly one content type, which in turn is made up of *site columns*.

If you look at a publishing page in Edit mode, you can see several editable field controls.

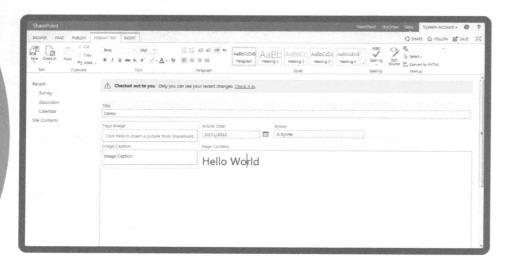

These editable fields are defined by which site columns are available in the underlying content type. To put it another way, editable field controls on page layouts have their data stored in the site columns that define them. You see an example of creating a custom page layout in the next section, but for now it's useful to understand that when you create a custom page layout, you first select the content type on which it is based. From there you can select from the available site columns to be used as field controls.

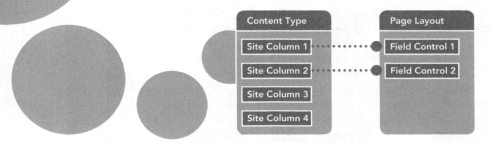

To gain a better understanding of how all these concepts are related, the out-of-the-box page layout Image on Left can be analyzed. This page layout is based on the Article Page content type. The content type has a Publishing HTML site column named Page Content. The Image on Left page layout has an editable field control in it called `PublishingPageContent`, which is directly related to this site column. In turn, any page that uses the Image on Left page layout, when edited, can have Page Content information entered and saved from the field control.

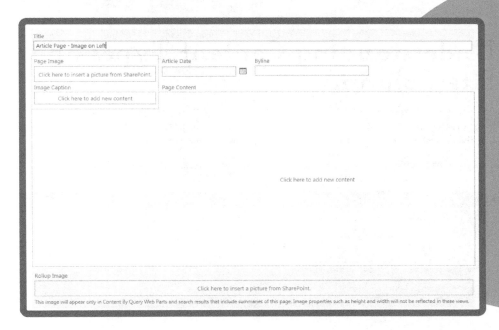

All page layouts in SharePoint are based on the Page content type or another content type that is inherited from the Page content type. When creating your own page layouts, the simplest way to start is by basing them on any of the out-of-the-box Page Layout content types. If you find that you need to have different editable fields in your page layout than those available in the out-of-the-box content types, you can create your own content type (inheriting from either the Page Layout or Page content type), add extra site columns, and base your page layout off of it.

Page Layout Structure

To better understand the structure of page layouts, here is a sample of a simple page layout. This page layout includes just a rich HTML field and a Web Part zone:

```
<%@ Page language="C#"
 Inherits="Microsoft.SharePoint.Publishing.PublishingLayoutPage,
Microsoft.SharePoint.Publishing,Version=15.0.0.0,Culture=neutral,
PublicKeyToken=71e9bce111e9429c" %>

<%@ Register Tagprefix="SharePointWebControls"
 Namespace="Microsoft.SharePoint.WebControls"
 Assembly="Microsoft.SharePoint, Version=15.0.0.0, Culture=neutral,
 PublicKeyToken=71e9bce111e9429c" %>

<%@ Register Tagprefix="WebPartPages"
 Namespace="Microsoft.SharePoint.WebPartPages"
 Assembly="Microsoft.SharePoint, Version=15.0.0.0, Culture=neutral,
 PublicKeyToken=71e9bce111e9429c" %>

<%@ Register Tagprefix="PublishingWebControls"
 Namespace="Microsoft.SharePoint.Publishing.WebControls"
 Assembly="Microsoft.SharePoint.Publishing, Version=15.0.0.0,
 Culture=neutral, PublicKeyToken=71e9bce111e9429c" %>

<%@ Register Tagprefix="PublishingNavigation"
 Namespace="Microsoft.SharePoint.Publishing.Navigation"
 Assembly="Microsoft.SharePoint.Publishing, Version=15.0.0.0,
 Culture=neutral, PublicKeyToken=71e9bce111e9429c" %>

<asp:Content ContentPlaceholderID="PlaceHolderPageTitle"
 runat="server">
 <SharePointWebControls:FieldValue id="PageTitle" FieldName="Title"
  runat="server"/>
</asp:Content>

<asp:Content ContentPlaceholderID="PlaceHolderMain" runat="server">
 <div class="MainContent">
  <PublishingWebControls:RichHtmlField
   FieldName="PublishingPageContent" runat="server"/>
 </div>
 <div class="WebParts">
  <WebPartPages:WebPartZone runat="server" Title="Web Parts"
   ID="WPZ1"></WebPartPages:webpartzone>
 </div>
</asp:Content>
```

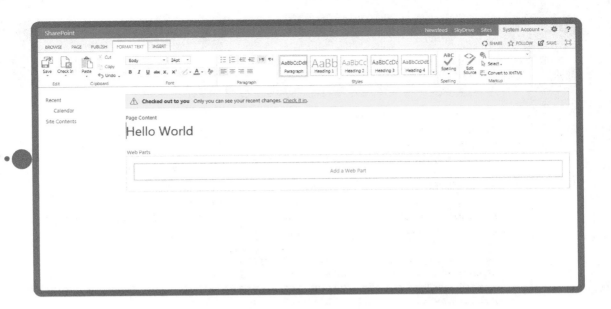

Like ASP.NET pages, the page layout begins with @ Page, but instead of referencing a master page, it simply states that the page layout is written in C# and inherits code from the SharePoint Server PublishingPageLayout code. Then there are several controls registered that are used throughout the page layout. After those Register tags, everything else in the page layout must be contained inside of a content placeholder. In this code, there are two content placeholders: PlaceHolderPageTitle, which overrides content in the master page's HTML <title> section, and PlaceHolderMain, which is the main content section in the master page.

Inside the first placeholder you see <SharePointWebControls:FieldValue>, which is a value control and is used to simply display a field (rather than allow it to be editable as you see next). In this case, PageTitle displays inside the HTML <title> section. In the next placeholder you see a <PublishingWebControls:RichHtmlField>, which is a field control that will be editable when the page is in Edit mode. Lastly, there is a Web Part zone, which is defined as <WebPartPages:WebPartZone>; this enables the content author to add any number of Web Parts to this page.

NOTE

Web Part zones are not the only place in which content authors can place and configure Web Parts. Content authors can place Web Parts anywhere within Wiki page content areas and in publishing HTML field controls. This is a powerful feature, but Web Part zones provide a nice way to have a designated area that arranges Web Parts horizontally or vertically in a controlled fashion.

EXAMPLE: CREATING A CUSTOM PAGE LAYOUT WITH SHAREPOINT DESIGNER 2013

1. Open your SharePoint Server site in SharePoint Designer 2013.

2. From the **Site Objects** menu on the left side, click **Page Layouts**.

3. From the ribbon, click **New Page Layout**.

4. From the New dialog box, use the following settings, and then click **OK**.

   - **Content Type Group**—Page Layout Content Types

   - **Content Type Name**—Article Page

   - **URL**—DemoLayout.aspx

   - **Title**—Demo Page Layout

5. Select the **Toolbox** pane on the right, scroll down to the bottom, and expand the section named **SharePoint Controls**.

6. If the Toolbox pane is not shown, click **View** from the ribbon and then **Task Panes ➤ Toolbox**.

7. Expand **Page Fields** and **Content Fields**. Page Fields shows all the site columns that were inherited from the parent content type. Content Fields shows all the site columns that were added to the actual content type from which the page layout was created.

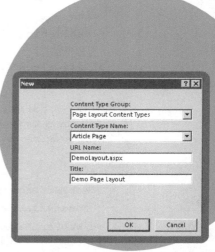

SharePoint Designer creates a basic page layout and opens it.

Replacing the GUID

When you drag fields from the Toolbox, SharePoint Designer unfortunately adds them with the behind-the-scenes SharePoint unique identifier (GUID) for the `FieldName`. So you end up with something like `f55c4d88-1f2e-4ad9-aaa8-819af4ee7ee8` instead of `PublishingPageContent`. If you want to improve your code readability, you can manually replace the GUID with the actual field name. To find the behind-the-scenes field name, navigate to Site Settings, and under Web Designer Galleries, click Site content types. Then click the content type that you are using for the page layout (in this case Article Page). From there, click the column that you are using for your field, and in your browser's URL, look for a section that starts with `Field=`. In this case you see `Field=PublishingPageContent`, so replace the GUID with `PublishingPageContent`.

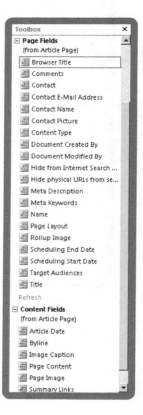

8. Add a field control to the page layout to allow authors to add content. Drag **Page Content** from the **Content Fields** into the `PlaceHolderMain`. Add an HTML `<div>` around the field control like this:

```
<div>
  <PublishingWebControls:RichHtmlField FieldName="f55c4d88-1f2e-4ad9-
    aaa8-
819af4ee7ee8" runat="server"></PublishingWebControls:RichHtmlField>
</div>
```

9. Add a Web Part zone to the page layout. For SharePoint Designer 2013 this can be done from the ribbon by clicking **Insert ➢ Web Part Zone**. If the button is grayed out, refresh the SharePoint Designer interface by pressing **F5**. Add the Web Part Zone in a `<div>` below the Page Content field like this:

```
<div>
  <WebPartPages:WebPartZone id="g_9A81CAACC0F1428EAEE87D345D2093C4"
  runat="server" title="Zone 1">
  </WebPartPages:WebPartZone>
</div>
```

10. Type **Ctrl+S** to save the page layout.

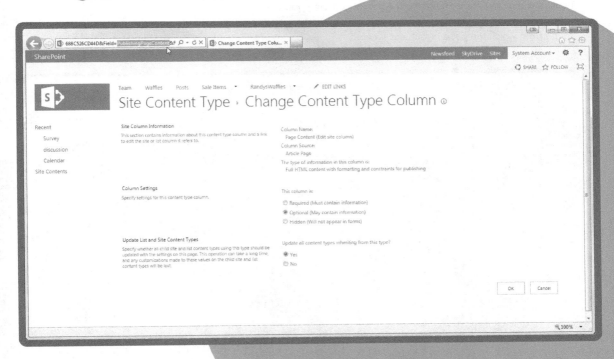

Using Edit Mode Panels to Hide and Show Page Layout Sections

Sometimes you may want to have a field control that shows only when a content author is editing the page; this is useful if you want to keep track of certain information on a page but not show it to regular users browsing the site. For example, a field control like that would come in handy if you want the author to be able to add and edit the article's date so that you can roll it up with a Web Part on another page and sort by date. Fortunately, doing this is a simple process.

EXAMPLE: ADDING AN EDITMODEPANEL AROUND THE FIELD CONTROL

1. Below the Web Part zone in the page layout from the previous example, add the following code:

```
<PublishingWebControls:EditModePanel runat="server">
</PublishingWebControls:EditModePanel>
```

2. Add the article date field control to the page layout. Drag **Article Date** from the **Content Fields** between the opening and closing <PublishingWebControls:EditModePanel> like this:

```
<PublishingWebControls:EditModePanel runat="server">
  <SharePointWebControls:DateTimeField
    FieldName="71316cea-40a0-49f3-8659-f0cefdbdbd4f" runat="server">
  </SharePointWebControls:DateTimeField>
</PublishingWebControls:EditModePanel>
```

3. Press **Ctrl+S** to save the page layout.

Completing your Custom Page Layout

Even though your page layout is created, you still need to check in a major version and test it before content authors can use it. This section describes how to do this.

EXAMPLE: PUBLISHING A PAGE LAYOUT

1. Click back on the **Page Layouts** item in the **Site Objects** menu in SharePoint Designer 2013, and then click the icon for DemoLayout.aspx.

2. On the ribbon, click **Check In**, select **Publish a Major Version**, and click **OK**.

Finally, you can test the new page layout by creating a page and switching its layout to the newly created page layout.

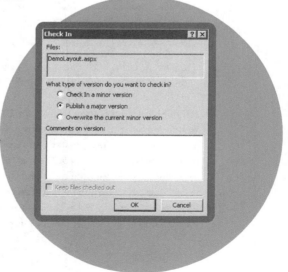

EXAMPLE: TESTING A PAGE LAYOUT

1. Click the **Settings menu ➤ Add a page**.

2. Give the page a name, and then click **Create**.

3. Select the new page layout from the ribbon by clicking **Page ➤ Page Layout ➤ Demo Page Layout**.

4. Edit the content and click **Save**. If you want other users to see the content, you also need to click **Publish**.

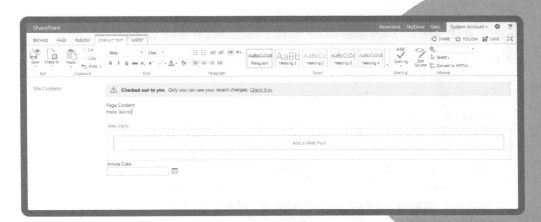

NOTE

The great thing about page layouts is if you make future changes to the page layout, all pages based on it will be updated automatically.

UPGRADING A SHAREPOINT 2010 MASTER PAGE TO 2013

Although creating custom SharePoint 2013 master pages from a starter master page is cool, you may be wondering what to do if you already have existing SharePoint 2010 branding that you want to use in SharePoint 2013. Unfortunately, you can't just apply a SharePoint 2010 master page to a 2013 site and have it function as expected. The master pages are set up similarly between the two versions though; for instance, they are both a similar file size and contain a ribbon that takes up a good portion of the code. That being said, there is a little work that needs to be done to properly update a 2010 master page to 2013. The easiest way to start is to compare your SharePoint 2010 master page to one of the starter master pages and make changes as needed.

Here are some of the high-level things that you need to think about changing for SharePoint 2013 master pages:

- The DOCTYPE should be XHTML 1.0 Strict or HTML5.

- The metatag that tells IE which version to target should be updated to IE10: `<meta http-equiv="X-UA-Compatible" content="IE=10" />`.

- Branding assets can be moved to the Master Page Gallery if you want, but it is also acceptable to keep them in the Style Library or the `_layouts` folder. Obviously, if you move the assets, their paths need to change in the master page.

- In SharePoint 2013, the main CSS file `corev15.css` is not automatically loaded, so you want to load it with `<SharePoint:CssRegistration Name="corev15.css" runat="server" />`.

- Many of the SharePoint controls in the `<head>` section and the beginning of the `<body>` section have been deprecated and/or replaced with new controls.

- CSS needs to be updated to reflect the new SharePoint 2013 CSS class naming used throughout the markup.

- The ribbon needs to be updated with either the one-line publishing ribbon or the much larger one from either an out-of-the-box or starter master page.

- The out-of-the-box search box control has been updated to: `<SharePoint:DelegateControl runat="server" ControlId="SmallSearchInputBox" Version="4"/>`.

- The available navigation `SiteMapProviders` have been updated including two that work with both structured and managed navigation: `GlobalNavigationSwitchableProvider` and `CurrentNavigationSwitchableProvider`.

- Be sure to check the list of required content placeholders from the "SharePoint Master Page Structure" section and update your master page accordingly.

These are just a few of the most obvious changes you need to make to a SharePoint 2010 master page to get it to work with SharePoint 2013. Because every master page is unique, there may be more issues that need to be addressed in your 2010 master page.

UNDERSTANDING SHAREPOINT SOLUTION PACKAGES

The SharePoint 2013 Design Manager includes a feature to export design packages, which is a great option for moving branding assets between site collections or environments. However, the feature itself doesn't provide much flexibility, and understanding its limitations can help you determine if the export design packages functionality will work well for your project. For example, the feature does not allow any flexibility for what gets packaged and instead includes all files that have been edited from the Master Page Gallery, Style Library, Theme Gallery, and Device Channels. The design package does not include

content pages, navigation settings, or anything from the term store. Another consideration is that this design package needs to be applied one site collection at a time, which can make applying updates more difficult if you have an implementation with more than one site collection. In general, many larger or more custom projects require additional functionality as part of the deployment, such as the ability to include custom code along with the branding assets. To truly create a customized branding solution, the best option is to make a SharePoint Solution or WSP and deploy it to production servers. The upcoming sections discuss some of the most common concepts related to branding deployments.

Customized and Uncustomized Files

Although the terms are generic sounding, customized and uncustomized files mean something specific in the SharePoint vernacular. If you've been around SharePoint for a while, you might have heard the terms *customized* and *uncustomized* as well as *ghosted* and *unghosted*.

All the files used to create the out-of-the-box sites are uncustomized and ghosted. Uncustomized is an attribute associated with a file that indicates that a file hasn't been modified. Ghosted means that the source of the file lives on the file system of the server and not in the content database. There is still a pointer in the content database (the ghost of the file) that tells SharePoint to look for the source of a file on the server's file system. In this case, when the page is requested, SharePoint still looks to the content database, but because the instance of the page does not include a source, the file is rendered from the file system.

Uncustomized files make it possible to have many copies of a file point to the same source—similar to how a template for a document works. For example, if you have many sites using the same page layout, you can make modifications to a single file, and every place that uses the uncustomized page layout is updated. This is helpful from a design perspective because it allows you to make changes easily.

A customized file is one that has been modified in any way through a mapped drive or by using SharePoint Designer. After a file has been customized, it becomes more difficult to apply updates on a broad scale. Because customized files are created by editing and because they limit the flexibility of applying updates, it is advisable to use care when making edits, especially in the production environment.

An unghosted file refers to a file whose source lives in the content database. In earlier versions of SharePoint, the terms customized and unghosted referred to the same concept, but with the introduction of sandbox solutions in SharePoint 2010, the meaning of the terms began to refer to uniquely different aspects.

For example, the export design functionality of Design Manager creates a sandbox solution to package branding files. The sandbox solution is never added to the file system of the server, therefore by definition its files are considered ghosted. But, the files it deploys are still in an uncustomized state. This is a bit tricky to follow at first since the terminology is vague. Technical aspects aside, the following list summarizes the most important considerations around this concept:

- Out-of-the-box files deploy in an uncustomized and ghosted state, which provides the greatest flexibility for updating on a broad scale. This can only be achieved with a full trust farm solution.

- Sandbox solutions deploy files in an uncustomized and unghosted state. These files must be deployed separately to each site collection, but updates can be broadly applied to files within the site collection.

- Once a file has been customized, it won't be updated with updates applied via a farm or sandbox solution.

- The export design functionality of Design Manager deploys files as a sandbox solution.

Uncustomized File — Customized File

For more information on customized and uncustomized files, see Andrew Connell's MSDN article here: `http://msdn.microsoft.com/en-us/library/cc406685.aspx`. It was written for SharePoint 2007 but the concepts still apply for SharePoint 2013.

Features and Solutions

The primary mechanism used to provision uncustomized instances of files in SharePoint is called a *feature*. A feature enables a developer to deploy files and other site customizations or functionality to a site collection or individual site. When activated, the feature deploys the files to SharePoint in an uncustomized state.

Although they have a generic-sounding name, features refer to something specific in SharePoint. Every feature includes a `Feature.xml` file that provides basic information (title, description, scope of deployment, and more), a unique ID, the name and location for an assembly, or one or more element manifest files. The element manifest file is what describes to SharePoint where to deploy the various files contained in the feature. When an assembly is referenced, usually it deploys files the same way that the element manifest would, except it requires compiled code instead of the Collaborative Application Markup Language (CAML) used by the elements file.

By themselves, features enable you to deploy branding assets in an uncustomized state, but the files related to the feature (`feature.xml`, element manifests, and the branding files to be deployed) ideally need a structured way to move everything around. SharePoint Solutions or, more simply, solutions are a sealed cabinet (`.CAB`) file with a `.WSP` extension. Solutions help to get files where they need to be in a safe way to help ensure the reliability of the SharePoint servers. They provide a mechanism for moving files between server farms like between development and production environments. In addition, solutions also provide a way to simultaneously deploy files across multiple servers in the farm.

SharePoint Branding Solutions

In SharePoint 2013 there are two types of solutions: farm solutions and sandboxed solutions. Farm solutions, which were available starting in SharePoint 2007, are typically deployed by server administrators and are definitely a preferred approach to the alternative of manually deploying files to multiple servers. However,

the challenge is that farm solutions can deploy almost any type of file to the server with full trust—from an administrator's perspective it is difficult to ensure that a farm solution isn't going to negatively impact a SharePoint farm. For this reason it is important to thoroughly test all farm solutions that are deployed.

From a branding perspective, farm solutions present a small challenge. Most custom branding files such as master pages, page layouts, CSS, or images are relatively harmless and easily could be deployed through the user interface or SharePoint Designer. But if you want to avoid customized files, sandboxed solutions are an option that can be uploaded and activated by Site Collection Administrators without a Farm Administrator's intervention.

In concept, a sandboxed solution is a safe way to deploy files to a specific site collection on your SharePoint server. Farm administrators can actually validate and monitor a sandboxed solution, which allows them to define automated policies about what is allowed and not allowed in the sandbox. Sandboxed solutions deploy in a partial trust state, so there are some limitations to the type of code that can be run in the sandbox. For the most part though, this shouldn't limit the ability to deploy most branding files. For more information on sandboxed solutions, see *Developing, Deploying, and Monitoring Sandboxed Solutions in SharePoint 2010* by Paul Stubbs (http://msdn.microsoft.com/en-us/magazine/ee335711.aspx).

Both farm solutions and sandboxed solutions are the preferred ways to deploy your branding files, but which one should you choose? Sandboxed solutions provide an additional layer of protection, which allows files to deploy to the server while minimizing the impact to the server. Because of this, they are the only option for deploying a custom branding solution to Office 365 SharePoint Online sites. However, sandbox solutions have limitations; they can't do some powerful things that farm solutions can do. For instance, you cannot create a feature receiver to automatically apply your branding when new sites are created. For this reason, typically larger or more complex branding solutions that aren't installed into the cloud are set up as farm solutions.

The following table shows the three options for getting files onto a server and their pros and cons:

USING A MAPPED DRIVE OR CREATING EXPORT FROM DESIGN MANAGER	SANDBOXED SOLUTIONS	FARM SOLUTIONS
Fine for development and small implementations	Option of choice for Office 365	Requires a farm administrator to deploy
Creates customized files	Deploys files to the site collection only	Files can be used by all site collections
Inflexible	Limited functionality	Greater flexibility
	Low risk	More risk

You can download the completed Visual Studio solution for the WaffleNET example you saw earlier from the downloadable code for this chapter. This can serve as both a great educational tool for learning how to create a SharePoint branding solution, or it could be modified and used directly in your own SharePoint projects.

NOTE

For a detailed explanation of creating a branding solution for SharePoint 2013, you can read *Deploying Branding Solutions for SharePoint 2010 Sites using Sandboxed Solutions* by Ted Pattison (http://msdn.microsoft.com/en-us/library/gg447066.aspx).

SUMMARY

- HTML-based master pages created with the Design Manager feature in SharePoint 2013 were intended to be used with publishing sites. For truly custom branding that applies across SharePoint including collaboration sites, it may be necessary to create custom master pages by hand the classic way.

- In traditional ASP.NET websites, ASPX content pages refer to master pages that provide a unified look and feel. Content pages have content controls that can override content placeholders in the master page.

- SharePoint master pages work similarly to ASP.NET except that pages don't refer directly to a specific master page; instead, they reference Site or System master pages that can be applied from either the Site Settings menu in publishing sites or with PowerShell or SharePoint Designer 2013. SharePoint master pages also have a set of required content placeholders that are used throughout the various pages of a SharePoint site.

- Collaboration sites have the Minimal Download Strategy (MDS) feature turned on by default. This feature speeds up page loading but requires the use of AjaxDelta controls placed throughout your master page, surrounding areas that dynamically change from page to page.

- Starter master pages like those available at `http://startermasterpages.codeplex.com` are useful for creating new custom SharePoint branding.

- Page layouts are another big part of SharePoint branding. They are based on content types, which define site columns that can eventually be used as editable field controls in pages.

- SharePoint branding should be packaged into a solution package known as a WSP for deployment to production servers. Solutions can be created as either farm (which runs at the whole farm) or sandboxed (which runs at the site collection). If you are deploying to Office 365 and SharePoint Online you should use a solution marked as sandboxed.

8

ADVANCED
SHAREPOINT
BRANDING TASKS

What's In This Chapter

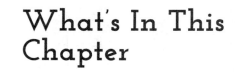

With any SharePoint branding project, most people think only about the major tasks, such as creating the master page and working with the HTML and CSS. Although these tasks are certainly the biggest ones, a number of other important tasks are usually required to fully achieve the intended creative design. This chapter is a collection of topics to help you create a refined and polished final product.

WORKING WITH NAVIGATION

SharePoint 2013 provides many valuable options for controlling the way navigation looks using just the web user interface. However, several things can be changed only by editing controls directly in master pages. Whether you look at the global navigation at the top of the page or the current navigation, (Quick Launch) that shows on the left, SharePoint primarily uses two controls to show navigation: SiteMapDataSource and AspMenu. If you want to have better control of how navigation shows in your branding, it's a good idea to understand these two controls.

SiteMapDataSource

The `SiteMapDataSource` control is essentially a data source that can be used by controls in ASP.NET to display information about the hierarchical arrangement of sites and pages throughout your SharePoint site. The most typical use for `SiteMapDataSources` is to show navigation information, but they can also be used for tree views and breadcrumbs. A typical `SiteMapDataSource` might look like this:

`ShowStartingNode`—This setting tells the control whether to render the starting node. In this case it's set to **False** because the root node of a SharePoint navigation hierarchy is often just the parent container and is not intended to be rendered.

`SiteMapProvider`—This is the most critical setting in the control; it can point to one of many `SiteMaps` available by default in SharePoint. You may want to change this setting to tightly control what SharePoint shows for navigation items.

```
<asp:SiteMapDataSource ShowStartingNode="False"
SiteMapProvider="SPNavigationProvider"
id="topSiteMap" runat="server" StartingNodeUrl="sid:1002"/>
```

`Id`—The ID shows how navigation controls refer to this `SiteMapDataSource`.

`StartingNodeUrl`—This is a confusing setting, but essentially it tells SharePoint where to look for the beginning of the navigation elements. `sid:1002` is a code that SharePoint understands as the topmost navigation element in its navigation. This is something that would not be changed in a typical custom master page.

Looking at the out-of-the-box Seattle master page, you can see that Microsoft surrounds the `SiteMapDataSource` with a delegate control like this:

```
<SharePoint:DelegateControl runat="server"
 ControlId="TopNavigationDataSource" Id="topNavigationDelegate">
 <Template_Controls>
 <asp:SiteMapDataSource ShowStartingNode="False"
  SiteMapProvider="SPNavigationProvider" id="topSiteMap"
  runat="server" StartingNodeUrl="sid:1002"/>
 </Template_Controls>
</SharePoint:DelegateControl>
```

It does this so that `Seattle.master` can be applied to any site in SharePoint, whether you have SharePoint Foundation or SharePoint Server, and even if the site is a publishing site or a team site. The delegate control swaps out the sitemap with the appropriate choice for that site automatically. If you want to have more control over this process, you can remove the delegate control from around the `SiteMapDataSource` and set the `SiteMapProvider` to match your wanted navigation.

You can see all the available Sitemaps for your SharePoint server by looking at the `web.config` file in the root of the web server. (Typically this would be located on the server in a subfolder of `C:\inetpub\wwwroot\wss\VirtualDirectories\`.) If you search the `web.config` file for `<providers>`, you see a section that includes many different sitemaps and a brief description of each. The sitemaps are different depending upon what version of SharePoint is installed and what site template was used to create the site you are looking at. Many of these sitemaps aren't appropriate for either the latest version of SharePoint or even for navigation controls.

SharePoint Foundation 2013 uses the sitemap named `SPNavigationProvider` to show basic navigation in the top link bar and Quick Launch navigation. SharePoint Server, on the other hand, has more options available, which include the old 2010-style Structured Navigation and the new Managed Navigation based on Managed Metadata term sets. Here are the various publishing navigation sitemaps:

- `GlobalNavigation`—Shows Structured Navigation items in the global navigation for this website. This navigation is shown at the top of the page in most websites.

- `CurrentNavigation`—Shows Structured Navigation items to display in current navigation for this website. This navigation is shown on the side of the page in most websites.

- `GlobalNavigationTaxonomyProvider`—Similar to `GlobalNavigation` but used for Managed Navigation instead of Structured Navigation.

- `CurrentNavigationTaxonomyProvider`—Similar to the `CurrentNavigation` but used for Managed Navigation instead of Structured Navigation.

- `GlobalNavigationSwitchableProvider`—Shows `GlobalNavigation` or `GlobalNavigationTaxonomyProvider` depending on which is selected in the Navigation Settings.

- `CurrentNavigationSwitchableProvider`—Shows `CurentNavigation` or `CurrentNavigationTaxonomyProvider` depending on which is selected in the Navigation Settings.

AspMenu

The `AspMenu` control is what actually renders navigation items based on a selected `SiteMapDataSource`. Here is a sample AspMenu control from a typical SharePoint master page:

`DataSourceID`—Refers to the specific `SiteMapDataSource` that can provide the data for the navigation that will be rendered.

`UseSimpleRendering`—This property was added with SharePoint 2010 to indicate whether a simple HTML unordered list is used for rendering the navigation or if the legacy ASP.NET table-based rendering will be used. You should typically set this to **True** unless you have a good reason not to do this. For example, if you have styled navigation from SharePoint 2007 that you are bringing forward to SharePoint 2013 and don't have time to restyle the rendering.

```
<SharePoint:AspMenu ID="TopNavigationMenu" Runat="server"
  EnableViewState="false" DataSourceID="topSiteMap"
  AccessKey="<%$Resources:wss,navigation_accesskey%>"
  UseSimpleRendering="true" UseSeparateCss="false"
  Orientation="Horizontal" StaticDisplayLevels="2"
  AdjustForShowStartingNode="true"
  MaximumDynamicDisplayLevels="2" SkipLinkText=""
/>
```

`Orientation`—This property can be set to **Horizontal** or **Vertical** depending on which direction you want to render the navigation. Obviously, you would want to use horizontal for top navigation and vertical for side navigation.

This control has a lot of different options available to change its behavior, but the following two properties are probably the most important to understand. They indicate how many levels of navigation to show normally and how many will show when you hover over an item and show its children as fly-outs. These are two settings that many designers would like Microsoft to include in the web interface's navigation settings because it would be useful for site owners to be able to change them easily as opposed to them being editable only through code.

`StaticDisplayLevels`—This property represents the number of levels of hierarchical navigation nodes that SharePoint shows by default in the navigation. For example, if the `AspMenu` orientation is set to **Horizontal** and this property is set to **2**, you can see the first and second levels of navigation shown in a line horizontally by default on the page.

`MaximumDynamicDisplayLevels`—This property represents the number of levels of hierarchical navigations that show dynamically as fly-outs. The levels that show here are counted after the number of levels that are set to show for `StaticDisplayLevels`. For example, if `StaticDisplayLevels` is set to **3** and `MaximumDynamicDisplayLevels` is set to **2**, you see the first three levels of navigation shown on the page automatically; then you see the next two levels of navigation as dynamic fly-outs only when you mouse over their parent nodes. The actual navigation that shows is determined by a

number of other factors, such as if you use structured or managed navigation and whether the navigation settings in the UI are set to show subsites.

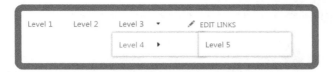

Tree View

The tree view is an interesting feature that provides an expandable view of the site structure shown as a hierarchical tree. You have probably seen it used in collaboration sites, in the bottom of the left navigation.

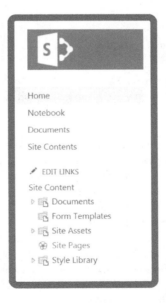

If you don't see the tree view on your site, there is an easy menu for showing or hiding it available from **Site Settings ➢ Look and Feel ➢ Tree view.** From this menu you can hide or show either the tree view or the entire Quick Launch menu for the SharePoint site.

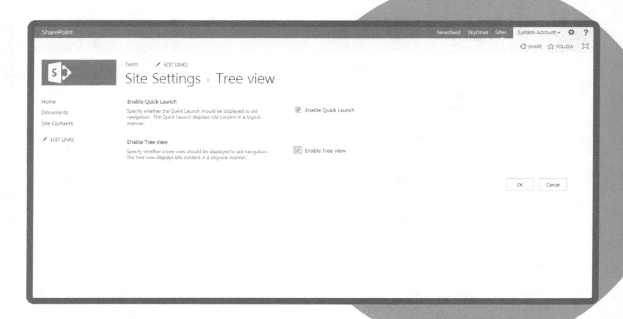

In a lot of ways, the tree view is difficult to work with from a branding perspective. This is mostly because it adds an expandable area inside of a scrolling iFrame to an already cramped place on the page, but also because there is a lot going on dynamically in the HTML for the tree view. It's tempting to just say you aren't going to support the tree view in a custom branded SharePoint site, but if you work on a collaborative intranet site, this option might not be wise. Many business users find value in the tree view because it adds in metadata navigation for navigating or filtering the navigation options using metadata terms.

Because the tree view is used primarily as a self-contained piece of functionality, you can add the tree view to your master page simply by copying the default delegate control from either the default Seattle.master or a starter master page. Here is the standard code that creates the tree view:

```
<SharePoint:DelegateControl runat="server"
 ControlId="TreeViewAndDataSource">
 <Template_Controls>
  <SharePoint:SPHierarchyDataSourceControl
   runat="server"
   id="TreeViewDataSourceV4"
   RootContextObject="Web"
   IncludeDiscussionFolders="true" />
  <SharePoint:SPRememberScroll runat="server"
   id="TreeViewRememberScrollV4"
   onscroll="javascript:
    _spRecordScrollPositions(this);"
   style="overflow: auto;">
   <SharePoint:SPTreeView id="WebTreeViewV4"
    runat="server" ShowLines="false"
     DataSourceId="TreeViewDataSourceV4"
     ExpandDepth="0"
     SelectedNodeStyle-CssClass="ms-tv-selected"
    NodeStyle-CssClass="ms-tv-item"
     SkipLinkText="" NodeIndent="12"
    ExpandImageUrl="/_layouts/15/images/
     tvclosed.png?rev=23"
    ExpandImageUrlRtl="/_layouts/15/images/
     tvclosedrtl.png?rev=23"
    CollapseImageUrl="/_layouts/15/images/
     tvopen.png?rev=23"
    CollapseImageUrlRtl="/_layouts/15/images/
     tvopenrtl.png?rev=23"
    NoExpandImageUrl="/_layouts/15/images/
     tvblank.gif?rev=23">
   </SharePoint:SPTreeView>
  </SharePoint:SPRememberScroll>
 </Template_Controls>
</SharePoint:DelegateControl>
```

USING TRADITIONAL BREADCRUMBS

Breadcrumbs—those fun, little navigational links frequently seen at the top of websites—are one thing that SharePoint 2013 doesn't handle well out-of-the-box. For SharePoint 2013, Microsoft decided to remove the useful (but fairly ugly) hierarchical breadcrumbs that were available in a pop-out menu at the top left of the ribbon for SharePoint 2010. However, by default there is something similar to a bread-crumb shown in a large font near the top of the page body.

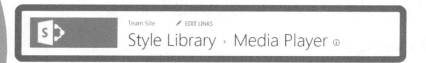

This section is rendered using the `SPTitleBreadcrumb` control as well as a content placeholder. Here is the actual code as it is seen in `Seattle.master`:

```
<SharePoint:AjaxDelta id="DeltaPlaceHolderPageTitleInTitleArea"
 runat="server">
 <asp:ContentPlaceHolder id="PlaceHolderPageTitleInTitleArea"
  runat="server">
  <SharePoint:SPTitleBreadcrumb runat="server"
   RenderCurrentNodeAsLink="true"
   SiteMapProvider="SPContentMapProvider"
   CentralAdminSiteMapProvider="SPXmlAdminContentMapProvider">
   <PATHSEPARATORTEMPLATE>
    <SharePoint:ClusteredDirectionalSeparatorArrow
     runat="server" />
   </PATHSEPARATORTEMPLATE>
  </SharePoint:SPTitleBreadcrumb>
 </asp:ContentPlaceHolder>
</SharePoint:AjaxDelta>
```

Although this is useful for showing list and library information and looks a lot like breadcrumbs, the user actually isn't provided with traditional breadcrumb functionality that shows the parent sites above the current page.

Fortunately, there is a traditional ASP.NET control that you can use in your master pages, which is a close approximation of typical website breadcrumbs, known as `SiteMapPath`. Here is the simplest way to use it in your master page and an example of the result:

```
<SharePoint:AjaxDelta ID="SiteMap" BlockElement="true" runat="server">
 <asp:SiteMapPath runat="server"/>
</SharePoint:AjaxDelta>
```

Home > Level 2 Site > **Level 2 Site**

The control also takes a property `SiteMapProvider` that enables you to pass in a specific provider, much like the `AspMenu` you learned about earlier. However, it is typically best to leave this property blank because you are essentially telling SharePoint to use the default `SiteMapProvider` for the specific type of site that is viewed.

CREATING A DYNAMIC BACK TO HOME LINK

If you followed the custom master page example in Chapter 7, you have seen the use of `$SPUrl` tokens to make a dynamic link back to the top of the site collection. This token can be useful when creating branding that applies to larger SharePoint sites, especially those with multiple sites or site collections.

WARNING

The `$SPUrl` token is only available to SharePoint Server because it is related to the publishing features. If you use a Foundation site, you must manually make relative links such as `/_catalogs/masterpage`, which would go to the top of the web application root and then navigate down to `_catalogs` and `masterpage`.

$SPUrl has two available tokens, ~site and ~sitecollection, which can navigate to either the top of the current site or the top of the current site collection, respectively. Here is an example of using $SPUrl to find a CSS file by looking at the root of the site collection:

```
<SharePoint:CssRegistration ID="CssRegistration1"
 name="&lt;% $SPUrl:~sitecollection/_catalogs/masterpage/
  WaffleNet/style.css %&gt;"
 runat="server" after="SharepointCssFile" />
```

Notice that the entire $SPUrl is surrounded by <% and >%, which are essentially HTML escaped versions of the ASP.NET inline open and close tags <% … %>. They tell ASP.NET that there is some code that needs to be interpreted in this section.

Although this usage of $SPUrl is fairly straightforward, you can also see some instances in which the token shortcut is used without the $SPUrl section. This is because some controls are wired to understand the tokens by themselves. SPLinkButton is one such control. Here is an example of an SPLink-Button wrapped around a SiteLogoImage to create a logo that links back to the top level of a site collection:

```
<SharePoint:SPLinkButton runat="server"
 NavigateUrl="~sitecollection/_catalogs/masterpage/waffles/logo.png">
 <SharePoint:SiteLogoImage ID="myLogo" LogoImageUrl="&lt;%
  $SPUrl:~sitecollection/_catalogs/masterpage/waffles/logo.png %&gt;"
  AlternateText="Back to Home" runat="server" />
</SharePoint:SPLinkButton>
```

Notice that the NavigateUrl property of SPLinkButton only has the ~sitecollection token, whereas the LogoImageUrl property of SiteLogoImage needs the full $SPUrl and the beginning and end tags to function properly.

HANDLING ANONYMOUS USERS

Anonymous users, those visitors to your site that are just browsing the pages or that have no credentials to authenticate, have unique needs that may need to be addressed in your SharePoint branding. You must first decide if your site will support anonymous browsing. By default SharePoint has anonymous access turned off for web applications, so if you decide to enable it there are a couple things you need to do to provide access.

EXAMPLE: TURNING ON ANONYMOUS ACCESS

1 From **Central Administration** on the server, click **Manage web applications**.

2 Select the desired web application, and from the ribbon click **Authentication Providers**.

3 From the list of authentication providers, click **Default**. If you have more than one authentication provider, you must click the zone that anonymous users would be accessing the site from.

4 Check the box for **Enable Anonymous Access**, and click **Save**. The page does not refresh when you click Save in this dialog box, so just close the box after clicking **Save**.

At this point the web application permits anonymous users to reach the site, but you still need to allow anonymous access for the particular SharePoint site.

5 On your SharePoint site, click **Site Settings ➤ Users and Permissions ➤ Site permissions**.

6 From the ribbon, click **Anonymous Access**.

7 In the Anonymous Access dialog, select **Anonymous users can access: Enter Web site** and click **OK**.

Your site is now enabled for anonymous access, but if you have custom branding assets, they all need to be checked in as major versions and published before anonymous users can see the site. You can learn more about this process from Chapter 7.

Now that you have a site that is viewable anonymously, there are a few more things to consider, namely whether the ribbon should show and how anonymous users can authenticate into the site. Typically, anonymous users are consumers of content on your site and won't need to edit pages or lists. Because of this, they usually don't need to see the ribbon at the top of SharePoint. This is especially true for public-facing SharePoint sites, where the ribbon is not only unnecessary but also changes the typical scrolling behavior of the website.

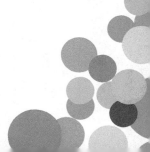

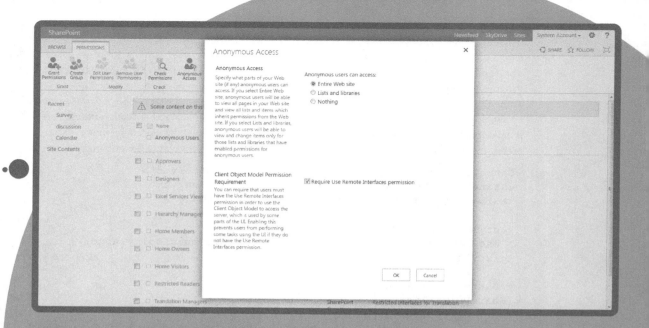

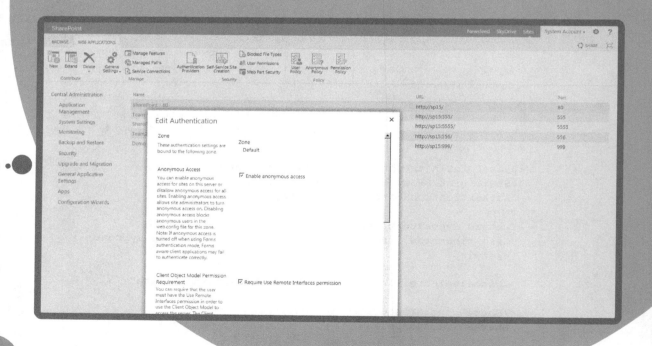

Hiding the ribbon is already handled if you use the Design Manager to create an HTML master page, or if you use the shorter `PublishingRibbon` control in a custom master page. This is not the case if you use SharePoint Foundation or the longer ribbon code included with the out-of-the-box master pages. If you want to manually hide the ribbon, you can use `SPSecurityTrimmedControl` to show and hide content based on whether the user is anonymous or authenticated via the `AuthenticationRestrictions` property. This property can be set to either `AnonymousUsersOnly` or `AuthenticatedUsersOnly` to show content to users based on their authentication status. Here is an example that would hide the ribbon for anonymous users. It could be placed anywhere in the master page, but for readability it might be best to add this code right before the ribbon code:

```
<SharePoint:AjaxDelta id="DeltaLogin" runat="server">
 <SharePoint:SPSecurityTrimmedControl runat="server"
  AuthenticationRestrictions="AnonymousUsersOnly">

  <style type="text/css">
   #s4-ribbonrow, #suiteBar { visibility:hidden;display:none; }
  </style>

 </SharePoint:SPSecurityTrimmedControl>
</SharePoint:AjaxDelta>
```

In the middle of the control is a style that can hide the ribbon; the style will be added only to the page for anonymous users.

Another thing to consider when hiding the ribbon for anonymous users is that you will also be hiding the default login control, which is included at the top right of the ribbon. This can be a problem for users that do need to authenticate because they will see the site in anonymous mode first and not have a way to log in. One way to handle this is to educate your users about how they need to navigate manually to `/_layouts/15/Authenticate.aspx` (or any URL in Site Settings) to launch the authentication process. Although this would save you some effort, it's not the most elegant solution. Luckily, you can use the same `SPSecurityTrimmedControl` to add in the welcome menu (which is also the login control when you aren't yet authenticated) for anonymous users only. Here is the update code that includes a style to hide the ribbon and the welcome control:

```
<SharePoint:AjaxDelta id="DeltaLogin" runat="server">
 <SharePoint:SPSecurityTrimmedControl runat="server"
  AuthenticationRestrictions="AnonymousUsersOnly">

  <style type="text/css">
   #s4-ribbonrow, #suiteBar { visibility:hidden;display:none; }
  </style>

  <wssuc:Welcome runat="server" EnableViewState="false" />

 </SharePoint:SPSecurityTrimmedControl>
</SharePoint:AjaxDelta>
```

This simply adds a Sign In link to the page rather haphazardly; you may want to spend some more time styling it to match with the rest of your branding.

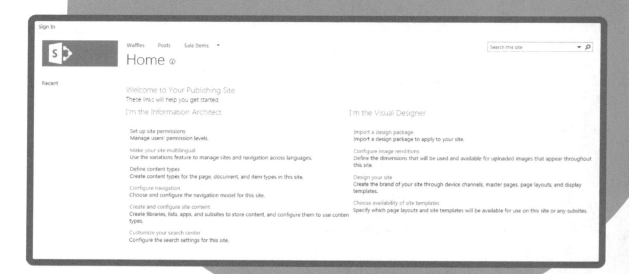

WARNING

Depending on the master page that is used, particularly master pages that are created with the Design Manager, the welcome control is registered at the top of the master page with the prefix `wssucw` and other times it is registered to the prefix `wssuc`. This frustrating inconsistency can cause the preceding code to have an error. If you run into this error, you can change the line to `<wssucw:Welcome runat="server" EnableViewState="false">`.

WORKING WITH DEVICE CHANNELS

If you've read Chapter 5, "Using the Design Manager to Start a Design in SharePoint," or played with the Design Manager, you have probably seen the option (typically listed as step 2) for Managing Device Channels. This topic was moved from Chapter 5 because in a lot of ways it doesn't make sense to think about device channels until after you understand the basics of making master pages.

Device channels are a feature of SharePoint Server publishing, so you cannot use them with Foundation or basic team sites. They can be thought of simply as a way of declaring rules for specific devices that can then be used to decide which master page to apply to a site or even to change certain parts of a page only for those devices. For example, you could set up a device channel for Apple iOS devices and another for Microsoft Surface tablets and show different branding, either subtly changed or completely different, depending upon which device is used to browse your SharePoint site.

Device channels work by looking for keywords in the browser's user agent, a string of text that is sent to the server by every browser to identify its characteristics. For example, here is the user agent string for the Safari browser on Apple's iPad:

```
Mozilla/5.0 (iPad; U; CPU OS 3_2_1 like Mac OS X; en-us)
AppleWebKit/531.21.10 (KHTML, like Gecko) Mobile/7B405
```

Because user agent strings can change as new OS versions are released, you can use a portion of the string (like "iPad") as a wildcard keyword when targeting browsers with device channels.

NOTE

Device channels are not the same thing as media queries in CSS3. Device channels enable you to change the display based on the browser that is visiting your site, whereas media queries enable you to change styles based on browser capabilities such as resolution, orientation, width, height, and so on. You can actually use both of these technologies together to create truly responsive mobile experiences in SharePoint.

Creating a Device Channel

Creating Device Channels in SharePoint 2013 is actually simple; you can access the menu from either the Design Manager or through **Site Settings** ➢ **Look and Feel** ➢ **Device Channels**. If you haven't created any device channels yet, you see the list contains only the default device channel applied to all of SharePoint. The following fields are used to define Device Channels:

- **Active**—Use this check box to mark device channels as activated or deactivated on your site.

- **Name**—The name that shows in the user interface for this specific device channel.

- **Alias**—The identifier that can be used with Device Channel panels, which you learn more about in a bit.

- **Description**—Optionally, you can give the device channel a description.

- **Device Inclusion Rules**—Enables you to specify user agent substrings that SharePoint can use to decide what device channel to apply. You can enter several substrings on separate lines, and SharePoint will look through all of them.

You could try to create a device channel for the iPad but that device would be a little difficult for everyone to test. Instead, you can create a device channel for a freely downloadable browser such as Google's Chrome browser. Device channels can be created for any browser that sends a user agent string, not just mobile devices. If you want to find out what the user agent string looks like for a particular browser, you can use a free web service such as http://whatsmyuseragent.com/.

The user agent string for the latest version of Google Chrome is as follows:

```
Mozilla/5.0 (Windows NT 6.1; WOW64) AppleWebKit/537.11 (KHTML, like
Gecko) Chrome/23.0.1271.97 Safari/537.11
```

To make a device channel that matches this, you need to pick a substring inside of this text that you think would be unique to the browser you are targeting. In this case the word "Chrome" appears in the user agent so that should work well.

To create a new one click New Item and fill in the following fields; then click Save:

- **Name**—Chrome
- **Alias**—Chrome
- **Device Inclusion Rules**—Chrome
- **Active**—Checked

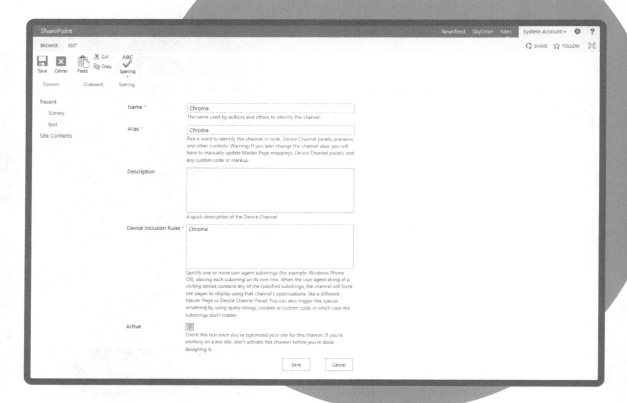

At this point you have a device channel created, but you need to apply a master page to the device channel before you can see it in action.

NOTE

If more than one device channel could match a specific browser, SharePoint applies whichever channel appears first in this list. If you need to change the order of the device channels, there is an easy method via the Reorder Channels button on the ribbon for the device channel page.

Applying a Master Page to a Device Channel

Applying a master page to a specific device channel is also easy. Start by clicking **Site Settings** ➢ **Look and Feel** ➢ **Master page**. Now that you have a device channel created, you can see more than one option under the **Site Master Page** settings. In this case you have one for Chrome, and you always see the Default device channel. The default behavior is to have all new device channels set to follow the default channel; in other words, they will show whatever master page is already set for the site.

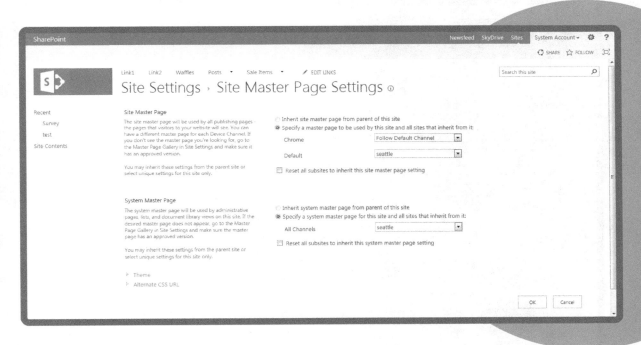

From here you can set the master page from the Chrome device channel to a unique master page and have everything else use the default setting. For example, you could select the WaffleNet master page from the previous chapter to display only for Chrome browsers, and have everyone else continue to see the default Seattle master page.

You have a few options for testing your newly applied device channel. Obviously, the easiest way to test would be to just download Chrome and visit the site to see a different master page than you would from Internet Explorer. But what if you don't have Chrome, or more commonly, what if you don't have the expensive mobile device you are trying to make a device channel for? Microsoft gives you an easy way to test any device. Simply append `DeviceChannel=YourDeviceChannel` to the end of the URL like this:

```
http://RandysWaffles/Pages/default.aspx?DeviceChannel=Chrome
```

This allows you to choose a device channel and see the site through that browser's "eyes." You can also access this feature from any page that you are editing: from the ribbon click the **Page** tab and then in the **Page Actions** section click **Preview**.

Device Channel Panels

Applying master pages to device channels is a great way to completely change the look of a site based on the browsing device, but in some cases it can introduce more maintenance overhead to manage multiple master pages. What if you want to have one master page but change out specific parts of the UI based on the browsing device? Microsoft has provided a control for this purpose, the Device Channel Panel. (Say that three times fast!)

Device Channel Panels are available from the Snippet Gallery for adding to HTML-based Design Manager master pages, but for this chapter you will focus on using the actual control in custom master pages that you create without the Design Manager. Device Channel Panels can be used in either master pages to affect all pages in a site, or they can be added to individual page layouts to affect certain pages. Here is what the code looks like for a typical Device Channel Panel. First, you need to add a register tag at the top of the master page or page layout to bring in the publishing web controls:

```
<%@Register Tagprefix="Publishing"
 Namespace="Microsoft.SharePoint.Publishing.WebControls"
 Assembly="Microsoft.SharePoint.Publishing, Version=15.0.0.0,
 Culture=neutral, PublicKeyToken=71e9bce111e9429c"%>
```

Then wherever you want the special content to appear, add the Device Channel Panel like this:

```
<Publishing:DeviceChannelPanel runat="server"
 IncludedChannels="Chrome">
 This will only show for Chrome!
</Publishing:DeviceChannelPanel>
```

The key property for the panel is the IncludedChannels, which tells SharePoint which device channel aliases to look for to include this content. You can list more than one channel alias, separating them by commas. In this case This will only show for Chrome! would show only when the Chrome device channel is applied. After you do any testing with this, be sure to change the master page settings back to **Follow Default Channel** at least until you get the hang of things; otherwise, you might have a different master page applied for the channel when working on future examples.

The previous code example was rather arbitrary; a more useful exercise for Device Channel Panels would be to change the arrangement of the page based on the device channel. For example, you could hide the Quick Launch left menu for devices such as the iPhone only. In the following code, the Device Channel Panel is set to override the applied styles if an iPhone device channel is being applied. Keep in mind you would need to set up a corresponding device channel with an alias of "iPhone" that targets an iPhone Safari browser user agent before you could use this panel. This code could be placed anywhere in a master page, but for readability, it might make sense to place it directly above the Quick Launch controls.

```
<Publishing:DeviceChannelPanel runat="server"
 IncludedChannels="iPhone">
 <style type="text/css">
  #sideNavBox { display: none; }
  #contentBox { margin-left: 20px; }
 </style>
</Publishing:DeviceChannelPanel>
```

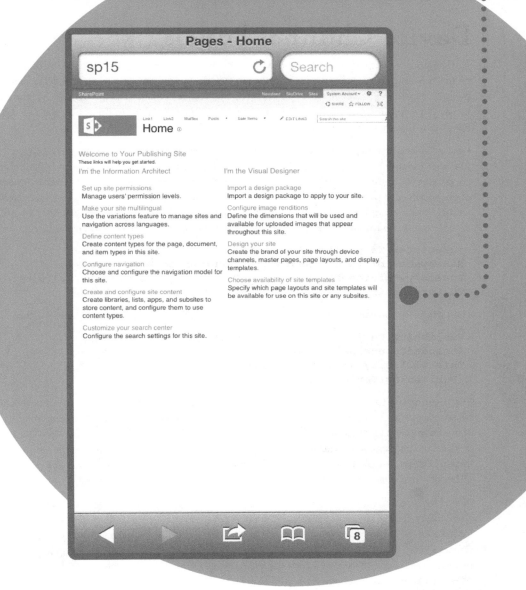

When this Device Channel Panel code displays, the styles hide the Quick Launch menu and decrease the left margin on the main content area to expand to fill the extra room. If you have an iPhone, you can test the Device Channel Panel; if not, you can use one of the methods previously shown to preview the site as an iPhone.

WARNING

One thing that you can't use Device Channel Panels for is Web Part zones. You can embed preconfigured Web Parts in Device Channel Panels, but zones are not supported. If you need Web Parts to leverage device channels, you can actually use JavaScript to check which panel is being applied and react accordingly. For more information about this, see "Plan device channels in SharePoint Server 2013" at http://msdn.microsoft.com/en-us/library/jj862343.aspx.

WORKING WITH MY SITES

If you have done any work with previous versions of SharePoint, you have probably heard of My Sites, which enable users to easily share information about themselves and their work in a central location. After My Sites are configured, you can access your My Site from several of the links on the top right of the ribbon including **Newsfeed**, **SkyDrive**, **Sites**, and from **USER NAME** ➤ **About Me**.

My Sites Architecture

Architecturally speaking, My Sites are a bit different than dealing with a normal SharePoint site. At the highest level you must know that My Sites have both a My Site host, which is a shared Site Collection between all users, and a personal site, which is a separate site collection created for each My Site user. Pages such as the Newsfeed and About Me are served from the shared My Site host, whereas pages such as SkyDrive and Sites are served from your personal site.

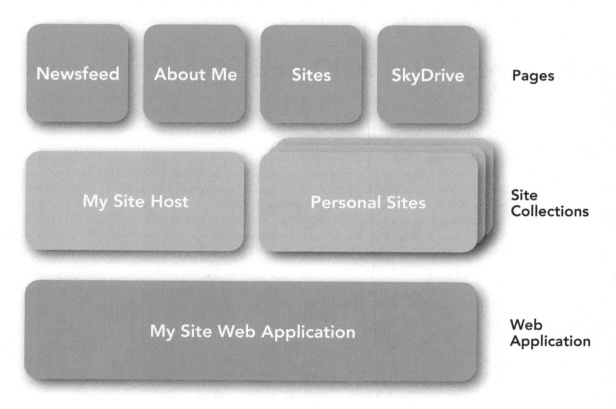

You can tell the difference between them by looking at the URL; pages that use the personal site typically have /personal/<name of user>/ in the URL. You can learn more about how My Sites are configured by reading "Plan for My Sites in SharePoint Server 2013" at http://technet.microsoft.com/en-us/library/cc262500.aspx.

Because of the way My Sites are set up with a shared Site Collection for the host and individual site collections for the personal sites, actually applying branding to these site collections becomes a bit more challenging than a typical SharePoint site. If you had rights to the My Site host site collection, you could certainly still map a drive to the master page gallery and create and edit master pages, and they would affect all of the user's Newsfeeds. But for the personal sites, you would be editing only one user's master page. Any new personal site would not show the branding because new personal sites are generated on-the-fly when a user first clicks on one of the My Sites links. In general, applying branding to My Sites is better left to a SharePoint Solution (WSP) created with Visual Studio. For more information on creating a Visual Studio solution for My Sites, see the Starter SharePoint My Site Customization CodePlex project at http://drisgill.com/go/mysites-solution. This project is currently set up for 2010 but the concepts should be similar for 2013.

NOTE

My Sites is an area of SharePoint in which the Design Manager cannot be used to create HTML-based master pages. If you want to brand My Sites, you must create a custom master page.

My Sites 2010 and 2013 Differences

In SharePoint 2010, branding My Sites involved two master pages; the My Site host used a special master page called mysite.master, whereas the personal site used the typical default.master. In SharePoint 2013, both sections use mysite15.master for almost everything specific to My Sites. However, there are still some instances inside of My Site in which you can create typical SharePoint sites. For example, if you create a personal team site or blog site inside of your My Site, these sites would use the typical seattle.master rather than the specific mysite15.master. Another key difference between SharePoint 2010 and 2013 master pages is that in 2010, Microsoft added a global navigation bar across the top of the My Sites pages. Alternatively, SharePoint 2013 My Sites shares the same top Suite Bar as a typical SharePoint site would. This section focuses on the mysite15 master page because anything that uses the default seattle master page can be branded using methods learned throughout the other chapters in this book.

In many ways, the default My Site branding is similar to typical SharePoint branding with a few key changes. The following diagram highlights the major differences between a My Sites master page and a typical SharePoint master page.

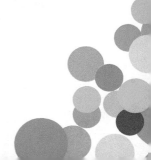

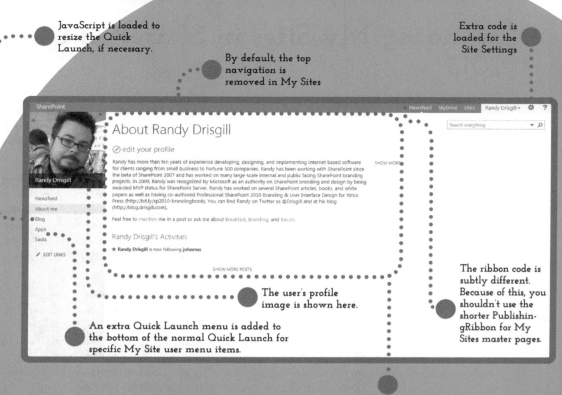

JavaScript is loaded to resize the Quick Launch, if necessary.

By default, the top navigation is removed in My Sites

Extra code is loaded for the Site Settings

The user's profile image is shown here.

An extra Quick Launch menu is added to the bottom of the normal Quick Launch for specific My Site user menu items.

The ribbon code is subtly different. Because of this, you shouldn't use the shorter PublishingRibbon for My Sites master pages.

PlaceholderMain loads in the main content of the My Sites.

To achieve these changes, `mysite15.master` has different code from `seattle.master`. To brand SharePoint 2013 My Sites, you must understand these differences to create a master page that reflects the rest of your site's branding.

Branding My Sites in SharePoint 2013

Much like creating branding for traditional SharePoint sites, you have some options for actually creating the My Sites branding. With My Sites you shouldn't work directly with a production server. Instead, you should have a local development environment, either a physical or virtual machine, for quickly making changes and seeing the results in real time. When you are happy with your My Sites branding, refer to the link in the previous section for instructions on packaging them as a SharePoint solution.

You can easily map a drive to the Master Page Gallery of the My Site host and work directly with master pages. Just like with typical SharePoint branding, if you want to make something that looks almost exactly like the out-of-the-box My Site branding, you may want to start by making a copy of `mysite15. master` and making changes there. However, most designers find it easier to use a starter master page to create more complex My Site branding. You can download a starter master page for My Sites from `http://startermasterpages.codeplex.com`. Work with it the same way you did for the custom master pages in Chapter 7.

Chances are good you will already have existing SharePoint 2013 branding by the time you need to make My Site branding. You can reuse most of your HTML markup, as well as any CSS and images that you used for your standard SharePoint branding. Just remember that the page content is driven by the My Sites experience. Specifically for My Sites, the branding should avoid sweeping changes to the main content of the page, and instead focus mostly on color and font changes. Unless you are getting into creating custom-developed Web Parts or controls, most My Site branding initiatives leave the arrangement of the My Site pages as they are by default. The following completed My Site branding could match with the WaffleNet branding from Chapter 7.

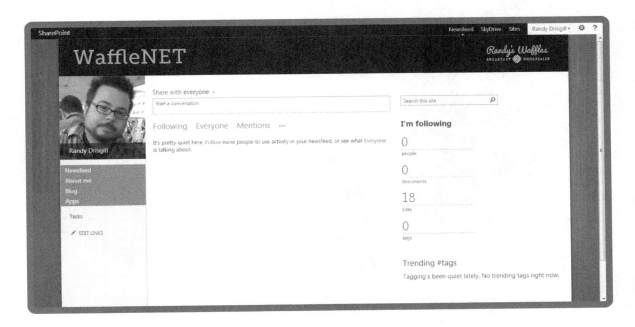

Applying a My Site master page is a bit more challenging, though. By default, publishing isn't turned on for My Sites, so you won't see the typical **Site Settings ➤ Master page** option. To apply the master page, you can either activate publishing features for the My Site host, use SharePoint Designer 2013 (by right-clicking the master page ➤ **Set as Default Master Page ➤ Set as Custom Master Page**), or you can use Visual Studio or PowerShell code to apply the master page. For information on using PowerShell to apply a master page, see Todd Klindt's blog post "How to use PowerShell to set the Master Page in SharePoint 2010" at `http://drisgill.com/go/powershell-masterpage`.

UNDERSTANDING SHAREPOINT ONLINE

Throughout this book, branding SharePoint 2013 is mostly discussed when it is installed in your own farm. As of the writing of this book, that is by far the most common way SharePoint is used, but Microsoft is keen to move SharePoint installations into its cloud-based offering known as Office 365. Microsoft refers to SharePoint in Office 365 as SharePoint Online.

As a designer, you may wonder how SharePoint Online affects the branding process. Interestingly enough, the SharePoint Online differences are drawn along a division between whether the site is public-facing or an intranet site.

WARNING

Writing about SharePoint Online is a lot like trying to hit a moving target. Microsoft treats the 2013 version of SharePoint Online as a versionless product. What you see today in SharePoint Online for the user interface, menus, and even functionality could be vastly different than how it looked at the time of this writing.

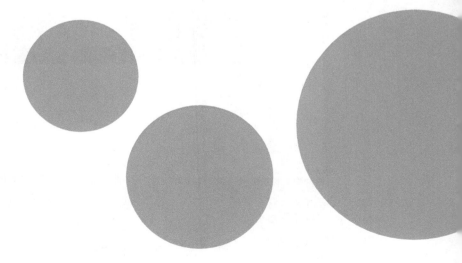

SharePoint Online Intranet Sites

The great thing about branding intranet sites in SharePoint Online is that there isn't much difference from branding traditional intranet sites for SharePoint installed in the farm. For instance, see if you can tell which of the following two screen shots is a team site in SharePoint Online and which is a farm-based team site.

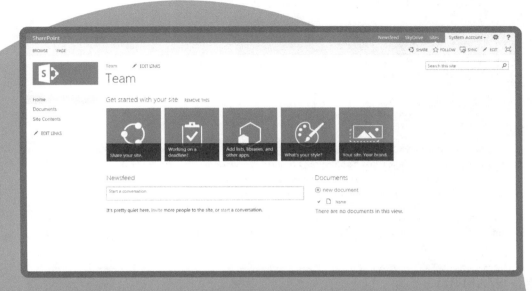

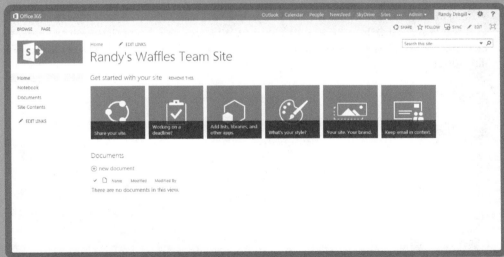

If you said the second one is the SharePoint Online site, you are correct! Pretty much the only thing that visually differentiates a SharePoint online intranet site from a farm-based one is the Suite Bar at the top of the ribbon. In SharePoint Online, this bar shows a logo for Office 365 on the left, and you can see more options related to navigating to the other sections of Office 365 on the right side of the bar. That being said, under the covers there are some significant differences in SharePoint Online worth mentioning.

Publishing Sites in SharePoint Online

As you have learned in previous chapters, SharePoint branding is often enhanced by the abilities that come with the publishing features that are included with SharePoint Server in a typical farm-based install. For SharePoint Online, there are some subtle nuances that dictate which sites support the publishing features based on what license edition you have. This can be confusing because all editions of SharePoint online include the ability to have one site designated as a public website, which has some aspects of publishing, as you will learn about in the next section.

Small Business editions of Office 365 include just one team site, which does not include publishing, plus the public website. Enterprise editions of Office 365 come with a team site collection at the root web application for the domain that does not include publishing; however, they do include the ability to create new publishing site collections underneath that root web application. For more information on Office 365 editions and SharePoint Online, see: `http://www.microsoft.com/en-us/office365/compare-plans.aspx`

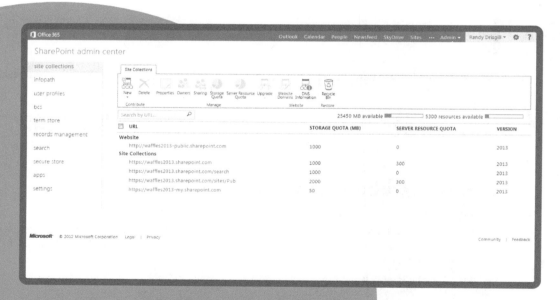

Mapping a Drive to SharePoint Online

You can create SharePoint Online branding much like you have in the other chapters of this book for traditional SharePoint branding. In previous chapters you used the Design Manager and worked with custom master pages; in both cases mapping a drive to the Master Page Gallery was an important step. You can still use Design Manager (if you have a publishing site) and you can still map drives to Share-Point Online, but the process of getting authenticated before mapping the drive can be a little challenging in SharePoint Online. One trick is to make sure to check the boxes to both **Remember Me** and **Keep Me Signed In**, before you click the **Sign In** button. This ensures that you can seamlessly map a drive from Windows to the SharePoint site.

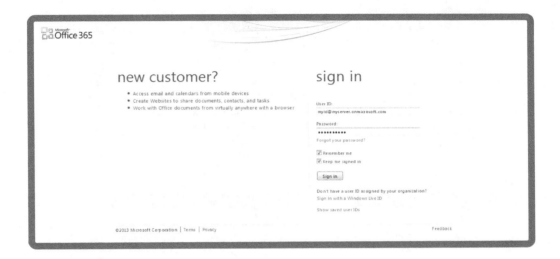

If you still run into trouble logging in and mapping a drive to SharePoint Online, see "How to configure and to troubleshoot mapped network drives that connect to SharePoint Online sites in Office 365 for enterprises" at `http://support.microsoft.com/kb/2616712`.

Sandboxed Solutions

Probably the biggest difference for working with SharePoint Online is the lack of ability to add farm-based Visual Studio solutions. SharePoint 2013 adds the concept of apps to help traditional developers build powerful solutions and still deploy them to SharePoint Online, but unfortunately the SharePoint App model doesn't make it easy to deploy and apply branding to SharePoint Online. Instead, to deploy branding to a SharePoint Online site, you can use a sandboxed solution. For more information on sandboxed solutions see "Sandboxed solutions overview" at `http://technet.microsoft.com/en-us/library/ee721992(v=office.14).aspx`. This article talks about creating solutions for SharePoint 2010 but the concepts are similar.

SharePoint Online Public Sites

As previously mentioned, all SharePoint Online editions have the ability to create one public-facing website ideal for small businesses that is based on SharePoint 2013. These public sites are worth noting because this is one area of SharePoint Online in which SharePoint deviates a lot from what is available in a farm install. If you have played with public sites in SharePoint Online prior to 2013, you probably were less than thrilled with the implementation. Public sites in SharePoint Online 2010 were based on an older product named Office Live Small Business, which was wedged into the SharePoint 2010 interface and lacked many of the useful features used for SharePoint 2010 branding. For SharePoint 2013, Microsoft completely retooled the public site experience to more closely match the typical SharePoint 2013 branding experience. For instance, it includes the ability to work with master pages, page layouts, composed looks, and even some aspects of the Design Manager.

NOTE

For more information on creating a public site in SharePoint online, see Microsoft's article, "Set Up a Public Website" at http://drisgill.com/go/spo-public-site.

The first time you see a public site in SharePoint Online 2013, you can immediately notice that something is different from a traditional default SharePoint 2013 homepage. Although you can certainly see the hallmarks of a normal SharePoint 2013 site such as the ribbon and site logo, the bulk of the design looks nothing like the default Seattle master page or any of the usual composed looks. The UI is sparse, and there is a large background image floating behind the text.

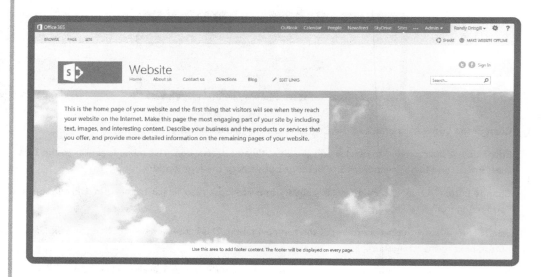

Not only does the site look different, but also the menus and options for SharePoint online have been changed some to focus the user on activities geared toward working with a public-facing website for small businesses. These changes include different ribbon menus, extra out-of-the-box master pages named after cities (such as Berlin, Lyon, and Tokyo), and new composed looks for small businesses, such as hotels and restaurants.

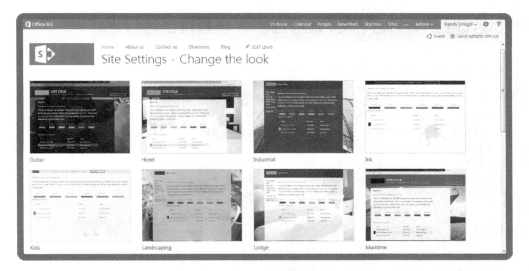

SharePoint Online public sites even include some custom controls such as persistent headers and footers that can be edited in one place and shown on many pages.

Probably the most interesting difference in SharePoint Online public sites is the Site tab on the ribbon. This tab includes several helpful items for working with a small business website. If you browse to the homepage of your public site, and click the Site tab, you can see the following options.

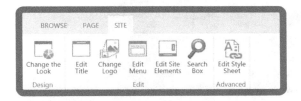

● **Change the Look**—A shortcut to the Change the Look menu from **Site Settings**.

● **Edit Title**—A dialog menu to quickly edit the site title and description. This menu is similar to the Title, Description, and Logo menu from Site Settings but without the logo options.

● **Change Logo**—A dialog menu to quickly change the site logo. Also similar to the Title, Description, and Logo menu from Site Settings.

● **Edit Menu**—Opens the quick editing of the top navigation. This is the same as clicking the Edit Links button next to the navigation.

● **Edit Site Elements**—One of the more interesting options in this menu. Clicking this puts the page into a mode where you can edit some common elements that all pages share; this includes the Header and Footer sections. Any edits made here will persist across all pages. This item has no similar functionality in a farm install of SharePoint.

● **Search Box**—A dialog menu for hiding the search box.

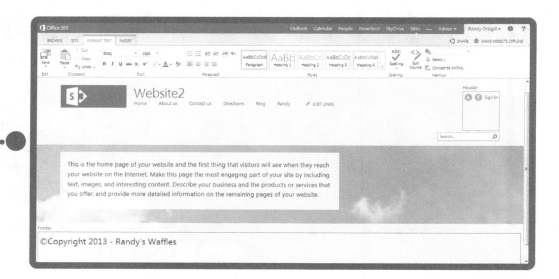

- **Edit Style Sheet**—A dialog box for editing the already applied Alternate CSS style sheet. You learned about Alternate CSS in Chapter 6, "Cascading Style Sheets and SharePoint," but this option is different than any available in a farm install of SharePoint. This enables you to quickly edit and save changes to the Alternate CSS in the web UI without having to use a text editor.

After you get past some of these changes for SharePoint Online public sites, you can use many of the same techniques you learned about throughout this book to create branding for them. For example, you can still use the Design Manager to create HTML master pages and page layouts, and you can still map a folder to the master page gallery and create custom master pages. Just remember that public-facing sites have different needs than internal intranet sites. Be sure to also take into account that the default pages in a SharePoint Online public site are set up with different page layouts than farm installs of SharePoint, and they can include things such as editable persistent headers and footers. Be sure to thoroughly test your pages in your new branding before letting the public view the site.

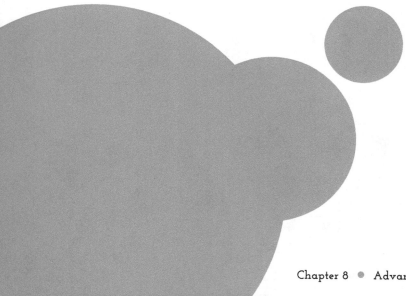

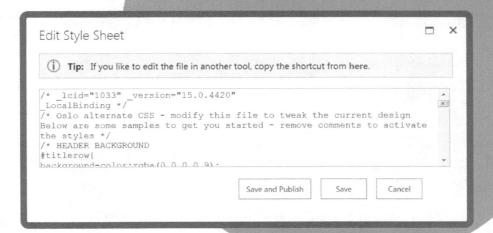

NOTE

Public Sites in SharePoint Online include a button at the top right labeled either **Make Website Online** or **Make Website Offline**. These options can be useful when you are first building the site or if you make large sweeping changes. You can edit the site when it's offline and then bring it back online when your edits are finished.

SUMMARY

- SharePoint navigation has several settings that are only available by editing code in master pages. This includes the AspMenu, which actually shows the navigation and the `SiteMapDataSource`, which provides data to the AspMenu.

- Two of the most commonly changed properties of AspMenu are `StaticDisplayLevels` and `MaximumDynamicDisplayLevels`, which control how many levels of navigation show normally and as fly-outs when you hover over parent items.

- The tree view is useful specifically on collaboration sites for showing a scrollable hierarchy of the site contents as well as providing metadata navigation and filtering.

- Traditional breadcrumbs were not included with SharePoint 2013 out-of-the-box. The `SiteMapPath` control can be used to show breadcrumbs in your SharePoint site.

- The `$SPUrl` tokens can be used in SharePoint Server websites to create links that dynamically point back to the top of a site or site collection.

- Anonymous users have unique needs in SharePoint sites. You can hide the ribbon from displaying to anonymous users, but be sure to also include a link for them to log in if they have credentials on the site.

- Device Channels can be used to show certain master pages or even parts of a master page to devices based on their browsers' user agent strings.

- My Sites use a unique master page named `mysite15.master` to apply its branding. This master page is similar to the default SharePoint branding but is simplified considerably. Also, My Sites branding is typically packaged in a solution package (WSP) so that it can be applied programmatically as new personal sites are created.

- Office 365 includes SharePoint Online intranet sites, which are very similar to traditional farm-based SharePoint sites. You can also create one public site in SharePoint Online that can be used to easily style a public-facing website for small businesses. This concept is unique to Office 365 and not included with a farm install of SharePoint.

9

CREATING CONTENT ROLLUPS WITH SHAREPOINT WCM

What's In This Chapter

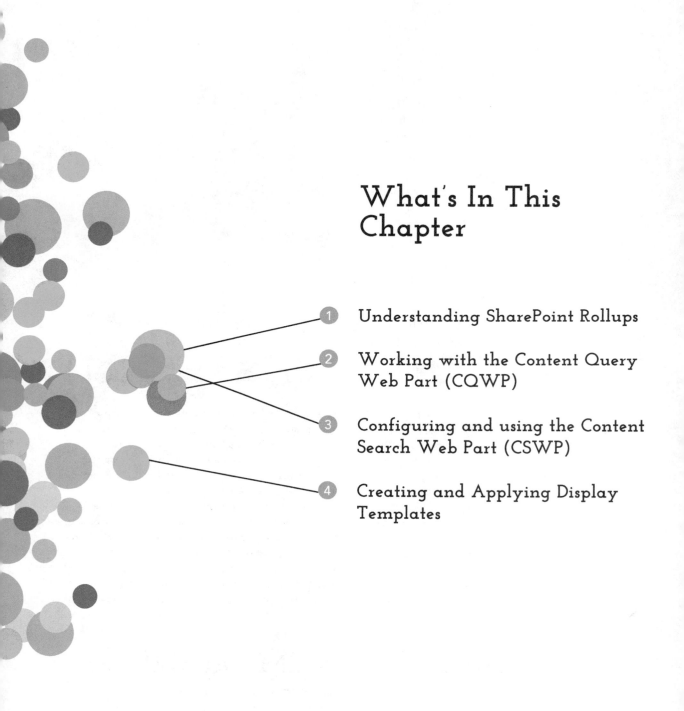

Much of this book has focused on the specific ways to customize the look and feel of a SharePoint site. For branding and designing in SharePoint, master pages, CSS, and page layouts are usually the first things that someone thinks about. However, to implement a custom design means that in many instances you have to also consider how to style some of the functional areas of the site. This chapter discusses the basics of creating one of the most common functional areas that SharePoint branders and designers will encounter—rolling up and styling content with SharePoint WCM Web Parts.

AN INTRODUCTION TO ROLLUPS IN SHAREPOINT

Chapter 4, "Planning for Branding," talks about creating an information architecture, taxonomy, wire frames, and realistic design comps. That process should be fairly technology-agnostic and similar to designing almost any type of site. Some SharePoint specifics are discussed, but for the most part that process should be fairly common to any design project. The chapters following Chapter 4 walk you through the various techniques required to create the major elements of your design within SharePoint, which to this point have been mostly static. This chapter discusses how to customize the rollup Web Parts that deliver dynamic content to SharePoint pages. The ability to combine a custom look and feel with dynamic elements is one of the more powerful aspects of SharePoint. For example, think back to the design for Randy's Waffles where a section on the homepage displayed products. You could have just hard-coded the HTML for those products in a page layout or a Content Editor Web Part (CEWP). But imagine if one of the products changed pricing and you needed to update the information. In a static website, that means you'd have to go to every page where that product price is displayed and make the change. In large sites this could mean updating several pages. The good news is that there's a better way!

Understanding WCM Capabilities

SharePoint is a robust Web Content Management (WCM) platform that enables you to efficiently manage content. One of the most basic concepts of WCM is that content can be created in a single place and surfaced throughout the site wherever it is needed. In other words, rather than needing to

copy the same piece of content to make it show in several places, WCM enables you to create it once and control the rollup of that content to make it display where you need it. In the example for Randy's Waffles, this means creating products and surfacing the content for them wherever the design dictates, such as on the homepage and potentially other pages throughout the site. If you need to update a product's pricing, you can simply edit the single product details page, and then wherever that product is displayed the updated pricing will appear, whether it is on one page or several pages.

This has far-reaching practical implications beyond editing products on fictional websites. An example of a product-centric site is one of the easiest to demonstrate, but here are a few other common examples of rollups that might apply in your environment:

- **News**—Different departments often create content to share with the rest of an organization. Content can be actual press releases or just general information. You can use rollups so that these pieces of content can be displayed in a common location on the homepage. Similarly, if content is tagged with metadata, you can roll them up to other more specific pages as needed.

- **Events**—Similar to the news scenario, events occur at specific dates and times. As sites across your organization create their own events, it is common to have these events roll up to a central place so that users can get a consolidated view of what is happening in an organization.

- **Related documents**—One of the more complex rollup scenarios, related documents requires you to tag content with metadata so you can roll up a specific tag as needed. For example, if you have a Project Management Office site and want to add a Web Part to roll up all content tagged as a Project Plan and related to a SharePoint Project, you can create content organically but make it surface to the website without someone from within the department specifically seeking it out.

These are just a few of the more common scenarios you might consider as you plan your site. SharePoint 2013's WCM capabilities have significantly improved over previous versions, and this opens up a huge number of possible scenarios. The topics covered in this book provide a foundation for styling simple scenarios as well as give you a starting point for more complex scenarios.

Before Getting Started with Rollups

There are a few concepts that might be worth reviewing before diving into rollups. Chapter 2, "Share-Point Overview," discusses the various versions of SharePoint along with a brief overview of Web Content Management (WCM), also referred to as *publishing* in SharePoint. The techniques referenced in this chapter require publishing functionality, so a basic understanding of these concepts covered in Chapter 2 will be helpful.

To further complicate things, although the rollup options discussed in this chapter are all considered publishing functionality, not all options are available across all versions of SharePoint with publishing. Therefore, each section in this chapter briefly covers in which SharePoint versions the respective functionality is available. This is just a reminder to keep your eyes open because the techniques and functionality covered in this chapter might not be available to everyone based on the version of SharePoint you are using.

NOTE

For a more detailed comparison of different versions of SharePoint, see the following: http://technet.microsoft.com/en-us/library/jj819267.aspx. Although the title references SharePoint Online, all versions, including on-premises versions, are covered.

USING THE CONTENT QUERY WEB PART (CQWP)

Since SharePoint Server 2007, the Content Query Web Part (CQWP) has been the primary way to roll up content. The CQWP is included in all versions of SharePoint 2013 where it is possible to enable publishing. This Web Part is fairly straightforward and does exactly what its name implies: It rolls up content based on a specific query. This is a common task on just about any dynamic website. The CQWP Web Part was designed to be reusable so that whenever a need to display content rolled up from within the site arose, a user could add the Web Part to a page, define a specific query, and have the content presented on the page. This is obviously much more efficient than writing a custom Web Part every time you want to display some rolled up content. The user can also change the query, as well as the results it produces, without the need of a developer.

How the CQWP Works

After you define your query, the CQWP looks for content matching your query throughout the site collection. Then it displays the results, which are presented using predefined XSL templates. You can style these XSL templates or even create your own for further flexibility. The Web Part results are *security trimmed*, meaning that CQWP respects SharePoint user security permissions. This means that if a user doesn't have access to view the content, the Web Part won't display it.

Although displayed CQWP results are customizable via XSL, few folks consider themselves XSL experts. Working with XSL can be tricky and difficult to debug when you make a mistake. For example, if you make a typo in your XSL, you'll quickly realize that something isn't correct. But the challenge is that big mistakes fail the same way that minor typos do, making it tedious to find your exact error. Those mistakes will break (until it's fixed) every web part that uses the XSL. Patience is important when creating custom XSL for the CQWP; even experienced designers deal with many of the same challenges.

Unlike the Content Search Web Part (CSWP), discussed later in the section "Using the Content Search Web Part (CSWP)," the CQWP doesn't rely on search, and instead queries down through the site structure of a site collection. This means that returned results display as soon as content is modified. Note that the CQWP can display results only from within the site collection where it is being used.

For many sites, the CQWP is perfectly suited to meet your content rollup needs. However, you might find the Web Part limiting for larger implementations with more complex requirements. No matter the size of your implementation, the CQWP is likely to be to used. Understanding how to customize the CQWP is a useful skill for any SharePoint designer.

Customizing the Content Query Web Part

You can customize your CQWP in many ways, but the general customization process begins with creating custom content for your rollup, then moves into creating custom styles, and ends with applying these custom styles to your CQWP.

EXAMPLE: CREATING THE CONTENT FOR YOUR CQWP

1. From the homepage of your newly branded Randy's Waffles site that you set up in Chapters 5 and 6, click the **Settings menu ➤ Site contents**.

2. At the bottom of the site contents page, click the **New subsite** link.

3. On the New SharePoint Site menu, enter the following settings:

   ● **Title**—Breakfast Talk

   ● **Description**—You can optionally type a description for the new site.

   ● **URL name**—BreakfastTalk

   ● **Select a template**—Click the **Publishing** tab and choose the **Publishing Site** template.

   ● **User Permissions**—Leave the default setting **Use Same Permissions As Parent Site**.

   ● **Navigation Inheritance**—Select **Yes** to use the same items in the top navigation as the parent.

4. Click Create.

5. When the site is created, click the **Settings menu ➤ Add a Page**. In the Add a Page dialog box, enter **Article1** for the name and click **Create**.

6. When the page is created, click the **Page** tab on the ribbon; then click the **Page Layout** drop-down and select the **Image on Left** layout option.

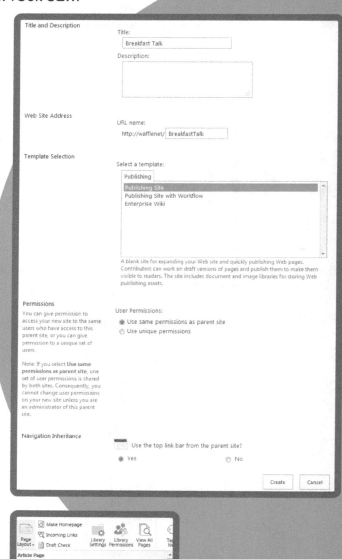

7. In the Page Image field control, click the **Click here to insert a picture from SharePoint** link, and on the Edit Image Properties dialog, click the **Browse** button for the Selected Image input field.

8. On the Select an Asset dialog, click in the Location (URL) field and type `http://<yoursite>/` `_catalogs/masterpage/Waffles` then press **Enter**. (Replace *<yoursite>* with the actual URL of your site, such as `http://wafflenet`.) The Location (URL) field will change to a relative URL to the Waffles folder in the Master Page Gallery.

9. Within the Select an Asset dialog box, click the **Assets** folder to open it; then select one of the images in the folder (BlogPhoto1.jpg, for example) and click **Insert**.

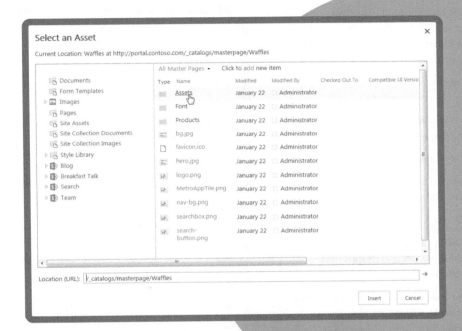

10. On the Edit Image Properties dialog, click **OK**.

11. Fill in the remaining fields on the Article1 page.

   - Type today's date in the Article Date field.

   - Type a name in the Byline field.

   - Add some content to the Page Content field as well.

   - (Optional) You can fill in the Image Caption if you want, but this content won't be included in the rollup later.

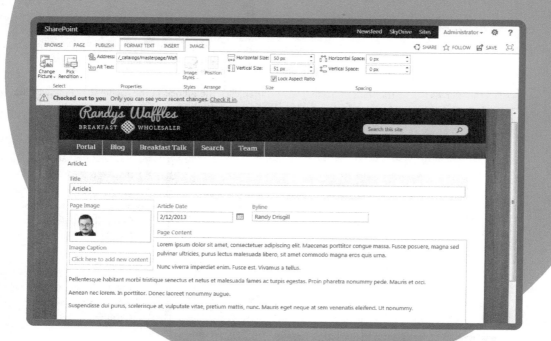

NOTE

If you need to insert some placeholder text quickly, you can take advantage of a couple hidden features in Microsoft Word that generate placeholder text. In a Word document, type =lorem() and press Enter to generate several paragraphs of Lorem Ipsum text that you can copy and paste into SharePoint as filler text. If you want more control over the content of the placeholder text, you can specify how many paragraphs and sentences you want to include. For example, if you typed =lorem(5,4) and press Enter, you generate five paragraphs of lorem ipsum text, each containing four sentences. (You can also use =rand() to the same effect, but this generates actual words and sentences instead of the fake lorem ipsum text.)

12. After you add content to your page, click the **Publish** tab on the ribbon and click **Publish**.

13. Create three more pages in the Breakfast Talk site, using different images, article dates, bylines, and content.

Now that you have created some content that you can roll up, it's time to get to work on styling the CQWP. For this particular rollup, you add the CQWP to the homepage of your site and have it roll up the articles from the newly created Breakfast Talk site. Because space on the homepage is limited, you need to truncate the text of the articles so that just a snippet of the article text shows. The remainder of the article is truncated and is followed by an ellipsis (...). You also need to include a picture of the post author, the author's name, and the date of the post.

You first want to edit the XSL style sheet containing the different templates that you can apply to the CQWP. Then add a CQWP to your site's homepage, configure it to roll up the content you just created, and apply your item style to the rollup, as shown in the following steps:

EXAMPLE: STYLING YOUR CQWP

1. Navigate back to the homepage of your site collection, and click the **Settings menu ➤ Site Contents**.

2. Click **Style Library**; then click the **XSL Style Sheets** folder to open it.

3. Click the **ellipsis (…)** to the right of ItemStyle, and then click the **ellipsis** in the menu after Follow. Click **Check Out**.

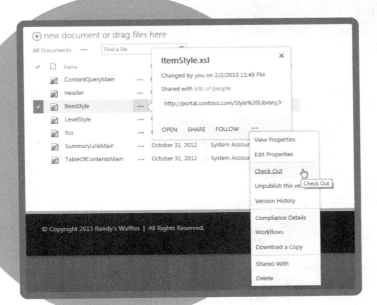

NOTE

You can also select **ItemStyle** by clicking the check box to the left of the filename and using the **Check Out** button in the **Files** tab on the ribbon.

NOTE

For a refresher on how to map a drive, refer to Chapter 5.

4. Map a network drive to the root of your site (for example, `http://wafflenet/`).When your mapped drive opens, browse to the **Style Library ➤ XSL Style Sheets** folder.

5. Before going further, make a backup copy of ItemStyle.xsl and save it somewhere on your computer. This way, you can quickly revert to the original contents of the file if you make a mistake. Keep in mind that if the custom XSL you add to ItemStyle.xsl doesn't have the correct syntax, none of the Content Query Web Parts that use ItemStyle.xsl can display any content in the site, so it's a good idea to keep a backup copy of this file somewhere. You can always revert to a previous version of this file using SharePoint's version history, or you can copy the contents from another copy of ItemStyle.xsl from a different SharePoint site collection. Generally, making a backup is considered the best option.

6. Open **ItemStyle.xsl** in the editor of your choice.

7. At the top of ItemStyle.xsl in the `<xsl:stylesheet ...` declaration section, place the cursor after the line `xmlns:cmswrt="http://schemas.microsoft.com/WebParts/v3/Publishing/runtime"` and press **Enter** to create a new line. Then add the following to the new line:

```
xmlns:ddwrt="http://schemas.microsoft.com/WebParts/v2/DataView/runtime"
```

```
<xsl:stylesheet
  version="1.0"
  exclude-result-prefixes="x d xsl msxsl cmswrt"
  xmlns:x="http://www.w3.org/2001/XMLSchema"
  xmlns:d="http://schemas.microsoft.com/sharepoint/dsp"
  xmlns:cmswrt="http://schemas.microsoft.com/WebParts/v3/Publishing/runtime"
  xmlns:ddwrt="http://schemas.microsoft.com/WebParts/v2/DataView/runtime"
  xmlns:xsl="http://www.w3.org/1999/XSL/Transform" xmlns:msxsl="urn:schemas-microsoft-com:xslt">
```

8. Scroll to the end of the ItemStyle.xsl file. In the second to last line, place the cursor in front of the closing `</xsl:stylesheet>` tag and press **Enter** to create a new line above it and add the following:

NOTE

This step uses templates from Waldek Mastykarz's blog post at http://blog.mastykarz.nl/generating-short-description-content-query-web-part/. Although the blog post references SharePoint 2007, the concepts and code still work perfectly fine in SharePoint 2013. You can copy the templates with names that start with `Imtech` from this blog post if you would rather not type them out.

```xsl
<xsl:template name="CustomPostRollup"
 match="Row[@Style='CustomPostRollup']" mode="itemstyle">
 <xsl:variable name="SafeLinkUrl">
  <xsl:call-template name="OuterTemplate.GetSafeLink">
   <xsl:with-param name="UrlColumnName" select="'LinkUrl'"/>
  </xsl:call-template>
 </xsl:variable>

 <div class="customBlogItem">
  <div class="customBlogImage">
   <xsl:value-of select="@PublishingRollupImage"
    disable-output-escaping="yes"/>
  </div>
  <xsl:value-of select="@Title"/> - <xsl:value-of select="
   ddwrt:FormatDateTime(string(@ArticleStartDate),1033,
   'MMM dd yyyy')" /><br/>
  <a href="{$SafeLinkUrl}">
   <xsl:call-template name="Imtech.GenerateSummary">
    <xsl:with-param name="Content"
     select="@PublishingPageContent" />
    <xsl:with-param name="Length" select="80" />
    <xsl:with-param name="Suffix" select="'...'"/>
   </xsl:call-template>
  </a>
  <div class="customClear"></div>
 </div>
</xsl:template>

<xsl:template name="Imtech.GenerateSummary">
 <xsl:param name="Content"/>
 <xsl:param name="Length"/>
 <xsl:param name="Suffix"/>
 <xsl:variable name="cleanContent">
  <xsl:call-template name="Imtech.RemoveHtml">
   <xsl:with-param name="String" select="$Content"/>
  </xsl:call-template>
 </xsl:variable>
 <xsl:call-template name="Imtech.SubstringBeforeLast">
  <xsl:with-param name="String"
   select="substring($cleanContent, 1, $Length)"/>
```

continues

continued

```xml
  <xsl:with-param name="Char" select="' '"/>
 </xsl:call-template>
 <xsl:if test="string-length($cleanContent) &gt; $Length">
  <xsl:value-of select="$Suffix" disable-output-escaping="yes"/>
 </xsl:if>
</xsl:template>

<xsl:template name="Imtech.RemoveHtml">
 <xsl:param name="String"/>
 <xsl:choose>
  <xsl:when test="contains($String, '&lt;')">
   <xsl:value-of select="substring-before($String, '&lt;')"/>
   <xsl:call-template name="Imtech.RemoveHtml">
    <xsl:with-param name="String" select="substring-
after($String,
     '&gt;')"/>
   </xsl:call-template>
  </xsl:when>
  <xsl:otherwise>
   <xsl:value-of select="$String"/>
  </xsl:otherwise>
 </xsl:choose>
</xsl:template>

 <xsl:template name="Imtech.SubstringBeforeLast">
  <xsl:param name="String" />
  <xsl:param name="Char" />
  <xsl:param name="subsequent"/>
  <xsl:choose>
   <xsl:when test="contains($String, $Char)">
    <xsl:if test="$subsequent = 1">
     <xsl:value-of select="$Char"/>
    </xsl:if>
    <xsl:value-of select="substring-before($String, $Char)"/>
    <xsl:call-template name="Imtech.SubstringBeforeLast">
     <xsl:with-param name="String" select="substring-
after($String,
      $Char)" />
     <xsl:with-param name="Char" select="$Char" />
     <xsl:with-param name="subsequent" select="1"/>
    </xsl:call-template>
   </xsl:when>
   <xsl:otherwise>
    <xsl:if test="$subsequent != 1">
     <xsl:value-of select="$String"/>
    </xsl:if>
   </xsl:otherwise>
  </xsl:choose>
 </xsl:template>
```

9 Save the ItemStyle.xsl.

10 Return to the browser and refresh the Style Library/XSL Style Sheets page. Select the check box next to ItemStyle.xsl; click the **Files** tab on the ribbon and click **Check In**. Choose to publish a major version and click **OK**.

You have just added some custom styles to the ItemStyle.xsl. First, you added a line in the declaration section that helps the XSL to properly format dates. Then you added several templates to the ItemStyle file. The first one (the one you use to apply to a CQWP) is called `CustomPostRollup` and tells the CQWP how to format the data it rolls up. The additional styles that begin with `<xsl:template name="Imtech...>` are referenced by the `CustomPostRollup` to truncate the text the rollup displays and also to help clean up the display by stripping out the HTML markup.

Now it's time to put all these pieces together and add a CQWP to your homepage and apply your custom item style template. If you added any placeholder Web Parts to your homepage while following the examples in Chapter 5, you will delete them in the following example.

EXAMPLE: ADDING AND CONFIGURING THE CQWP

1 Navigate to the homepage of your site and click the **Edit** button on the ribbon. (If you don't see the Edit button, click the Settings menu ➤ Show Ribbon.)

2 If you added a Web Part in Zone 2 in Chapter 5 you can delete it by hovering over the Web Part title, clicking the drop-down arrow that appears toward the right side, and selecting **Delete** from the Web Part menu. Click **OK** when you are prompted to delete the Web Part.

3 In Zone 2, click the **Add a Web Part** link.

4 From the Web Part menu at the top under **Categories**, click **Content Rollup**, and then under **Parts** click **Content Query**. Then click **Add**.

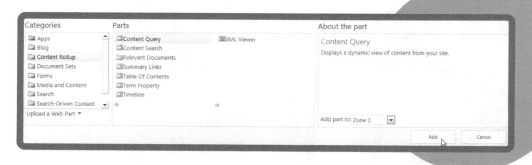

5 In the Content Query Web Part that you just added, click the **open the tool pane** link. Alternatively, you can click the drop-down arrow that appears toward the right side of the Web Part header when you hover over it, and select **Edit Web Part**.

6. In the tool pane that appears to the right of your page content, expand the **Query** section by clicking the plus symbol or the Query header, and select the option to **Show items from the following site and all subsites**; then click the **Browse** button.

7. In the Select Site dialog that appears, click the **Breakfast Talk** site, and then click the **OK** button.

8. In the Content Type section, change the first drop-down to **Page Layout Content Types**, and then make sure the second drop-down is set to **Article Page**.

9. Expand the **Presentation** section of the tool pane, and in the Grouping and Sorting section, change the Sort items by drop-down to **Article Date**.

10. Below the Sort items by section, change **Limit the number of items to display** from 15 to **4**, and in the Styles section, change the Item style drop-down to **CustomPostRollup**.

11. In the Fields to display section, fill in the fields as follows:

   - **Link**—URL Path;
   - **Title**—Byline;
   - **PublishingRollupImage**—Page Image;
   - **ArticleStartDate**—Article Date;
   - **PublishingPageContent**—Page Content;

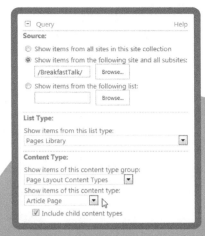

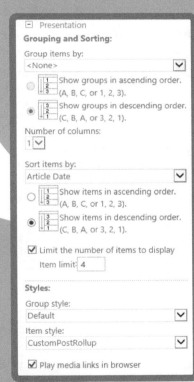

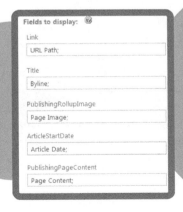

12. Expand the Appearance section of the tool pane, and change the Title field to **Breakfast Talk** and then click **OK**.

13 Click the **Publish** tab on the ribbon, then click the Publish button to publish the page.

There you have it! Your custom CQWP now displays the page image, the author, the article date, and a limited text preview of the content.

Breakfast Talk

Ryan Keller - Jun 17 2013
Nunc viverra imperdiet enim. Fusce est.
Vivamus a tellus. Pellentesque habitant...

Jonathan Mast - Apr 04 2013
Mauris et orci. Aenean nec lorem. In
porttitor. Donec laoreet nonummy...

John Ross - Feb 26 2013
Suspendisse dui purus, scelerisque at,
vulputate vitae, pretium mattis, nunc....

Randy Drisgill - Jan 22 2013
Lorem ipsum dolor sit amet, consectetue
adipiscing elit. Maecenas porttitor...

NOTE

This particular rollup is also set up to utilize the rollup image field that is built in to the out-of-the-box article pages in SharePoint 2013, which enable you to display a different picture on your rollup than you do on the actual article page, just as you could in previous versions of SharePoint. If you want to use the rollup image field to display in your rollup instead of the page field, you would change the value of the `PublishingRollupImage` field in the Fields to display the section to Rollup Image instead of Page Image. If you aren't sure if content authors on your site are going to use the Page Image or the Rollup Image, you can set the rollup to look for both images by typing Page Image; Rollup Image; in the field. The page image takes precedence over the rollup image in this case (if you reversed the order, the rollup image would take precedence), but if there isn't a page image set on the page, the rollup image will display.

USING THE CONTENT SEARCH WEB PART (CSWP)

As mentioned in the previous section, the CQWP became the primary way to do rollups in SharePoint since its introduction in SharePoint Server 2007. Chapter 2 covered several of the new enhancements to SharePoint. One of the biggest changes to SharePoint 2013 is the addition of the Content Search Web Part (CSWP), which leverages SharePoint search to roll up the content.

NOTE

As of this writing, the CSWP is only available in SharePoint Server 2013 Enterprise with sites that have enabled publishing. It is currently not available in any of the SharePoint Online SKUs from Office 365, but Microsoft has stated that it intends to add the functionality in the future.

The CSWP can show any content as long as SharePoint search can crawl the content and add it to the index. There are a number of benefits to this approach:

You can roll up content across site collection boundaries. In SharePoint, a single search service can crawl, index, and provide results for whatever web applications are associated with it. This means that if you can find a piece of content with a search, the CSWP can surface the content. When you perform a search, you type in a search query and click the **Search** button before receiving results. For the CSWP, you specify the search query in the Web Part configuration settings to return the content you want to roll up.

The CSWP has better performance than the CQWP. Because the CSWP is based on the SharePoint search feature, it has excellent performance even when querying with complex rules and filters.

● **You can style the CSWP using HTML, CSS, and JavaScript.** While the CQWP uses XSLT for styling the results, that is often difficult to debug, so the CSWP uses display templates for styling. Display templates are based on HTML and they can be used with CSS and JavaScript to easily style results.

Keep in mind that, similar to CQWP, the content that the CSWP returns is security trimmed. If a user doesn't have access to a specific piece of content then it isn't included within the results.

● **NOTE**

One important thing to consider about this Web Part is that just as with SharePoint search, content needs to be checked in, published, and crawled by the search index before it is available to be returned by the Web Part.

Prepping for the CSWP

Because the CSWP shows content that has been indexed by the SharePoint search crawl, it is a good idea to ensure you have some content indexed before looking at the options available in the CSWP. In the following example you create content that can be used in later examples, in which you will finish the original Randy's Waffles example (from Chapter 5 and Chapter 6) by adding a CSWP to the bottom-left corner that rolls up publishing pages in a subsite.

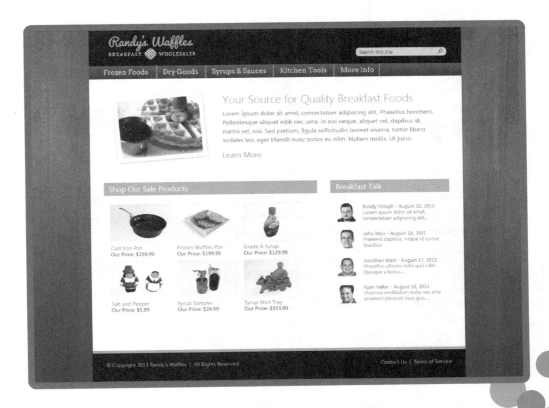

Checking your FURL Setting

The following example contains one tricky step in relation to how pages are created in SharePoint 2013. Essentially, if you have friendly URLs (FURLs) turned on in the navigation settings, the URL for a subsite behaves differently than if you have friendly URLs turned off. This becomes important in later examples because when FURLs are on, newly created pages under a subsite have URLs that look like they belong to the root site, for example: `http://rootsite/subpage`. Alternatively, if FURLs are turned off, the pages look like they normally do in SharePoint: `http://rootsite/subsite/pages/subpage.aspx`.

You can check your FURL setting by navigating to Site Settings and under Look and Feel, click Navigation. Scroll down to Managed Navigation: Default Page Settings. From there you can check the setting for Create Friendly URLs for New Pages Automatically to see whether FURLs are turned On or Off. The default behavior is for SharePoint to automatically create friendly URLs for all new pages.

You can use whichever setting you prefer here, but make note of it as there will be extra steps to follow if you have FURLs turned On.

The CSWP examples in this chapter assume you are using managed navigation on your site. In general the examples work with structured navigation just fine, but the steps may be different for you. If you haven't worked with managed navigation before you may want to review Chapter 3, "Working with the SharePoint 2013 User Interface." Pay particular attention to the warning in the section titled "Working with Navigation in SharePoint 2013"; this describes an issue you might run into when first configuring managed navigation on your site.

EXAMPLE: CREATING CONTENT FOR THE CSWP

1. Create a publishing-based subsite named **SaleItems**.

2. Inside of the new subsite create a new publishing page.

3. Switch the page layout to **Article Page - Image on Left**.

4. Add a Page Image, a product price for the Byline, and Page Content. You can use fake content if you'd like, but make the image fairly small in size—about 150px wide by 100px tall.

NOTE

For a refresher on how to map a drive, refer to Chapter 5.

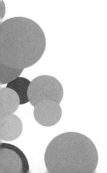

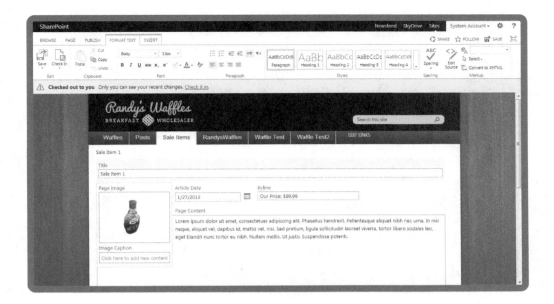

5. After entering the page content, save, check-in, and publish the page.

6. The example later in the chapter looks best with six results, so repeat steps 2 through 5 for five more pages; try to enter different content for each page so that you see different results when the CSWP rolls them up.

Now that the pages are created, it's a good time to consider the previous warning about FURLs. If you have FURLs turned Off, you don't need to do anything extra at this time. If FURLs are turned On (the default setting), there are some extra steps that need to be performed. Follow these steps after you have created all the publishing pages.

EXAMPLE: ORGANIZING PAGES WITH FURLS

1. Click the **Settings menu** ➢ **Site Settings** ➢ **Site Administration** ➢ **Term Store Management**.

2. In the menu on the left, expand the folder for your site collection, and then expand the node for your navigation. If SharePoint created the node for you the node is called **Site Navigation**.

3. Click the drop-down next to your navigation node and select **Create Term**, and type **Sale-Items**. You'll use this term as a parent for the subpage terms that are auto-generated. It's important not to name this term exactly the same as the name of your subsite, otherwise SharePoint will have problems navigating to the node.

4. Click on the new term Sale-Items and then on the right side of the page click the Navigation tab. Change the Navigation Node Type radio button to **Simple Link or Header** and click the **Save** button.

5. For each publishing page that you created earlier, click the drop-down that is next to the name of the corresponding node, and then select **Move Term**. In the dialog that appears, select **Sale-Items** and click **OK**.

Now that you have content created and arranged properly under the subsite you need to get the content indexed by SharePoint search. If you have continuous crawling turned on for your SharePoint search, the new pages will eventually be crawled automatically. Otherwise, follow the next example to include the new pages in the search index.

EXAMPLE: CRAWL THE NEW PUBLISHING PAGES

1. On your SharePoint server, open **SharePoint 2013 Central Administration**.

2. Under **Application Management**, click **Manage Service Applications**.

3. Scroll down and click the first entry for **Search Service Application**.

4. From the left menu under **Crawling**, click **Content Sources**. The page will refresh quickly, and then click **Start All Crawls**.

5. The status updates to **Starting....** Wait a minute or two and then check the status by clicking **Refresh**. Eventually, the crawl finishes and the status changes to **Idle**.

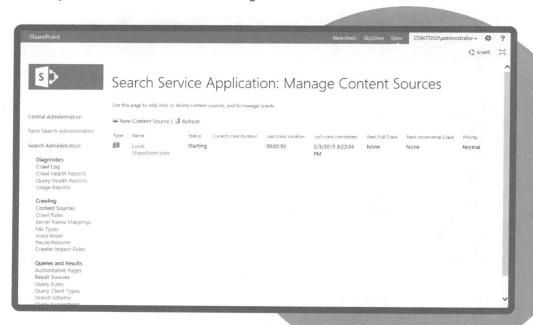

WARNING

If you have never run a crawl on your site before you must run a full crawl, which may take a while to complete.

When the status changes to Idle, your search index should be updated to include the new pages. You can check to see if they have been indexed by searching for the new pages' content on your SharePoint site. If the search results include your new pages, they were successfully added to the index. If your new pages aren't in the results then you need to go back and check to make sure they were published and ensure that SharePoint search is set up to crawl the site properly.

Now that you have publishing pages created and indexed by SharePoint search you can add a CSWP to a publishing page to look at the available options the CSWP provides. Like the Content Query Web Part example earlier, this example uses the homepage design of Randy's Waffles from Chapter 5. If you haven't been following along with the previous chapters you can create a new publishing page, but the example steps will be different. Because the CSWP is an Enterprise feature, you must have a publishing site on SharePoint Server with an Enterprise License to follow along with the example.

EXAMPLE: ADDING A CSWP TO A PUBLISHING PAGE

1. Navigate to the homepage of your site and put the page in Edit mode.

2. If you added a Web Part in Zone 1 in Chapter 5 you can delete it by hovering over the Web Part title, clicking the drop-down arrow that appears toward the right side, and selecting **Delete** from the Web Part menu. Click **OK** when you are prompted to delete the Web Part.

3. In Zone 1, click the **Add a Web Part** link.

4. From the Web Part menu at the top under **Categories**, click **Content Rollup**, and then under **Parts** click **Content Search**. Click **Add.** The CSWP is loaded on the page and by default shows recently updated pages.

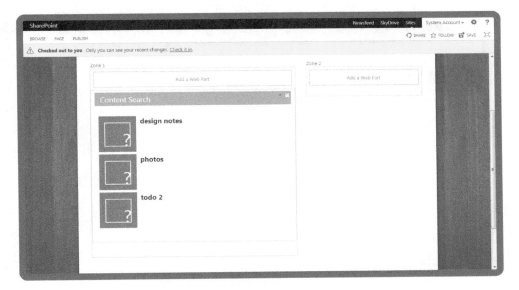

Whew, that was a lot of work just to look at a Web Part, but it is necessary to fully understand how queries work for the CSWP. In the next section you take a look at some of the options that are available for queries in the CSWP.

Understanding CSWP Queries

Take a quick look at the Web Part properties for the CSWP by clicking the little arrow drop-down on the right side of the CSWP title and selecting **Edit Web Part**. The very first option in the Web Part properties menu under the Search Criteria section is the **Change query** button.

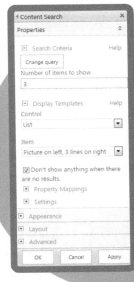

Clicking this button opens a dialog with a powerful query builder that includes several tabs with options for querying content. The next few sections look at the most commonly used options that are available in these tabs.

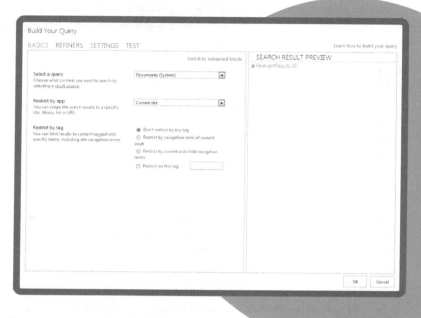

Basics Tab

The Build Your Query dialog opens to the first tab called Basics. Under the Basics section you are provided with a few initial options for querying content:

- **Select a query** — Provides a drop-down of content sources that can be selected for querying content.
- **Restrict by app** — Filters the query to only return results from a specific location.
- **Restrict by tag** — Filters the query to only return results tagged with specific metadata.

As you select and make changes to your options, the Search Results Preview pane on the right updates automatically to show the relevant results. You can check this preview after trying new options and see if the query returns results that you expected.

You might also notice the **Switch to Advanced Mode** link in the upper-right corner of the left section of the query builder. By default, the query builder opens in Quick Mode, which is more simplistic and designed for users who aren't intimately familiar with the Keyword Query Language (KQL) used by SharePoint search. You can learn more about KQL by viewing the links at the end of this section.

Advanced Mode has two major features beyond the default Quick Mode:

- You can view and modify the KQL that is being built for you. If you'd like to add additional keyword or property filters, the Advanced Mode provides an interface for adding these to your query to bring back more specific results.
- Advanced Mode actually adds another tab at the top of the query builder for sorting. The sorting tab enables you to control the order of the results that are shown in the CSWP.

Refiners Tab

The Refiners tab works similar to the SharePoint refinement panel when you do a search. Here you can filter results based on whether content matches one or more managed properties that are enabled as refiners in the SharePoint search settings. You can choose multiple values to refine if necessary; as you add refiners, the result preview to the right changes.

Settings Tab

The Settings tab has four options that go a bit beyond the typical rollup scenarios you might encounter, but essentially they help define the performance behavior of the CSWP. This is useful in more complex or high-traffic implementations as well as the URL Rewriting behavior that's used with the new SharePoint 2013 Catalog feature.

Test Tab

The test tab displays the full KQL for the query you've built. This can be helpful with learning how KQL works. You can see the KQL that is generated from all of the settings you've selected in the other tabs and potentially use similar KQL in Advanced Mode for future queries.

NOTE

For more information about the Content Search Web Part, see "Introducing the Content Search Web Part" at http://sharepoint.microsoft.com/blog/Pages/BlogPost.aspx?pID=1053.

"Configure Search Web Parts in SharePoint Server 2013" gives additional information on working with search Web Parts including the Content Search Web Part at http://technet.microsoft.com/en-us/library/jj679900.aspx.

"Building Search Queries in SharePoint 2013" from MSDN provides additional details about building queries with Keyword Query Language (KQL) and FAST Query Language (FQL) at http://msdn.microsoft.com/en-us/library/jj163973.aspx.

To learn more about building queries for the CSWP, check out Chris O'Brien's post on the topic at http://www.sharepointnutsandbolts.com/2012/10/using-content-search-web-part-and.html.

Customizing the CSWP

Now that you have a better understanding of how queries are made for the CSWP, you can put the knowledge to use by rolling up the publishing pages you created earlier. This example uses the master page and styles from the Randy's Waffles branding that was created in Chapters 5 and 6. Follow along with these steps without using the Randy's Waffles branding, but the styles will be different from the screen shots. You can download the completed Randy's Waffles master page and CSS from the code downloads for this chapter.

Although this is a simple example, it illustrates some key points; you could use these same methods to roll up pages across site collections or even do things such as filter the pages based on meta tags.

NOTE

This example continues from the previous one so if you don't already have the Build Your Query dialog open, be sure to edit your homepage, put the CSWP in Edit More, and click the Change query button at the top of the Web Part properties on the right side of the page.

EXAMPLE: ROLLING UP PUBLISHING PAGES WITH THE CSWP

1 Make sure the Basics tab is set to **Quick Mode**. If it's set to Advanced Mode, switch it back.

2 From the **Basics** tab, choose these options:

- Select a query—**Items matching a content type (System)**.

- Restrict by app—**Specify a URL** .

- For the URL box, think back to the "Prepping for the CSWP" section when you looked at whether FURLs were turned on or off. If FURLs were left on, enter the parent term you created `http://`YOURSERVER/`Sale-Items`. If FURLs were turned off, enter the name of the subsite you created `http://`YOURSERVER/`SaleItems`.

- Restrict by tag—**Don't restrict by any tag.**

- Restrict by content type—**Article Page.**

- Add additional filters—Leave this set to the default or clear out the field.

NOTE

As you make changes, the Search Results Preview window updates to reflect these. By choosing to query only items matching a content type and by restricting the content type to Article Page, your CSWP shows only pages that use page layouts that are based on the Article Page content type like Article Page - Image on Left. You also restricted the query to only show items under the subsite by entering the URL for that site or the parent term.

WARNING

Restricting queries to specific URLs can be difficult to work with depending on how your server is configured. If you are running into problems getting the query to return results in the preview window you may want to change the setting for Restrict by app back to Current site collection. Your results won't be as specific, but at least you can complete the example properly.

3. Change the sorting to arrange the pages by the date and time that the page was created. To do this, click the **Switch to Advanced Mode** link.

4. Click the **Sorting** tab and change the **Sort by** drop-down to **Created.** Then change the direction to **Ascending.** When you are in Advanced Mode, the Search Results Preview doesn't automatically update. To see your changes, click on the **Test** tab.

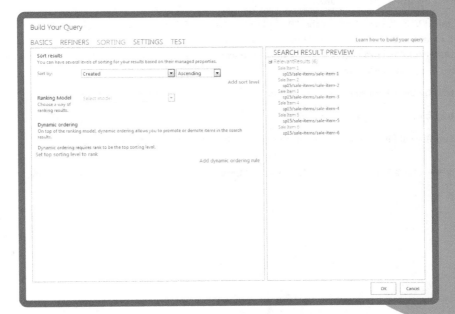

5. At this point the query is complete; click **OK** at the bottom of the dialog window.

6. Next, you can change some of the display properties to see what the CSWP would look like with paging turned on. To do so, from the Web Part properties menu on the right side of the page, under **Display Templates,** switch **Control** to **List with Paging.** For **Item** select **Picture on left, 3 lines on right.**

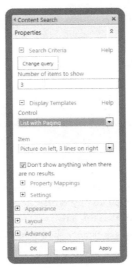

NOTE

By default, the Web Part properties menu has the **Number of Items to Show** option set to show three items at a time. Earlier you created six pages that can display in this query result. Therefore the CSWP shows the pages three items at a time with a next and previous arrow.

7. Click **OK** on the Web Part properties menu.

8. Save the page to see the end result.

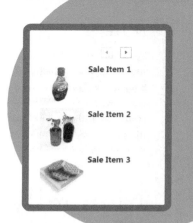

The CSWP has a handy paging menu at the top right that enables you to scroll through the result pages. At this point you have a working CSWP querying the correct results, but the display doesn't really match the original example. In the next section, you will learn how to create a display template that makes some simple changes to the display of the query results.

WORKING WITH DISPLAY TEMPLATES

Display templates are made up of HTML and JavaScript files that control how results are presented when the content is returned from the CSWP query or other search Web Parts, such as the Search Results and the Refinement Panel. As you learned earlier in the chapter, styling the CQWP involves working with XSL, a language many people find challenging to work with. The switch to an HTML- and JavaScript-based approach is probably a welcomed change for many SharePoint veterans.

Display templates are stored in the Master Page Gallery of your site collection. Microsoft was kind enough to include several out-of-the-box display templates that can be used to style Web Parts like the CSWP (they are also great for learning how to create your own display templates). At the end of the previous example you actually used out-of-the-box display templates to show the items arranged in pages. If you edit the Web Part again and look at the Web Part properties under Display Templates, you can see two drop-downs: Control and Item. These correspond to two different types of display templates that are used together to style results:

- **Control Template**—Defines the overarching behavior of the group of items that are returned. By default there are three options: List, List with Paging, and Slideshow. List is the most straightforward of the options, simply showing the results one after each other. You saw List with Paging in action in the previous example, and Slideshow shows off the results using a fancy style with the items dynamically rotating from one to the next on the page.

- **Item Template**—Defines the style for each of the individual items that are returned from the query. There are several out-of-the-box options available to show items in various styles.

Although the out-of-the-box templates are a good starting point, many custom branding projects require the creation of your own custom display templates. Because the CSWP uses HTML and JavaScript to style results, customizing the display of CSWPs should be more approachable by designers than styling CQWPs using XSL.

Manually Changing Property Mappings

In the previous example, you used the **List with Paging** Control display template and the **Picture on left, 3 lines on right** Item display template; together these created a display with a paging control. In addition, for each item, the photo was on the left and the title was on the right. Notice that the byline you added to all the pages (which had the sale price) doesn't show up in the CSWP at this point. Although you set the display template to show three lines on the right, only the title shows. This is because of *property mappings*, which are how display templates receive content from the results of the query.

If you expand the Property Mapping section of the CSWP Web Part properties menu you can actually see what shows for each of the three lines. By default, Line 1 is set to show the Title of the content and Line 2 is set to show the Description. However, in the previous example nothing was shown on the second line because the publishing pages you created earlier didn't have descriptions set. One way of correcting this is to change Line 2 from showing the description to showing the Article Byline. If you wanted to do this, you would check the box for **Change the Mapping of Managed Properties for the Fields in the Item Display Template** and then change the drop-down for Line 2 to `ArticleByLineOWSTEXT` (which is the behind-the-scenes name for the managed property that corresponds to the Article Byline).

Instead of changing the property mappings manually, in the next few sections, you learn how to create a new display template that displays items in rows of three as well as changing the Line 2 property mapping to automatically pull the byline information by default.

Creating a Display Template

When you work with display templates, it rarely makes sense to start one from scratch; instead, you would typically modify a copy of whichever out-of-the-box display template is most similar to your intended display. It's also worth noting that every display template includes both an HTML file and a JavaScript file that share the same root filename. You always want to edit the HTML file, because SharePoint automatically generates the JavaScript file by interpreting the HTML file. The following example walks you through starting a new display template by copying an existing one.

EXAMPLE: CREATING A NEW DISPLAY TEMPLATE

1. From a drive you've mapped to your Master Page Gallery, navigate down to the Display Templates subfolder, where all the display templates live. Each subfolder holds different types of display templates, such as templates for searches and filters. The CSWP uses display templates in the Content Web Parts folder.

2. Navigate down to the **Content Web Parts** folder. There are many default display templates listed in here that you can use to learn from. In the next step, you will make a copy of the **Picture on left, 3 lines on right** display that you selected previously when you configured your CSWP.

3. Make a copy of `Item_Picture3Lines.html` and rename it **`WaffleDisplay.html`**. When you do this SharePoint automatically generates a corresponding JavaScript file.

4. Open `WaffleDisplay.html` in your editing program of choice and you should see the following display template code.

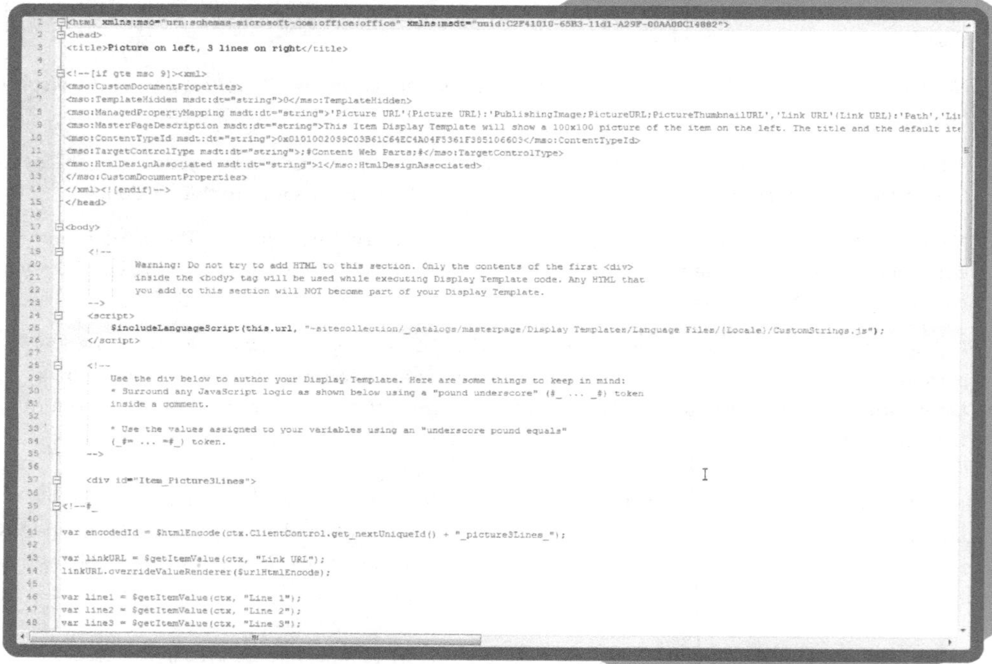

```
<html xmlns:mso="urn:schemas-microsoft-com:office:office" xmlns:msdt="uuid:C2F41010-65B3-11d1-A29F-00AA00C14882">
<head>
<title>Picture on left, 3 lines on right</title>

<!--[if gte mso 9]><xml>
<mso:CustomDocumentProperties>
<mso:TemplateHidden msdt:dt="string">0</mso:TemplateHidden>
<mso:ManagedPropertyMapping msdt:dt="string">'Picture URL'{Picture URL}:'PublishingImage;PictureURL;PictureThumbnailURL','Link URL'{Link URL}:'Path','Lin
<mso:MasterPageDescription msdt:dt="string">This Item Display Template will show a 100x100 picture of the item on the left. The title and the default ite
<mso:ContentTypeId msdt:dt="string">0x0101002039C03B61C64EC4A04F5361F385106603</mso:ContentTypeId>
<mso:TargetControlType msdt:dt="string">;#Content Web Parts;#</mso:TargetControlType>
<mso:HtmlDesignAssociated msdt:dt="string">1</mso:HtmlDesignAssociated>
</mso:CustomDocumentProperties>
</xml><![endif]-->
</head>

<body>

    <!--
            Warning: Do not try to add HTML to this section. Only the contents of the first <div>
            inside the <body> tag will be used while executing Display Template code. Any HTML that
            you add to this section will NOT become part of your Display Template.
    -->
    <script>
        $includeLanguageScript(this.url, "~sitecollection/_catalogs/masterpage/Display Templates/Language Files/{Locale}/CustomStrings.js");
    </script>

    <!--
        Use the div below to author your Display Template. Here are some things to keep in mind:
        * Surround any JavaScript logic as shown below using a "pound underscore" (#_ ... _#) token
        inside a comment.

        * Use the values assigned to your variables using an "underscore pound equals"
        (_#= ... =#_) token.
    -->

    <div id="Item_Picture3Lines">

<!--#_

var encodedId = $htmlEncode(ctx.ClientControl.get_nextUniqueId() + "_picture3Lines_");

var linkURL = $getItemValue(ctx, "Link URL");
linkURL.overrideValueRenderer($urlHtmlEncode);

var line1 = $getItemValue(ctx, "Line 1");
var line2 = $getItemValue(ctx, "Line 2");
var line3 = $getItemValue(ctx, "Line 3");
```

Now that you have made a new display template by copying an existing one, you are almost ready to update it with your own custom display template code. But before you start making changes, the next section walks you through the copied display template code and explains how it works.

Understanding the Display Template

A lot goes on inside a typical display template, and the one just created is no exception; some areas of the code are noteworthy for customization and others can typically be ignored. The following list looks

at the display template code from top to bottom, describing the areas that you should keep in mind when creating a custom display template and skipping over the unimportant sections:

- The title of the HTML page (between `<title>` and `</title>`) is used to surface the name of the display template in the Web Part properties menu. In this case the title is **Picture on left, 3 lines on right**. This is what you selected in the **Display Templates ➤ Item** drop-down on the Web Part properties menu in the CSWP example.

- Next, you see a group of XML tags that start with `<mso:`—Most of these should not be changed. The exception is `ManagedPropertyMapping`, which you use to surface extra property mappings on the Web Part properties menu. The syntax for adding new mappings looks like this (note that each property mapping is separated by a comma):

```
'AuthorVar'{Author Name}:'Author',
```

  In this case `AuthorVar` is used in the actual display template HTML file, `Author Name` shows as a select box in the Web Part properties menu for property mappings, and `Author` is the default option that was selected in that drop-down.

- Next, there is a section that has a comment warning you not to add HTML to this part of the display template.

- After that, you will see a `<script>` tag that includes a call to `$includeLangageScript`. This section is used to call in other JavaScript files. You will not be making any changes to this section.

- Next, you will see a div tag. In this case `<div id="Item_Picture3Lines">`. This is the main container for the editable section of the display template. You MUST leave this div tag here, but you can change the ID that is associated with it.

- Inside of this div you see several lines of HTML and JavaScript code. All JavaScript is escaped by surrounding it with `<!--#_` and `_#-->` and all display variables are surrounded with `_#=` and `=#_`. Later, when you edit and save this file, SharePoint will convert these escaped pieces of JavaScript into functioning code.

In addition to the aforementioned escaped characters, this section of the file consists of typical JavaScript that you would use within traditional web pages including some extra SharePoint fanciness added in. You will see a few SharePoint functions used throughout the sample display templates; here is a description of a few of the more common functions used:

- `$getItemValue`—Retrieves the value of managed properties that were defined in the MSO section at the top of the display template. For example, `$getItemValue(ctx, "Line 2");` retrieves whatever managed property is applied for the display template from Line 2 in the Web Part properties menu.

- `$htmlEncode`—Encodes a given string so that it is safe for displaying as HTML

- `$urlHtmlEncode`—Encodes a given string so that it is safe for using as a URL.

- `Srch.ContentBySearch.getPictureMarkup`—Returns HTML markup for a given image including references to the proper image rendition.

Along with these functions there is an object named `ctx` (short for context) used throughout the display templates. This object refers back to the result set returned from the CSWP query. Here is a list of some of the more important uses for the `ctx` object in the default display templates:

- **ctx.ClientControl**—Returns information from the actual Web Part on the page that shows the display template. Frequently used to retrieve a unique ID for this Web Part instance. This ID is then appended to HTML elements in the display template to give the elements their own unique IDs. Without this, each item might use the same exact HTML IDs in its HTML elements, making styling and scripting difficult.

- **ctx.ListData**—Returns information about the set of results provided by the query. Used in the control display templates because they show the group of items returned from the query.

- **ctx.CurrentItem**—Returns the data for the current item being processed by an item display template.

- **ctx.CurrentItemIdx**—Returns the index number of the current item being processed by an item display template. This number starts from zero for the first item instead of one, so if you do any sort of conditional formatting, you may need to increment the index value by 1 to get the actual position starting from 1.

Customizing the Display Template

Now that you have some background on how the display template is set up, you can look at the changes required for the Waffle Display template to work properly. If you get lost following this example, you can download the completed display template from the downloads for this chapter:

EXAMPLE: CREATING A CUSTOM DISPLAY TEMPLATE

1. Change the title of the display template to the following:

   ```
   <title>Waffle Display</title>
   ```

2. Update the `ManagedPropertyMapping` for Line 2 to include a default setting that points to the byline. To do this, scroll down to the MSO section and find the `ManagedPropertyMapping` line. Replace this part:

   ```
   'Line 2'{Line 2}: 'Description'
   ```

   With this code:

   ```
   'Line 2'{Line 2}:'ArticleByLineOWSTEXT'
   ```

3. Add some JavaScript to insert a CSS break after every third item. To do this, find the first instance of `<!--#_` and add the following code inside of it (add the code before the line that starts with `var encodedID`).

   ```
   var customRowEnd = "";

   if((ctx.CurrentItemIdx + 1) % 3 == 0){
    customRowEnd = "<div style='clear:both;'></div>";
   }
   ```

   This code sets an initial string variable called `customRowEnd` and then looks at the index counter for the current item and decides if it is divisible evenly by 3. If the item is divisible by 3, `customRowEnd` will be set to show a div with a CSS style that adds a break.

4. Remove the default display; you will replace it with a new display in step 6. To do this, find the section of code that begins with:

   ```
   <div class="cbs-picture3LinesContainer"
   ```

5. Remove this entire section of code, including the start and end tags, leaving only the following code at the bottom of the display template:

```
  </div>
 </body>
</html>
```

6. Add in the custom display code before the closing `</div>`:

```
    <div class="customProductsItem">
     <!--#_if(!linkURL.isEmpty){_#-->
      <!--#_if(!pictureMarkup.isEmpty){_#-->
       <a class="customProductsImage" href="_#= linkURL =#_">
        _#= pictureMarkup =#_
       </a>
      <!--#_}_#-->

      <!--#_if(!line1.isEmpty){_#-->
       <a href="_#= linkURL =#_">_#= line1 =#_</a><br/>
      <!--#_}_#-->

      <!--#_if(!line2.isEmpty){_#-->
       _#= line2 =#_
      <!--#_}_#-->
     <!--#_}_#-->
    </div>

    <!--#_if(!customRowEnd.isEmpty) {_#-->
     _#= customRowEnd =#_
    <!--#_}_#-->
```

NOTE

Although this code may look confusing, it's actually not hard to understand once you get used to the markup. Everything surrounded by `<!--# #-->` is JavaScript, and everything surrounded by `#= =#` is a managed property or variable being output by the display template. You will see several places in which conditional JavaScript is used to determine whether a variable is empty before it is displayed.

When this display template is rendered in the browser, the resulting code shows the product image, line 1, line 2, and then `customRowEnd`, which is a variable that adds a break after every third item. The following pseudocode shows an example of what could be output from this display template for each item:

```
<div class="customProductsItem">
 <a class="customProductsImage" href="LINK TO ITEM">
  <img src="IMAGE SOURCE" />
 </a>
 <a href="LINK TO ITEM">TITLE</a></br>
 BYLINE
</div>
<div style="clear: both;"></div>
```

7 These are all the changes needed for the display template. Save the file and SharePoint can regenerate the corresponding JavaScript file.

8 To finish the example, edit the SharePoint page that has your CSWP, and bring up the Web Part properties menu by clicking **Edit Web Part**. Make the following changes:

- **Search Criteria ➤ Number of items to show**—6
- **Display Templates ➤ Control**—List
- **Display Templates ➤ Item**—Waffle Display

9 You should also check to make sure the **Property Mappings** now shows ArticleByLineOWSText for Line 2. When all those settings are in place, click **OK**.

10 Assuming no errors display, **Save** and **Publish** the page.

If you have any errors, SharePoint tries to guide you in the right direction to show which part of the display template caused the error. Like all debugging in SharePoint, it pays to go slow and make small changes when you work on a new display template. The nice thing about display templates compared to XSL and the CQWP is you can see changes to the display templates by just saving the HTML file and refreshing your browser.

If you have the completed Randy's Waffles master page from Chapter 5 and have applied the CSS from Chapter 6 to your site, you should already see custom styling for the products. The CSS from the Randy's Waffles branding that applies to the display template is as follows:

```css
.customProductsItem {
 padding-right: 14px;
 float: left;
 padding-bottom: 15px;
}
.customProductsImage {
 display: block;
 padding-bottom: 2px;
}
.customProductsImage img {
 border: 1px solid #dddddd;
}
```

The finished product uses the query from the CSWP and the custom display template you created in the previous example to show two rows of sale products with images, titles, and a price (which you entered into the byline field).

If you are comfortable working with JavaScript, you can easily take this example to the next level. Perhaps you create a highlight effect for the photos or maybe add code that parses the value of the product's price and conditionally highlights heavily discounted prices in the display.

CQWP VERSUS CSWP

Throughout this chapter we've covered the two primary Web Parts that roll up content in WCM. There's quite a bit of information to take in, both for using the Web Parts and for customizing them. But the big question is how to best apply all of this new information to the various scenarios you might find in your implementation. For many readers, the decision regarding which method you use for rolling up content is made for you, simply because the CQWP is available in more versions of SharePoint whereas the CSWP is (as of this writing) only available with SharePoint Server 2013 Enterprise. If do find yourself in a position where you need to decide which approach is better, the following chart breaks down some of the major factors you might want to consider:

NOTE

Although currently not available with O365 as of this writing, Microsoft has stated it plans to make the CSWP available in the future.

	CQWP	CSWP
You have SP Server Enterprise	●	●
You have SP Server or O365*	●	
Need Cross Site Collection Rollups		●
Migrating existing SP2010 WCM site	●	
Security Trimming	●	●
Content Availability	Immediate	Requires Search Crawl
Have a less complex site structure with simple rollup requirements	●	
Need to dynamically rollup a high volume of content		●
Display Customization	XSLT	HTML and JavaScript
Storing for results	Using custom XSL	●
Paging for results		●
Friendly URLs (FURLs) for content		●
Flexibility for mobile		●

There is also a possibility that you end up using both Web Parts in your SharePoint implementation. For simpler rollup scenarios, the CQWP is useful. Although the CSWP is flexible and powerful, it also requires an additional level of complexity because it leverages search. In practice, there tends to be a bit more effort involved to configure and customize the CSWP, which could be overkill if you're just rolling up a few pages.

So overall, which one is best? As with many things in SharePoint, the ultimate answer is, "It depends." The good news is that SharePoint 2013 provides more options than ever for rolling up your content. It is now possible to do things that previously would have required a significant custom effort to re-create. Whether it is search-driven content, supporting mobile sites, or something else, SharePoint 2013 provides a powerful and flexible set of Web Content Management capabilities. And if you are familiar with the way SharePoint rolled up content in the past, the classic approach to content rollup is still available! There's something for everyone to create beautiful and engaging SharePoint sites with dynamic content.

SUMMARY

- SharePoint is a robust Web Content Management (WCM) platform that enables you to more efficiently manage content. The most basic principle of WCM is the idea of creating a single piece of content and being able to surface that content wherever it might be needed.

- The CQWP is included in all versions of SharePoint 2013 where it is possible to enable publishing. The Web Part is fairly straightforward and does exactly what its name implies: it rolls up content based on a specific query. This is a common task on just about any dynamic website.

- The results returned from the CQWP are styled with XSL, which can be customized.

- One of the biggest changes to SharePoint 2013 is the addition of the Content Search Web Part (CSWP), which leverages SharePoint search to roll up the content.

- *Display templates* are made up of HTML and JavaScript files that control how results are presented when the content is returned from the CSWP query or other search Web Parts, such as the Core Search Results and the Refinement Panel.

- When it comes to deciding between CQWP and CSWP you may end up using both. Or the version of SharePoint you are using might make the choice for you.

10

COMPOSED
LOOKS AND
CUSTOM
BRANDING

What's In This Chapter

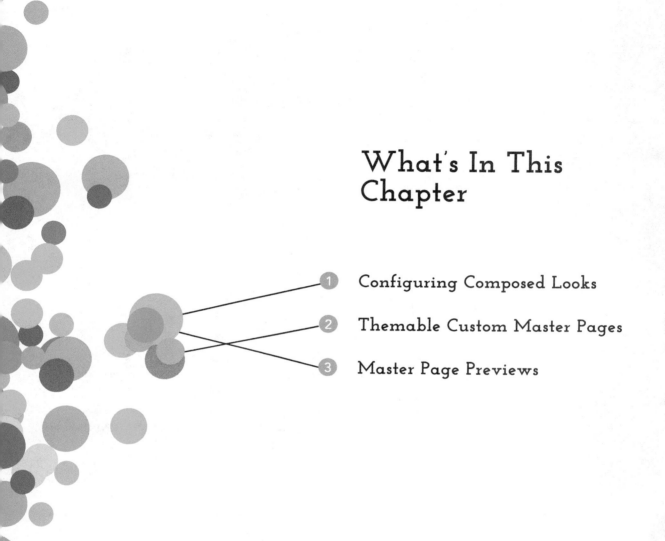

1. Configuring Composed Looks

2. Themable Custom Master Pages

3. Master Page Previews

In Chapter 3, "Working with the SharePoint 2013 User Interface," you learned about how to use composed looks to apply style to a SharePoint 2013 site without a lot of effort. Although it's great that Microsoft provides several composed looks with SharePoint, you may want to create your own composed looks and make them available to your site owners for use on their sites. The cool thing about composed looks is you can provide a base master page design, and users can change the colors, fonts, and background images without knowing anything about CSS or master pages.

UNDERSTANDING COMPOSED LOOKS

To begin understanding composed looks, you should check out the composed looks gallery by clicking **Site Settings ➤ Web Designer Galleries ➤ Composed looks.** By default, this page has a list of all the composed looks included with SharePoint.

In this list, all the column names are behind-the-scenes names that correspond to friendly labels that you would see when you go to the Change the Look menu.

Composed Looks ⓘ

All Items

✓	Name	Master Page URL	Theme URL	Image URL	Font Scheme URL	Display Order
	Orange	/_catalogs/masterpage/seattle.master	/_catalogs/theme/15/palette015.spcolor			10
	Sea Monster	/_catalogs/masterpage/oslo.master	/_catalogs/theme/15/palette005.spcolor	/_layouts/15/images/image_bg005.jpg	/_catalogs/theme/15/fontscheme003.spfont	20
	Green	/_catalogs/masterpage/seattle.master	/_catalogs/theme/15/palette013.spcolor			30
	Lime	/_catalogs/masterpage/seattle.master	/_catalogs/theme/15/palette026.spcolor			40
	Nature	/_catalogs/masterpage/seattle.master	/_catalogs/theme/15/palette006.spcolor	/_layouts/15/images/image_bg006.jpg	/_catalogs/theme/15/fontscheme001.spfont	50
	Blossom	/_catalogs/masterpage/seattle.master	/_catalogs/theme/15/palette002.spcolor	/_layouts/15/images/image_bg002.jpg		60
	Sketch	/_catalogs/masterpage/oslo.master	/_catalogs/theme/15/palette008.spcolor	/_layouts/15/images/image_bg008.jpg	/_catalogs/theme/15/fontscheme003.spfont	70
	City	/_catalogs/masterpage/seattle.master	/_catalogs/theme/15/palette004.spcolor	/_layouts/15/images/image_bg004.jpg		80
	Orbit	/_catalogs/masterpage/seattle.master	/_catalogs/theme/15/palette009.spcolor	/_layouts/15/images/image_bg009.jpg		90
	Grey	/_catalogs/masterpage/seattle.master	/_catalogs/theme/15/palette032.spcolor			100
	Characters	/_catalogs/masterpage/seattle.master	/_catalogs/theme/15/palette007.spcolor	/_layouts/15/images/image_bg007.jpg	/_catalogs/theme/15/fontscheme002.spfont	110
	Office	/_catalogs/masterpage/seattle.master	/_catalogs/theme/15/palette001.spcolor			120
	Breeze	/_catalogs/masterpage/seattle.master	/_catalogs/theme/15/palette003.spcolor	/_layouts/15/images/image_bg003.jpg		130
	Immerse	/_catalogs/masterpage/oslo.master	/_catalogs/theme/15/palette010.spcolor	/_layouts/15/images/image_bg010.jpg		140
	Red	/_catalogs/masterpage/seattle.master	/_catalogs/theme/15/palette022.spcolor			150
	Purple	/_catalogs/masterpage/seattle.master	/_catalogs/theme/15/palette031.spcolor			160
	Wood	/_catalogs/masterpage/oslo.master	/_catalogs/theme/15/palette011.spcolor	/_layouts/15/images/image_bg011.jpg	/_catalogs/theme/15/fontscheme002.spfont	170
	Current	/_catalogs/masterpage/seattle.master	/_catalogs/theme/15/Palette001.spcolor			0

The following shows the new item menu from the composed looks gallery (**Site Settings** ➢ **Web Designer Galleries** ➢ **Composed looks**) on the left and the menu you see when you select a composed look (**Site Setting** ➢ **Look and Feel** ➢ **Change the Look**) on the right:

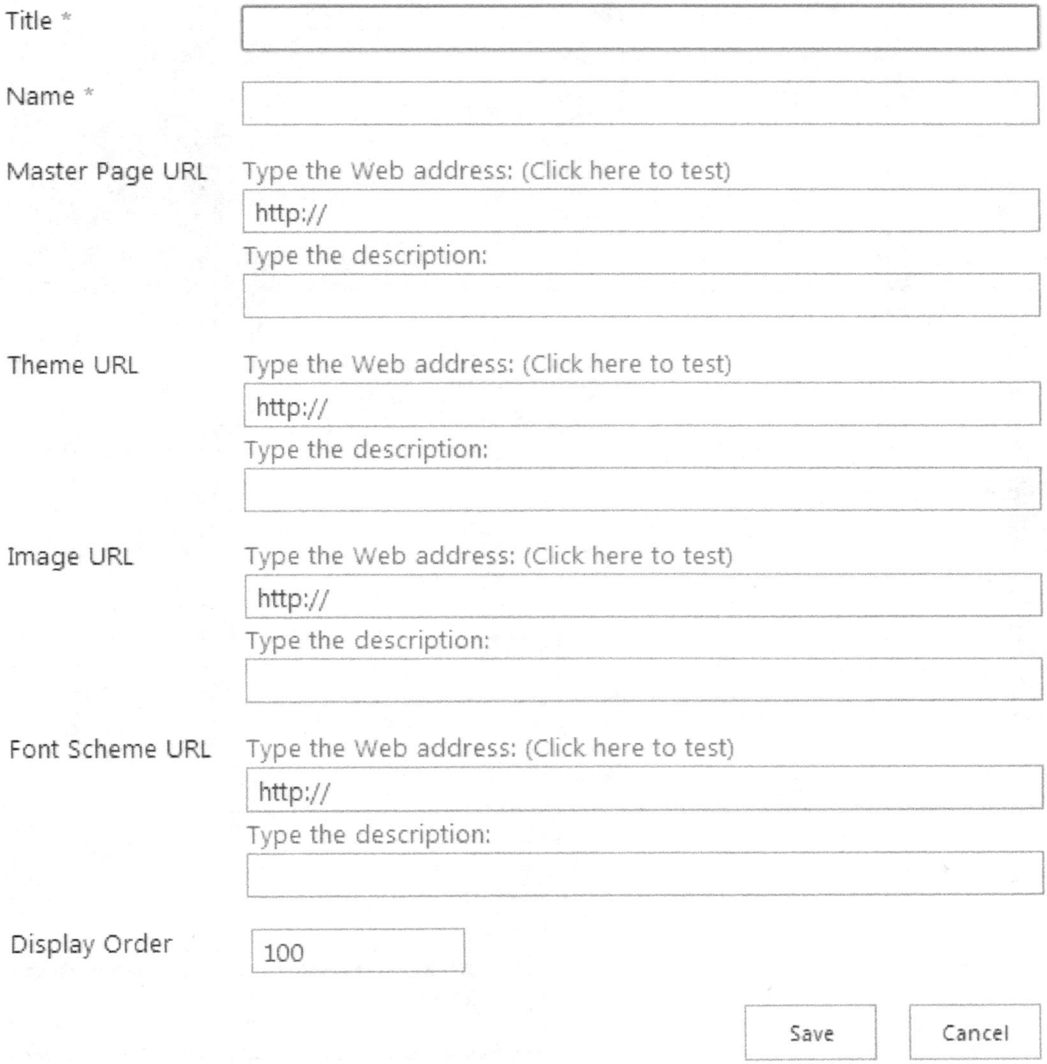

Title *

Name *

Master Page URL   Type the Web address: (Click here to test)

http://

Type the description:

Theme URL   Type the Web address: (Click here to test)

http://

Type the description:

Image URL   Type the Web address: (Click here to test)

http://

Type the description:

Font Scheme URL   Type the Web address: (Click here to test)

http://

Type the description:

Display Order   100

Save   Cancel

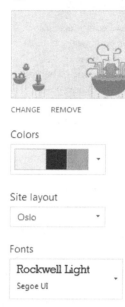

CHANGE   REMOVE

Colors

Site layout

Oslo

Fonts

Rockwell Light
Segoe UI

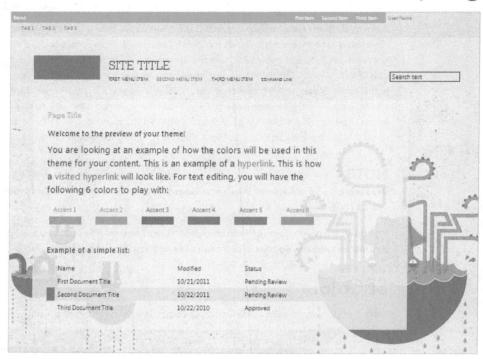

The following list details what each setting in the composed looks gallery represents and how it relates to the Change the Look menu.

- **Title**—The title for the list item that is created for each composed look.

- **Name**—The name or label that appears next to the look in the Change the Look menu.

- **Master Page URL**—A reference to the preferred master page that goes with the composed look. In the Change the Look menu, this shows in the Site Layout drop-down. This can be confusing terminology because Site Layout could be confused with page layouts, which are a different concept.

- **Theme URL**—Another confusing option because themes were the overarching name for functionality that was similar to composed looks in SharePoint 2010. In the composed looks gallery, Theme URL refers to an XML file that lists preferred colors for the composed look. This is shown in the Change the Look menu as Colors.

- **Image URL**—References the URL for a background image to be used in the composed look. On the Change the Look menu, this is represented by the image thumbnail in the top left of the screen.

- **Font Scheme URL**—Refers to an XML file that lists preferred fonts for this composed look. On the Change the Look menu, this is simply shown as Fonts.

- **Display Order**—This number represents the sort order from low to high that the composed look shows on the first page of the Change the Look menu with all the thumbnail previews.

One interesting thing about the composed looks gallery is that each item simply represents a suggestion for the Change the Look menu. In reality the user can select a composed look and then change the background image, colors, master page, and fonts from all the available options. This can be a good thing because it gives the user a much larger array of options from which to mix and match.

Creating SPFont and SPColor Files

Before you learn about using composed looks with your own master page, you should create a simple composed look to use with one of the default master pages. To get started with this you'll want to make some simple font and color XML files for the composed look. These files live in /_catalogs/theme/15, which is actually one level above the master page gallery that you may have mapped earlier in the book. If you haven't already done so, go ahead and map a drive to the root of your SharePoint server instead of the master page gallery. From there, simply navigate to the _catalogs/theme/15 folder. You can see a long list of files that end with the extensions .spfont and .spcolor; these represent all the default color and font options for composed looks.

NOTE

Depending on your Explorer window settings you may have to turn off hidden files in order to see the _catalogs folder.

You need to make copies of fontscheme001.spfont and Pallete001.spcolor. Name the copies **BreakfastFonts.spfont** and **BreakfastColors.spcolor**, respectively.

SPColor

Start by opening BreakfastColors.spcolor in a text editing program.

```xml
1   <?xml version="1.0" encoding="utf-8"?>
2   <s:colorPalette isInverted="false" previewSlot1="BackgroundOverlay" previewSlot2="BodyText"
    previewSlot3="AccentText" xmlns:s="http://schemas.microsoft.com/sharepoint/">
3       <s:color name="BodyText" value="444444" />
4       <s:color name="SubtleBodyText" value="777777" />
5       <s:color name="StrongBodyText" value="262626" />
6       <s:color name="DisabledText" value="B1B1B1" />
7       <s:color name="SiteTitle" value="262626" />
8       <s:color name="WebPartHeading" value="444444" />
9       <s:color name="ErrorText" value="BF0000" />
10      <s:color name="AccentText" value="0072C6" />
11      <s:color name="SearchURL" value="338200" />
12      <s:color name="Hyperlink" value="0072C6" />
13      <s:color name="Hyperlinkfollowed" value="663399" />
14      <s:color name="HyperlinkActive" value="004D85" />
15      <s:color name="CommandLinks" value="666666" />
16      <s:color name="CommandLinksSecondary" value="262626" />
17      <s:color name="CommandLinksHover" value="0072C6" />
18      <s:color name="CommandLinksPressed" value="004D85" />
19      <s:color name="CommandLinksDisabled" value="B1B1B1" />
20      <s:color name="BackgroundOverlay" value="D8FFFFFF" />
21      <s:color name="DisabledBackground" value="FDFDFD" />
22      <s:color name="PageBackground" value="FFFFFF" />
23      <s:color name="HeaderBackground" value="D8FFFFFF" />
24      <s:color name="FooterBackground" value="D8FFFFFF" />
25      <s:color name="SelectionBackground" value="7F9CCEF0" />
26      <s:color name="HoverBackground" value="7FCDE6F7" />
27      <s:color name="RowAccent" value="0072C6" />
28      <s:color name="StrongLines" value="92C0E0" />
```

The bulk of the file is color definitions that start with `<s:color...` and include the name of the color and a hexadecimal value like you would use to represent colors in CSS. One thing to note in these colors is that they will sometimes be listed with eight digits instead of the normal six. These are 8-bit aRGB colors, where the first two digits represent the alpha (or transparency) value in hex, followed by the normal CSS hex color digits.

The other thing to note is the second line in the file, which defines some important parameters for this color file:

- `isInverted`—Used primarily by the color drop-downs in the SharePoint ribbon. If `isInverted` is set to `True`, SharePoint knows to invert the color options in the color dropdowns so that the default text colors start lighter and go darker to let them show better on a dark background.

- `PreviewSlot1`, `PreviewSlot2`, and `PreviewSlot3`—These refer to the colors drop-down that shows in the Change the Look menu. Each slot points to a color value in the preceding list of colors. For example, `Pallete001.spcolor` uses `BackgroundOverlay`, `BodyText`, and `AccentText` for its color slots. In the Change the Look menu you can see the colors white, gray, and blue, respectively, because they are defined by the hex settings for each of those colors in the color list.

When you understand the way the file is set up, changing colors is actually not that complicated. You can make a simple edit to the color file by changing the value for `BodyText` to a noticeable red color.

Replace this line:

```
<s:color name="BodyText" value="444444" />
```

With this color and save the file:

```
<s:color name="BodyText" value="B22222" />
```

Because you are changing a color that is referenced in a `PreviewSlot`, in this case `BodyText`, you can see this color in the drop-down when selecting the composed look.

SPFont

To familiarize yourself with an SPFont file, look at the `BreakfastFonts.spfont` file:

```xml
<?xml version="1.0" encoding="utf-8"?>
<s:fontScheme name="Bodoni" previewSlot1="title" previewSlot2="body" xmlns:s="http://schemas.microsoft.com/sharepoint/">
    <s:fontSlots>
        <s:fontSlot name="title">
            <s:latin typeface="Bodoni Book" eotsrc="/_layouts/15/fonts/BodoniBook.eot" woffsrc="/_layouts/15/fonts/BodoniBook.woff"
            ttfsrc="/_layouts/15/fonts/BodoniBook.ttf" svgsrc="/_layouts/15/fonts/BodoniBook.svg"
            largeimgsrc="/_layouts/15/fonts/BodoniBookLarge.png" smallimgsrc="/_layouts/15/fonts/BodoniBookSmall.png" />
            <s:ea typeface="" />
            <s:cs typeface="Segoe UI Light" />
            <s:font script="Arab" typeface="Segoe UI Light" />
            <s:font script="Deva" typeface="Nirmala UI" />
            <s:font script="Grek" typeface="Segoe UI Light" />
            <s:font script="Hang" typeface="Malgun Gothic" />
            <s:font script="Hans" typeface="Microsoft YaHei UI" />
            <s:font script="Hant" typeface="Microsoft JhengHei UI" />
            <s:font script="Hebr" typeface="Tahoma" />
            <s:font script="Hira" typeface="Meiryo UI" />
            <s:font script="Thai" typeface="Tahoma" />
            <s:font script="Armn" typeface="Segoe UI Light" />
            <s:font script="Beng" typeface="Nirmala UI" />
            <s:font script="Cher" typeface="Gadugi" />
            <s:font script="Ethi" typeface="Ebrima" />
            <s:font script="Geor" typeface="Segoe UI Light" />
            <s:font script="Gujr" typeface="Nirmala UI" />
            <s:font script="Guru" typeface="Nirmala UI" />
            <s:font script="Knda" typeface="Nirmala UI" />
            <s:font script="Khmr" typeface="Khmer UI" />
            <s:font script="Laoo" typeface="Lao UI" />
            <s:font script="Mlym" typeface="Nirmala UI" />
            <s:font script="Mymr" typeface="Myanmar Text" />
            <s:font script="Orya" typeface="Nirmala UI" />
            <s:font script="Sinh" typeface="Nirmala UI" />
            <s:font script="Syrc" typeface="Estrangelo Edessa" />
```

This file has a little extra going on. On line two the `<s:fontScheme>` tag is set up similarly to the `<s:color>` tag in the SPColor file in that it defines some `previewSlots` referenced in the following list of `fontSlots`. Inside of the `fontSlots` node, you see several `fontSlot` child nodes, each with a "name" that defines the slot. Inside of each `fontSlot` node you see an `<s:latin>` node that configures the actual fonts that will be used for this slot plus several nodes that tell SharePoint what fonts to use if the default language is set to a foreign language that doesn't use Latin type faces. Focusing on the `latin` node, you can see that it defines the following properties:

- **Typeface**—The name of the font that shows in the Change the Look menu.

- **EOTSRC**—Points to the URL for an .EOT font file.

- **WOFFSRC**—Points to the URL for a .WOFF font file.

- **TTFSRC**—Points to the URL for a .TTF font file.

- **SVGSRC**—Points to the URL for an .SVG font file.

- **Largeimgsrc**—Points to the URL for an image that represents the font in the Change the Look menu. This image shows the user a sample of what the font will look like for the first `previewSlot`.

- **Smallimgsrc**—Points to the URL for an image that represents the secondary font in the Change the Look menu. This image shows the user a sample of what the font will look like for the second `previewSlot`.

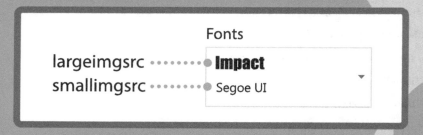

If you have never created fonts for use on the web, you may be confused by the EOT, WOFF, TTF, and SVG settings here. They represent the four common font formats that the different browsers use to show custom fonts. If you want more information on how web fonts work, check out http://www. fontsquirrel.com, which has many web fonts available for download and a generator that creates the EOT, WOFF, TTF, and SVG files for you.

To make life easy, a sample web font is provided that you can download from the code for this chapter to create your SPFont file. Download the Arvo font and then copy the entire Arvo folder into /_catalogs/theme/15/Arvo. This includes EOT, SVG, TTF, and WOFF fonts as well as two images you can use for the largeimgsrc and smallimgsrc. With these files in place, you can change the first latin slot on line 5 to match this and then save the file:

```
<s:latin typeface="ArvoRegular"
eotsrc="/_catalogs/theme/15/Arvo/Arvo-Regular-webfont.eot"
woffsrc="/_catalogs/theme/15/Arvo/Arvo-Regular-webfont.woff"
ttfsrc="/_catalogs/theme/15/Arvo/Arvo-Regular-webfont.ttf"
svgsrc="/_catalogs/theme/15/Arvo/Arvo-Regular-webfont.svg"
largeimgsrc="/_catalogs/theme/15/Arvo/ArvoRegularLarge.png"
smallimgsrc="/_catalogs/theme/15/Arvo/ArvoRegularSmall.png" />
```

Creating a Simple Composed Look

Now that you have created SPFont and SPColor files, you can use them to build a simple custom composed look. For this example, you can use an existing background image and one of the existing out-of-the-box master pages.

EXAMPLE: CREATING A SIMPLE COMPOSED LOOK

1. Navigate to **Site Settings** ➤ **Web Designer Galleries** ➤ **Composed Looks**.

2. Click **new item** at the top of this page to create a new composed look.

3. Enter the following options for the composed look:

   - Title—**Breakfast**
   - Name—**Breakfast Theme**
   - Master Page URL—`/_catalogs/masterpage/oslo.master`
   - Theme URL—`/_catalogs/theme/15/BreakfastColors.spcolor`
   - Image URL—`/_layouts/15/images/image_bg117.jpg`
   - Font Scheme URL—`/_catalogs/theme/15/BreakfastFonts.spfont`
   - Display Order—**5**

   The master page URL points to the out-of-the-box Oslo master page, which shows off a little more of the background image than the Seattle master page does. Theme URL and Font Scheme URL point to the new color and font files you created in the previous section. Rather than make your own image for this example, you can use one that comes with SharePoint. In this case, Image URL points to a photo of some food on a table that is included in the SharePoint install folder on the server. Finally, Display Order tells SharePoint to show this theme near the top of the Change the Look menu.

4. When you have the options set to match these, click **Save**.

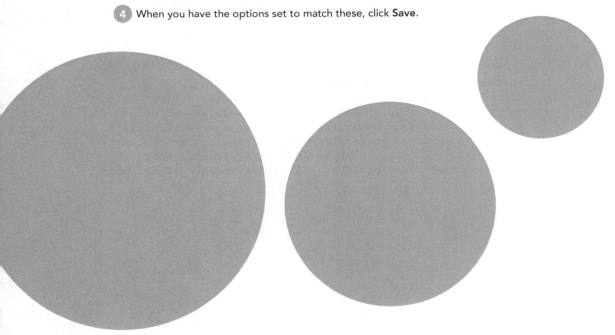

Title *	Breakfast
Name *	Breakfast Theme
Master Page URL	Type the Web address: (Click here to test)
	http://sp15/_catalogs/masterpage/oslo.master
	Type the description:
Theme URL	Type the Web address: (Click here to test)
	http://sp15/_catalogs/theme/15/BreakfastColors.spcolor
	Type the description:
Image URL	Type the Web address: (Click here to test)
	http://sp15/_layouts/15/images/image_bg117.jpg
	Type the description:
Font Scheme URL	Type the Web address: (Click here to test)
	http://sp15/_catalogs/theme/15/BreakfastFonts.spfont
	Type the description:
Display Order	5

Created at 1/7/2013 6:30 PM by ☐ System Account

Last modified at 1/13/2013 7:38 PM by ☐ System Account

Save   Cancel

NOTE

You could browse a selection of background photos that are included with SharePoint by looking on your server in the SharePoint 15 folder under \ TEMPLATE\IMAGES. The background images are all of the format image_bg*.jpg.

At this point the composed look is created, and you can select it from the Change the Look menu by clicking **Site Settings ➢ Look and Feel ➢ Change the Look**. Because Display Order was set to 5, the new composed look should be either the first or second option in the list. If you have already applied a composed look to your SharePoint site, you see that the composed look shown first is labeled **Current.** You can already see that the Breakfast Theme is showing the breakfast table background image that was set earlier.

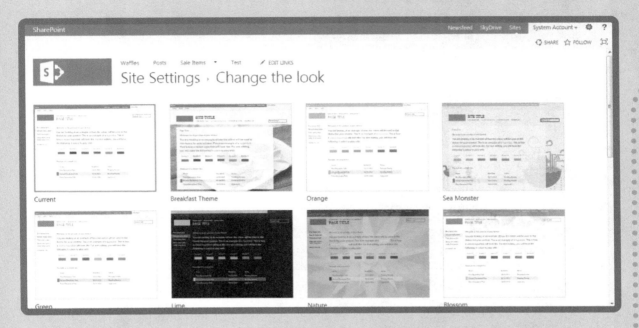

Click the thumbnail for the newly created **Breakfast Theme** and you will see that all the settings for the composed look show as the default settings on this screen. The breakfast table image shows on the top left; the BodyText red color you added shows in the drop-down. If you click the color drop-down and hover over this color, you can see some text that tries to describe the applied colors. In this case SharePoint says, "This palette is primarily White with Red and Dark Blue." Interesting enough, you entered a hex value for the color but SharePoint knows to show the user-friendly text that says the color is red. The Site Layout also shows that the Oslo master page is selected, and then the Fonts drop-down shows the font you added earlier, Arvo Regular, as the default primary font. This drop-down shows an image thumbnail of the font, not the actual font rendering in the browser. On the right side of the menu, you see a preview of what everything should look like when it's put together. You'll learn more about that preview later in the "Creating a Master Page Preview" section.

If you want to change any of the options, you can do that now. All the available values are made up of options created for the other available composed looks.

EXAMPLE: CHOOSE AND APPLY A COMPOSED LOOK

1. When you have the options set how you like them, click **Try It Out.**

2. From here click **Yes, Keep It** to apply the composed look to your SharePoint site.

Without doing a lot of work, you now have a SharePoint site that shows a custom background image, some custom colors, and even custom fonts. Although this is handy, you can actually push the envelope even further by applying composed looks to your own customer master pages.

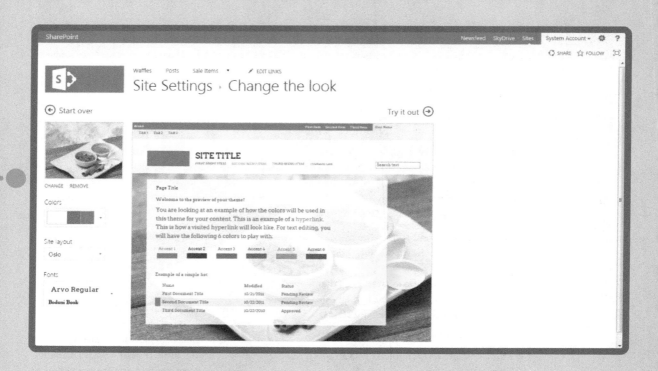

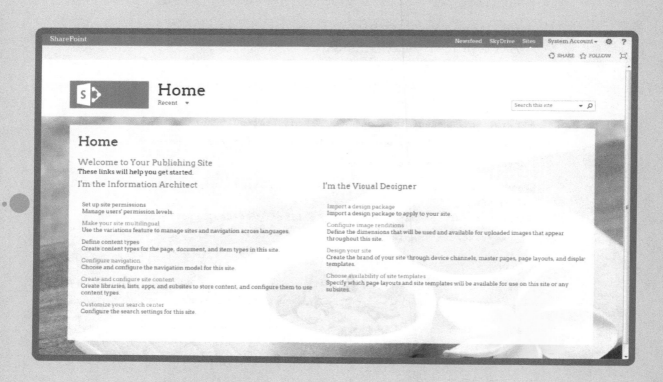

APPLYING A COMPOSED LOOK TO CUSTOM BRANDING

When a composed look is applied to a SharePoint 2013 site, SharePoint makes a copy of the applied CSS and updates the colors, fonts, and background image to match the composed look settings. When this happens, behind the scenes SharePoint looks for specific CSS comments that describe these changes. If you ever looked at how SharePoint 2010 applied theme comments to custom CSS, this concept is virtually identical for SharePoint 2013 composed looks.

SharePoint looks for and applies the composed look settings to any CSS, whether it is out-of-the-box SharePoint CSS or your own custom CSS, as long as the CSS meets two key criteria:

- Your custom CSS must be located in a "themeable" location. The following locations and any subfolders beneath them are valid themable locations:

  - In the SharePoint server's root folder:

    `15\TEMPLATE\LAYOUTS\1033\STYLES\Themable`

  - At the top level of a site collection in one of these folders:

    `/Style Library/Themable/`

    `/Style Library/en-us/Themable/`

> **WARNING**
> Depending upon your SharePoint edition and the site template used to create your SharePoint site, these folders may not be created for you automatically. In those cases you can simply create the folder yourself and themes will work.

- Your custom CSS must be loaded from a master page using the CssRegistration tag like this:

  ```
  <SharePoint:CssRegistration ID="CssRegistration1"
  name="/Style Library/en-us/Themable/style.css" runat="server"
  after="SharepointCssFile" />
  ```

  SharePoint will not apply a composed look to your CSS if you try to load it with a standard HTML link tag, like this:

  ```
  <link rel="stylesheet" href="/Style Library/en-us/Themable/style.css"
  type="text/css" media="screen" />
  ```

> **NOTE**
> If you use the Design Manager to create an HTML master page, SharePoint typically converts an HTML `<link>` tag to the appropriate CssRegistration tag automatically for you.

These two criteria are what SharePoint looks for to apply composed looks to custom CSS called from a master page. However, there is one more thing required to actually select a master page from the Site Layout drop-down in composed looks: a preview for the master page. This is what shows in the list of

composed look thumbnails as well as the large preview section on the right of the Change the Look menu. Although it may seem like these previews are showing static thumbnail images or even functioning master pages, in actuality they are generated from a special type of preview file. You learn more about creating this preview file later in the "Creating a Master Page Preview" section.

Composed Look Theme Tokens

When a composed look is applied to a site, SharePoint finds and replaces special CSS comment tokens. Here is a list of the tokens that SharePoint looks for. In each case, SharePoint will find the token and modify the next line of CSS, injecting a value derived from the composed look that is applied to the SharePoint site:

- `ReplaceBGImage`—Replaces a background image with the image assigned in the applied composed look image URL.
  ```
  /* [ReplaceBGImage] */
  background-image:url("background.png");
  ```

- `ReplaceFont`—Replaces a font with one of the fonts from the Font Scheme URL defined in the applied composed look.
  ```
  /* [ReplaceFont(themeFont:"body")] */
  font-family: sans-serif;
  ```

- `ReplaceColor`—Replaces a color with one of the colors from the Theme URL defined in the applied composed look.
  ```
  /* [ReplaceColor(themeColor:"BodyText")] */
  color:#444;
  ```

- `RecolorImage`—Recolors images using either Tinting or Filling. Tinting is useful for shifting the colors of a multicolor image, whereas Filling is more useful for changing a single, solid color icon with transparency like a PNG.
  ```
  /* [RecolorImage(themeColor:"BodyText",method:"Filling")] */
  background-image:url("icon.gif");
  ```

If you want to get a good idea of how these tokens work, you can see how Microsoft uses them by viewing the source for COREV15.CSS on your server. You can see several hundred of these comments sprinkled throughout the CSS file; each one represents a change that would occur in the master page when a composed look is applied to it.

NOTE

COREV15.CSS is located on the server in the SharePoint 15 folder under: \TEMPLATE\LAYOUTS\1033\STYLES\Themable\COREV15.CSS

Now that you've learned about how composed looks work and what token can be applied to custom CSS, it's time to give it a try. You can use the WaffleNet branding created in Chapter 7, "Creating SharePoint Branding," to do so. If you haven't finished that example yet, you can get the completed code from the Chapter 7 downloads file. You also need a drive mapped to the root of your SharePoint site, much like the earlier example for creating SPFont and SPColor files.

The examples in this chapter assume you have a SharePoint publishing site in a site collection created at the root of your SharePoint server. If your site is in a site collection that was not created at the root, some of the paths to files may need a reference like /sites/sitename.

EXAMPLE: ADDING COMPOSED LOOK TOKENS TO CUSTOM CSS

1. Using a mapped drive, navigate to _catalogs/masterpage. Make sure you already have a subfolder named **WaffleNet** with the WaffleNet master page example loaded into it.

2. Edit **WaffleNet.master** in your editor of choice. You will be adding a CSS reference to a new themeable CSS file. After the CssRegistration tag add the following line, and save the file:

```
<SharePoint:CssRegistration ID="CssRegistration2" name="&lt;%
$SPUrl:~sitecollection/style library/themable/WaffleThemed.css %&gt;"
runat="server" after="style.css" />
```

At this point the referenced CSS file doesn't exist, but you will create it in the next few steps. Since you are already working in the WaffleNet folder, now is a good time to create a preview file for the master page. Remember that a preview file is required to select the master page from the Change the Look menu. In this example, you can cheat a little and use one of the existing preview files. You learn more about creating a real preview file later in the "Creating a Master Page Preview" section.

3. From your mapped drive navigate up one folder from the WaffleNet directory to the masterpage root. Find **Oslo.preview** and copy it; then navigate back to the WaffleNet folder and paste it in. Rename the file **WaffleNet.preview**.

4. To publish both the master page and the preview file, navigate to **Site Settings ➢ Web Designer Galleries ➢ Master Pages and Page Layouts**. Navigate to the **WaffleNet** folder; then click the drop-down next to each file, and select **Publish a Major Version**. Click **OK** on the dialog window.

NOTE

Preview files always match the corresponding master page filename exactly, only with a .preview extension instead of a .master extension. If you ever change the master page filename, you should also change the corresponding preview filename and vice versa.

EXAMPLE: CREATING THE WAFFLETHEMED.CSS FILE

1. Using the drive mapped to the root of your SharePoint site, navigate to **Style Library**. If there is not a folder named **Themable** there, create it now, and then navigate to that folder.

2. Create a new file named **WaffleThemed.css** and open in it your favorite editor.

3. Add CSS and composed look tokens only for areas of the design that you want to be specifically controlled by composed looks. There may be other out-of-the-box styles that pick up on composed

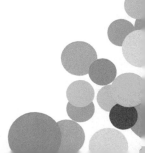

look changes, but the ones defined here will be the only custom areas in your design that can purposely use the composed look. Add the following lines of code and then save the file:

```
.ms-backgroundImage {
 /* [ReplaceBGImage] */
 background-image: url(
   /_catalogs/masterpage/wafflenet/bg.jpg) !important;
}
.customBread .ms-core-pageTitle  {
 /* [ReplaceColor(themeColor:"BodyText")] */
 color: #00b3ff !important;

 /* [ReplaceFont(themeFont:"title")] */
 font-family: "Segoe UI Semilight","Segoe UI","Segoe",
  Tahoma,Helvetica,Arial,sans-serif !important;
 font-size: 30px !important;
}
```

The first rule uses a `ReplaceBGImage` token to replace the default wood grain background image if the composed look applies one. If not, the line after the `ReplaceBGImage` will continue to apply the standard background image.

The second rule changes the page title that appears in the breadcrumb area of the page. `ReplaceColor` first changes the color to match the composed look `BodyText` color setting. Then `ReplaceFont` changes the font to the title font from the composed look font setting. Finally, the font size is changed to 30px; this has nothing to do with composed looks, but it can help you see the changes over the original smaller font size.

WARNING

Because CSS references can sometimes load out of order, it's a good idea to add `!important` to the end of the styles to ensure the composed look takes precedent over other CSS code. Each line in the previous example already has `!important` added to it.

EXAMPLE: CHECKING IN THE WAFFLETHEMED.CSS FILE

1. Because the WaffleThemed.css file lives in the Style Library, it needs to be checked in as a major version before you can use it. From the SharePoint Site click the **Settings** gear, and from the drop-down click **Site contents**.

2. From the **Site contents** menu, click the blue square for **Style Library** and then click **Themable**.

3. Click the ellipses "…" next to **WaffleThemed** and then the second set of ellipses "…" in the pop-up menu; then click **Check In**. Next to **Version** select **1.0 Major Version (Publish)** and click **OK**.

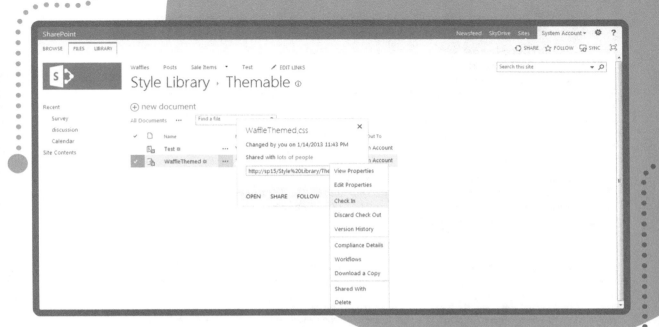

EXAMPLE: APPLYING YOUR COMPOSED LOOK TO YOUR CUSTOM THEME

1. Navigate to **Site Settings ➤ Look and Feel ➤ Change the Look** and then from the list of thumbnails select **Breakfast Theme**.

2. The default **Site Layout** is set to the **Oslo** master page. Now that you have a preview file created for **WaffleNet**, you can select the drop-down and choose WaffleNet. Remember you used a copy of Oslo's preview file, so the preview on the right will look like that master page.

3. Click **Try It Out**. Unlike the preview on the previous page, this preview window actually shows your custom master page with the composed look applied to it. Click **Yes, Keep It** to apply the composed look to your custom branding.

After SharePoint is done "thinking," you see that the composed look is applying the custom background image of the breakfast table and the page title is showing with the red BodyText color and uses the custom Arvo font.

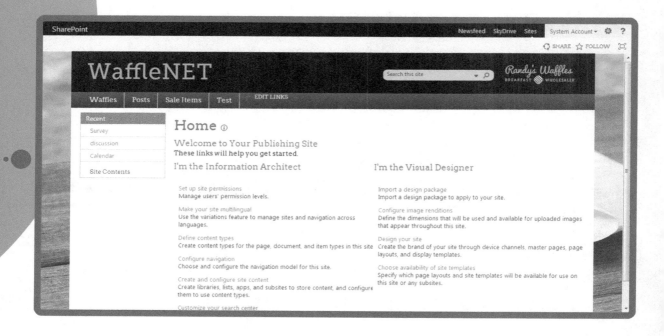

Because SharePoint enables you to change the default settings that are applied with a composed look, having this preview file allows your custom master page to be selectable with the other composed looks. This makes it possible to mix and match settings to make a variety of new looks.

CREATING A MASTER PAGE PREVIEW

When you applied the composed look in the previous section, you saw a preview for the Oslo master page in both the composed look thumbnail and the larger preview when selecting the look. This was because you copied the preview file from the Oslo master page. These thumbnail and larger previews are actually generated by iFramed HTML created from that preview file. Because those two pages show the thumbnail and preview at different sizes, SharePoint is actually scaling the iFramed HTML as needed to fill the necessary sizes.

This preview file for Oslo looked nothing like your custom master page in the previews from the previous example. To get your custom master page to show, you need to create a custom preview file to match your custom master page. The process of creating a custom preview file is actually kind of tricky because it is mostly an HTML file, not a master page file, yet it has special markup that is unlike any traditional HTML file or even a typical master page. To make matters worse, recall that the same preview file shows as a small thumbnail and a larger preview, which means the markup needs to stretch and compress according to the size of the preview that is shown.

Preview File Structure

Before getting too deep into creating a preview file, you should look at the basic structure of one of the default previews. Use your mapped drive to navigate to _catalogs/masterpage and open **Oslo.preview** in your text editor. You can see that the file is broken into four areas by three [SECTION] identifiers.

Throughout the CSS and HTML sections of the preview file, you can notice bracketed tokens that are used to inject strings into the markup. The following sections cover some of the key tokens that you see in previews.

```
1    Palette001.spcolor
2    [SECTION]
3    SharePointPersonality.spfont
4    [SECTION]
5    [ID] .dgp-pageHyperLinkVisited
6    {
7        color: [T_THEME_COLOR_HYPERLINKFOLLOWED] !important;
8    }
9    [ID] #dgp-pageContainer
10   {
11       background-color: [T_THEME_COLOR_PAGEBACKGROUND];
12       color: [T_THEME_COLOR_BODYTEXT];
13       width: 100%;
14       height:100%;
15       background-image: url('[T_IMAGE]');
16       background-size: cover;
17       font-family: [T_BODY_FONT];
18   }
19   [SECTION]
20   <div id="dgp-pageContainer">
21       <div class="dgp-pageContent">
22           <div class="dgp-suiteBar">
23               <div class="ms-tableRow">
24                   <div class="dgp-suiteBarLeft">
25                       <div class="dgp-globalleft">
26                           [BRANDSTRING]
27                       </div>
28                       <div class="dgp-globalright">
29                           <span class="dgp-spacing">[SUITELINK1]</span>
30                           <span class="dgp-spacing">[SUITELINK2]</span>
```

Default SPColor: This is the name of an SPColor file like the one you created earlier. SharePoint shows these colors in any preview thumbnail that uses this master page on the first Change the Look menu before any composed look has been selected.

Default SPFont: Similar to the previous section, this defines the default SPFont file that will be used in any preview thumbnail that uses this master page on the first Change the Look menu before any composed look has been selected.

CSS that is specific to the preview file: This is a large section of CSS that is used to style HTML only in this preview file. Each CSS rule begins with an **[ID]** that is a token that will be different for each available composed look. This unique token is what allows several small iFramed HTML thumbnail previews to show from the same HTML page on the Change the Look menu, but yet have each one styled differently by CSS.

This CSS resembles the CSS from the actual master page, but in a simplified manner and with one striking difference: the width and heights are all represented by percentages. This is required because of the two different-sized previews that show in Change the Look.

HTML that is specific to the preview file: The last section is the HTML markup for the preview. Again this markup is like a simplified HTML version of what shows in the related master page.

CSS Tokens

- **[ID]**—As you just learned, this token injects a unique identifier before each CSS rule to make them stand out when shown in a grid of composed look thumbnail previews.

- **[T_HEIGHT]** and **[T_WIDTH]**—The height and width of the preview window.

- **[T_IMAGE]**—The URL of the optional background image.

- **[T_IMGHEIGHT]** and **[T_IMGWIDTH]**—The height and width of the background image.

- **[T_THEME_COLOR_<SLOTNAME>]**—The color value for a given slot name in the SPColor file.

- **[T_THEME_COLOR_<SLOTNAME>_AA]**—Like the previous item but shows the color including the two extra hex digits needed to show alpha transparency for the color.

- **[T_<SLOTNAME>_FONT]**—The font value for a given slot name in the SPFont file.

HTML Tokens

The HTML tokens are a little different from the CSS tokens. Where the CSS tokens refer to settings from the composed look like fonts, color, and a background image, the HTML tokens are strings that are predefined by Microsoft to be used as placeholders in the HTML design of the preview. For instance, one token injects fake top navigation, whereas another injects a fake search box.

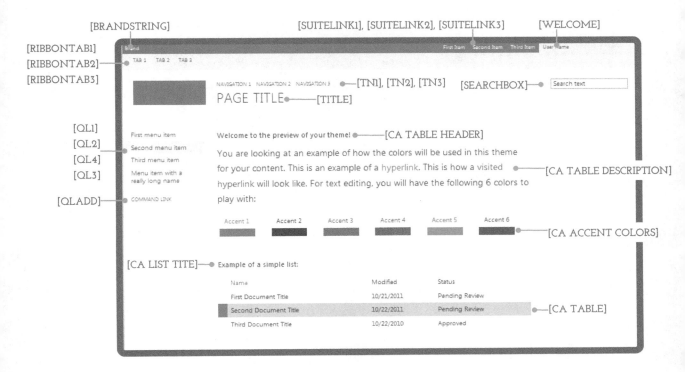

Creating a Custom Preview File

The process of creating the actual preview file for the WaffleNet master page would take up quite a few pages and take a lot of time to follow. Instead this section discusses the general steps for making your own preview, and includes some tips for making the task a little easier. You can also download the completed preview file from the chapter downloads for studying later

EXAMPLE: MAKING YOUR OWN PREVIEW

1. Begin by copying one of the out-of-the-box master page previews, either `Seattle.preview` or `Oslo.preview` from `_catalogs/masterpage`. The two are subtly different, so check out a preview of both from the Change the Look menu before deciding which is the most similar to your custom design. Copy the preview file to the same folder as your custom master page, and rename it to the same exact filename with a `.preview` extension.

2. Open the file in a text editor, and in the first two sections enter default SPColor and SPFont filenames. For example, the WaffleNet preview starts with this code:

```
BreakfastColors.spcolor

[SECTION]

BreakfastFonts.spfont

[SECTION]
```

NOTE

The references do not include a path; SharePoint knows to look for them in `_catalogs/theme/15`.

3. Skip over the next section with all the CSS rules, and go to the final section with the HTML; you'll come back to the CSS after the HTML. The default HTML in the Oslo and Seattle previews is fairly easy to read and modify; it represents a much more simplified version of the corresponding master pages. The preview HTML has a parent element of `<div id="dgp-pageContainer">` and contains many child divs with style classes that describe their contents, including divs for the suite bar / ribbon, top navigation, page title, logo, left navigation, search box, and some fake page content.

4. Modify the out-of-the-box preview file HTML to look similar to your custom branding. You want to try to get the broad strokes right; the preview does NOT need to be an exact replica of the master page. Ultimately, you must decide how close you want the preview to look to your custom branding. Use the HTML tokens that are already in the out-of-the-box preview; arrange them with your custom HTML to get a nice preview.

5. Jump back up in the code to the previous CSS section. For this section there are a couple things that you need to handle.

First, update any of the existing out-of-the-box preview CSS that represents colors, fonts, and images from composed looks that you are NOT using in your custom branding. For instance, most of the WaffleNet page text is dark gray no matter what composed look is applied. Because of that the WaffleNet preview has changes like the following:

```
[ID] .dgp-contentBoxTableHeader
{
    color: [T_THEME_COLOR_BODYTEXT];
    font-family: [T_BODY_FONT];
    font-size:1.125em;
    margin:1% 0 2% 0;
}
```

Is changed to:

```
[ID] .dgp-contentBoxTableHeader
{
    font-size:1.125em;
    margin:1% 0 2% 0;
}
```

For WaffleNet the color and font-family were removed; they instead inherit a color and font-family from the body.

● Next, after you make any necessary changes to the default preview CSS, add any custom CSS you need to make your preview look like the master page. In some ways you can leverage copy and pasting from your existing custom CSS file styles, but remember a couple things:

  ● You don't want to just paste in all your custom CSS; you need only a small percentage of the CSS to style this much simpler preview file.

  ● Every CSS rule you add should not only begin with the unique identifier token [ID] but you also want to change the selectors to be unique from your typical custom branding. This may be a little confusing, but the need for uniqueness is because the previews are shown inside of iFrames, inside of whatever master page is currently applied to your site. If you use the same exact selector names as you did in the applied custom branding like the WaffleNet master page, it can make inspecting and debugging CSS tricky. In the WaffleNet preview, all the custom CSS classes begin with prvCustom.

  ● You should strive to have all the height and width references use percentage-based measurements so that the preview scales properly. Having said that, you can certainly get by with some less important measurements set as pixels, especially if they are small pixel sizes.

  ● In general, background images besides the main background image should be avoided or used sparingly. The out-of-the-box preview files for Oslo and Seattle use little, colored rectangles in place of most images. This is because if you want to use custom background images you need to create smaller versions of the originals in an image-editing program so that the smaller-scaled versions look good—plus they still need to have CSS that allows them to scale appropriately. This means having a special -ms-filter in CSS to handle IE8's lack of CSS3 support. The WaffleNet preview includes a few custom background images; you can download the final preview code to see how they are handled.

6 When you think you have the preview file set up the way you like, save the file. Before you test the previews though, create a new composed look that uses the WaffleNet master page. Follow the steps from earlier in this chapter, but use the following settings for the composed look:

- Title—**WaffleNet**
- Name—**WaffleNet Theme**
- Master Page URL—`/_catalogs/masterpage/WaffleNet/WaffleNet.master`
- Theme URL—`/_catalogs/theme/15/BreakfastColors.spcolor`
- Image URL—`/_catalogs/masterpage/WaffleNet/bg.jpg`
- Font Scheme URL—`/_catalogs/theme/15/BreakfastFonts.spfont`
- Display Order—**2**

7 With this composed look created, you can then go to the Change the Look menu and see the thumbnail preview in the list of composed looks. Compare it to your custom SharePoint branding. Be sure to also click the composed look and see the bigger preview in the next menu. Make sure the preview looks good at both scales.

Remember the goal here is to get it close to the master page look and feel, but it doesn't need to be an exact mirror image. If you need to debug the HTML or CSS, you can use tools such as IE's F12 toolbar or Firefox's Firebug, but be aware that the HTML is buried deep in the source, and the inspection tool often does not bring up the exact location in the HTML source. If you need to make changes to the preview file, open it in your text editor and make changes at any time. Whenever you click Save, the composed look preview should update accordingly.

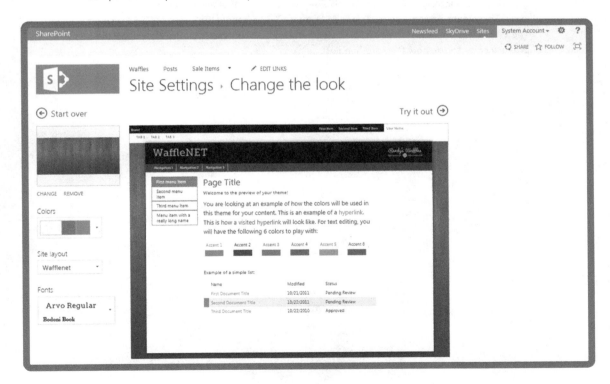

SUMMARY

- Composed looks in SharePoint 2013 enable users to change the look and feel of a site without a lot of work.

- Composed looks set default options for a master page, background image, colors, and fonts, which can then be changed by a user before the composed look is applied to a site.

- Composed look fonts and colors are defined by XML files that end in `.spfont` and `.spcolor`, accordingly.

- Master pages can use CSS comments that have specific tokens, which will receive values from an applied composed look in order to change background images, colors, and fonts. For these tokens to work, the CSS must live in a themable location.

- Custom master pages will not show up as options in the Change the Look menu unless they have a corresponding `.preview` file with a matching filename.

- Composed look preview files are based on a unique file structure that defines default colors, fonts, preview-specific CSS and HTML markup, as well as special tokens that will inject helpful values. The HTML and CSS in previews represent a simpler version of the master page branding that they represent. The CSS in previews should be based on percentage sizes to allow for scaling between two different preview sizes that SharePoint uses in the Change the Look menu.

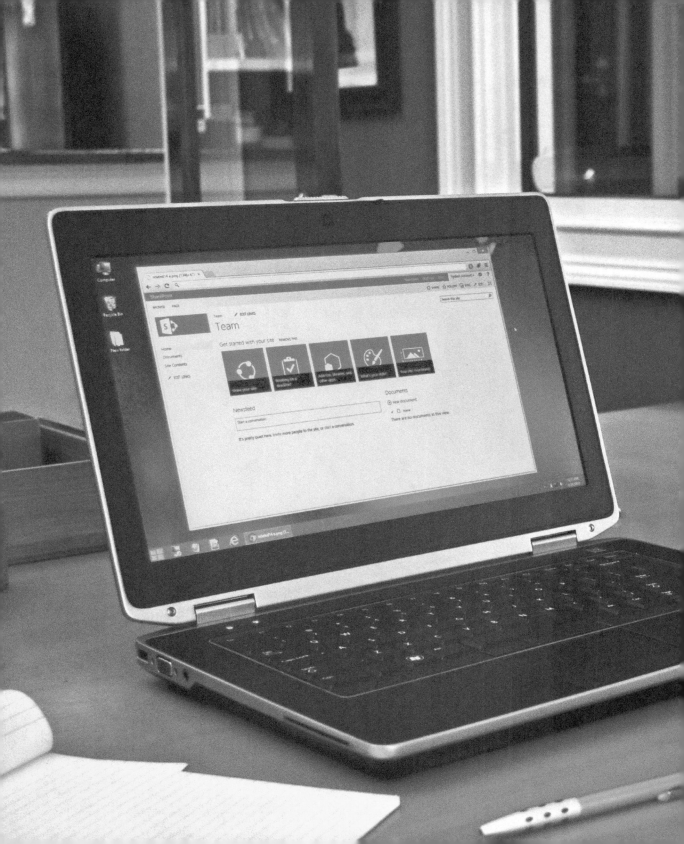

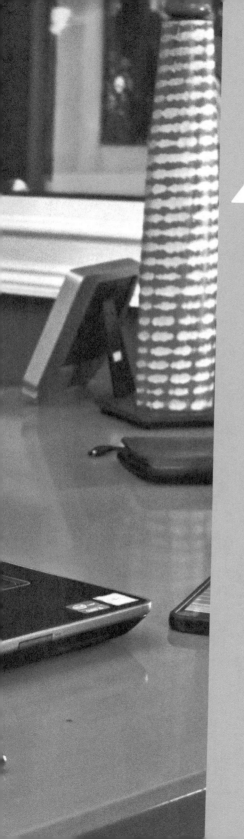

4

Other Branding Concepts

11

MODERN WEB DESIGN AND SHAREPOINT

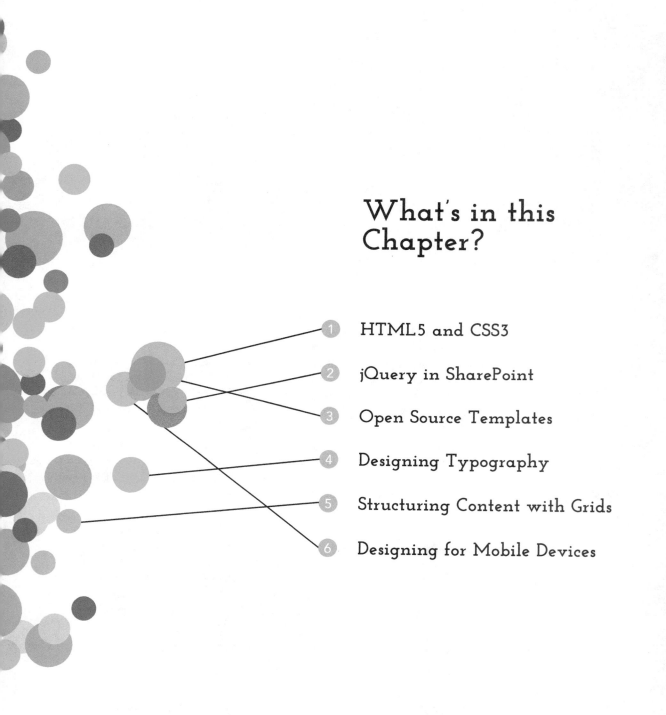

What's in this Chapter?

One of the most frequently asked
user interface questions that came up for
SharePoint 2010 was, "Does it support HTML5?"
Chances are most people asking this question are interested in both
HTML5 and CSS3, which are two technologies almost always lumped together,
probably because they both entered the web development scene around the
same time. When designers talk about modern web design techniques, they
are usually referring to HTML5, CSS3, and other technology such as web fonts
and jQuery.

The answer to the question of whether SharePoint 2010 supported HTML5 was always yes and no because SharePoint is browser-based software. Ultimately, whether a website shows HTML5 and CSS3 depends on browser support. SharePoint 2010 was basically coded to meet IE8 HTML standards, and IE8 was not known for its excellent support for modern HTML techniques. The out-of-the-box Share-Point 2010 master pages even had code in them to instruct Internet Explorer 9 to render the page in IE8 mode. With a little work, you could certainly make modern HTML techniques work in SharePoint 2010, but ultimately you weren't guaranteed a good experience throughout a SharePoint site.

Fast forward to SharePoint 2013 and the story has changed for the better. SharePoint 2013 is coded with IE9 and IE10 in mind, using standards-based HTML. IE8 is the lowest IE browser version supported in SharePoint 2013, and many special tweaks were added to the HTML and CSS to support IE8's lesser rendering capabilities. This is good news for those that want to use modern design techniques such as HTML5 and CSS3.

You may not realize it, but all HTML master pages created with Design Manager are HTML5, and almost all the custom master page examples in this book are based on HTML5 as well. This is all great for fans of modern web design, but unfortunately the two default out-of-the-box master pages (Seattle and Oslo) use the old XHTML 1.0 Strict DOCTYPE instead of the new HTML5 one. Interesting enough, even without a valid HTML5 DOCTYPE, Oslo and Seattle still show HTML5 and CSS3 content properly in most modern browsers. When it comes to IE rendering, SharePoint 2013 includes a key meta tag in the out-of-the-box master pages:

```
<meta http-equiv="X-UA-Compatible" content="IE=10" />
```

This tag essentially tells IE that the markup was written for IE10 and to use that rendering mode if it's available.

This chapter looks at some of the ways that modern design techniques can be used with SharePoint 2013. This includes discussing HTML5, CSS3, web fonts, jQuery, and more.

HTML5

When you look at modern web design, between HTML5 and CSS3, much of the exciting new features are found in CSS3. That said, some new features in HTML5 are worth discussing:

- New tags for <video> and <audio> to embed various types of media on the page without a plug-in such as Silverlight or Flash
- A <canvas> tag that enables you to draw on the page using JavaScript
- Several new semantic HTML markup tags including <section>, <article>, <header>, <nav>, and <footer>, which can be used to organize HTML code better
- New form elements and input types such as color and date fields
- Support for Scalable Vector Graphics (SVG)
- Geolocation to identify the physical location of the browser
- New concepts such as drag and drop and persistent local storage

For a full list of new features included with HTML5, see http://www.w3schools.com/html/html5_form_input_types.asp.

Out of these noteworthy new features, two of the more visual additions that come with HTML5 are particularly interesting because they add features that formerly required plug-ins like Flash or Silverlight. These features are videos and canvases, and they are discussed in the following sections.

NOTE

Some of the examples in this chapter that show off HTML5 and CSS3 techniques require a modern browser such as IE9. If you need to use these features with older browsers such as IE8, you should look into technology such as Modernizr and polyfills. Modernizr is a JavaScript library that can detect browser capabilities as well as add support for new semantic HTML5 elements, whereas polyfills are JavaScript libraries that add in functionality that mimics some of the more advanced HTML5 and CSS3 features such as the video and canvas tags.

For more information on Modernizr and polyfills, check out http://modernizr.com/docs/.

HTML5 Video and SharePoint

The basic markup for adding video in HTML5 looks like this:

```
<video poster="thumbnail.png" width="320" height="240">
  <source src="movie.mp4" type="video/mp4">

  Your browser does not support the video tag.
</video>
```

To try out the new HTML5 video features in SharePoint, it might be tempting to start a new HTML5 master page and add a Script Editor Web Part for adding the video markup, but none of this is actually needed. This is because SharePoint 2013 uses HTML5 by default when you use the ribbon to add video to a page. If you remember, Chapter 3, "Working with the SharePoint 2013 User Interface," has a section titled "Working with Videos," which includes an example for adding video to the page.

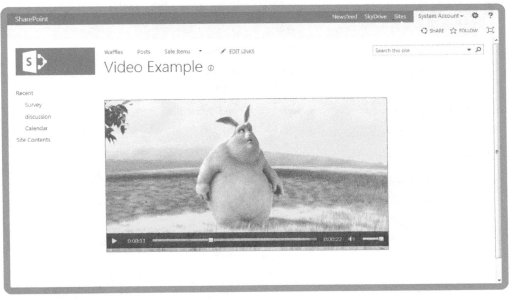

©2008, Blender Foundation www.bigbuckbunny.org

If you view source on a SharePoint 2013 page that has video added, you will find code similar to this buried in the HTML:

```
1  <video id="ctl00_ctl39_g_30d4ad6a_b051_470f_ac13_484bef390683" width="640" height="360" data-mediatitle="Media Web
   Part" poster="/Style Library/Media Player/VideoPreview.png" src="/_layouts/15/clientbin/mediaplaceholder.mp4"
   onloadstart="" data-init="1"><source src="/SiteAssets/big_buck_bunny_trailer_480p_high.mp4" data-label="Media Web Part"
   type="video/mp4">
2
3      <object id="ctl00_ctl39_g_30d4ad6a_b051_470f_ac13_484bef390683" type="application/x-silverlight-2" data=
       "data:application/x-silverlight-2," width="100%" height="100%">
4          <param name="source" value="/_layouts/15/clientbin/mediaplayer.xap?rev=zuBbpwS4QIoVfmLpIUt3Og%3D%3D">
5          <param name="enableHtmlAccess" value="true">
6          <param name="windowless" value="true">
7          <param name="background" value="#80808080">
8          <param name="initParams" value="mediaTitle=Media Web
           Part,mediaSource=/SiteAssets/big_buck_bunny_trailer_480p_high.mp4,previewImageSource=/Style Library/Media
           Player/VideoPreview.png,videoSetSource=,startPlayBackAt=0">
9
10         <a href="http://go.microsoft.com/fwlink/?LinkID=124807" style="text-decoration: none;"><img src=
           "http://go.microsoft.com/fwlink/?LinkId=108181" alt="Get Microsoft Silverlight" style="border-style: none"
           ></a><a href="/SiteAssets/big_buck_bunny_trailer_480p_high.mp4" class="media-link" title="Download Media"><span
           class="media-title">Download Media</span></a>
11     </object>
12 </video>
```

This includes the standard HTML5 `<video>` tag with some options such as a poster or preview image and the height and width of the video. Inside of the HTML5 video tag is where you would normally put some messaging to notify users that their browser can't display HTML5 video properly. Instead of doing that, SharePoint includes an `<object>` tag, which loads a Silverlight player. Although not everyone in the world has the Silverlight player, this is a nice feature to include as a fallback in case HTML5 doesn't work in the user's browser.

For more information on the specifics of how video works in HTML5, check out `http://www.w3schools.com/html/html5_video.asp`.

Adding an HTML Canvas to SharePoint

Another interesting feature of HTML5 is the `<canvas>` tag. The canvas enables you to draw in two dimensions using standard JavaScript. For example, the following code would draw a blue square inside of an HTML5 canvas:

```
<script>
 var ctx=document.getElementById("myCanvas").getContext("2d");
 ctx.fillStyle="#0fff00";
 ctx.fillRect(0,0,150, 150);
</script>
```

For more information on drawing with the HTML5 canvas, see `https://developer.mozilla.org/en-US/docs/HTML/Canvas/Tutorial/Drawing_shapes`.

The following example uses code from this Mozilla Developer Network article to draw a smiley face in a canvas tag added to SharePoint 2013. The example uses the default Seattle master page, which displays HTML5 fine in most modern browsers. If you are a purest, you might consider creating a new master page with the Design Manager because it creates master pages that use the HTML5 DOCTYPE.

EXAMPLE: USING HTML CANVAS TO DRAW A SMILEY FACE

1. Create a new page by clicking **Settings Menu ➤ Add a page.** In the dialog that opens, give the new page a name such as **Canvas Example** and click **Create.**

2. When the new page opens, leave the cursor in the **Page Content** field. From the ribbon click **Insert ➤ Web Part.**

3. Navigate to **Categories ➤ Media and Content ➤ Parts ➤ Script Editor,** and then click **Add.**

4. From the Script Editor Web Part, click **EDIT SNIPPET.**

5. Add the canvas tag, give it an ID of **canvas** for referencing, and give it a width and height of 200 pixels:

```
<canvas width="200" height="200" id="canvas"></canvas>
```

6. Next, add code from the smiley face example from the URL earlier. This code makes a reference to the canvas tag's ID and then creates a drawing path using arcs and moveTo to move the "pen" around the canvas. The code also applies a stroke to the path; without this stroke the path would be transparent.

```
<script type="text/javascript">
  var ctx = document.getElementById('canvas').getContext('2d');
  ctx.beginPath();
  ctx.arc(75,75,50,0,Math.PI*2,true); // Outer circle
  ctx.moveTo(110,75);
  ctx.arc(75,75,35,0,Math.PI,false);   // Mouth (clockwise)
  ctx.moveTo(65,65);
  ctx.arc(60,65,5,0,Math.PI*2,true);   // Left eye
  ctx.moveTo(95,65);
  ctx.arc(90,65,5,0,Math.PI*2,true);   // Right eye
  ctx.stroke();
</script>
```

7. With the code complete, click **Insert**.

8. Save and publish the page.

WARNING

Sometimes SharePoint won't show the canvas drawing immediately after the page is saved. If this happens, just refresh your browser, and the smiley face drawing should show.

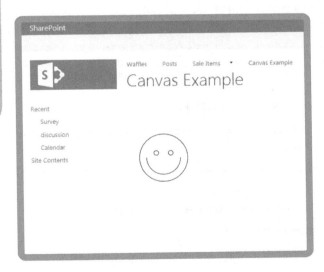

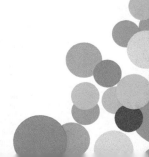

CSS3

You can learn a lot about working with CSS in Chapter 6, "Cascading Style Sheets and SharePoint," including a brief overview of how SharePoint 2013 uses a lot of CSS3 in the out-of-the-box CSS. This chapter just highlights the fact that SharePoint 2013 can show almost any CSS3 that your browser can actually render. You can see this in action in the following example.

EXAMPLE: ADDING CSS TO SCRIPT EDITOR WEB PART

1. Edit the page from the previous example, and then from the Script Editor Web Part, click **EDIT SNIPPET**.

2. Add `<div class="shadowbox">` around the `<canvas>` tag like this:

```
<div class="shadowbox">
<canvas width="200" height="200" id="canvas"></canvas>
</div>
```

3. Add the following CSS to the previous section. This styles the shadowbox div by adding a height, width, and border as well as a border-radius to round the corners and a box-shadow to add a drop shadow behind the div:

```
<style type="text/css">
 .shadowbox {
  width: 200px;
  height: 200px;
  border: 1px solid black;
  border-radius: 10px;
  box-shadow: 5px 5px 10px #999999;
 }
</style>
```

4 Click **Insert** and then save and publish the page.

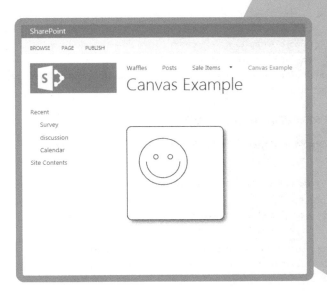

This was a simple example of using CSS to style a div; for more CSS3 ideas, you can explore the CSS3 examples at `http://www.css3.info/preview/`.

JQUERY

If there is one technology that has forever changed the face of web development over the past decade it would have to be the release of the jQuery JavaScript library. You have probably heard a lot about jQuery over the past couple years, but if you don't know what it is, here is a description from the official jQuery website (`http://jquery.com/`):

> jQuery is a fast, small, and feature-rich JavaScript library. It makes things like HTML document traversal and manipulation, event handling, animation, and Ajax much simpler with an easy-to-use API that works across a multitude of browsers. With a combination of versatility and extensibility, jQuery has changed the way that millions of people write JavaScript.

Before jQuery existed most JavaScript was written by hand, and any visual quirks between different browsers had to be handled manually with fixes and workarounds. Dynamic websites were more difficult to code and had to be updated constantly to support new browser versions as they were released. jQuery changed all this by providing one open source code base for JavaScript that enables anyone to quickly and easily control many aspects of an HTML page. Today, if you can think of a visual technique, someone has probably already coded an open source jQuery plug-in that can implement it quickly and easily. Sites such as Facebook and Twitter use technology similar to jQuery to provide dynamic user experiences that many users expect in modern web design.

Although there were some quirks when using jQuery with SharePoint 2010, SharePoint 2013 works great with jQuery. Microsoft has actually based a lot of the SharePoint 2013 App model on the idea that client-side scripting such as jQuery can be used to create rich applications that interact with SharePoint data without needing to understand the intricacies of C# development. You will learn more about how apps work with SharePoint 2013 in Chapter 12, "Designing Apps."

Loading jQuery in SharePoint

When using jQuery with SharePoint 2013, the first step is to figure out how to load the jQuery library. Certainly you could load jQuery for just one page if you want to with a Content Editor or Script Editor Web Part, but chances are you want to use jQuery in multiple pages throughout your site. The following sections highlight a few ways you can load jQuery into SharePoint along with some pros and cons for each option.

WARNING

If jQuery is loaded more than once on the same page, you could run into errors. Keep this in mind if you are including custom controls or Web Parts that might include jQuery themselves. Some of the following methods listed can be used to make sure jQuery loads only once. You can also use JavaScript to check if jQuery is not already loaded via this conditional: if (typeof jQuery == 'undefined')

Link to Content Delivery Network (CDN) in the Master Page

Content Delivery Networks, or CDNs, are a collection of servers located around the world providing centralized hosting for commonly used Internet files. Two of the most popular CDNs for jQuery are hosted by Microsoft and Google. Here is an example of what the reference would be to either of them; the most common location for this reference would be near the bottom of the <head> section of your master page:

```
<script type="text/javascript"
  src="http://ajax.aspnetcdn.com/ajax/jQuery/jquery-1.9.0.min.js">
  </script>

<script type="text/javascript"
  src="http://ajax.googleapis.com/ajax/libs/jquery/1.9.0/jquery.min.js">
  </script>
```

Both these links point to the minified or compressed version of the library for use in production environments; if you want to use the more human readable uncompressed version for debugging, you can remove .min for either reference. Also, keep in mind that as jQuery evolves, new version numbers will be released, and you may someday want to update your references to reflect a newer version.

PROS	CONS
Easy method for loading jQuery into SharePoint.	Referencing external Internet URLs from a corporate intranet may be against company policy.
The file will be served from a fast server located somewhere close to the user's location.	The CDN could conceivably experience an outage, or more likely, the user's connection to the public Internet could go down. Although this outage is beyond your control, to users this can seem like a bug if they can browse the intranet but can't load the public URL for the CDN.
Chances are the user's browser already has the library cached from loading it for another website that referenced the same CDN.	Does not ensure jQuery is loaded only once on your page.

Link to a Local Copy from the Master Page

This method is similar to the CDN method except you download the latest jQuery library from jQuery.com and add the file to your site collection. There are many places you could put the file, but with the new mapped drive features of SharePoint 2013, it would probably be easiest to add the library to the same place your master page is located in the Master Page Gallery. After the library is added to the same location as your master page, you can reference it much like these code examples do:

From a custom master page located in a site collection at the web root, use this code:

```
<script type="text/javascript"
 src="/_catalogs/masterpage/MyMasterPageFolder/jquery-1.9.0.min.js">
</script>
```

If you use the Design Manager to create an HTML-based master page and your master page and jQuery are located in the same folder, you can reference jQuery without a path, and SharePoint can handle making the correct reference on conversion to a master page.

```
<script type="text/javascript" src="jquery-1.9.0.min.js">
</script>
```

Easy method for loading jQuery into SharePoint.

The file will be located inside the corporate intranet.

Does not ensure jQuery is loaded only once on your page

Use a ScriptLink Tag in the Master Page

ScriptLink is a tag that SharePoint uses to load JavaScript while ensuring that a script is loaded only once as well as ensuring that any dependencies have been loaded first.

This is what a reference would look like to the jQuery library if it were copied to the Master Page Gallery of your site collection:

```
<SharePoint:ScriptLink ID="ScriptLink1" runat="server"
 Name="~sitecollection/_catalogs/masterpage/jquery-1.9.0.min.js" />
```

NOTE

If you use the Design Manager to create an HTML master page, you would need to surround the line with `<!--SPM:` and `-->`.

PROS

CONS

Ensures jQuery is loaded only once, assuming all other references to jQuery will use ScriptLink as well

Not really any cons to this method. Like the previous methods it requires editing a master page. If you can't edit the master page for some reason, see the next option.

Use a Custom Action to Load jQuery

Custom actions are a feature of SharePoint that enables you to extend the default user interface with custom code, such as adding a button to the ribbon programmatically. Similarly, a custom action can be created with Visual Studio, which automatically loads jQuery for an entire site collection. For more information on using Visual Studio to create this feature, see the blog post by Bijay Kumar, "Call jQuery to SharePoint page using Custom Action" at `http://drisgill.com/go/jquery-action`.

PROS

CONS

Loads jQuery for an entire site collection

Does not require editing a master page

Requires writing custom code with Visual Studio that can create a feature that needs to be activated on the server

Using jQuery with SharePoint

Now that you know how to load jQuery into SharePoint, you can try a quick example. This example uses a SharePoint Server publishing site and the Design Manager feature to quickly create an HTML-based master page. If you don't have SharePoint Server or access to Design Manager, the steps may be different, but the concepts remain the same. For this example, you will add a button that hides and shows the SharePoint search box with a simple fade in and out effect.

EXAMPLE: USING JQUERY TO SHOW AND HIDE A SEARCH BOX

1. Start by navigating to **Site Settings ➤ Look and Feel ➤ Design Manager**.

2. On the left menu, click **Edit Master Pages ➤ Create Minimal Master Page**. Give it a name such as **jQueryDemo** and click **OK**.

3. From a mapped drive to your Master Page Gallery, open the new HTML master page for editing.

4. In your web browser, from the master page list in Design Manager, click **Conversion Successful** next to the new master page. Then at the top of the next page, click **Snippets**.

5. From the ribbon click **Search Box**; then copy and paste the snippet into the master page above the `PlaceHolderMain` snippet.

6. Navigate to the **Edit Master Pages** menu in **Design Manager**, and next to the master page, click the ellipsis (**...**) and then the second ellipsis in the dialog window. Click **Publish a Major Version** and then click **OK**.

7. Apply the master page from **Site Settings ➤ Look and Feel ➤ Master Page**. There is no navigation in the master page, so you may have to move around the site by typing in URLs.

8. To see the homepage, navigate back to the top-level URL for your site. At this point the master page isn't special, just a simple HTML5 master page with a search box.

9. In your editor, before the closing `</head>` tag, add the following line:

```
<script type="text/javascript"
  src="http://ajax.aspnetcdn.com/ajax/jQuery/jquery-1.9.0.min.js">
</script>
```

10. Now add an ID to the div around your search box so that jQuery can reference it properly. Update `<div data-name="SearchBox">` by adding `id="SearchBox"`, like this:

```
<div data-name="SearchBox" id="SearchBox">
```

11. Add a button above the search box div:

```
<button id="SearchToggle" type="button" style="margin:10px 0px;">
  Toggle Search
</button>
```

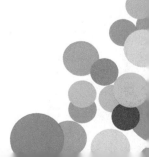

12 Now all you need is some jQuery to handle the button click. Add the following code to the bottom of the page, before the closing `</body>` tag:

```
<script>
$(document).ready(function(){
  $("#SearchToggle").click(function(){
    $("#SearchBox").toggle(500);
  });
});
</script>
```

This jQuery code waits until the HTML document is fully loaded and then it adds a click function to the SearchToggle button. When the button is clicked the SearchBox div toggles between a hidden and showing state. The 500 inside of the toggle function tells jQuery to fade the search box in and out over 500 milliseconds.

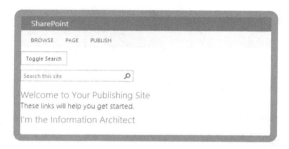

This is a rather simple example of the power of jQuery; for more information on how jQuery works, check out http://docs.jquery.com/.

HTML5 BOILERPLATE

One of the great things about modern web design is that folks are embracing the idea of creating free community resources. In the past few years, a new open source template concept has emerged that provides designers with a common standard starting point for projects that use HTML5, CSS3, and jQuery.

One popular open source template for modern web design is the HTML5 Boilerplate (sometimes abbreviated as H5BP). According to its website:

> 66 HTML5 Boilerplate helps you build fast, robust, and adaptable web apps or sites. Kick-start your project with the combined knowledge and effort of 100s of developers, all in one little package. 99
>
> *http://html5boilerplate.com*

Here is a list of some of the features included with HTML5 Boilerplate:

- A barebones starter HTML template that is mobile friendly
- Placeholder icons for both a favicon and Apple touch-enabled devices
- Google Analytics code
- The latest version of the minified jQuery library
- Modernizr to help support older browsers such as IE8
- Special open source CSS called Normalize.css to help render HTML elements consistently across different browsers
- CSS styles for media queries (for more information see the upcoming section on responsive design) as well as print styles

These features are great but you may wonder how well HTML5 Boilerplate plays with SharePoint 2013. Because HTML5 Boilerplate uses a lot of new and advanced techniques, there are actually a few things in it that don't work well with the SharePoint 2013 Design Manager HTML import process. Because of this you need to make some changes to the HTML5 Boilerplate to be able to use it with SharePoint Server 2013's Design Manager feature.

NOTE

The HTML5 Boilerplate codebase is constantly changing. This chapter was written with version 4.1.0. If you download a more recent version, the HTML-to-master page conversion process may require some adjustment before it works properly.

To follow along with this example, browse to `http://html5boilerplate.com/` and download the latest version of HTML5 Boilerplate.

NOTE

Although it would be tempting to just ignore HTML5 Boilerplate completely for SharePoint, the implications actually go further than you might think. Many modern web design templates, whether open source or for pay, are actually based on the HTML5 Boilerplate codebase. Keep this in mind if you ever work with one of these design templates; they may require the same modifications before converting them to working master pages.

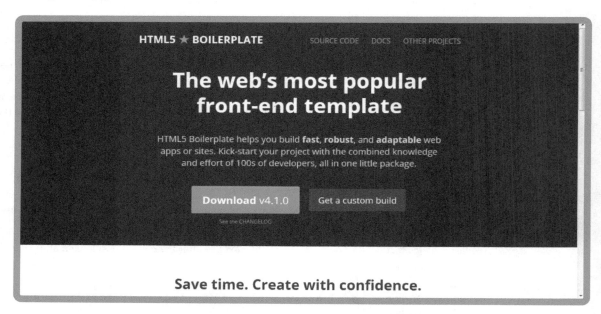

EXAMPLE: CHANGING HTML5 BOILERPLATE TO WORK WITH THE SHAREPOINT 2013 DESIGN MANAGER

1. From a mapped drive to your Master Page Gallery, make a new folder called **HTML5Boilerplate** and copy in all the files from the HTMLBoilerplate zip file.

2 Rename index.html to **HTML5Boilerplate.html** so that you can find it easily in the list of master pages and open it in an editor.

3 Take a look at the HTML source; there aren't a lot of lines of code, but there are some unique techniques used. If you try to convert the HTML to a master page now, you would see some strange behavior. The Design Manager would fail to give you a status for the conversion, and the details would say, "We couldn't find the converted file. After editing and saving your HTML design file, refresh this page."

4 This Design Manager confusion is caused by the code at the top of the HTML5 Boilerplate. Namely, the lines before the `<head>` tag that start with `<!--[if lt IE7>...` are lines used to add special CSS classes for old versions of IE. Although this technique is technically valid HTML, it causes issues for the Design Manager. To handle the issue, edit the top section so that it looks like this:

```
<!DOCTYPE html>
  <html class="no-js">
    <head>
```

5 With that change, the HTML would convert to a working master page in Design Manager, but you need to make a couple other minor changes to how the jQuery is loaded. Scroll down to the first reference to `jquery.min.js`, which is the code for loading jQuery from the Google CDN. The line sometimes gets changed automatically when the file is copied into SharePoint. Make sure the line doesn't say this:

```
<script src="/ajax/libs/jquery/1.9.0/jquery.min.js"></script>
```

Instead the line should be

```
<script
 src="//ajax.googleapis.com/ajax/libs/jquery/1.9.0/jquery.min.js">
</script>
```

6 If the line is incorrect, change it back at this time. The syntax for this URL may seem odd, but it is used to load either https or http depending on the protocol used on the site.

7 The last changes that need to be made are to the next line after the one you just looked at. By default it looks like this:

```
<script>
 window.jQuery || document.write('<script src="js/vendor/jquery-
 1.9.0.min.js"><\/script>')
</script>
```

This line is used as a fallback in case the CDN can't be loaded for some reason; in those cases jQuery will be called from a local directory. This line is technically correct, but SharePoint gets confused by it. Two changes need to be made:

- Split into three lines so that SharePoint can parse it properly

Change the jQuery path to include the path from the top of your site collection to the HTML5Boilerplate folder in your master page gallery. The following code shows how the code needs to change. If your site collection is not at the root, your reference may be different:

```
<script>
 window.jQuery || document.write('<script
 src="/_catalogs/masterpage/HTML5Boilerplate/js/vendor/jquery-
 1.9.0.min.js"><\/script>')
</script>
```

Save these changes; at this point the HTML file is ready to be converted to a master page. If you want to make more changes to the file, you can do them now, or you could wait until later after the conversion process.

CONVERTING AN HTML FILE TO A MASTER PAGE

1. From your SharePoint site navigate to **Site Settings** ➢ **Look and Feel** ➢ **Design Manager**

2. On the left menu, click **Edit Master Pages** ➢ **Convert an HTML File to a SharePoint Master Page.**

3. In the **Select an Asset** window, navigate to the **HTML5BoilerPlate** folder; select **HTML5Boilerplate. html** and click **Insert.**

4. When the page refreshes the master page should have converted successfully, so you can publish it and apply the master page to your site if you want.

At this point, HTML5 Boilerplate code is loaded into SharePoint, and you can take advantage of many of its features. The look and feel isn't pretty; essentially it just says, "Hello world! This is HTML5 Boilerplate." But that's the beauty of templates like this; you can use them as a jumping-off point to create anything you want using modern web design standards in SharePoint 2013.

WARNING

One thing to watch out for in templates such as HTML5 Boilerplate is code that is known as a *CSS reset*. These CSS resets help standardize the rendering of HTML elements across all the different browser platforms. Although this helps maintain a standard look across browsers, it can affect the out-of-the-box SharePoint styles as well. Be sure to test sites with CSS resets thoroughly before using in production. Usually you can see changes in the way SharePoint styles out-of-the-box menus, toolbars, and the ribbon.

In HTML5 Boilerplate this code is known as normalize.css. For the most part, normalize.css is less aggressive than CSS resets that are used in some other open source projects. Be sure to test them, especially in collaborative sites where users need to interact with menus and the ribbon.

WEB FONTS

When creating a great design, typography is one of the main concepts that comes into play. Outside of the web world, traditional and print designers have spent the last 30 years using thousands of different styles and types of fonts to create interesting and engaging content. Web developers have been trying to include aesthetically pleasing typography through the use of fonts since the beginning of HTML; however, until recently this has been limited to mostly relying on the default fonts installed on users' computers. With the advent of CSS3 and modern browser technology, however, web designers finally have a reliable mechanism for showing many fonts that go beyond those that the users already have installed on their computers.

Through the use of the CSS3 font-face rule, web designers can include licensed fonts with their CSS code. Using this new method, browsers can download the font source files and display text using the styles defined by the particular font. The following is a simple example of how font-face is used to show a unique font:

```css
@font-face {
  font-family: 'ArvoRegular';
  src: url('fonts/Arvo-Regular-webfont.eot');
  src: url('fonts/Arvo-Regular-webfont.eot?#iefix')
    format('embedded-opentype'),
    url('fonts/Arvo-Regular-webfont.woff') format('woff'),
    url('fonts/Arvo-Regular-webfont.ttf') format('truetype'),
    url('fonts/Arvo-Regular-webfont.svg#ArvoRegular') format('svg');
  font-weight: normal;
  font-style: normal;
}
```

This code was generated by a useful, free service available from http://www.fontsquirrel.com. .

Font Face Basics

The font face begins with `font-family: 'ArvoRegular'`. This is how you would refer to this font throughout your CSS file. After that, there are URLs listed for four different types of font sources. Although it would be a lot easier to include only one font source file, unfortunately, each web browser vendor uses different font types, and these four cover the most common browser needs:

- **EOT**—Embedded Open Type (EOT)
- **WOFF**—Web Open Font Format (WOFF)
- **TTF**—True Type (TTF)
- **SVG**—Scalable Vector Graphics (SVG)

Gathering all the font formats for each font you want to use can be a pain. Luckily, tools like the aforementioned Font Squirrel @font-face Generator can create the four formats for you based on whatever type you upload.

WARNING

Not every font creator enables their fonts to be embedded as web fonts. Be sure to check the licensing of all fonts before including them in your SharePoint site.

Along with the ability to add fonts directly to your server for users to see with the font-face rule, there are also services that can handle the entire process for you. Google Web Fonts (`http://www.google.com/webfonts`) is a free service that includes many open source fonts, even providing the hosting of these files and sample code to include them with your design. Another service called Typekit (`https://typekit.com`) provides a similar service but for licensed fonts. It has a fee associated with it but offers a free trial option.

Using Web Fonts with SharePoint 2013

Using web fonts with SharePoint 2013 is similar to how you would use them in traditional HTML. If you have followed along with the examples in this book, you have already used web fonts with the WaffleNet example from Chapter 7, "Creating SharePoint Branding." The following example includes a web font that is used for the body text.

EXAMPLE: USING A WEB FONT WITH SHAREPOINT

1. Acquire the source files, EOT, WOFF, TTF, and SVG for the font you want to display on the web. The aforementioned Font Squirrel can help you get the files that you need.

2. From a mapped drive to your Master Page Gallery, copy the images into the same folder as your master page. You may want to create a subfolder for the fonts to keep them organized and away from the rest of the site files.

3. If you don't already have a CSS file for the master page, create one and reference it in the master page or the HTML file. After you have a CSS file associated to the master page, open it for editing.

4. Add the font-face rule for your new font. Again, Font Squirrel can help you with the syntax if you aren't sure. Here is a sample font-face rule; in this example the font was copied to a subfolder named fonts. The code is exactly the same as the earlier example because web fonts work the same in SharePoint as they do in standard HTML.

5. Use the font-family reference in your CSS styles; for example, you could set the <body> to use the custom font. Here the font size is also increased so that the change is easier to see:

6. Save the CSS file and you should see the custom font load in your SharePoint site. Remember , if you want anonymous users to see the styles, you need to publish all the related assets including the master page, CSS, and all the font files.

Notice that much of the body content is now using the larger custom font; in this case the font is Arvo Regular.

```css
@font-face {
  font-family: 'ArvoRegular';
  src: url('fonts/Arvo-Regular-webfont.eot');
  src: url('fonts/Arvo-Regular-webfont.eot?#iefix')
   format('embedded-opentype'),
   url('fonts/Arvo-Regular-webfont.woff') format('woff'),
   url('fonts/Arvo-Regular-webfont.ttf') format('truetype'),
   url('fonts/Arvo-Regular-webfont.svg#ArvoRegular') format('svg');
  font-weight: normal;
  font-style: normal;
}


body {
font-family: 'ArvoRegular',arial,sans-serif;
  font-size: 120%;
}
```

SharePoint

Newsfeed   SkyDrive   Sites   System Account ▾   ⚙   ?

BROWSE   PAGE   PUBLISH

⟳ SHARE ☆ FOLLOW ✎ EDIT ⌷

Waffles   Posts   Sale Items • RandysWaffles •   ✎ EDIT LINKS

Search this site   ▾ 🔍

Home ⓘ

Recent

Survey

discussion

Calendar

Site Contents

Welcome to Your Publishing Site

These links will help you get started.

I'm the Information Architect

I'm the Visual Designer

Set up site permissions
Manage users' permission levels.

Import a design package
Import a design package to apply to your site.

Make your site multilingual
Use the variations feature to manage sites and
navigation across languages.

Configure image renditions
Define the dimensions that will be used and available
for uploaded images that appear throughout this site.

Define content types
Create content types for the page, document, and
item types in this site.

Design your site
Create the brand of your site through device channels
master pages, page layouts, and display templates.

Configure navigation
Choose and configure the navigation model for this
site.

Choose availability of site templates
Specify which page layouts and site templates will be
available for use on this site or any subsites.

Create and configure site content
Create libraries, lists, apps, and subsites to store
content, and configure them to use content types.

GRID-BASED DESIGN

The use of grids in traditional print design is another concept, like typography, that has been around for a long time. The idea is that it's easier to create an appealing page layout if you use tools such as a grid overlay to arrange content in a structured pattern. By overlaying the page with a grid, designers could arrange content into columns and rows (either symmetrically or asymmetrically) and as long as the grid was used, the page ended up looking nice to the reader.

One of the founders of grid-based design, Josef Müller-Brockmann, provides a good explanation about grids:

> " The grid system is an aid, not a guarantee. It permits a number of possible uses and each designer can look for a solution appropriate to his personal style. But one must learn how to use the grid; it is an art that requires practice. "

This image, provided by the Wikimedia Commons (`http://en.wikipedia.org/wiki/File:Grid2aib.svg`), shows a typical grid that might be used to align text in a page layout.

Vermont Symphony Orchestra

Winter 2007 Season	Aaron Copland **The Tender Land** January 2007	Eric Satie **Gymnopedie 1, 2** February 2007
	01/12/07 Middlebury College Center for the Arts 8:00 pm	02/03/07 Johnson State College Dibden Center for the Arts 8:00 pm
	01/19/07 Johnson State College Dibden Center for the Arts 8:00 pm	02/10/07 Castleton State College Fine Arts Center 8:00 pm
	01/26/07 Lyndon State College Alexander Twilight Theater 8:00 pm	02/17/07 Middlebury College Center for the Arts 8:00 pm

As web design has evolved over the years, so has the level of sophistication that has been applied to web page layouts. In recent years, the idea of using grids in web design has become popular. This popularity has increased since the introduction of open source web grid systems such as the 960 Grid System (http://960.gs). The 960 Grid System was created to target 1,024-pixel-wide displays, the most common low-end resolution for users at that time. After accounting for scroll bars and other things, the team settled on the standard web page size of 960-pixel-wide, which was easily divided by many numbers making it a good width from which to apply a grid system. Essentially, after 960 Grid is added to a website, the designer can easily create rows and columns that conform to a large variety of appealing combinations. You can learn more about working with 960 Grid from the articles linked from http://960.gs/.

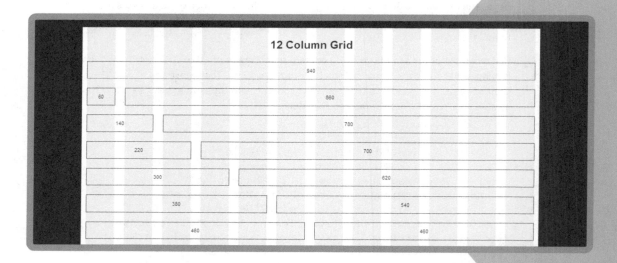

Much like HTML5 Boilerplate that you learned about earlier, there are some gotchas to using grid systems with SharePoint. Most notably is that many grid systems such as 960 Grid use CSS that aggressively resets the standard rendering for HTML elements across browser platforms. Although this helps the grid stay consistent, be sure to test the result on your SharePoint site.

EXAMPLE: USING 960 GRID WITH SHAREPOINT 2013

1 Begin by downloading the code from http://960.gs by clicking the **Big ol' DOWNLOAD button :).**

2 After the file is downloaded, you can see a folder inside the zip file called **code**. Map a drive to your master page gallery, make a subfolder for **960Grid**, and copy in all the files from the code folder. If you want you can rename demo.html to **960Grid.html** so that it's easier to find as a master page. Then just use the SharePoint Server Design Manager feature to convert the html file into a functioning master page without changing any of the code. These steps are similar to any of the previous Design Manager examples.

3 After the master page has been converted, you can make some changes by editing the HTML master page. The default 960Grid.html file (originally demo.html) includes some example styles and HTML markup that isn't needed in actual usage. Remove this reference: `<link rel="stylesheet" href="css/demo.css" />`.

4 Remove most of the sample 960 Grid content that is inside of `<div id="s4-bodyContainer">` leaving just the `<div class="container_12"></div>`. Then move the ContentPlaceHolderMain DIV and all its contents into the container_12 DIV. The section should look like this when you are done:

```
<div id="s4-bodyContainer">
 <div class="container_12">
  <div data-name="ContentPlaceHolderMain">
   <!--CS: Start PlaceHolderMain Snippet-->
   <!--SPM:<%@Register Tagprefix="SharePoint"
    Namespace="Microsoft.SharePoint.WebControls"
    Assembly="Microsoft.SharePoint, Version=15.0.0.0,
    Culture=neutral, PublicKeyToken=71e9bce111e9429c"%>-->
   <!--MS:<SharePoint:AjaxDelta ID="DeltaPlaceHolderMain"
    IsMainContent="true" runat="server">-->
    <!--MS:<asp:ContentPlaceHolder ID="PlaceHolderMain"
     runat="server">-->
    <!--ME:</asp:ContentPlaceHolder>-->
   <!--ME:</SharePoint:AjaxDelta>-->
   <!--CE: End PlaceHolderMain Snippet-->
  </div>
 </div>
</div>
```

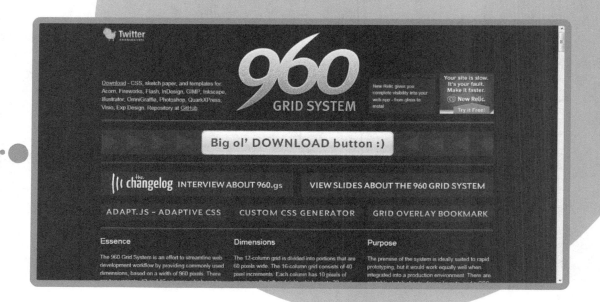

At this point the 960Grid is clean and ready to use with SharePoint; however, nothing is actually using the grid yet. You can save the master page, publish it, and apply it to your SharePoint site. Keep in mind that you didn't include any navigation snippets, so the interface will be minimal.

To take advantage of the grid though, you could create a new page layout using the Design Manager as you learned in Chapter 5, "Using the Design Manager to Start a Design in SharePoint." The downloads for this chapter include a completed Design Manager page layout that is arranged like this pseudo code:

```
<div class="grid_4">
 Page Image Snippet
 Image Caption Snippet
</div>
<div class="grid_8">
 Title Snippet
 Page Content Snippet
</div>
<div class="clear"></div>

<div class="grid_4">
 Web Part Zone 1 Snippet
</div>
<div class="grid_4">
 Web Part Zone 2 Snippet
</div>
<div class="grid_4">
 Web Part Zone 3 Snippet
</div>
```

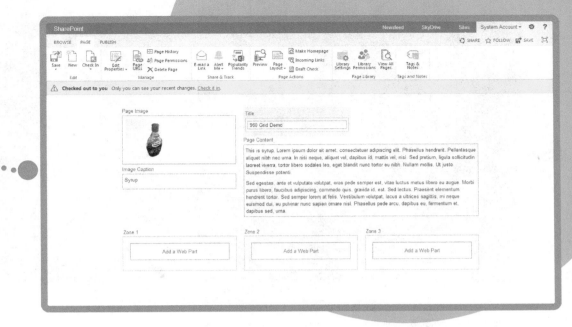

Although you can't see the gridlines, notice that the fields are arranged in a grid pattern. The first row contains a smaller column on the left with the Page Image, Image Caption, and a larger column on the right with the Title and Page Content. Then there is a second row split into three equal-sized columns with Web Part zones in them. In the page layout code, 960 Grid uses the classes `grid_4` and `grid_8` to set the grid column widths, and it uses `<div class="clear"></div>` to start new rows.

RESPONSIVE DESIGN

For modern web design, the hottest new topic is *responsive design*. It's probably no surprise to you that mobile devices have become incredibly popular in recent years. Almost everyone has a smartphone or tablet device, especially in the business world. In turn, web designers have had to struggle to not only keep up with designing websites to target all these small screens, but to also keep mobile style and content consistent with the traditional full-sized desktop browsing experience.

The idea of responsive design is one potential answer to this problem, providing a means of designing a website so that it looks good on a widescreen desktop browser but also scales intelligently to look right on the smallest of modern mobile devices. The topic of responsive design even came up during the 2012 U.S. presidential election, as one candidate's website used a responsive design to handle all browsers, and the other used two targeted designs split between desktop and mobile experiences. At the time of this writing, there isn't a clear-cut winner in this debate—even though the presidential race

was decided. The decision on whether one method or the other is right for a particular project is left to the designer.

The key to allowing responsive design to become as popular as it is today comes from the addition of media queries in CSS3. With media queries it's possible to target portions of a CSS style sheet to different devices based on the device's capabilities. Media queries consist of a media type (screen, print, and so on) and at least one expression that can check to see if a browsing device supports a specific media feature (device-width, resolution, device-aspect-ratio, and so on). For example, the following CSS would target the features of an iPad because its resolution falls between 768 and 1,024 pixels wide depending on the orientation of the device:

```
@media only screen and (min-device-width : 768px) and (max-device-
width : 1024px) {
  body {
    font-size: 16px;
  }
}
```

Any device that meets those screen-width specifications has the style rule inside the media query applied; in this case, the body has its font size changed to 16px.

You can learn more about media queries from `https://developer.mozilla.org/en-US/docs/CSS/Media_queries`.

For a list of media queries for common mobile devices, see `http://css-tricks.com/snippets/css/media-queries-for-standard-devices/`.

NOTE

Media queries are different than device channels. You can learn more about how these two concepts differ by reviewing device channels in Chapter 8, "Advanced SharePoint Branding Tasks."

In the next section, you will look at an existing responsive HTML design and use the Design Manager to create a simple master page that uses media queries to respond to mobile devices.

Creating a Responsive Master Page

You can use the Design Manager feature to convert a responsive HTML design into a SharePoint master page. Keep in mind that you need SharePoint Server with publishing enabled to use the Design Manager.

WARNING

The responsive master page that you create in this chapter is meant as an exercise in showing how responsive design can work in SharePoint. As such, it has been tested only minimally for the homepage of a publishing site. If you want to use this code in production—particularly if you want to use it for collaboration sites—more testing and changes may need to be made to accommodate all usage scenarios.

The bulk of the responsive awesomeness that you will see later in the example starts with an HTML5 design that has responsive CSS applied to it. You can get the initial HTML design from the chapter downloads. Before you try to convert this HTML into a working master page you should understand how it's set up. To do so, open the HTML page Responsive.html in a text editor.

```html
1    <!DOCTYPE HTML>
2    <html>
3    <head>
4        <meta charset="utf-8">
5        <title>Responsive SharePoint</title>
6
7        <!-- mobile zoom reset -->
8        <meta name="viewport" content="width=device-width, initial-scale=1.0" />
9        <!-- custom styles -->
10       <link rel="stylesheet" href="responsive.css" type="text/css" media="screen" />
11       <!-- enable media queries in some unsupported browsers -->
12       <script type="text/javascript" src="respond.min.js"></script>
13   </head>
14
15   <body>
16       <div class="customWidth">
17           <div class="customHeader">
18               <div class="customLogo">
19                   Replace Logo
20               </div>
21               <div class="customNav">
22                   <ul>
23                       <li><a href="#">Link1</a></li>
24                       <li><a href="#">Link1</a></li>
25                       <li><a href="#">Link1</a></li>
26                       <li><a href="#">Link1</a></li>
27                   </ul>
28               </div>
29               <h1 class="customTitle">
30                   Replace Title
31               </h1>
32               <div class="customSearch">
33                   Replace Search
34               </div>
35           </div>
36           <div class="customClear"></div>
37
38           <div class="customBody">
39               <div class="sideNavBox customRespond">
40                   Replace LeftNav
41               </div>
42               <div class="contentBox customRespond">
43                   Replace Main
44               </div>
45               <div class="customClear"></div>
46           </div>
47       </div>
48   </body>
49   </html>
50
```

For the most part, this is a straightforward HTML5 page, with header and body sections, and placeholders for a logo, top navigation, title, search box, left navigation, and main body content.

In the <head> section you can see a few interesting lines. First, there is this tag:

```
<meta name="viewport" content="width=device-width, initial-scale=1.0"
/>
```

The viewport tag is used for mobile devices such as smartphones, which have the capability to load a page initially larger than the actual browser size. These devices enable the user to zoom in and out with finger gestures to see more or less of the page. The viewport tag tells these devices how to load the page, including the initial width and zoom scale. On the Responsive.html page, this is set to the most basic option of zooming into the page to show the entire contents of the page on first load. When you work with a responsive design, this tag is necessary because you want to control the mobile browsing experience at different sizes.

After the viewport tag, the style sheet is loaded for the page, and after that you will see JavaScript that includes `respond.min.js`. Respond.js is the name of a lightweight polyfill that adds support for CSS3 media queries to older browsers such as IE8. This is needed because the responsive HTML leverages media queries extensively, and you need something to handle IE8's lack of media query support. For more information on Respond.js see `https://github.com/scottjehl/Respond`.

Everything else in the HTML file is normal HTML5 markup; most of the magic happens in the included CSS style sheet.

Responsive CSS

The style sheet `Responsive.css` (available for download) is broken into three major sections to handle the three supported browsers sizes. When you are looking at making responsive CSS there are two basic approaches you can decide between. You can make the CSS either *desktop first* or *mobile first*; in other words, the design will either start out as a desktop design that is reduced as the browser gets thinner, or it is a mobile design that expands as the browser gets wider. Although you could use either method, `Responsive.css` uses a desktop first design because SharePoint is primarily a desktop web application. (At least in 2013—for future versions this could change.) Because of this design decision the CSS file starts out with desktop styles, then has styles for a medium browser width, and it ends with mobile styles.

Looking at `Responsive.css` you see that the first section of CSS is the default desktop CSS. There are styles that set a minimum and maximum width for the page content to allow the page to be centered and look good, but not stretch too far if the resolution is high. The elements are arranged as you would normally see them in SharePoint; they are in two main rows, the header section with the site logo, top navigation, site title, search, and a body section with the left navigation and main body content. Many of the elements float on the same line as other elements and spread across the width of the page.

The next section begins with this line:

```
@media only screen and (max-width: 767px) {
```

This is a media query that looks only at devices smaller than the width of a tablet, such as the iPad when it is in portrait mode. Anything above that width shows the standard desktop CSS, but devices smaller than 768 pixels wide show this CSS (unless they are even smaller and fall into the next category). In this media query the example CSS does a few things. Most notably, the body style font size is reduced a little, the left navigation is hidden while the main content area is increased to 100 percent, and the logo and navigation are split into separate rows to allow for more room for navigation to show across the screen.

The last section begins the mobile media query like this:

```
@media handheld, only screen and (max-width: 480px), only screen and
(-webkit-min-device-pixel-ratio: 2) and (max-device-width: 1500px) {
```

This media query is a bit more complex than the previous one. It starts by checking for devices that describe themselves as handheld, which is typically an older designation for phones that aren't considered smartphones. Next, the media query checks for devices that are no bigger than the typical mobile phone screen width of 480 pixels wide. Lastly, the media query checks for devices that have high-pixel density such as the retina iPhone and iPad as well as some Android devices, but will target them only if they are less than 1,500 pixels wide. If a device meets any of those criteria, the mobile media query styles will be rendered. The goal here is to target smaller mobile devices without catching bigger tablet devices.

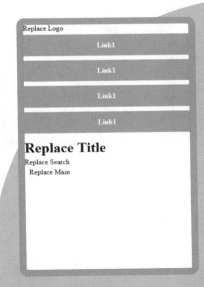

The CSS in this last mobile section makes a few changes to the display. First, the body size is increased because mobile devices are a little harder on the eyes. Next, the page width is changed to auto to allow the page to expand and contract as needed, and most of the padding, margin, and floating are turned off for the major sections. The biggest change is the navigation, which is changed from displaying inline to block, placing them vertically down the page—an orientation that lends itself well to mobile device browsing. Also, the navigation items are increased in size and gain a background color to make them more finger-friendly.

EXAMPLE: USING A RESPONSIVE DESIGN IN SHAREPOINT

1. Map a drive to your Master Page Gallery and create a subfolder named **Responsive**. Then copy in all the HTML, CSS, and JavaScript from the example.

2. Use the Design Manager to convert the HTML into a functioning master page. If you need a refresher on these steps, see the previous examples in this chapter or Chapter 5.

3. After you have the HTML file converted to a master page, you can click its name in the list of master pages in the **Design Manager** under the **Edit Master Pages** step. This brings up the preview screen; if you resize your browser, you see that the media queries are already working and applying different styles to the different browser sizes.

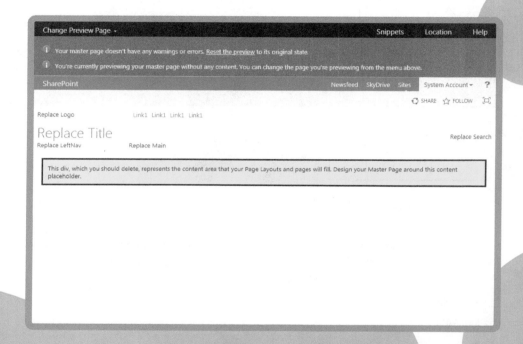

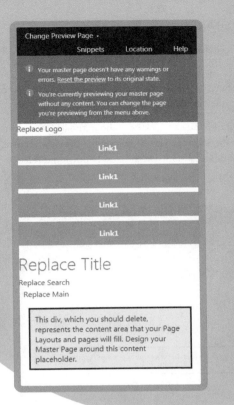

④ Although the media queries work at this point, you can do a few things to make the experience nicer. Start by adding the following snippets to the HTML master page. Each snippet can replace the comment that corresponds to it in the HTML master page:

- **Site Logo**

- **Site Title**

- **Search Box**

- **Vertical Navigation**

- **Replace Main** should be replaced with the PlaceHolderMain snippet that is already included on the page.

⑤ The last snippet to add is the **Top Navigation**, but you need to change two options before you cut and paste it. Under **Customization - Top Navigation (AspMenu)** change **Important** ➢ **StaticDisplayLevels** to **1**; expand **Behavior** and change **MaximumDynamicDisplayLevels** to **1** as well. Click **Update** before copying the code. Then in the HTML master page, replace the entire <UL> structure with the snippet. There is also a rogue <A HREF> in this snippet that has no navigation item; you should remove this because otherwise it will be styled with an empty blue box like the other navigation items in the mobile view. Do a **Find** on your HTML master page to find and delete this line:

```
<a name="startNaviation"></a>
```

6 At this point the HTML master page is ready to go, but there are a couple changes to make to `Responsive.css` for SharePoint-specific styling. Rather than list the code here, replace your existing CSS with the finished `Responsive.css` from the chapter downloads.

By replacing this CSS you have added several things. In the desktop section, the styles are updated for the body container, top navigation, left navigation, and the welcome page to allow them to look nice in SharePoint. This section is fairly similar to what you would do after converting any HTML design to a master page. For the next section, the medium-sized media query, there are no updates needed for SharePoint.

The last section, the mobile media query, gets the bulk of the updates to handle SharePoint-specific elements that need to look different on the smaller screen. Here is a list of some of the main styling changes that were made:

● The ribbon is hidden because it would be difficult to use at this size.

● The search box size is increased.

● All the top navigation styles gain the `!important` property to ensure they get applied in SharePoint. This is a quick-and-easy way to override the more specific SharePoint styling.

● For the top navigation, the fly-outs and their corresponding arrow indicators are hidden. Also, the Edit button that shows if you have navigation editing rights is hidden. These concepts would have behaved incorrectly in the mobile view, so it's best to hide them.

● Some page-level styles are changed, specifically for the default homepage of a publishing site to allow the page layout columns to adjust from being side by side to displaying vertically down the page.

With all these changes in place, the responsive master page is completed. The final result shown here is the default homepage of a publishing site at different browser sizes.

DESKTOP

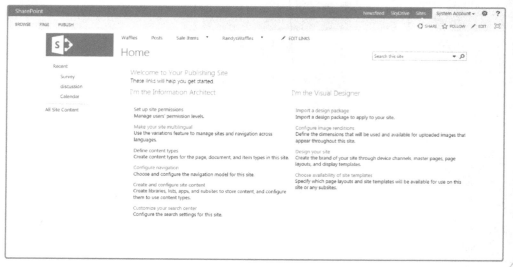

MEDIUM

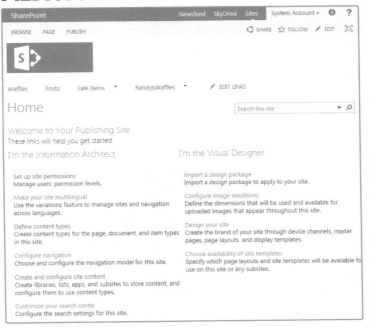

MOBILE

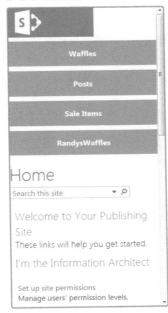

SUMMARY

● SharePoint 2013 was created with modern web design techniques in mind. It even uses HTML5 and CSS3 concepts in the default code base. For example, HTML5 is used for loading videos and CSS3 is used for adding shadows behind elements.

● The jQuery JavaScript library can be used with SharePoint 2013 to perform a variety of dynamic user interface effects including animations.

● Modern web design templates can be used with SharePoint 2013, but there are some gotchas when it comes to using certain templates with the Design Manager, specifically in regard to some of the techniques used in the common open source HTML5 Boilerplate template.

● Web fonts can easily be referenced in custom SharePoint 2013 branding to add unique typography.

● Grid-based designs like the one provided with 960 Grid can be used with SharePoint 2013 to enable easier creation of layouts with uniformly aligned rows and columns.

● SharePoint 2013 lends itself well to the use of responsive design in custom branding. Responsive design is a technique that enables website layouts and styles to adapt based on different browser features, such as the height and width of mobile devices like tablets and phones.

12

DESIGNING APPS

What's in this Chapter:

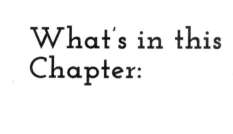

SharePoint 2013 and Office 2013 introduce
a new app model fit for the cloud. In this new
app model you can write code in any language,
framework, or platform that you choose. This is
possible because your app does not actually run on the SharePoint server.
The core design principal in SharePoint 2013 is that no user code runs on the
server. This chapter teaches you what you need to design and brand apps that look and
feel like the SharePoint site on which they are hosted.

SHAREPOINT CLOUD APP MODEL

In the past, you could write full trust applications, sandboxed solutions, and applications that ran on the client, either WPF or mobile devices. Although full trust applications and sandboxed solutions (including Silverlight) are still supported, they are not the future direction of SharePoint development and are deprecated in Office 365.

The key to the SharePoint app model and the flexibility it delivers comes from the fact that the code is not running on the SharePoint server. That means the SharePoint server is free to change as frequently or infrequently as the SharePoint product team wants to with less impact on your app. This is especially important as SharePoint Online in Office 365 becomes a more popular way that users deploy Share-Point. If your app is not running on the SharePoint server, where is it running? The answer is any place you want. You learn about the various hosting options for your SharePoint app in this chapter.

There are a number of ways that you can surface your app in SharePoint, even though it runs outside of SharePoint. This chapter covers the three user experience options for your app and provides more detailed examples of each of these in action.

The last piece of the app puzzle is branding. If your app runs outside of SharePoint, how do you make your app look and feel like the SharePoint site it is installed in? There are a number of ways to pull context and style information from SharePoint and use this to style your app. You see examples of these in this chapter.

This chapter offers only a brief look into the new app model focusing on what you need to get started designing and branding apps. You learn how to use the new browser developer tool Napa and dive a little into Visual Studio to build apps. Although this chapter is on the SharePoint app model, the Office 2013 app model is nearly identical, and the same tools and techniques you learn for SharePoint also apply to building Office apps.

NOTE

The SharePoint app model is similar conceptually to developing Facebook applications. If you have built Facebook applications, you can leverage those skills to build SharePoint apps. Similarly, after you learn how to build SharePoint apps, you can then leverage those skills to build Facebook apps.

HOSTING OPTIONS

A SharePoint app is a web application hosted outside of the SharePoint server. There are two basic hosting options: SharePoint-hosted and cloud-hosted (or a combination of the two).

SharePoint-Hosted

SharePoint-hosted apps are a bit of a misnomer because the app is not actually hosted in SharePoint. These are browser-only apps. That is, the web pages are stored in SharePoint and delivered to the browser as HTML pages. All the code runs on the client side. There is no server-side code allowed. These are simple apps to create from a designer's perspective because there is only HTML, CSS, and JavaScript code involved.

Later in the "Creating and Branding SharePoint-Hosted Apps" section of this chapter you use the new browser-based Napa tools to create and brand a SharePoint-hosted app. The SharePoint-hosted app can also include other declarative SharePoint items such as list templates and modules. But the primary UI is an HTML web page that uses JavaScript to interact with the SharePoint server's REST API or the client-side object model (CSOM).

Cloud-Hosted

Cloud-hosted apps are SharePoint apps hosted outside of SharePoint. This may or may not be in a cloud-hosting environment. The only requirement is that it is not running on SharePoint. Therefore, this could be a cloud-hosting environment such as Windows Azure, Amazon AWS, or Rackspace. It could also be on-premise in your enterprise environment. For example, you can run SharePoint in your own data centers. You can have another server in the same data center running Internet Information Server (IIS) and hosting the apps for your SharePoint farm.

The general term used by SharePoint to describe the hosting models is *cloud-hosted*. Microsoft is working to make Windows Azure be the first and best option for hosting your SharePoint and Office apps. You see how this is critical in the autohosted option in the next section.

Provider-Hosted

The first cloud-hosting model is *provider-hosted*. Provider-hosted means that you as the provider of the application are responsible to host the application some place. Windows Azure is probably the best choice to do this, but any platform capable of serving up web pages can work. This can be Windows Azure, Amazon AWS, Google Compute, or another web-hosting provider like Rackspace.

The benefit of using the provider-hosted option is that you control the development platform. You can use any framework and any version, such as .Net, PHP, Java, Ruby, and so on. You also control the software installed on the server and the versioning. The downside to provider-hosted apps is that you own the server and must maintain and service the server and applications. Also, you are responsible for the costs associated with hosting the app.

In this book, you do not build provider-hosted apps. You can learn all the branding techniques using SharePoint-hosted and autohosted apps. Then apply that knowledge when you build a provider-hosted app.

Autohosted

Autohosted apps are cloud-hosted apps that are automatically hosted for you by Office 365. Auto-hosted apps have the ease of deployment of a SharePoint-hosted app but have the power of a provider-hosted app. In an autohosted app Office 365 works under the covers to create a Windows Azure Web Sites instance and a Windows Azure SQL Database on-the-fly for you and deploys your app and data to this newly provisioned site.

The benefit to this model is that you do not need to worry about finding and maintaining a hosting environment for your apps. One interesting aspect for autohosted apps is that for every app install there is a single and unique Windows Azure Web Sites site and Windows Azure SQL Database created. When the app is uninstalled, the instance of the website and database are also destroyed. This differs from the provider-hosted model where every installation of your app points back to a single instance of your app, which would potentially isolate users and customers in a multitenant app.

NOTE

To learn more about the hosting option for SharePoint apps visit MSDN at http://msdn
.microsoft.com/en-us/library/fp179887.aspx.

User Experience Options

As you've seen, there are several options for hosting your app. There are also various user experience options available. The user can interact with your app in three ways: through an immersive full-page app, as an App Part, or as a custom action. You could also use any combination of these three user experiences together in a single app. The following sections explore what these mean for users and designers. Later in the "Branding Autohosted Apps" section of this chapter you learn to build all three of these user experiences.

Immersive Full-Page App

The immersive full-page app is the default entry point for SharePoint apps. In this type of app, the user is redirected to the URL that is defined as the start page for the app. The start page is located outside of SharePoint, and the user navigates to this web page. As a SharePoint user and developer, this is probably the hardest idea to understand. The experience is as if you typed a new address in the browser and navigated to a new site. You may wonder, how is this a SharePoint app?

The glue that holds the SharePoint site and the full-page app together is the branding. When the app is started by SharePoint, it not only navigates to the start page URL, it also sends along some other information about the user and the site that launched the application. Using this additional information you can brand the site to look like the SharePoint farm that it belongs to. Later in the "Branding Autohosted Apps" section of this chapter you learn how to use branding to make the full-page app tie back to the SharePoint site it was launched from.

App Part

The traditional way to surface applications in SharePoint has been through Web Parts. In the new app model there is a different way called App Parts. App Parts look and behave similar to Web Parts except they are actually just an iFrame window to a web page hosted by your app. Your app is still hosted some place depending on the hosting model you chose. The App Part enables you to surface a page to the user in a frame on the SharePoint site.

The branding of App Parts is important because the App Part sits on a branded page of the SharePoint site. It will be painfully obvious when the App Part is not branded or branded incorrectly. The App Part can reference the styles of the host SharePoint site to correctly style all the elements in the App Part.

Custom Action

There are two ways for your app to interact with custom actions: using the ribbon or using a menu item. Both methods provide entry points for your app to interact with the user. The branding associated with custom actions enables you to add ribbon items and launch dialog windows. These are not visual branding elements though so they will not be covered in this book. You can read more about creating custom actions on the MSDN site at http://msdn.microsoft.com/en-us/library/jj163954.aspx.

In the next section, you learn how to bring all these concepts together to create apps for SharePoint 2013 using the Napa browser tool and Visual Studio 2012.

CREATING AND BRANDING SHAREPOINT-HOSTED APPS

Building and branding SharePoint-hosted apps using the Napa online code editor is the best way to start branding. Napa is itself a SharePoint app that enables you as a designer or power user to quickly build SharePoint-hosted apps using only your web browser. After you add the Napa app to your SharePoint developer site, you are ready to begin creating SharePoint apps. Apps created with Napa are SharePoint-hosted apps that are based on a SharePoint Master Page that contains a reference to the SharePoint-themed CSS file. You can use this CSS to brand your app. The following sections walk you through the process of installing Napa and creating your first SharePoint app. The Napa tool is rapidly adding new features. You explore only a few of these features in this book, but you can to learn more about the tool from `http://dev.office.com`.

Napa Office 365 Development Tools

You can create SharePoint-hosted apps using Visual Studio, but as a designer you may feel more comfortable building apps using only your browser. Napa makes it incredibly easy to start. First, you need to create a developer site in Office 365.

You can sign up for a free site at `http://msdn.microsoft.com/en-us/library/fp179924.aspx`. The sign-up process is straightforward.

WARNING

Both Napa and Office 365 are frequently updated by Microsoft. The code shown in this chapter may appear differently for you depending on any changes that may have occurred since this book has been published.

EXAMPLE: CREATING A NAPA ACCOUNT

1. Enter your basic contact information.

2. Specify a new Office 365 user ID. This is not only the tenant administrator for your new site, but it is also the name of your new domain. For example, you could create a user called `Administrator` and a new domain called `WaffleApps`. This results in a login id of `administrator@WaffleApps.OnMicrosoft.com` for the site `https://WaffleApps.SharePoint.com`.

3. Enter a code that will be sent to your mobile phone.

4. Click **Create My Account** to start the provisioning process.

   This is the site that will be used throughout this chapter. If you work along with the book, replace the administrator and WaffleApps names with the user and domain name that you used when you signed up for your Office 365 account.

Installing Napa

When your new Office 365 developer site has been provisioned, you can download the Napa app. If you start from an existing SharePoint tenancy, remember that you can install the Napa app only in a site collection based on the developer site template.

There are two common ways to add an app to your site. The first is to choose **Add an App** from the Settings menu in the top right of the site page located between your username and the help icon.

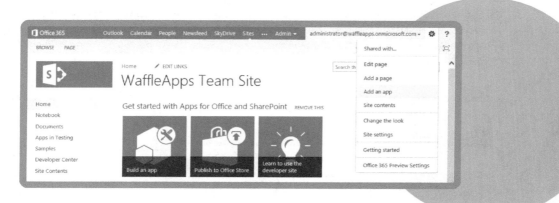

The second way to add an app is to click on the **Site Contents** link on the left side of the site page. This opens the Site Contents page. The Site Contents page shows all installed apps and has an **Add an App** icon as the first item on the page. Clicking this takes you to the same place as clicking the **Add an App** from the Settings menu.

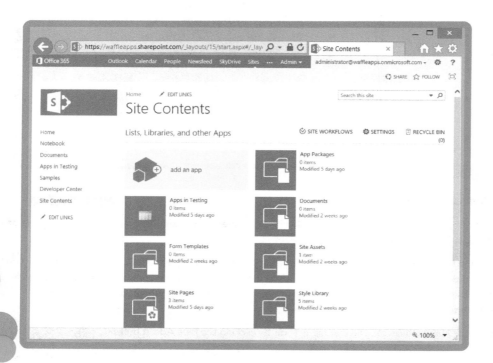

The Add an App page, /_layouts/15/addanapp.aspx, lists the apps you can add. These are basic apps that come with SharePoint, such as a Document Library, Custom List, and Task. If you are new to SharePoint 2013, remember that to simplify the concept count, all these items like Document Libraries and Lists are considered apps. There is also a filtered list of apps from your organization. These are apps that have been installed in the Corporate Catalog. The Corporate Catalog is a central store of apps approved by your administrators. The Corporate Catalog also enables enterprises to side load apps without installing them in the SharePoint Store, which is run by Microsoft.

On the Add an App page, you want to install the Napa app, which is located in the SharePoint Store. The SharePoint Store is Microsoft's online store for developers to publish apps and for consumers to discover, purchase, and install apps. Think of this just like other apps stores you are familiar with such as Apple's iTunes Store, Google's Play Store, or the Microsoft Store for Windows 8 or Windows Phone 8. You can click the SharePoint Store link on the left to browse to the SharePoint Store website.

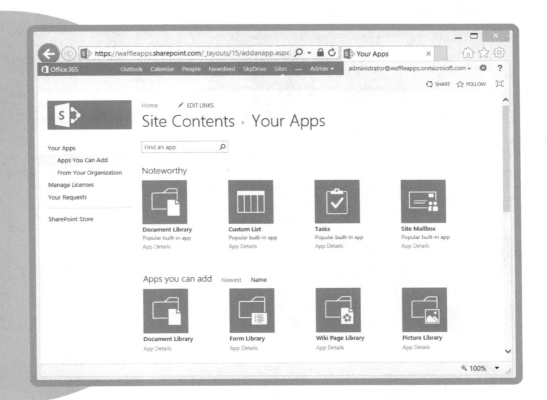

EXAMPLE: INSTALLING THE NAPA APP

1. On the SharePoint Store website, type **Napa** in the **Find an App** search box on the upper-right side of the page. There will most likely be only one result.

2. Click the Napa icon to open the app details page. The app details page shows you a number of screen shots of the app. It also has some details such as the version, rating, and release date. There is also a link to the app support site, http://go.microsoft.com/fwlink/?LinkId=258346, which is simply a tutorial article on the MSDN website.

3. Install the Napa Office 365 Development Tools by clicking the blue **Add It** button.

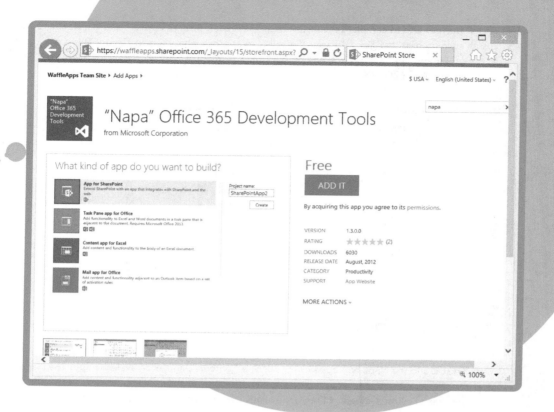

4. Sign in with a Microsoft account (previously known as a Live ID). Note that this cannot be your `.onmicrosoft.com` account.

5. Click the green **Continue** button to confirm the installation of the Napa app. After the confirmation screen you will be prompted to choose the sites to install the app on. In this case you may have only the one developer site, which is selected by default.

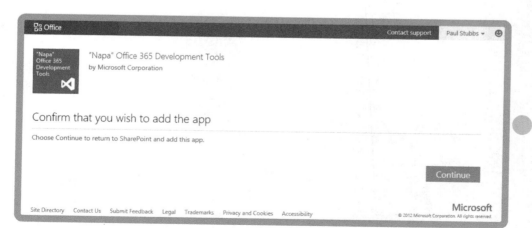

6. Click **Return to Site** to complete the installation. The Trust It prompt appears and is a standard OAuth style prompt that gives the user the ability to approve what the app can do. This is an all-or-nothing prompt. If you cancel and do not trust the app, the app will not be installed. The Napa app requires full control on the site collection and access to basic user information.

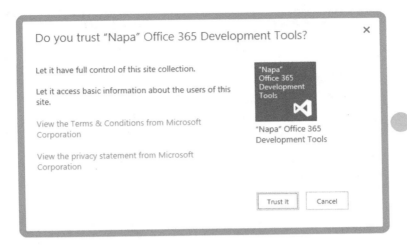

7. Click **Trust it** and the Napa app appears in your Site Contents page as an available app. The Napa app icon appears with the new tag, indicating it was recently installed. If you hover over the app icon, you see an ellipses appear. Clicking the ellipses shows you more details about the app.

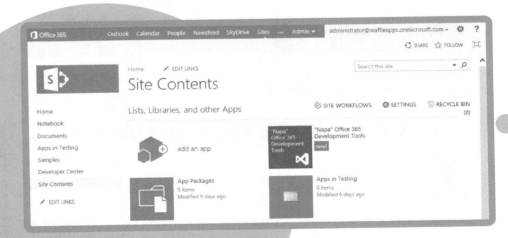

Creating Your First SharePoint App

The Napa app enables you to create SharePoint-hosted apps. As you learned earlier, SharePoint-hosted apps are client-side only and contain no server-side code. When you click the Napa app to launch it you see that the app is a full-page immersive app.

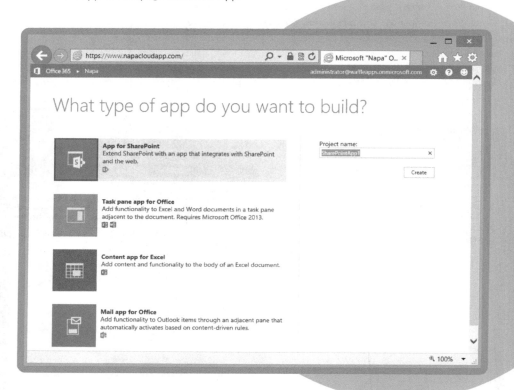

This starting page is the page where you can select the type of app to build. Currently there are four app types supported by Napa: App for SharePoint, Task Pane App for Office, Content App for Excel, and Mail App for Office. This book focuses on building apps for SharePoint, but many of the techniques you learn here also apply to building apps for Office.

For your App for SharePoint project you can either change the project name or keep it as the default, in this case SharePointApp1. You then simply click **Create** and in a few seconds your new SharePoint app project is created and ready for editing directly in the browser. The Napa editor is amazing for a browser-only code editor. Many of the conveniences of a full Visual Studio editor are available, such as color coding, instance highlighting, indenting, and bracket matching. There is even JavaScript code completion and snippets. And because this is a cloud-based tool, expect these features to improve and more features to be added frequently.

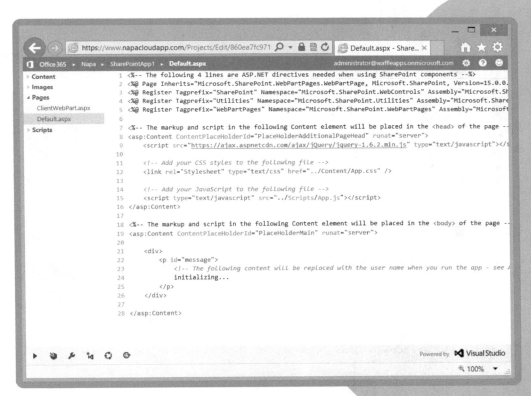

The project structure of the SharePoint-hosted app consists of two web pages. The Default.aspx is the starting page for the app and provides the immersive full-page experience. The second page is the ClientWebPart.aspx page. This provides the client App Part experience. The other pages are common pages to most web projects. There is a CSS page, an application icon image, and a JavaScript file. You can explore these in more detail.

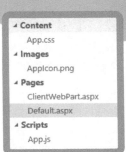

The Default.aspx page should be familiar to you if you have done SharePoint development before. You can see in the following code that the page has a number of SharePoint assembly references. The most interesting one is a Page reference to the SharePoint master page, ~masterurl/default .master.

```
<%@ Page Inherits="
Microsoft.SharePoint.WebPartPages.WebPartPage,
Microsoft.SharePoint,
Version=15.0.0.0,
Culture=neutral,
PublicKeyToken=71e9bce111e9429c"
MasterPageFile="~masterurl/default.master"
language="C#" %>
```

The next two items in the page are content controls. The first content control is for the header information and has the ID of PlaceHolderAdditionalPageHead. This header control contains the references to the JQuery JavaScript library, your CSS file in your project called App.css, and a reference to your JavaScript file called App.js.

```
<%-- The markup and script in the following Content element will be
 placed in the <head> of the page --%>
<asp:Content ContentPlaceHolderId="PlaceHolderAdditionalPageHead"
 runat="server">
 <script src="https://ajax.aspnetcdn.com/ajax/
 jQuery/jquery-1.6.2.min.js"
 type="text/javascript"></script>

 <!-- Add your CSS styles to the following file -->
 <link rel="Stylesheet" type="text/css"
  href="../Content/App.css" />

 <!-- Add your JavaScript to the following file -->
 <script type="text/javascript" src="../Scripts/App.js"></script>
</asp:Content>
```

The second content control has the ID of PlaceHolderMain and represents the body or main content of the app. The default project template outputs the username in a div tag. This is where you put the UI for your application.

```
<%-- The markup and script in the following Content element will be
 placed in the <body> of the page --%>
<asp:Content ContentPlaceHolderId="PlaceHolderMain" runat="server">

 <div>
  <p id="message">
   <!-- The following content will be replaced with the
    user name when you run the app - see App.js -->
   initializing...
  </p>
 </div>

</asp:Content>
```

The ClientWebPart.aspx page appears as an App Part when the app is installed. In the following code, you can see that the App Part is a simple html page. It contains a head section with references to the SharePoint client-side object model (CSOM). It also contains a reference to your app.css style sheet. Inside the body tag there is a div that contains a span. You put the contents of your app in the span.

```
<!-- The following tells SharePoint to allow this page to be hosted
 in an IFrame -->
<WebPartPages:AllowFraming runat="server" />

<html>
 <head>
  <!-- Add your CSS styles to the following file -->
  <link rel="Stylesheet" type="text/css"
   href="../Content/App.css" />

  <!-- The following scripts are needed when using the
   SharePoint object model -->
  <script type="text/javascript"
   src="https://ajax.aspnetcdn.com/ajax/4.0/1/MicrosoftAjax.
   js"></script>
  <script type="text/javascript"
   src="/_layouts/15/sp.runtime.debug.js"></script>
  <script type="text/javascript"
   src="/_layouts/15/sp.debug.js"></script>
 </head>

 <body class="partBody">

  <div class="partDiv">
   <span class="partContent">
    Your content goes here...
   </span>
  </div>

 </body>
</html>
```

The App.js file contains some sample code that you can use to start creating your app. The most interesting code is the initialization code. You want to make sure that the SharePoint client object model is loaded and that the client context is ready. When this is ready you can execute your initialization code; in this case it is the function called sharePointReady(). The sharePointReady() function gets a reference to the SharePoint client context and sets the global variable called *context*. Next, the sample code calls the getUserName() function. The getUserName() function gets the user object from the server asynchronously and sets the paragraph object that has the ID equal to "message" with the user title.

```
var context;
var web;
var user;

// This code runs when the DOM is ready. It ensures the SharePoint
// script file sp.js is loaded and then executes sharePointReady()
$(document).ready(function () {
 SP.SOD.executeFunc('sp.js', 'SP.ClientContext', sharePointReady);
});

// This function creates a context object which is needed to use the
// SharePoint object model
function sharePointReady() {
 context = new SP.ClientContext.get_current();
 web = context.get_web();

 getUserName();
}

// This function prepares, loads, and then executes a
// SharePoint query
// to get the current users information
function getUserName() {
 user = web.get_currentUser();
 context.load(user);
 context.executeQueryAsync(onGetUserNameSuccess,
 onGetUserNameFail);
}

// This function is executed if the above call is successful
// It replaces the contents of the 'helloString' element with the
// user name
function onGetUserNameSuccess() {
 $('#message').text('Hello ' + user.get_title());
}

// This function is executed if the above call fails
function onGetUserNameFail(sender, args) {
 alert('Failed to get user name. Error:' + args.get_message());
}
```

The last file in the default project is the App.css style sheet. You can see in the following code that there are three classes defined that set some basic attributes. These are actually applied in the ClientWebPart. aspx page.

```
.partBody
{
 margin: 0;
 padding: 0;
 border: 0;
}

.partDiv
{
 margin: 0;
 padding: 0;
 border: 0;
 position: relative;
 width: 300px;
 height: 200px;
 background-color: #0000FF;
 font-family: 'Segoe UI', Arial, Helvetica, sans-serif;
 color: #FFFFFF;
 font-size: 14pt;
}

.partContent
{
 position: absolute;
 top: 5px;
 left: 5px;
}
```

The default project template from Napa is just a starting point that shows some examples of what is possible. You are free to expand the project in any way that makes sense for your app. This code runs in the browser, so you could write to any version of HTML you prefer that is supported by SharePoint. The best way may be to push forward with modern browsers that support HTML 5 or above, but that is a decision for you to make.

The manifest properties are the last important piece of the project. You can access these properties by clicking the Properties icon on the bottom left. The manifest Properties dialog contains information about the project, such as the Name, Title, Icon, and Start Page URL. You can see these same properties again when you open the project in Visual Studio.

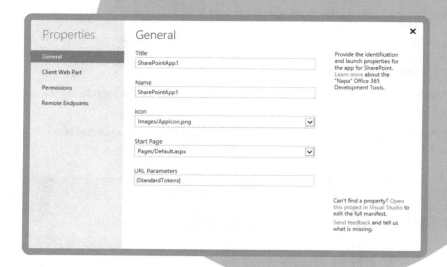

At this point you have not made any changes to the default project, but it is ready to run. Click the **Play** icon on the bottom left to compile and package, install, and run the project. Notice that the app has a blue menu bar at the top. This menu bar is provided by the master page and, among other things, provides a hook or anchor back to the SharePoint site that the app belongs to. Without this menu bar, which is a suggested best practice that all apps have, there would be no way to know this app was part of the SharePoint site.

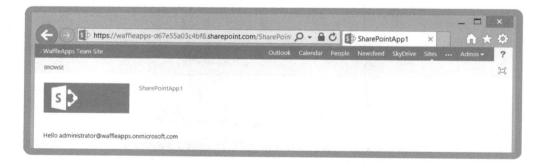

NOTE

The URL for this app is `https://waffleapps-d67e55a03c4bf8.sharepoint.com/SharePointApp1/`. SharePoint creates a new site-to-host app, which has the site name plus a random number. This provides a separate security domain enforced by the browser.

So far you have created an App Part as part of the default project. Just like you do with Web Parts, you can insert an App Part onto a SharePoint page. The App Part shows your app in a frame on an existing SharePoint page that may contain a combination of Web Parts and App Parts.

EXAMPLE: INSERT AN APP PART ON A SHAREPOINT PAGE

1. Using the link on the top left of the app, navigate back to the SharePoint site. On the homepage, you see a document library called **Apps in Testing**, which now contains at least one project, called Share-PointApp1. This is the project you just created.

2. You can add the App Part to this page as well. Click **Edit** on the top right of the page to put the page in edit mode. When in edit mode, click the **Insert Ribbon** tab.

3. Click the **App Part** icon to open the Parts dialog window. The Parts dialog lists a number of parts installed with SharePoint by default. You also see your SharePointApp1 App Part.

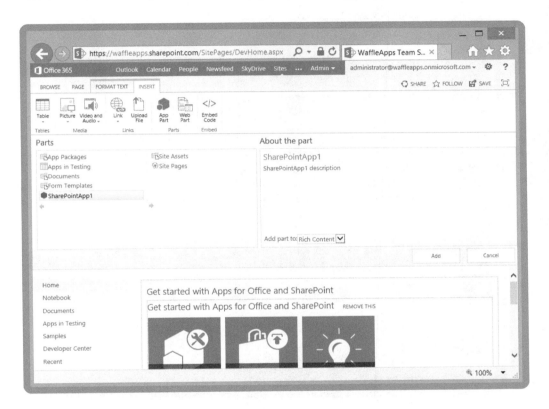

4. Select the SharePointApp1 App Part on the left pane to see the details in the right pane. These details come from the manifest properties.

5. Click **Add** to add the SharePointApp1 App Part to the page. The App Part is inserted into the page, and the page is still in edit mode.

6. Click the **Save** button on the ribbon to save the page and exit edit mode.

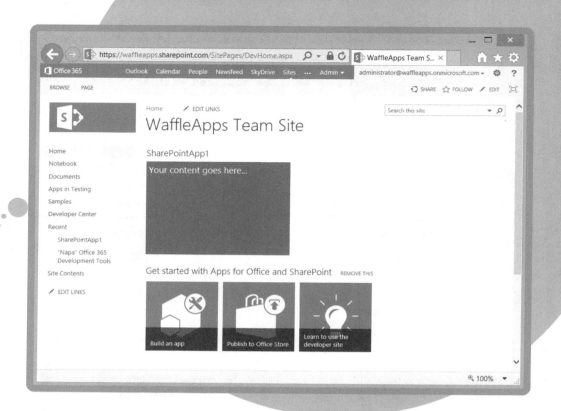

The Napa tool is a great tool for web developers to easily create SharePoint-hosted apps. The tool doesn't require installing Visual Studio and reduces the concepts to get started building apps. Now that you have created your app you are ready to start branding.

Branding your App with CSS and Styles

One of the first things you want to do after creating your app is brand it to match the branding of the host website, which is the site where the app is installed. To do this you need to use the style sheet from the host web, which is part of the app template. The SharePoint-hosted app derives from a simple master page; this is the *app template*. The app template provides some basic features such as the navigation bar at the top of the page. It also provides the basic placeholders for the two content controls: `PlaceHolderAdditionalPageHead` and `PlaceHolderMain`.

To achieve the look and feel of the host site for your app using the style sheet, use the host's style definitions in your app. For example, add the style called `ms-accentText` to your paragraph tag with the id of message. It will look like the following code.

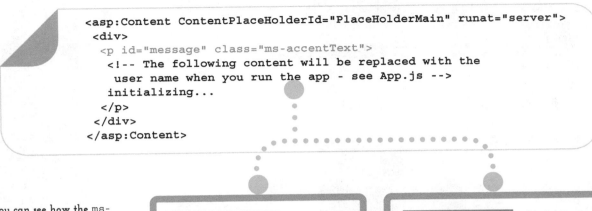

```
<asp:Content ContentPlaceHolderId="PlaceHolderMain" runat="server">
 <div>
  <p id="message" class="ms-accentText">
   <!-- The following content will be replaced with the
    user name when you run the app - see App.js -->
   initializing...
  </p>
 </div>
</asp:Content>
```

You can see how the ms-accentText changes the Hello administrator@waffleapps.onmicrosoft.com message when you run the app.

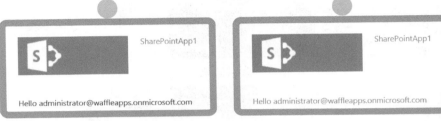

Many of the host web style sheet classes like the one you just used are also defined on MSDN at http://msdn.microsoft.com/en-us/library/jj220046. Although it is outside the scope of this book to enumerate all the available styles, you will see a few common examples here. You should become familiar with the standard styles and guidelines for creating SharePoint apps. The goal of any app design is to be consistent with the host web styles. See Chapter 6, "Cascading Style Sheets and SharePoint," for a detailed CSS explanation.

To see examples of how some of the styles render when you change the look and feel of your site, run the following code to your app:

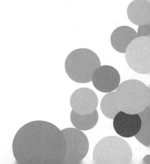

```
<div>
 <p class="ms-core-pageTitle">Page Title (ms-core-pageTitle)</p>
 <h1>Heading 1</h1>
 <h2>Heading 2</h2>
 <h3>Heading 3</h3>

 <p class="ms-webpart-titleText">
  Web Part Title (ms-webpart-titleText)</p>
 <p class="ms-dlg-heading">Dialog Heading (ms-dlg-heading)</p>
 <p class="ms-commandlink">
  Command Link (ms-commandLink)</p>
 <p class="ms-accentText">Accent Text (ms-accentText)</p>
 <p class="ms-error">Error Text (ms-error)</p>
 <p class="ms-disabled">Disabled Text (ms-disabled)</p>
</div>
```

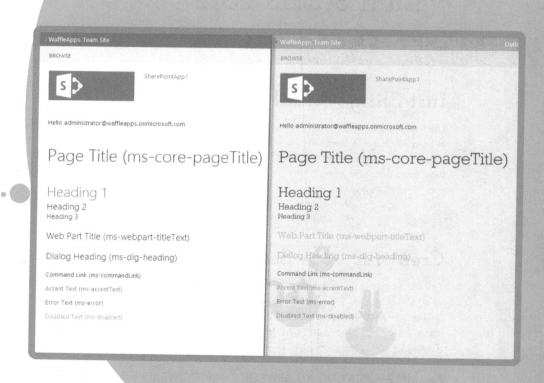

BRANDING AUTOHOSTED APPS

In the previous section you learned how to use Napa to build SharePoint-hosted apps. Although this was a good starting point for learning, you actually want to build your real-world apps as cloud-hosted apps. Cloud-hosted apps give you room to grow and fully leverage not only the SharePoint platform, but also the hosting platform where the app resides.

In this section, you learn how to use Visual Studio to develop autohosted SharePoint apps. You also learn how to apply branding to these apps that complement the SharePoint site they are surfaced in.

Visual Studio 2012

Visual Studio is an amazing development tool for building SharePoint applications. However, this book is not about Visual Studio, so it doesn't go into great detail about the tool. The goal is to show you enough so that you can understand the branding parts.

Installing Visual Studio

The first thing you need to do is install Visual Studio 2012. You can find detailed instructions on doing so at `http://msdn.microsoft.com/en-us/library/e2h7fzkw.aspx`. After you have Visual Studio installed, you need to install the Microsoft Office Developer Tools for Visual Studio 2012. The Office tools are a separate add-on for Visual Studio that enable you to create Office 2013 and SharePoint 2013 apps. The tools download page has a link under the tools section at `http://msdn`
`.microsoft.com/en-us/office/apps/fp123627` to download the tools. The tools are actually installed using the Microsoft Web Platform Installer (WebPI) tool.

Creating your Second SharePoint App

You can now try your hand at creating the same app you just built in the previous section, but this time using Visual Studio. The great thing about developing SharePoint 2013 apps is that you do not need SharePoint installed on the same machine. Unlike SharePoint 2010, you can now develop applications without ever installing SharePoint. In this case, you can use the Office 365 site that you created in the beginning of this chapter.

EXAMPLE: CREATING AN APP FOR SHAREPOINT USING VISUAL STUDIO

1. Launch Visual Studio 2012 with elevated permissions. Building apps for SharePoint 2013 requires administrator rights.

2. Create a new App for SharePoint 2013 called SharePointApp2.

3. Tell Visual Studio where the SharePoint developer site is that you want to use to build the app.

4. Choose the hosting option for the app. By default it is set to Autohosted, which is the type of hosting you want to use for this chapter.

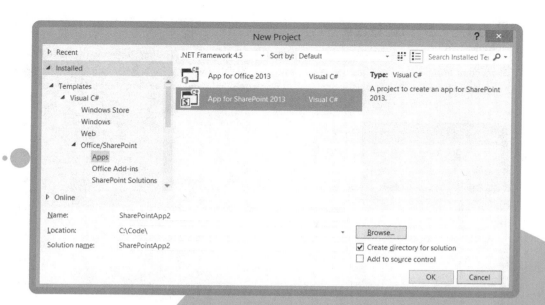

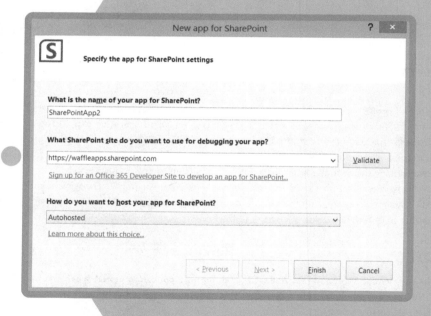

Project Structure

The Autohosted solution created by Visual Studio has two projects. The first project is the actual SharePoint app project. This has the same name you provided when you created the solution. In this case it is called SharePointApp2. It contains an AppIcon.png image and an AppManifest.xml file.

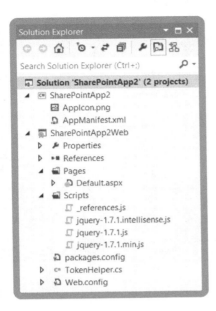

The second project is your actual web project. This is the project that contains your app logic and pages. In this case, Visual Studio creates a standard web project called SharePointApp2Web. The project has the Default.aspx page as the start page for your application. You learn more about how to brand this page in the next section. The web project also contains a Scripts folder with jQuery JavaScript files. You want to replace this with the latest version of jQuery from `http://www.jquery` `.org`. There is one last file called TokenHelper.cs. The TokenHelper file contains helper code to help you do advanced coding using the OAuth security tokens passed by SharePoint. As a designer, the discussion of OAuth is outside the scope of the book.

NOTE

By default, Visual Studio uses an ASP.NET Web Forms Application project when creating the autohosted app. You can simply delete this web project and add another project type, such as an ASP.NET MVC 4 Web Application.

Running and Debugging

You can start debugging your SharePoint app just like any other Visual Studio project by pressing F5. When you press F5, Visual Studio does a number of steps to make the experience easy. First, the project is compiled and packaged. Next, you need a temporary place to host the web app while debugging, so Visual Studio starts a local web server and deploys your web project. Then Visual Studio automates the deployment and starts the app on the SharePoint server. All these steps take a few minutes the first time to complete, and you will be prompted to trust the app as well. Note that there is no branding whatsoever on the page. Remember that the SharePoint-hosted app you created in Napa had a blue navigation bar at the top and the host CSS styles. In the cloud-hosted apps, you are responsible for providing the branding.

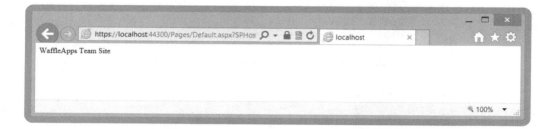

In the cloud-hosted apps you can run server-side code. Note that the title of the host web displays here. In the following code, which is the Default.aspx code, there is no code or HTML to display the host web title.

```
<%@ Page Language="C#" AutoEventWireup="true"
CodeBehind="Default.aspx.cs"
Inherits="SharePointApp2Web.Pages.Default" %>

<!DOCTYPE html
PUBLIC "-//W3C//DTD XHTML 1.0 Transitional//EN"
"http://www.w3.org/TR/xhtml1/DTD/xhtml1-transitional.
dtd">

<html xmlns="http://www.w3.org/1999/xhtml">
  <head runat="server">
  <title></title>
</head>
<body>
  <form id="form1" runat="server">
   <div>
   </div>
  </form>
 </body>
</html>
```

The code behind for the default.aspx page contains code on the load event that retrieves the SharePoint client context from the page request and parses it with the token helper. The client context enables you to use the client-side object model (CSOM) to retrieve the Title property of the app web. You can see the complete code in the following listing.

```csharp
using System;
using System.Collections.Generic;
using System.Linq;
using System.Web;
using System.Web.UI;
using System.Web.UI.WebControls;

namespace SharePointApp2Web.Pages
{
 public partial class Default : System.Web.UI.Page
 {
  protected void Page_Load(object sender, EventArgs e)
  {
   // The following code gets the client context and
   // Title property by using TokenHelper.
   // To access other properties, you may need to
   // request permissions on the host web.

   var contextToken = TokenHelper.
   GetContextTokenFromRequest(Page.Request);
   var hostWeb = Page.Request["SPHostUrl"];

   using (var clientContext =
    TokenHelper.GetClientContextWithContextToken(
    hostWeb, contextToken, Request.Url.Authority))
   {
    clientContext.Load(clientContext.Web, web => web.
     Title);
    clientContext.ExecuteQuery();
    Response.Write(clientContext.Web.Title);
   }
  }
 }
}
```

Chrome Control

The chrome control is a control provided by SharePoint to display the navigation bar at the top of your application. The chrome control visually ties the app with the site from which the app was launched. Remember that your app is just a redirect to another web page outside of SharePoint, and the chrome control provides a hyperlink back to the SharePoint site. Without the chrome control, the user would not know that the app is related to the host SharePoint site in any way. You are not required to use the chrome control, but you must provide a link back to the SharePoint if you want to conform to the SharePoint UX guidelines at `http://msdn.microsoft.com/en-us/library/jj220046.aspx`. The chrome control also provides a custom drop-down menu and a link to a help page, as well as a link to the host SharePoint site's CSS file, just like the App Template did for SharePoint-hosted apps. It is a good idea to add the chrome control to your app.

EXAMPLE: ADDING THE CHROME CONTROL TO YOUR WEB PAGE

1. Load the JavaScript libraries that are dependencies for the chrome control. You can do this declaratively in HTML by pulling the libraries from a content delivery network (CDN) endpoint. Add the following code to the head section of your Default.aspx page:

```
<head runat="server">
 <title></title>
 <script
  src="//ajax.aspnetcdn.com/ajax/4.0/1/MicrosoftAjax.js">
 </script>
 <script
  src="//ajax.aspnetcdn.com/ajax/jQuery/
  jquery-1.7.2.min.js">
 </script>
 <script src="/Scripts/ChromeControl.js">
 </script>
</head>
```

Notice in the previous code that there is also a script reference to the ChromeControl.js. This is just a helper script that you write to dynamically load the script from the host SharePoint site. You can name this script anything you want. You can find more examples of this script on MSDN at `http://msdn.microsoft.com/en-us/library/jj163201`.

2. Create a new file under the Scripts folder called ChromeControl.js and add the following code. The code simply loads the `SPHostUrl/_layouts/15/SP.UI.Controls.js` file.

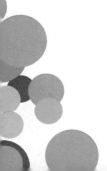

```
var hostweburl;

// Load the SharePoint resources.
$(document).ready(function () {

 // Get the URI decoded app web URL.
 hostweburl =
  decodeURIComponent(
   getQueryStringParameter("SPHostUrl")
 );

 // The SharePoint js files URL are in the form:
 // web_url/_layouts/15/resource.js
 var scriptbase = hostweburl + "/_layouts/15/";

 // Load the js file and continue to the
 // success handler.
 $.getScript(scriptbase + "SP.UI.Controls.js")
});

// Function to retrieve a query string value.
// For production purposes you may want to use
// a library to handle the query string.
function getQueryStringParameter(paramToRetrieve) {
 var params =
  document.URL.split("?")[1].split("&");
 var strParams = "";
 for (var i = 0; i < params.length; i = i + 1) {
  var singleParam = params[i].split("=");
  if (singleParam[0] == paramToRetrieve)
   return singleParam[1];
 }
}
```

3. After all the required JavaScript libraries are loaded, declaratively add the chrome control to your page. There are more options available to the chrome control that you see next, but for now here is the shortest amount of code to display the chrome control.

```
<div id="PlaceHolderChromeControl"
  data-ms-control="SP.UI.Controls.Navigation"
  data-ms-options=
   '{
    "appTitle" : "SharePointApp2"
   }'>
</div>
```

4. Run the project to see the chrome control.

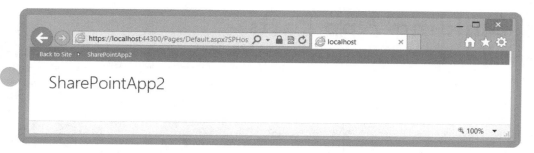

There are other options on the chrome control that are worth examining. The data-ms-options property is an array of option properties. In the previous example you used only the appTitle property. In the following code you can see that there are many more available. First, there are two icons that you can provide. The first is the appIconUrl, which is the icon that appears under the colored menu bar at the top of the page next to the appTitle. The second is the appTitleIconUrl, which is a small 24-by-24 pixel icon that appears in the menu bar at the top. In this example, you see a small waffle icon. Both of these icons are available with the downloads for this chapter.

```
<div id="PlaceHolderChromeControl"
 data-ms-control="SP.UI.Controls.Navigation"
 data-ms-options=
  '{
   "appIconUrl" : "/Images/AppIcon.png",
   "appTitleIconUrl" : "/Images/WaffleIcon.png",
   "appTitle" : "SharePointApp2",
   "appHelpPageUrl" : "/Pages/Help.aspx",
   "settingsLinks" : [
    {
     "linkUrl" : "/Pages/About.aspx",
     "displayName" : "About"
    },
    {
     "linkUrl" : "/Pages/Config.aspx",
     "displayName" : "App Config"
    }
   ]
  }'>
</div>
```

The appHelpPageUrl enables you to provide a link to a help page. The last property is the settings-Links. The settingsLinks is an array of menu items that appear on the right side of the menu bar as a drop-down menu of links. In the previous example there are two menu items, one for the **About** page and one for a **Configuration** page. The chrome control renders with these additional properties.

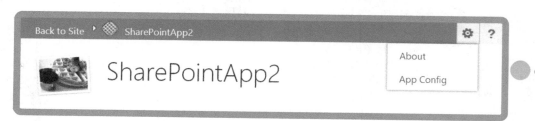

Building App Parts

As mentioned previously, you can think of App Parts as Web Parts for Apps. They are created and used just like Web Parts, but they are actually just an iFrame that points to your App Part page in your app. Because the App Part is hosted in a frame on an existing page that does not require a visual control linking it back to the host site, you do not use the chrome control. In other words, the App Part lives on a page that already has the branding and navigation at the top of the page. You do not want to duplicate the navigation again inside of your App Part.

To the user, App Parts and Web Parts are the same. To a developer, they achieve the same goal but are implemented differently. You can create an App Part by adding a Client Web Part project item to your app solution in Visual Studio. The following steps will walk you through the process of creating an App Part and adding code to the part.

EXAMPLE: CREATING AN APP PART

1. In Visual Studio, add a new Client Web Part project item to the SharePoint app project. Remember there are two projects in your solution: the SharePoint app project and the web project.

2. Use the default name of ClientWebPart1.

3. The project system of Visual Studio creates the ClientWebpart.aspx page in your web project for you. Visual Studio creates a new ClientWebPart1 element in the manifest of the SharePoint app project as well.

4. The aspx file that Visual Studio creates for you has a script block to reference the style sheet of the SharePoint host that the App Part is installed. Use the following code to add the `link` element to reference the `/layouts/15/defaultcss.ashx` CSS file. This is the same file that is added when you use the chrome control.

```
<script type="text/javascript">
 // Set the style of the client web part page to be
 // consistent with the host web.
 function setStyleSheet() {
  var hostUrl = ""
  if (document.URL.indexOf("?") != -1) {
   var params =
    document.URL.split("?")[1].split("&");
   for (var i = 0; i < params.length; i++) {
    p = decodeURIComponent(params[i]);
    if (/^SPHostUrl=/i.test(p)) {
     hostUrl = p.split("=")[1];
     document.write(
      "<link rel=\"stylesheet\" href=\"" +
      hostUrl +
      "/_layouts/15/defaultcss.ashx\" />");
     break;
    }
   }
  }
  if (hostUrl == "") {
   document.write("<link rel=\"stylesheet\"
    href=\"/_layouts/15/1033/styles/
    themable/corev15.css\" />");
  }
 }
 setStyleSheet();
</script>
```

5. Now that the host CSS file is referenced in your App Part, you can use any of the style elements on the page. Add the following div snippet to your page. This is the same code that you used in the SharePoint-hosted page that was created with Napa.

```
<body>
 <form id="form1" runat="server">
 <div>
  <p class="ms-core-pageTitle">
   Page Title (ms-corepageTitle)</p>
  <h1>Heading 1</h1>
  <h2>Heading 2</h2>
  <h3>Heading 3</h3>

  <p class="ms-webpart-titleText">
   Web Part Title (ms-webpart-titleText)</p>
  <p class="ms-dlg-heading">
   Dialog Heading (ms-dlg-heading)</p>

  <p class="ms-commandlink">
   Command Link (ms-commandLink)</p>
  <p class="ms-accentText">Accent Text (ms-accentText)</p>
  <p class="ms-error">Error Text (ms-error)</p>
  <p class="ms-disabled">Disabled Text (ms-disabled)</p>
 </div>
 </form>
</body>
```

6. Press F5 to run the project. When the project starts you will be on the Full Page of your app.

7. Navigate back to the host site, put the page in edit mode, and insert the App Part.

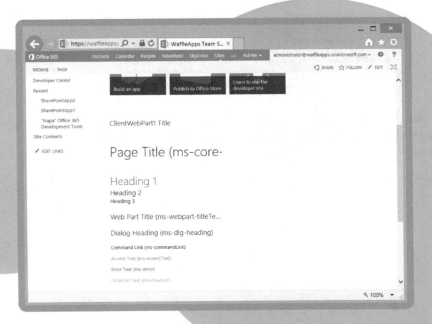